LENSEN

The Damned Inheritance

OTHER BOOKS BY GEORGE ALEXANDER LENSEN

Report from Hokkaido: The Remains of Russian Culture in Northern Japan

Russia's Japan Expedition of 1852 to 1855

The Russian Push Toward Japan; Russo-Japanese Relations, 1697–1875

The World Beyond Europe: An Introduction to the History
of Africa, India, Southeast Asia, and the Far East

Russia's Eastward Expansion (edited)

Revelations of a Russian Diplomat: The Memoirs of Dmitrii I. Abrikossow
(edited)

Korea and Manchuria Between Russia and Japan 1895–1904:
The Observations of Sir Ernest Satow, British Minister to Japan and China
(edited)

The Soviet Union: An Introduction

The d'Anethan Dispatches From Japan 1894–1910. The Observations
of Baron Albert d'Anethan, Belgian Minister Plenipotentiary
and Dean of the Diplomatic Corps (translated and edited)

The Russo-Chinese War

Trading under Sail off Japan, 1860–99. The Recollections of Captain
John Baxter Will, Sailing-Master and Pilot (edited)

Faces of Japan: A Photographic Study

Russian Diplomatic and Consular Officials in East Asia. A Handbook
(compiled)

Japanese Diplomatic and Consular Officials in Russia. A Handbook
(compiled)

April in Russia: A Photographic Study

Japanese Recognition of the U.S.S.R.: Soviet-Japanese
Relations, 1921–1930

War and Revolution: Excerpts from the Letters and Diaries of the
Countess Olga Poutiatine (translated and edited)

The Strange Neutrality: Soviet-Japanese Relations
during the Second World War, 1941–1945

The Damned Inheritance

The Soviet Union and
the Manchurian Crises
1924–1935

George Alexander Lensen

THE DIPLOMATIC PRESS
TALLAHASSEE, FLORIDA

PUBLISHED BY

THE DIPLOMATIC PRESS, INC.
1102 Betton Road
Tallahassee, Florida 32303

© 1974 George Alexander Lensen

PRINTED AND BOUND IN THE UNITED STATES
ROSE PRINTING COMPANY, INC., TALLAHASSEE

To the memory of
Dan M. Ulrich
one of my most gifted graduate students
the petals of whose blossoming life
were scattered by a gust
of leukemia

Preface

When the Communists came to power in Russia they renounced tsarist imperialism and imperialistic acquisitions. They spoke of transferring to China without compensation the Chinese Eastern Railway, which had been constructed with Russian and French capital in Manchuria. With time, however, strategic and economic considerations reasserted themselves and the Soviet revolutionaries, turned statesmen, found it increasingly difficult to divest themselves of the railway and of the subsidiary enterprises they had inherited from the old regime. When Manchurian and Chinese officials sought to seize the railway, the Soviet Union defended her treaty rights by force. As in 1900, Russian troops invaded Manchuria, though this time they withdrew promptly once the railway had been secured.

During the Sino-Soviet dispute of 1929 Japan sympathized with the USSR, aware that her own railway rights would be attacked next if the Chinese seizure of the CER went unpunished. But the swiftness and effectiveness of the Russian strike renewed the specter of the Soviet menace in Japan. The Manchurian Incident in turn aborted the relatively friendly feelings that had developed in the USSR toward Japan since the Japanese recognition of the Soviet Union in 1925 and turned lingering Russian mistrust into dire apprehension as the Japanese armies advanced within striking distance of Siberia. Still, the Soviets reciprocated Japanese noninterference and did everything they could to avoid a conflict with Japan, who was immeasurably stronger than China. They even sold the CER, over which they had fought with China, to the Japanese puppet state of Manchukuo for a fraction

vii

of its worth to remove the major source of friction with Japan and to deprive the Kwantung Army of the opportunity to stage another "incident."

In spite of Soviet efforts to maintain peace—efforts repeatedly acknowledged by British and American diplomats—speculation abounded about the "inevitability" of war between Japan and the USSR. To some extent the war scare was part of the bargaining process over the CER; to some extent it was for domestic considerations, to obtain acceptance of the enormous army budgets and to arouse patriotic fervor. Even the anti-Communist witch hunts in China, Manchukuo and Japan did not preclude peaceful relations with the USSR. They were a tool of ultranationalists to gain control at home and to curry favor or to silence opposition in the capitalist world.

In giving an unbroken account of the CER controversy, which formed a link between the Manchurian crises of the 1920s and the 1930s and dominated the course of Soviet-Japanese relations from 1931 to 1935, I have shunted aside a number of issues for the sake of clarity. The nonaggression pact question and the debate over the "inevitability" of war between Japan and the USSR are discussed following the settlement of the CER controversy; Soviet-Japanese economic relations, anti-Communism in Japan, and the Soviet-Japanese-American triangle have been relegated to the Appendix. In his detailed review of my *Japanese Recognition of the USSR,* the Soviet historian G. V. Nezadorov complains that I made only passing reference to the Soviet proposal of 1926 for a nonaggression pact.[1] Although I have devoted an entire chapter to

---

[1] G. V. Nezadorov, "Amerikanskii istorik o sovetsko-iaponskikh otnosheniiakh 20-kh godov," 169—72.

the nonaggression pact question in this volume, I have left out material on cultural contacts. It is impossible to include everything and still focus on a meaningful theme.

In writing this book I have relied heavily on the foreign relations documents published by the Soviet Ministry of Foreign Affairs in Russian. While I have not seen the original documents, I am satisfied on the basis of spot checks that I made whenever I found translations of individual Soviet documents in the Japanese, British or American archives, that the published Soviet documents are about as accurate as the foreign relations documents published by other states, with minor editing occurring here and there and with embarrassing documents, if any, probably deleted rather than altered. Of particular value were the detailed resumés made by the foreign commissars and other leading Soviet officials of their conversations with Japanese diplomats and statesmen.

The foreign relations documents published in Japan have not yet reached the period under discussion. The Japanese archives collection microfilmed for the Library of Congress contained a number of pertinent reels, but the most useful Japanese source was the secret history of the negotiations between Japan and the Soviet Union, compiled by Tanaka Bunichiro, a Japanese Foreign Service Officer, on the basis of unpublished Foreign Office documents in 1942 and declassified and reprinted in 1969. Written for Foreign Office use, it proved to be relatively reliable. Its interpretations were marred by about the same degree of prejudice as the Russian documents.

A third mine of information was the British Foreign Office Archives, preserved in the Public Record Office Annex in London, where I obtained hundreds of photocopies of unpublished secret and confidential dispatches and of uninhibited, handwritten comments in the minutes pertaining to the diplomatic correspondence. For color, wit and penetrating analysis they are unsurpassed.

In the wake of the Cold War and of the rehabilitation of Japan, a number of American historians, working primarily with Japanese sources, have sought to mute the charges of Japanese aggression by contending that Japanese expansion had been partly a reaction to the Soviet menace. This study shows that no such menace actually existed in the 1930s and that the USSR was genuinely desirous of maintaining amicable relations with Japan. I have quoted heavily from the unpublished comments of British officials, who were basically anti-Russian and pro-Japanese, to bolster my thesis, lest it be felt that I was misled by the extensive use of Soviet documents.

The British documents for this period were opened to the public in the mid-1960s; the 1934 volume of the Soviet documents was published in 1971, but received in the United States only in 1972. This book is based, therefore, to a large extent on new material, not available to authors who touched on the subject earlier. Japanese and Chinese names have been rendered in Oriental fashion, surname first.

I wish to express my sincerest thanks and admiration to the staff of the Public Record Office Annex—Mr. T. J. Donovan (Officer I/C), Mr. A. Harrington, Mrs. M. McManus and Miss I. Appelman—for their friendly and efficient assistance in letting me see any documents I required and in obtaining photocopies thereof. I am indebted also to librarians at the M. E. Saltykov-Shchedrin State Public Library and the Library of the Academy of Sciences in Leningrad, the Lenin Public

Library in Moscow, the Library of the University of Helsinki, the National Diet Library in Tokyo, the Hoover Library at Stanford, the Herbert Hoover Presidential Library, the Library of Congress, the East Asian Library at Columbia University, the Russian collection of the New York Public Library, and the Robert Manning Strozier Library of the Florida State University. My research was subsidized in part by awards from the Inter-University Committee on Travel Grants, the National Endowment for the Humanities, the American Council of Learned Societies, the American Philosophical Society, and the Florida State University Research Council. I am grateful to four of my graduate students—Captain Dean E. Maskell, Major James F. Osborn, Captain William R. Farrell, and Mr. Benjamin P. Field—for proofreading the galleys and preparing the index during my stay in Moscow on the Senior Scholar Exchange between the American Council of Learned Societies and the Academy of Sciences of the USSR. Last but not least, I owe thanks to Dr. Donald D. Horward, chairman of the Department of History at the Florida State University, and to my colleagues in the department for making my periodic absences possible.

GEORGE ALEXANDER LENSEN

Tallahassee, Florida
March 1973

Contents

ILLUSTRATIONS

"The Chinese Eastern Railway is a *damnosa hereditas* which has come down to the Soviets from Czarist Russia. It was a wild and reckless military adventure that never brought any additional strength or profit to Russia but was, on the contrary, a running sore and a source of weakness. This kind of adventure, however, is one that is extremely difficult to liquidate."

Sir John Pratt, April 23, 1932.

"In a way Manchuria is somewhat like a football field, with China, Japan and Russia each furnishing a team. These three teams take turns to sit on the grandstand or to enter the contest, siding either with one team or the other as they wish."

Wang Ching-chun, February 1932.

"The history of this triangular struggle, which began in earnest at the close of the Sino-Japanese war of 1894–95, has produced many startling changes and sudden crises, and will doubtless continue to do so."

W. R. C. Green, September 27, 1932.

"National friendships and national enmities are both ephemeral. Friendships in particular give way to a very little friction, while enmities are softened by the finding of a common enemy."

Japan Weekly Chronicle, March 15, 1934.

"By 'liquidating' most of her interests in the Far East, Soviet Russia has turned herself from what the Japanese regarded as the 'Muscovite menace' into the 'dark horse' of the Pacific."

Colonel P. T. Etherton and H. Hessell Tiltman, 1932.

1

Revolutionary Idealism and National Interests

When the Communists seized power in Petrograd in the winter of 1917, they were flushed with idealism. Their condemnation of imperialism was not confined to the imperialism of other powers. They decried the wrongdoings of their own country and pledged rectification. In July 1918 Commissar of Foreign Affairs Georgii Chicherin offered to cancel the indemnities which China owed to Russia for damage inflicted during the Boxer uprising in 1900 and to give up Russia's special rights in China. Speaking before the Fifth Congress of Soviets, he stated dramatically: "We renounce the conquests of the tsarist government in Manchuria and we restore the sovereign rights of China in this territory, in which lies the principal trade artery—the Chinese Eastern Railway . . . ." He held out that "if part of the money invested in the construction of this railroad by the Russian people were repaid by China, China might buy it back without waiting

1

for the term stipulated in the agreement violently imposed on her."[1]

As the Red Army swept east during the Russian civil war, Moscow sought to allay Chinese apprehensions. On July 25, 1919, Deputy Commissar of Foreign Affairs Lev Karakhan issued a declaration in which he proclaimed that the Red Army was not the bearer of coercion, enslavement or conquest. The Communists in their eastward drive, he asserted, were "bringing liberation to the peoples from the yoke of the foreign bayonet, from the yoke of foreign gold, which were strangling the enslaved peoples of the East and among them first of all the Chinese people."[2]

Karakhan referred back to Chicherin's speech and repeated Moscow's willingness to discuss the annulment of old treaties and to negotiate the surrender of the Chinese Eastern Railway, which ran through Manchuria. "The Soviet government," he proclaimed, "does away with all special privileges, with all business establishments of Russian merchants on Chinese soil. Not one Russian official, pope or missionary has the right to interfere in Chinese affairs, and if he commits a crime, he must in fairness be tried by a local court. In China there must be no authority, no court, other than the authority and court of the Chinese people."[3]

But the military government which held sway in Peking at this time did not respond to the Soviet overture and did not accept the Soviet offer to enter upon negotiations concerning the railway.[4]

[1] Allen S. Whiting, *Soviet Policies in China 1917–1924*, 28–29.

[2] *Izvestiia*, August 26, 1919; M. S. Kapitsa, *Sovetsko-kitaiskie otnosheniia*, 32–33.

[3] Whiting, 28–29; Xenia Joukoff Eudin and Robert C. North, *Soviet Russia and the East 1920–1927*, 128; *Izvestiia*, August 26, 1919; Kapitsa, 32–33.

[4] "In strict law," an American China specialist contends, "the offer might in due course have been considered forfeited by want of takers." (O. Edmund Clubb, *China and Russia*, 171.) There is indirect evidence, however, that rival

The Chinese Eastern Railway (CER) had been built by Russia in the wake of the Sino-Japanese War of 1894–95 as a shortcut from Siberia to the Maritime Province. The Trans-Siberian Railway, on which work had begun in 1891, had been projected to run along the left bank of the Amur River, then southward, at a right angle, to Vladivostok. The diagonal route through Manchuria had constituted a saving of almost 600 miles and, it had seemed at the time, a corresponding savings to Russia in time and money.[5] Humiliated by Japan, China had agreed to the project, partly in payment for Russian participation in the Tripartite Intervention which had denied to Japan acquisition of the Liaotung Peninsula, partly to give teeth to a secret Russo-Chinese alliance, concluded in 1896, by facilitating dispatch of Russian forces to defend China in the event of renewed Japanese aggression.[6]

The CER had been constructed by the Chinese Eastern Railway Company, a private concern financed by the Russo-Chinese Bank. Although the bank, like the railway company, had been in private hands, the tsarist government had guaranteed the expenses and financial

---

Chinese leaders may have replied. The counselor of the Japanese embassy in Moscow, Amau Eiji, informed a British colleague in 1932 that Sun Yat-sen had dissuaded Lenin from abandoning all Russian rights over the railway in 1919. Sun had allegedly suggested a postponement, lest the railway merely pass into the hands of Chang Tso-lin, the warlord in control of Manchuria. (William Strang to Sir John Simon, No. 491, Moscow, September 5, 1932, "Confidential," Great Britain, Foreign Office Archives, FO 371/16178. Most British documents bear three numbers: the number indicated by the author of the document, the number assigned to it by the Foreign Office, and the number under which it can now be found in the Public Record Office Annex. The citations in this book refer to the first and third categories of numbers.)

[5] *Survey of International Affairs 1925*–[hereafter cited as *"Survey"*], II, 337–38.

[6] Japanese ultranationalists later were to adduce the Russo-Chinese alliance as an argument that the CER had been constructed by Russia as a hostile act against their country. In negotiating permission for the construction of the CER, the Russians had paid a generous bribe to the Chinese statesman Li Hung-chang, but this had been common practice in those days and had hardly constituted a "violent imposition."

obligations of the railroad, so that, in the words of the British minister at Peking, "although the railway belonged in theory to a private company, it came very near in practice to being a Russian government concern."[7] Likewise, while the land on which the railroad had been built had remained legally Chinese—an agreement in 1909 had confirmed Chinese sovereign rights—the railway zone had been administered by Russian officials.[8]

The construction of the CER had proved to be a mixed blessing for Russia. On one hand, it had constituted a great strategic gain; the railway had seemed to secure Russian domination of Manchuria and the consolidation of Russian power on the Pacific shores. On the other hand, the very strategic importance of the railway had aroused the apprehensions and opposition of the other powers and had plunged Russia into bitter conflicts, notably the Russo-Chinese War of 1900 and the Russo-Japanese War of 1904–1905.[9]

Until the overthrow of the tsarist regime in 1917, the CER had been solely under Russian management with Russian officials in key positions and the entire railway zone under Russian civil administration. The company had had a Chinese president, but he had not controlled the operations of the railway.[10] With the outbreak of the Russian civil war the railroad had been transformed by its Russian officials into a base of resistance to the Communists. General Dmitrii Khorvat, who had been general manager of the railway since

---

[7] Sir Miles W. Lampson to A. Henderson, No. 930, Peking, July 2, 1930, "Confidential," FO 371/14699.

[8] *Ibid.*

[9] For a detailed narrative of the Russo-Chinese conflict along the CER in 1900 and of the resulting Russian occupation of Manchuria, which contributed to the outbreak of the Russo-Japanese War, *see* George Alexander Lensen, *The Russo-Chinese War.*

[10] Whiting, 26; *Survey* 1925, 338.

1902, had become also director general and then commissioner of an All-Russian Provisional Government.[11] An attempt by Communist supporters to seize the railway had been thwarted, and they had been deported to the Soviet Union.[12]

In December 1917 the Soviet government had proclaimed the dismissal of Prince Nikolai Kudashev, the Russian minister to China, and of other representatives of the old regime who had refused to recognize it and support its policy of a separate peace with the Central Powers.[13] It had informed the Chinese envoy to Russia also of the removal of Khorvat as general manager of the railway and had taken the opportunity to propose to the Chinese government the formation of a mixed Soviet-Chinese liquidation commission concerning the CER question.[14] As the Chinese had not yet recognized the Soviet regime themselves, they had continued to work with the old diplomatic and railway officials. But though Khorvat had remained in office, the Soviet move had weakened his position, and in January 1918 he had been forced to concede Chinese authority over the railway in an agreement with the local Chinese commander Sze Shao-chang, and a Chinese, Kuo Chung-hsi, the governor of Kirin, had been appointed president of the CER.[15]

[11] Peter S. H. Tang, *Russian and Soviet Policy in Manchuria and Outer Mongolia 1911–1931*, 115.

[12] Tien-fong Cheng, *A History of Sino-Russian Relations*, 96-97.

[13] Order of the foreign commissar, dated November 26 (December 9), 1917, USSR, Ministry of Foreign Affairs, *Dokumenty vneshnei politiki* [hereafter cited as "DVP"], I, 43-44. According to the compilation of the old mission's official correspondence and the brief historical sketch of its activity concerning "the protection of Russian interests in China," Kudashev's dismissal had come in January 1918, after he had thrice failed to answer Foreign Commissar Leon Trotskii's offer to remain at his post in the service of the Soviet government. (*Sobranie dokumentov, kasaiushchikhsia deiatel'nosti Rossiiskoi Missii v Kitae za period 1 Noiabria 1917 g.-po 31 Dekabria 1920 g.*, 4.)

[14] Polivanov to Chinese envoy, "Not earlier than the end of November 1917," transmitted on or after December 9, DVP, I, 46-47.

[15] Cheng, 97. Kuo Chung-hsi is romanized also as Kuo Tsung-hsi. Whiting gives the name as Kuo Hsiang-chi. (Whiting, 27.)

The position of the Soviet government concerning the status of the CER had been stated in the instructions of the Foreign Commissariat to the international sections of the regional Soviets of Workers' and Peasants' Deputies on February 22, 1918: "In regard to the Chinese Eastern Railway it should be kept in mind that the treaty of 1896, recognized by us and so far not repudiated by China, remains in force and that consequently China retains her sovereign rights over the territory through which the railway runs, and is obligated to protect it, without interfering in the internal regulations of the railway and in our self-government. . . ."[16]

While the Western powers were preparing to intervene in Russia (in order to prevent German seizure of Allied war supplies, evacuate Czechoslovak troops willing to continue the struggle against the Central Powers, contain the spread of Communism, and be on the spot should the breakup of the Russian empire offer opportunities for the acquisition of spheres of influence, if not of territory) Japan tried, by means of a bilateral military pact with China, to maneuver herself into a position to edge out Khorvat and step into Russia's place as the dominant power in the CER zone.[17] During the Siberian Intervention itself the Japanese tried to seize control of the CER by various stratagems, but Western, particularly American, opposition thwarted their plans, and in 1919 the administration of the railway was entrusted temporarily to an Inter-Allied Committee.[18]

[16] Instructions of Foreign Commissariat, signed by Chicherin and Karakhan, DVP, I, 110-11.

[17] George F. Kennan, The Decision to Intervene, 86; Whiting, 28.

[18] Tang, 123-25. Years later, an American scholar related the failure of the League of Nations to undo the Japanese conquest of Manchuria to the history of the Siberian Intervention. "The 'new psychology' theorists who were so dis-

British and American representatives at Harbin reported in 1920 that the Japanese commander-in-chief had organized Chinese bandit raids on the CER to demonstrate the inadequacy of Chinese military protection and provide an excuse for Japanese seizure of the railway.[19] So transparent were the Japanese efforts, however, that they aroused strong anti-Japanese feeling in China and the Japanese minister at Peking requested his own recall.[20] The threat of an immediate take-over receded, but it was obvious to the British that Japan had not "permanently renounced all ambition of eventually capturing this line."[21]

In announcing the placement of the Siberian and the CER lines under the protection of the Allied military forces, the Inter-Allied Committee pledged to administer and defend them "without impairing the sovereign rights of the Russian people and with the cooperation of a Russian staff and employees."[22] When China objected on the ground that the CER ran through her territory, the Allies agreed to place the protection of the railway in Chinese hands.[23]

---

turbed by the recent failure of the peace machinery to function might have spared themselves this mental shock, had they been more conversant with the spirit of jealousy, suspicion and downright deceit which characterized the actions of the nations involved in this Siberian affair." (Paul Hibbert Clyde, "Manchuria and Siberia: 1918," 53.)

[19] FO 371/5312—779, China 1920, pp. 181-83; Sir B. Alston to Foreign Office, No. 282, Peking, June 8, 1920, "Secret," *Ibid.*, pp. 60A–60B.

[20] Sir A. Geddes to Foreign Office, No. 636D, Washington, September 14, 1920, FO 371/5312-779, China 1920, pp. 177–78.

[21] FO 371/5312-779, China 1920, 221A–22B. "Japan will never withdraw her troops from the line altogether until she evacuates Vladivostok," the British minister wrote the following year; "and even then it is doubtful if she will, but we have no means of forcing her to do so that I know of." (FO 371/6604-788, China 1921, pp. 123-24.)

[22] "Declaration of the Inter-Allied Railway Committee of March 14th, 1919," FO 371/5311-186.

[23] Tang, 125.

The assumption by Khorvat of full administrative authority over the Russian population in the CER zone[24] elicited a protest from the Chinese Foreign Office, which insisted that China had not abrogated her power of government by the concessions agreement of 1896.[25] A general strike of Russian employees in March 1920 (partly because Khorvat's use of railway funds for political purposes had left them without salaries) provided General Pao Kuei-ch'ing, who had succeeded Kuo as military governor of Kirin and concurrently as president of the CER in August 1919, with the opportunity to remove Khorvat and to assume the administration as well as the policing of the CER himself.[26]

When Soviet Russia had nationalized all banks, emigré officials of the Russo-Asiatic Bank had transferred the head office to Paris and there had reorganized the Russo-Asiatic Bank—la Banque Russo-Asiatique—with the assistance and protection of the French government. The French had a vested interest in the continued operation of the bank, because the Russo-Asiatic Bank had come into being in 1910 as a merger of the Russo-Chinese Bank (composed itself of a group of French banks and the St. Petersburg International Bank) with the French Banque du Nord.[27] Furthermore, the vast operations of the Russo-Asiatic Bank, which in 1917 had 114 branches and agencies, included ownership of the greater part of the shares of French companies such as the Sungari

[24] Approximately 150,000 Russians resided at Harbin and another 50,000 in other parts of the railway zone. (FO 371/5310-779, China 1920, p. 235.)

[25] J. N. Jordan to Earl Curzon, No. 54, Peking, January 31, 1920, FO 371/5310-779.

[26] Chinese Foreign Office Note, March 1, 1920, FO 371/5310-779.

[27] "Extract from L'Information Financière dated 6/6/28," in the Japanese Foreign Office Archives microfilmed for the Library of Congress, hereafter cited as "Japanese Archives," document S 619224, reel S 172, p. 507; Tang, 42, 117.

Mills Company, which operated the major grain mills in the Far East and supplied the city of Harbin with most of its electricity.[28]

As heir to the Chinese Eastern Bank, the Russo-Asiatic Bank claimed ownership of the CER, which had been financed through the former. Taking advantage of a clause in the statute of the CER, which stipulated that the board of directors of the railway could reside either in St. Petersburg or in Peking, the bank had convened and reorganized the board in Peking in April 1918. In October 1920 the Russo-Asiatic Bank signed an agreement with the Chinese government, which had just withdrawn its recognition of the diplomatic and consular representatives of the Provisional Government and had asserted its jurisdiction over the CER zone. The bank consented to China's assumption of "supreme control" over the railway in trust for Russia until China could make an arrangement concerning the railway with a Russian government she recognized.[29]

Moscow rejected the claim of the Russo-Asiatic Bank to act for the CER. As the Soviet envoy Adolf Ioffe argued in October 1922, if the bank was a Russian institution, it had been nationalized by the Soviet government; if it was a French institution it could not own the railway, because according to the contract of 1896 the shares of the railway could be held only by Russians or Chinese.[30] But with the dissolution of the Inter-Allied Commission at Chinese insistence in 1922, the Chinese, in the absence of a Russian govern-

[28] "Notice" of the Franco-Asiatic Bank, Japanese Archives, doc. S 619224, reel S 172, p. 504.

[29] Tang, 126-30; Tao Shing Chang, "International Controversies over the Chinese Eastern Railway," 113, 128–29; Whiting, 139, 155; Pao-chin Chu, "V. K. Wellington Koo," 239–42.

[30] Tang, 117, 133.

ment which they recognized, continued to deal with the Russo-Asiatic Bank as the nominal owner of the railway.[31]

When the Karakhan declaration had been made in 1919, Moscow had not relinquished anything that it had actually possessed. The Soviet renunciation had been partly propagandistic, designed to arouse Chinese sympathy and undermine the position of the other powers. Yet it had also been an expression of the idealism of the early years of Bolshevik rule, when the treaties with China and Japan, on which Russian legal rights pertaining to the CER were based, had seemed unworthy of a Communist government and the belief had prevailed that world revolution was about to destroy the old order.

By 1922 the situation had changed. Victory in the long and bloody civil war and the withdrawal of foreign troops from Russian soil had strengthened the bargaining position of the Soviet leaders, who had become transformed, in the words of one author, "from revolutionists operating within Russia into Russian statesmen conducting world revolution."[32] The concept of world revolution remained on the drawing board, but immediate attention was turned back to traditional national interests.

The civil war and the flight of a large part of the

[31] Lampson to Henderson, No. 930, July 2, 1930, FO 371/14699, p. 2; Tang, 128. The Russo-Asiatic Bank was liquidated in October 1926. In order to save those parts of the business which still had exploitation value and to compensate the creditors of the bank, the reconstruction and management of the remaining assets were entrusted to a new bank, the Banque Franco-Asiatique, constituted in January 1928 by virtue of a mandate concluded between the liquidators of the Russo-Asiatic Bank and a financial group including the Banque Robert Weyl, Sauerbach et Compagnie and the Banque Benard Frères. Established for a period of ninety-nine years, the Franco-Asiatic Bank had hopes of playing an active part in the economy of Manchuria, particularly in the building of new railways and harbors. (Japanese Archives, reel S 172, document 619224, pp. 506-14.)

[32] Whiting, 25.

bourgeoisie and intelligentsia had left the Russian economy in shambles. The Russian Far East was in dire need of Manchurian foodstuffs. Control of the CER now seemed necessary in order to ensure the delivery of these foodstuffs, to keep open swift communication with Vladivostok, and to prevent Japanese domination of the area. As the railway was a profitable enterprise and possession of great strategic importance, the Soviet leaders were in no position to part with it as a revolutionary gesture.[33]

The contract for the construction and operation of the CER had provided for free transfer of the railway to the Chinese government "eighty years from the day on which the line is finished and traffic is in operation." It had stipulated that the Chinese government could purchase it "thirty-six years from the day on which the entire line is finished and traffic is in operation" by "repaying in full all the capital involved, as well as all the debts contracted for this line, plus accrued interest."[34] Since the railway had begun functioning in July 1903, China would have been eligible according to the contract to receive it free of charge in 1983; she would have had the right to purchase it after 1939.[35] But, as noted, Chicherin had offered to sell the CER to China[36] ahead of schedule and Karakhan had echoed the willingness to part with it.

The lengthy dispute which developed over the terms on which the Russians would sell the railroad was due

[33] *Ibid.,* 30, 132; Eudin and North, 130–31. For a contemporary appraisal of the importance of the railway to Russia, see A. N. Ventsel', "Znachenie Kitaiskoi Vostochnoi zheleznoi dorogi v dal'nevostochnom voprose."

[34] Victor A. Yakhontoff, *Russia and the Soviet Union in the Far East,* 369; USSR, Academy of Sciences, Institut Kitaevedeniia, *Russko-kitaiskie otnosheniia,* 77.

[35] Yakhontoff, 31; Mo Shen, *Japan in Manchuria,* 336.

[36] Chicherin had been prepared to sell the southern branch, between Harbin and Changchun, to Japan, because it really formed part of the South Manchurian Railway, owned by the latter. (Whiting, 28–29.)

in part to the existence of two versions of the Karakhan declaration. One version had been published in a pamphlet by Vladimir Vilenskii (Sibiriakov), East Asian expert of the Council of People's Commissars. It had been cabled to Peking by Iakov Ianson, representative of the People's Commissariat of Foreign Affairs of Siberia and the Far East, in French and had been certified by Karakhan as a true copy. The other version had been printed in *Izvestiia* and other publications. The former version had provided for transfer of the CER and related concessions without compensation; the latter had contained no such clause.[37] A declaration made by Karakhan in September 1920 had promised the return to China free of charge of "all that was ravenously taken from her by the tsar's government and by the Russian bourgeoisie," but had not enumerated what was included in this category. It had held out transfer of the railway to China after rules and regulations for Russian use of the railway had been drawn up jointly by Chinese and Soviet officials, including officials of the Soviet-dominated Far Eastern Republic.[38]

Ioffe made it clear in Peking in November 1922 that the Karakhan declaration did not annul "the legal and just interests of Russia in China" and that should Russia cede to China her rights to the railway, "this fact would not annul Russia's interests in the Chinese Eastern Railway, which comprises a part of the great Siberian Railway connecting one sector of Russia with the other."[39] When Karakhan himself succeeded Ioffe

[37] Whiting attributes the deletion of the clause to a change in policy. (Whiting, 33.) Kapitsa, on the other hand, contends that the clause had been merely in a preliminary draft, not in the final declaration, and that its inclusion in the Vilenskii pamphlet and subsequent transmission by wire had been a careless error. (Kapitsa, 35.)

[38] Whiting, 149.

[39] Eudin and North, 131; Lampson to Henderson, No. 930, p. 2.

as envoy to Peking in the fall of 1923, he sought to secure Chinese respect for "the legal rights of the USSR" in return for Soviet respect for Chinese sovereignty in the railway zone. Moscow rejected, in the words of a contemporary Soviet author, "all [foreign] claims to the Chinese Eastern Railway, including those of the Russo-Asiatic Bank with its French protector." As he put it: "Soviet Russia cannot tolerate a situation under which counterrevolutionary groups hostile to her possess property belonging to the USSR on Chinese territory and receive the acknowledgment of the Chinese administration."[40]

The Sino-Soviet agreement of May 31, 1924, whereby the Peking government recognized the USSR, tacitly acknowledged Soviet ownership of the CER by reiterating that it could be redeemed by China with Chinese capital, though the terms and manner of transfer were left for negotiation at a special conference. The agreement confirmed the railway's transformation in October 1920 from a line with political and military overtones to a strictly commercial enterprise. It prohibited the existence within the respective territories of China and the USSR of groups seeking the violent overthrow of each other's governments or the encouragement of propaganda against each other's political and social systems. The agreement provided for joint Sino-Soviet management of the railway and stipulated that its future must be determined by the Republic of China and the USSR "to the exclusion of any third party or parties."[41]

Since Marshal Chang Tso-lin rather than the Peking government was in actual control of the Autonomous

---

[40] Tang, 148.
[41] Aitchen K. Wu, *China and the Soviet Union*, 347–50; Yakhontoff, 398–401; USSR, Academy of Sciences, Institut Kitaevedeniia, *Sovetsko-kitaiskie otnosheniia*, 90–92.

Three Eastern Provinces, as the Chinese called Manchuria through which the CER ran, the Soviets signed an agreement with his government too. Concluded at Mukden, and thus known as the Mukden Agreement, on September 20 of the same year, it was similar to the Peking agreement, except that it provided for the free transfer of the CER twenty years earlier, that is in 1963.[42]

Both agreements provided for the principle of equal representation between Soviet and Chinese nationals. But while the Peking agreement was supplemented by a declaration that "the application of this principle is not to be understood to mean that the present employees of Russian nationality shall be dismissed for the sole purpose of enforcing the said principle," the Mukden agreement was accompanied by a declaration which provided for the dismissal by either side of persons whose presence or activity constituted a menace to the other side. Although couched in reciprocal language, the declaration was directed primarily against White Russians.[43] There is evidence that Chang may even have consented not to employ White Russians on the railway or elsewhere.[44]

An agreement for the provisional management of the CER, concluded at Peking in March 1924 and incorporated in the general agreement of May 31, provided for a board of directors of ten persons, five of whom, including the president of the board (who was also

[42] *Sovetsko-kitaiskie otnosheniia*, 94–96; Tang, 153; O. Edmund Clubb, *China and Russia*, 210–11. The Mukden Agreement was approved by Peking in March 1925 as a supplement to its own agreement. For a discussion of the relationship between the Mukden government and the national government, see C. Walter Young, *Japan's Special Position in Manchuria*, I, 8–25.

[43] Yakhontoff, 387–404.

[44] James William Christopher, *Conflict in the Far East*, 78; M. S. Myers to MacMurray, No. 201, March 27, 1929, United States, Department of State, *Foreign Relations of the United States*, hereafter abbreviated as "FRUS," 1929, II, 190–91.

director-general or *tupan*) were to be appointed by China, five, including the vice president of the board, by the Soviet Union. There was to be a board of auditors of five persons, two of them, including the chairman, appointed by China, three by the Soviet Union. The railway continued to have also a general manager, who was to be Russian, and two assistant managers, one Russian and one Chinese. The above officers were to be appointed by the board of directors; the appointments were subject to confirmation by the Soviet and Chinese governments. The board of directors was to appoint also the chiefs and assistant chiefs of the various railway departments, the positions being divided between the two countries. If a citizen of one country was chief of a department, a citizen of the other was to be assistant chief of that department.[45]

On October 3 the senior Chinese director of the railway informed his White Russian and Chinese colleagues that Chang Tso-lin had ordered their dismissal and that a new Soviet-Chinese board of directors would take their place.[46] The following day the old general manager, Boris Ostroumov, and three colleagues (I. A. Mikhailov, S. L. Gondatti, and M. I. Sepunin were arrested and placed in solitary confinement.[47]

[45] Chu, 256–57; Lampson to Henderson, No. 930, p. 3.

[46] Sir R. Macleay to Foreign Office, No. 286R, Peking, October 7, 1924, FO 371/10267–760.

[47] They were held in solitary confinement for over half a year without being shown a copy of the charges against them. As the *Morning Post* pointed out on April 3, 1925, since Ostroumov was about 60 years old and Gondatti over 70 and since both were seriously ill, they would be "condemned to death in prison for no crime at all" if detained any longer. Tried and convicted eventually on a trumped-up charge of "violation of official duties," Ostroumov remained in prison for another five months, when he was released belatedly, after joint appeals by the ministers of France, Great Britain, the United States, and Japan, under an amnesty issued many months earlier. (*Survey* 1925, II, 345; Great Britain, *Parliamentary Papers, China,* No. 3 [1926], p. 85; FO 371/10951–760.) For the text of the indictment, see FO 371/10951, China 1925, p. 50 ff. For a detailed analysis of the day-by-day proceedings and the disregard by the Chinese court of the various articles of the Statutes of Criminal Procedure, see Consul Herbert

A Soviet engineer, A. N. Ivanov, was appointed as the new general manager and another Soviet citizen, A. A. Eismont, as the assistant general manager. General Pao Kuei-ch'ing was reconfirmed in his position as president of the CER. Except for the changes in personnel, the managerial organization remained essentially the same as that negotiated between the Chinese government and the Russo-Asiatic Bank four years earlier.[48]

On paper, Chinese equality in the administration seemed assured. Yet in reality the USSR retained a dominant position. The provision that the various railway posts be filled on the basis of equal representation of the citizens of both countries was negated in part by the stipulation that appointments be made "in accordance with the ability and technical, as well as educational, qualifications of the applicants," because there was a shortage of qualified Chinese railroad personnel.[49] The appointment of a Soviet general manager proved to be a crucial advantage for the USSR. By not attending board of directors meetings or by abstaining from voting, the Russians could block action by the board of directors, because all board decisions required the consent of not less than six members, thus leaving the Soviet general manager in control of

---

Phillips to Ambassador Sir R. Macleay, No. 121, Harbin, November 10, 1925, FO 371/11666–766. As Phillips concluded: "From first to last the whole case was conducted as a political prosecution and only the barest form of proper legal procedure was observed."

[48] Chang, "International Controversies," 129.

[49] Chu asserts that the equal representation clause was diluted further by the provision that employees of Russian nationality not be dismissed for the sole purpose of enforcing the principle of equal representation. (Chu, 269–70.) Since White Russian employees, whom the Soviets wished dismissed, were Russian by nationality but stateless or Chinese by citizenship, it is not clear whether the provision was to protect Soviet or Chinese interests. As will be seen, the Chinese opposed Ivanov's attempts to discharge all White Russians.

affairs.[50] Moreover, most of the department chiefs were Russian.[51]

The spread of Soviet influence in the railway zone was reflected in the dismissal of White Russian school officials and their replacement by Soviet officials in the spring of 1925, despite assurances by Chinese officials the preceding October that this would not be allowed to happen. "The control over the Russian schools throughout the Chinese Eastern Railway Zone, which the Soviet Government has now acquired," the British consul reported from Harbin, "affords first-class opportunities for propaganda work."[52]

The assistance that the Soviet general manager showed to Soviet organizations, such as the trade unions of officers and workmen of the CER, and his pressure for the dismissal of White Russians even if they had become naturalized Chinese citizens, irked the Chinese. So did Ivanov's cancellation of the annual subsidy of 175,000 gold rubles by the CER to the churches in Harbin and his attempt to introduce the *chervonets* as legal currency in the railway zone.[53]

On April 9 Ivanov issued an order in his own name that all employees of the CER who had not officially applied for registration as citizens of the USSR or the Republic of China by May 31 or whose registration had been refused would be dismissed. A rumor that the Soviet authorities planned to transfer those who became Soviet citizens to railways in the USSR and turn the CER into a health resort for employees starving in Russia swelled the ranks of emigrés who applied

[50] Whiting, 231; Tang, 182–86.

[51] For a detailed analysis of the organization of the CER and the positions held by Russians and Chinese, see Tang, 169–74.

[52] Phillips to Chargé d'Affaires C. M. Palairet, No. 24, Harbin, March 12, 1925, "Secret," FO 371/10951.

[53] Phillips to Macleay, No. 92, Harbin, November 22, 1924, "Confidential," FO 371/10951–760.

for Chinese citizenship. But the Chinese deemed that Ivanov had no authority to issue such an order and had done so in an attempt to Bolshevize the railroad.[54] As a heated dispute ensued, the emigré paper *Russkii Golos* remarked that it was "clear as day to everyone that the Soviet-Chinese friendship may not even be compared to a rosy-hued, but worm-eaten apple."[55] Reporting that the dispute between the Soviet and Chinese directors of the CER was becoming increasingly acute as Ivanov was "apparently pouring oil upon the flames" by his insistence that the above-mentioned order be carried out and General Pao, though appointed six months before, delayed to take up his post as president of the railway, the British consul general at Harbin warned that "it hardly seems possible for the situation to continue indefinitely without one or the other climbing down or a serious clash of some sort occurring."[56]

Chinese resentment was translated into action when Ivanov refused to continue transporting Chinese railway guards and troops on credit. To Marshal Chang Tso-lin, Ivanov's order, issued in November 1925 on his own responsibility as general manager,[57] seemed to be not only arbitrary but hostile, because it came in the wake of General Kuo Sung-lin's uprising against him.[58] To the Soviets, on the other hand, the order seemed necessary, because the Mukden government

---

[54] Phillips to Palairet, No. 40, Harbin, April 23, 1925, FO 371/10951–760. Russians who became Soviet citizens merely to retain their jobs were dubbed "Radishes," for they were red on the outside, white on the inside. (Ben Dorfman, "White Russians in the Far East," 166–67.)

[55] *Russkii Golos*, April 24, 1925, as translated in FO 371/10951–760.

[56] Phillips to Palairet, No. 43, Harbin, April 30, 1925, FO 371/10951–760.

[57] *Survey* 1925, 345.

[58] By the time the order was enforced, however, Chang's troops were not rushing to quell the rebellion, but were returning to their posts at Harbin. (Porter to Macleay, No. 6, Harbin, February 1, 1926, "Confidential," FO 371/11666–766.)

already owed the railway over eleven million dollars.

When the railway authorities at Kuanch'engtzu Station, on the basis of Ivanov's order, refused free passage to Mukden troops on January 16, 1926, the soldiers forcibly occupied a Harbin-bound mail train, seized the locomotive, removed the keys from the switches, and brought operations to a halt at the station and elsewhere on the line. The next day the soldiers commandeered the mail train and forced the crew to take them to Harbin without obtaining the necessary clearance and ignoring "closed" semaphores. This and other incidents on the 17th and 18th made railway communication dangerous and forced Ivanov to terminate it officially, though it had in fact already ground to a halt.[59] With disorderly Chinese "guards" in control of the entire southern line, Ivanov declared on January 21 that he was "unable to bear the responsibility for the safe passage of passenger and freight traffic," and decreed an end to all movement there.[60]

The following afternoon, on January 22, Ivanov and three Soviet directors of the CER were arrested by the forces of General Chang Huan-hsiang at Marshal Chang Tso-lin's behest[61] on the charge of disobeying martial law.[62]

On January 19 Karakhan had sent a note of warning to the Chinese Foreign Minister Wang Cheng-t'ing as well as to Chang Tso-lin.[63] Now, on January 22, he addressed another note to the former, demanding the

[59] Note of Ambassador Lev Karakhan to Foreign Minister Wang Cheng-t'ing, January 19, 1926, in DVP, IX, 37–39.

[60] Consul General Grandt to Foreign Commissariat, January 22, 1926, DVP, IX, 43–44.

[61] Karakhan to Wang Cheng-t'ing, January 22, 1926, DVP, IX, 44; Tang, 186–87.

[62] Porter to Macleay, No. 6.

[63] Sir R. Hodgson to Sir Austen Chamberlain, No. 104, Moscow, February 9, 1926, FO 371/11666–766.

immediate release of Ivanov. Wang replied the following day that the Foreign Ministry jointly with the Ministry of Communications had sent an energetic telegram
to the highest authorities of the Three Eastern Provinces to this effect.[64]

That day, on the twenty-third, Karakhan conveyed
to Wang a telegram from Chicherin, addressed to Tuan
Ch'i-jui, the chief executive of the Chinese Republic.
It had been dispatched on the twenty-second, before
the receipt of Wang's note. The ultimatum, for such
was the telegram, made clear Moscow's determination
to defend Russian interests in the Far East. Referring
to Ivanov's arrest by the Chinese military authorities
in Harbin following five days of systematic violation
of the CER agreement as "unheard of," Chicherin
declared that the USSR expected the Chinese government to take "the necessary measures for the peaceful
solution of the question" and not evade an investigation
of the violation of the railway agreement by either side.
He put forth the demand that "within a period of three
days complete order be restored on the CER, the treaty
be implemented, and Mr. Ivanov be freed." "If for
any reason the Chinese Government should not be
in a position to secure a peaceful solution of these
questions within the given period," Chicherin continued, "the Soviet Government asks the Chinese
Government to allow the USSR with her own forces
to assure the implementation of the treaty and to defend
the mutual interests of China and the USSR on the
CER."[65]

Wang replied two days later, on January 25, in the
name of Tuan that the latter, upon receipt of Chicherin's telegram, had twice telegraphed Chang Tso-lin

[64] DVP, IX, 45.
[65] Chicherin to Tuan Ch'i-jui, January 22, 1926, DVP, IX, 48; FO 371/11666.

to settle the incident and that Ivanov had been freed. Wang expressed confidence that everything would be resolved peacefully very soon and remarked that this would be to their mutual advantage, as the CER served the interests of both countries.[66]

Ivanov had been released as the result of an agreement signed the previous day at Mukden between Consul General Kravkovetskii and Kao, the commissioner for foreign affairs of the Three Eastern Provinces. It was a compromise settlement, whereby the Chinese, on one hand, recognized that they must pay for the transporation of their troops, while the Soviets, on the other hand, agreed to deduct the amount from China's share of annual profits.[67] But Ivanov's role in the incident had discredited him in the Soviet Union. In 1925 the Soviet directors of the CER had been split into two factions, with Ivanov and Consul General Ivan Grandt favoring a hard line toward the Chinese, Vice President V. P. Pozdeev a conciliatory policy. The departure of Pozdeev in the Spring of 1925 had been interpreted as a victory for Ivanov.[68] Now Ivanov himself was recalled and Eismont, who had been the real technical head of the railway, was going on leave and was not expected to return. Even Karakhan's transfer was rumored as a result of the affair.[69]

The chiefs of various railway departments also were being changed in deference to Chinese wishes and the Soviet consul general was reported to be on the verge of removal.[70]

Chinese efforts to shake off Soviet domination of

[66] DVP, IX 48–49.
[67] Tang, 187.
[68] Phillips to Palairet, No. 40.
[69] Porter to Macleay, No. 24, March 12, 1926, FO 371/11666–766.
[70] Porter to Macleay, No. 41, Harbin, April 20, 1926, FO 371/11666–766; Tang, 180.

the CER persisted. Chang Huan-hsiang, the Chinese civil administrator, rudely informed L. P. Serebriakov, deputy commissar of transport and former vice president of the CER whom Moscow sent to Manchuria in an effort to smooth relations, that he could not host a banquet for the Chinese administration until "all misunderstandings and strained relations" had been eliminated. Once this had been done, Chang declared pointedly, he himself "with the entire Chinese world" would feast Serebriakov "as a guest in our native country."[71]

In August Chang Tso-lin demanded the surrender by the CER of all its vessels and the liquidation of its educational section, all schools to be transferred to the Direction of Popular Education, under the commander-in-chief of the Three Eastern Provinces. Foreign Commissar Chicherin, in a note to the Chinese chargé d'affaires in Moscow, dated August 31, expressed the willingness of his government "to examine all questions at issue" connected with the Mukden agreement, but categorically protested against unilateral infringement by the Chinese side of Soviet treaty rights in Northern Manchuria. He warned that the Soviet government "cannot permit the actions of the Autonomous Government of the Three Eastern Provinces in violation of existing treaties" and called for "the immediate withdrawal of demands upon the head office of the Chinese Eastern Railway" and the examination of the questions by "the normally acting diplomatic organs of both Governments."[72]

[71] Chang Huan-hsiang to Serebriakov, April 10, 1926, FO 371/11666–766.

[72] Chicherin to Chinese chargé d'affaires, Moscow, August 31, 1926, enclosed in Hodgson to Chamberlain, No. 647, Moscow, September 8, 1926, FO 371/11666–766. Tang dismisses the Soviet protest as without foundation, "as no treaty rights of inland navigation had ever been granted to the USSR by China since the abolition of the unequal treaties between them." (Tang, 194.) The seizure

On September 2 Chinese authorities at Harbin, acting under Chang's instructions, seized eleven steamers
and thirty barges of the Sungari River fleet, operated
by the railway company, and its wharves, warehouses
and machinery, ejected its employees and hoisted the
Chinese naval flag on the vessels. On September 4
the Education Department of the CER was forcibly
dissolved and its officials locked out.[73]

Chicherin vented his indignation in a strongly
worded note to the Chinese chargé d'affaires on September 7. Asserting that the "unexampled actions"
of the Chinese local officials "not only violate rudely
the treaty relations between the [Soviet] Union and
the Chinese Republic but are absolutely inadmissable
between states enjoying normal diplomatic relations,"
Chicherin warned that "by permitting such actions on
the part of the authorities of the Three Eastern Provinces," the Chinese government created "serious difficulties for further normal diplomatic relations with
the [Soviet] Union" and must, therefore, bear "all
responsibility" for the deterioration in relations with
the USSR. Chicherin repeated his government's readiness "to subject to careful examination all questions
at issue arising from the agreement existing between
the two states," but insisted that the Chinese government "take urgent measures for the immediate reversal
of the above-mentioned violation of its rights and for
the cessation of a situation which may affect in the
most unpleasant manner further relations between
the countries."[74]

---

of the Russian vessels may have been in retaliation for the confiscation of Chinese
steamers at the Eggersheld wharves at Vladivostok in March of that year. (Macleay
to Foreign Office, No. 317 [R], Peking, September 16, 1926, FO 371/11666–766;
Chang, 173.)

[73] Macleay to Foreign Office, No. 317 (R); Clubb, *China and Russia*, 221.

[74] Chicherin to Chinese chargé d'affaires, Moscow, September 7, 1926, enclosed
in Hodgson to Chamberlain, No. 647.

Chicherin's language was strong. "The Soviet notes are quite as 'imperialistic' in tone as any that we should send," a British official remarked sarcastically.[75] But for the moment Russian protests remained confined to words and the recall of Karakhan to Moscow that month seemed to be a concession to Chang Tso-lin.[76] L. A. Savrasov, the Soviet vice president of the CER, adopted the soft approach that Serebriakov and Pozdeev had pursued and by agreeing to practically all the demands of his Chinese colleagues succeeded in reestablishing cordial relations with them.

Savrasov's efforts were nullified, however, when Chargé d'Affaires Chernykh appeared on the scene in November and took charge of the negotiations. Reverting to the hard line of Ivanov, Grandt and Karakhan, Chernykh injected purely political issues which were unacceptable to the Chinese. Irate, Yü Chung-han, the Chinese president of the CER, questioned the sincerity of Savrasov and Chernykh in an interview, published by the Japanese newspaper *Manshu Nichi-Nichi* in Dairen on November 13, and called them "coolies" and "jellyfishes." He declared that he would go ahead and make "independent amendments in compliance with the Soviet-Chinese and Mukden-Soviet agreements" and threatened that if the Russians did not submit to this, "the only remaining way will be the annexation of the Chinese Eastern Railway." Caught between Chernykh on one side and Yü on the other, Savrasov resigned in order to block a meeting of the board of directors and thereby pre-

---

[75] FO 371/11666–766, China, 1926, p. 233.

[76] Porter to Macleay, No. 24; Chang, 174. Emboldened, Chang established a Chinese land office in the railway zone to compete with the Railway Land Department in the leasing of land and in 1927 forced the railway administration to deposit half of its surplus funds in Chinese banks. (Lampson to Henderson, No. 930.)

vent a decision inimical to Soviet interests. But his move worsened the situation and the Chinese were about to proclaim martial law, abolish the board of directors and seize the railway, when Moscow cabled that his replacement, M. M. Lashevich, would leave at once for Harbin. A collision was temporarily avoided.

"The feeling among leading Chinese here against the Reds is very strong," the British consul reported. He noted that the Chinese president of the CER was "almost too outspoken in his denunciation of them for an official who is supposed to be conducting important and delicate negotiations." Pointing to the "impulsive and ambitious character" of General Chang Huan-hsiang, the civil administrator, he observed that "as far as personalities are concerned the stage is set for a Chinese *coup* as soon as an opportune moment arrives."[77]

In February 1927 the military governor of Shantung, Chang Tsung-ch'ang, an old associate of Chang Tso-lin and a prominent member of the National Pacification Army (Ankuochün) created by him, seized the Soviet freighter *Pamiati Lenina* and arrested her crew and passengers, including a number of Soviet diplomatic couriers and Fannie Borodin, the American wife of Mikhail Borodin, the Soviet adviser to the Kuomintang or Nationalist Party. Chang Tso-lin did not heed a Soviet demand for their release and when Mrs. Borodin and the couriers were freed by order of a Peking judge, Chang tried to have them rearrested, though they made good their escape. In late March Chang Tso-lin's police

---

[77] Porter to Macleay, No. 126, Harbin, November 26, 1926, FO 371/12464–788. "We have already heard of Monsieur Chernykh's ill-advised 'butting-in'; he appears to have stirred up a pretty kettle of fish (or jelly-fish)," Toller (?) remarked. (FO 371/12464–788, China, 1926, p. 235.)

arrested a number of Peking college students and demanded that the colleges in that city deliver to them other students suspected of Kuomintang and Communist affiliation.[78]

On April 6 Chang Tso-lin directed a raid by Chinese Police and gendarmes on a number of buildings in the Soviet embassy compound in Peking, including the office of the military attaché, whence instructions had gone to the advisers and instructors of Chinese revolutionary groups. Documents seized in the raid provided evidence of Soviet aspirations to Bolshevize China and for years to come sustained Chinese and Japanese fears of Communist subversion.[79]

Chang's motives had been partly domestic—to liquidate revolutionary opponents who had taken refuge in the Soviet embassy or were associated with it—but his action clearly violated the extraterritorial status and diplomatic immunity of the embassy compound and its foreign personnel, guaranteed by international law.[80] When Chang Tso-lin, who by now had

[78] Clubb, *China and Russia,* 221–23.

[79] The Soviet government branded the documents published by the Chinese as forgeries and implicated the Western powers, notably England, in conspiring with Chang to violate the diplomatic sanctity of its embassy in order to plant false documents about Soviet hostile intentions to justify their own plans against the USSR. Some of the published documents may have been fabrications, but most are regarded as authentic by reputable scholars. (C. Martin Wilbur and Julie Lien-ying How, *Documents on Communism, Nationalism and Soviet Advisers in China 1918–1927,* 8–37.) However, as G. A. Mounsey, head of the Far Eastern Department of the British Foreign Office, remarked: "Like so many similar documents, these deal more with aspirations than facts." (FO 371/13932–611.) Chang had gained the prior approval of the Western diplomats for a raid on the offices of Dalbank (Far Eastern Bank) and of the CER, adjoining but outside the Soviet embassy grounds. They had not sanctioned the invasion of the embassy complex, but, when it occurred, they made no attempt to dissuade the intruders; in fact, they seemed pleased that it had occurred. The attitude of the British was reflected in a raid on Soviet House in London the following month and in the severance of diplomatic relations with the USSR when the raiders found documents seeming to link the Soviet Union with Communist subversion in Great Britain. Only Japan had reservations about the Chinese raid, conscious perhaps of the dangerous precedent such action set. (Clubb, 223–27.)

[80] Tang, 199.

become head of the Peking government and thus was in a more powerful position than he had been as warlord of Manchuria, rejected Soviet protests, refused to return the seized documents, and executed the Chinese Communists arrested on the premises, the USSR recalled her major diplomatic representatives from Peking and the Peking government responded in kind.[81]

The Peking government was not the only government in China, however, and as General Chiang Kaishek, the head of the rival regime, sent a note to Chernykh denouncing Chang's raid on the Soviet embassy, it looked for a moment as if the Russians might retain their influential position in the south.

The Soviet Union's association with the revolutionary government of the Kuomintang in Canton dated back to 1923, when Sun Yat-sen had requested and received Russian aid. In 1924 Soviet advisers had begun reorganizing the Kuomintang on the pattern of the Russian Communist Party. Ideological differences had not prevented the pragmatic support of the Kuomintang in its anti-imperialist (anti-Western and anti-Japanese) struggle, just as it had not deterred Moscow's dispatch of military aid and advisers to Feng Yü-hsiang, one of the militarists in Peking, in his struggle against "imperialism." The Chinese Communist Party had collaborated with the Kuomintang, supporting its left wing without seizing control of it, hoping, in accordance with the theses of the Comintern, to radicalize the party from within.

But the right wing of the Kuomintang, headed by Chiang Kai-shek, who had succeeded Sun after his death, had become increasingly alienated from the left

---

[81] Robert C. North, *Moscow and Chinese Communists,* 113; Clubb, 224–25. Soviet consular personnel remained in China; the Chinese Chargé d'Affaires Cheng Yen-hsi, in Moscow.

wing, which was fostering peasant seizure of land, as many of the Kuomintang officers came from landed families. In contrast to the social revolution desired by the left-wingers, Chiang had come to stress nationalism and had begun to solicit the support of the industrial capitalists in the coastal cities; in May 1927 Nationalist troops had attacked labor unions and peasant associations in Changsha.

Although Soviet advisers and aid had played a major role in his conquest of Northern China, Chiang turned on his Communist allies when victory was within his grasp and their assistance threatened to mature into dictation. On April 12, only four days after his denunciation of Chang's raid on the Soviet embassy and before the first documents seized in the raid had been made public, Chiang suddenly attacked the Chinese Communists and the leftist workers who had fought on his side in the capture of Shanghai.

Belated Russian attempts to build up a Communist-led army that could unseat the recalcitrant generals of the Kuomintang acerbated the conflict between the Kuomintang Right and the Communists. Caught in the middle, the Kuomintang Left was forced to choose sides and also turned against the Communists and their foreign mentors. As Chinese Communists were killed by the tens of thousands, the Soviet advisers returned to the USSR.[82]

Like Chang Tso-lin, Chiang Kai-shek had struck primarily at the native Communists, but the Soviets could not refrain from siding with the latter. When they backed an unsuccessful uprising at Canton in December 1927, five Soviet consular officials were

[82] Clubb, *China and Russia,* 235–49.

executed by Nationalist troops[83] and the Nationalist government broke off relations with the USSR.[84]

[83] *Ibid.*, 252.

[84] According to North, China "terminated official relations." (North, 113.) Kapitsa denies that diplomatic relations were severed. He points out that the Chinese consulates in the USSR remained open and that the Chinese embassy in Moscow continued to function. The Soviet consulate general in Peking remained open, as did the consulates in Sinkiang (Urumchi, Kashgar, Kuldja, Sharasume, Chuguchak) and Northeast China (Shenyang [Mukden], Harbin, Tsitsihar, Hailar, Sakhalian and Man'chzhuria [Manchuli] Station). (Kapitsa, 190.)

2

Mounting Chinese Nationalism

When Chiang Kai-shek completed the conquest of Northern China in June 1928 and moved the seat of the central government from Peking to Nanking, all powers recognized his regime except the USSR. Yet the break in normal diplomatic relations between the Soviet Union and China did not signify the expulsion of the Russians from Manchuria, over which Nanking did not have direct control. As the British minister reported, "the Russian position in Manchuria was still far too strong to be vitally affected by the catastrophe that overtook Soviet diplomacy in other parts of China."[1]

Manchuria by this time was ruled by Marshal Chang Hsüeh-liang, who had seized power after his father, Chang Tso-lin, had been assassinated on his way back from Peking to Mukden. The Japanese, who had long supported Chang Tso-lin, had blown up his railway carriage because he had become too independent of

[1] Lampson to Henderson, No. 930; Conrad Brandt, *Stalin's Failure in China*, 113–18.

them and they had wished to replace him with General Yang Yu-t'ing, chief of staff of the Mukden armies. But Chang Hsüeh-liang had outfoxed Yang and a fellow-rival, Chang Yui-huai, the former minister of communications. He had invited them to his house for a friendly game of mahjong and, when they had arrived, had them slain by his bodyguards, announcing publicly that they had been tried for treason against the government of Mukden, found guilty, and executed.[2]

Although Chang Hsüeh-liang and his principal officers pledged allegiance to the Nanking government, they remained virtually independent, free to deal with the Japanese and Russians directly. Yet they shared with the central authorities a mounting nationalism and joined in the Kuomintang campaign to recover the rights and concessions forced from China by the foreign powers. Emboldened by the passivity with which the Soviets had withdrawn from China proper and believing that internal difficulties in the USSR precluded Russian resistance, the Manchurian authorities, with the blessing of Nanking, attempted to take control of the Chinese Eastern Railway.[3]

On December 22, following a propaganda campaign during which public officials, private citizens and newspapers had lambasted the Soviet Union's dominant position in the administration of the CER, Harbin police, on instructions from Mukden, forcibly seized the railway's costly telephone system. When the Rus-

[2] Consul General Tours to Chamberlain, No. 3, Mukden, March 31, 1929, FO 371/13891–638.
[3] G. Badham-Thornhill to Lampson, Peking, September 24, 1929, "Secret," FO 376/13955; Lampson to Henderson, No. 930; O. Edmund Clubb, *Twentieth Century China*, 160–62; Max Beloff, *The Foreign Policy of Soviet Russia 1929–1941*, I, 72; S. Iu. Vygodskii, *Vneshniaia politika SSSR 1924–1929 g.g.*, 300; Tang, 200; Whiting, 231.

sians did not oppose the move, even though the ownership of the telephone system had been confirmed eighteen months before,[4] Chang Hsüeh-liang went a step
further and on December 29 hauled down the flag of
the CER—a composite of the Chinese five-colored flag
on top and the Soviet flag below—and hoisted the new
sun-flag of the Kuomintang instead.[5]

As the new year began, the Chinese members of
the railway administration put forth various demands
to strengthen their role, including the demand that
henceforth the orders of the Soviet general manager
and other Soviet senior railway officials must be countersigned by their Chinese assistants.[6] Alarmed by the
train of events, the Soviet government on February
2, 1929, proposed to Mukden the discussion and settlement of disputed issues. When no reply to the note
was received, Boris Mel'nikov, the Soviet consul
general at Harbin, proceeded to Mukden in March
to defuse the explosive situation,[7] but, as the British
consul general reported, "only succeeded in considerably widening the breach."[8]

Mel'nikov and Chang Hsüeh-liang were equally
undiplomatic and their meeting "singularly stormy."
Mel'nikov accused the Chinese of violating the treaties
and agreements between their countries. Chang
retorted that it ill behooved a representative of the
Soviet government to speak of the violation of treaties
and agreements, for it itself had violated them
repeatedly. He rejected Mel'nikov's protest against

[4] FRUS 1929, II, 188; Kapitsa, 191–92.
[5] G. C. Hanson to MacMurray, No. 1869, Harbin, December 31, 1928, FRUS 1929, II, 186.
[6] Lampson to Henderson, July 2, 1920, pp. 3–4; Christopher, 75; Cheng, 150.
[7] Meyers to MacMurray, No. 201, March 27, 1929, FRUS 1929, II, 190–91.
[8] B. G. Tours to Lampson, No. 30, Mukden, May 4, 1929, FO 371/13915–638.

the employment by the Manchurian government of White Russians, and denied that the recent appointment of Boris Ostroumov, former general manager of the CER, as adviser to the Communications Commission was a breach of treaty. White Russian employees, he declared, were quiet, peaceable, and very satisfactory workers in contrast with Red Russians, who were turbulent and unsatisfactory and always caused trouble. He added that the Chinese were being humanitarian in providing the White Russians with the chance to earn a livelihood, while the Soviet government prevented them from returning home and only wished to persecute them.[9] When Mel'nikov taunted Chang that he was under the influence of foreign advisers, Chang retorted that the advisers were merely employees, whose counsel was followed only when it accorded with his own views, and asked rudely when Mel'nikov would leave Mukden. "At once," he shot back angrily and repaid the insult with the remark that he would return when the governor of Kirin would come to the city (that is, when Chang Tso-hsiang would displace Chang Hsüeh-liang).

Learning of Ostroumov's arrival in Mukden, Mel'nikov hastened back in April, but Chang would not see him, and Mel'nikov withdrew to Harbin "discomfited."[10]

On May 27 Chinese police stormed into the Soviet consulate general in Harbin and seized a number of

[9] "Regarding the employment of 'White' Russians," the American Consul M. S. Meyers reported, "it is reliably stated that there are secret stipulations attached to the Mukden Agreement providing that no 'White' Russians shall be employed as advisers or in other capacities by the Mukden Government. This, it is said, was unknown to General Chang at the time of the interview. It is understood that General Chang proposes to publish the secret part of the agreement if the Soviet Government presses this point. . . ." (Meyers to MacMurray, No. 201.)

[10] Tours to Lampson, No. 30.

documents, some of them partially burned, as they were retrieved from a stove in which the Russians had tried to destroy them when the building had been surrounded. Among the finds were masterfully made imitations of small American and Japanese metal seals that may have been used to reseal letters which had been opened and to get out Soviet correspondence and Communist propaganda under the guise of United States or Japanese correspondence.[11]

Contending that they had broken up a secret meeting of the Third International (the Comintern), the Chinese arrested over 80 persons, including 42 consular officials. The remainder, according to the Nanking government, were "important officials of the Chinese Eastern Railway, members of the Chinese Eastern Railway Labor Union, the Soviet Central Commercial Federation, the Soviet Mercantile Shipping Bureau, the Soviet Far Eastern Petroleum Bureau, and the Soviet Far Eastern National Trading Bureau, and Communist leaders of the Harbin special area, Chita, Khabarovsk, and other centers along the same railway."[12]

The Soviets denied that there had been any meeting whatsoever in the consulate general. They asserted that their countrymen had been in different rooms at the moment of the intrusion and that the visitors had been in the building on visa and passport business.[13] The Chinese countered that some of the Russians had come all the way from Manchuli (Manchzhuriia

[11] MacMurray to Secretary of State, No. 485, Peking, June 17, 1929, FRUS 1929, II, 196–97; Sir John Tilley to Foreign Office, Tokyo, June 13, 1929, FO 371/13931–F2692; FO 371/13931–F2960.

[12] "A Communication of the Nationalist Government of the Republic of China to the Signatories of the Treaty for the Renunciation of War," Chargé d'Affaires W. C. Chen to Henderson, London, August 27, 1929, FO 371/13954–632.

[13] Vygodskii, 299; Karakhan to Hsia Wei-sung, No. 45/2, May 31, 1929, DVP, XII, 334–37; Kapitsa, 193.

Station) and Suifeng, even though their passports could have been exchanged at the local Soviet consulates and that none of them was in possession of a new passport although they had been in the Harbin consulate general for over an hour. Nanking blandly asserted that when Chinese policemen saw through a window of the consulate general that the officials were hurriedly burning documents, "Chief of Police Shao was compelled to force an entrance to save the rest of the documents before the Russians could throw them all into the furnace."[14]

The documents, which were later published, contained evidence of the activity of Soviet agents in Manchuria. But while the Chinese asserted that they showed "conclusively" that there were plans to overthrow the Nationalist government and that they included material that was "startling,"[15] the British minister remarked that they "revealed nothing very startling" and that although the arrested persons were eventually sentenced to various terms of imprisonment, their trial had really been "inconclusive."[16] Foreigners in general believed that the immediate object of the raid had been to obtain evidence that would justify the removal of any remaining Soviet control from the administration of the CER.[17] The charge of Communist subversion, advanced by the Chinese in a book published in Nanking in English, was weakened by the condemnation of tsarist as well as Communist policy and the inference that Russia by

[14] The International Relations Committee, *The Sino-Russian Crisis,* 6–7. The book contains the text and some photocopies of the documents seized in the raid. Booklets with secret codes were allegedly found on some of those arrested.
[15] *Sino-Russian Crisis,* 8.
[16] Lampson to Henderson, No. 930.
[17] Chargé d'Affaires E. M. B. Ingram to Henderson, No. 897(4/14D), Peking. June 22, 1929; Acting Consul General L. H. Lamb to Lampson, No. 60, Harbin, June 5, 1929, "Confidential," FO 371/13932–611.

the "diplomatic display of friendship" had acquired the CER dishonestly, playing the role of "a man who rescues your estate from your adversary and keeps it for himself."[18]

The Soviet Union vehemently protested against the raid in a note from Deputy Foreign Commissar Karakhan to Acting Chargé d'Affaires Hsia Wei-sung in Moscow, dated May 31,[19] and demanded the immediate release of the arrested Soviet citizens and the return of the correspondence, money, and other things seized. Linking the attack with the raid on the Peking embassy on April 6, 1927, a White Russian attack on the Soviet consulate general in Shanghai on November 7, 1927, and the destruction of the Soviet consulate in Canton the following month, the USSR accused the Chinese of unwillingness or inability to conform with universally accepted norms of international law and usage, and in retaliation revoked the extraterritorial immunity of Chinese diplomatic and consular officials in the Soviet Union. Although declaring her desire to maintain friendly relations with the Chinese people, the USSR "most categorically" warned "the Nanking government and its organs" against "further trial of the long-suffering of the government of the Union of Soviet Socialist Republics by provocative acts and the violation of treaties and agreements."[20]

Moscow's warning to Nanking fell on deaf ears. Chinese diplomatic and consular officials packed their bags and departed from the Soviet Union on June 1.

---

[18] *Sino-Russian Crisis*, 1–19.

[19] A copy of the note was transmitted by Consul General Martynov to the chief of the central diplomatic representation of the Three Eastern Provinces at Mukden on June 4.

[20] DVP, XII, 334–37; FRUS 1929, II, 193–95; Lampson to Henderson, No. 930; *Peking and Tientsin Times*, June 3, 1929.

On July 4 a Soviet member of the board of directors of the CER committed suicide, "evidently," as the American consul reported, "because he realized matters were coming to a crisis, in which the Soviet side would suffer, and because he did not dare return to Moscow, to which place he had been recalled, to report failure and possibly to receive punishment there for this failure."[21] On July 9 Lü Jung-huan, president of the board of directors of the CER, appointed Fan Chi-kuan, a member of the board of directors, assistant general manager of the railway in place of Kuo Chung-hsi, who had been granted sick leave.[22] Lü ordered that Chinese be put in charge of the telegraphic, financial, traffic, commercial and motive-power departments and that all orders and communications of the Russian general manager of the railway must be countersigned by the Chinese assistant general manager.[23]

When Emshanov, former manager of the Perm Railway and commissar of transport who had replaced Ivanov, refused to comply with Lü's orders, the Chinese authorities at Harbin on July 10 swooped down on the railway line, took over its telegraph system, through which the Russian officials had been able to exchange secret communications with the USSR, shut down the Soviet Trade Mission (Torgpredstvo), the Far Eastern Trading Corporation (Dalgostorg), the offices of the Soviet Merchant Marine (Sovtorgflot),

---

[21] Hanson to MacMurray, No. 1991, Harbin, August 16, 1929, FRUS, 1929, II, 278–84.

[22] Kuo's illness and that of Tu Wei-ching, the American-educated chief of the traffic department of the railway, who was also given sick leave, consisted of their inability to speak Russian. The appointment of Fan, who had been educated in a Russian technical school in Harbin and knew Russian well, was to facilitate his assumption of Emshanov's duties shortly. (Hanson to MacMurray, No. 1969, Harbin, July 10, 1929, FRUS 1929, II, 198–99; also No. 1991.)

[23] Lampson to Henderson, No. 930; Tang, 200.

the oil and textile syndicates, and the railway trade unions.[24]

The Soviet vice president of the board of directors, A. V. Charkin, hastened to Lü to protest against these actions. Lü urged him to accept the Chinese stipulations concerning the powers of the Soviet general manager and the Chinese assistant general manager as well as their demand for parity in personnel and chiefs of principal departments, but Charkin, like Emshanov, refused because this would have been contrary to the Mukden Agreement of 1924.[25] Thereupon the Chinese began to arrest many Soviet employees on the charge of spreading Communist propaganda; some were deported at once, others were placed in detention camps.[26] On July 11 Lü removed Emshanov and Eismont as well as all Soviet department heads and immediately replaced them with Chinese and naturalized-Chinese White Russians, who began the wholesale dismissal of employees suspected of Soviet sympathies.[27]

[24] Lampson to Henderson, No. 930; Hanson to MacMurray. No. 1969; Tang, 200; Kapitsa, 200.

[25] Hanson to MacMurray, No. 1991.

[26] The Soviets later accused the Chinese of mistreating the prisoners. So bad were conditions according to Kapitsa that some of the Russians tried to commit suicide. (Kapitsa, 217) Although the American consul at Harbin on his first inspection of the Chinese internment camp on October 2 found "no evidence of cruel treatment, systematic or otherwise," he reported following another visit less than three weeks later that in the absence of stoves, "the prisoners must be suffering intensely, especially at night, when it is quite cold." He added that "besides cold, absence of bathhouses and lack of communication with the outside, the prisoners' complaints are that they have no knowledge of what charges have been brought against them, if any, and of how long they must remain prisoners." (Hanson to MacMurray, Harbin, October 5, as quoted in MacMurray to Stimson, No. 915, Peiping, October 21, 1929, FRUS 1929. II, 331–32; Hanson to MacMurray, Harbin, October 21, 1929, as quoted in MacMurray to Stimson, No. 943, Peiping, November 1, 1929, FRUS 1929, II, 341–42.)

[27] Emshanov was replaced by Fan Chi-kuan. Emshanov and Eismont left for the Soviet Union two days later. (Lampson to Henderson, No. 930; Hanson to MacMurray, No. 1969; Hanson to MacMurray, No. 1991; Tang, 200; Kapitsa, 200.)

The Chinese government asserted that Emshanov and Eismont had been removed solely because of their violation of article 6 of the Sino-Soviet agreement of 1924 by their engaging in "propaganda directed against the political and social system of China" and their conspiring "to overthrow the Chinese government, to destroy the Chinese Eastern Railway, and to perpetrate other outrages." It alleged that their dismissal had "no connection whatsoever with the question of the right of administrative control over the railway."[28] But Western observers were agreed that the charges against the Soviet officials were merely pretexts for the seizure of control, which the Chinese had been planning for some time. The American consul in Mukden called it their "pet scheme."[29]

In a secret report to Sir Miles W. Lampson, Colonel G. Badham-Thornhill, the British military attaché, charged that Chang and his advisers had "for some time past been working on an agreed policy of aggression vis-à-vis the Russian half of the administration." He saw Mukden's "real concern" in the railway's decline in profits, as the Soviet administrators poured money into opera houses, clubs, hotels and other institutions for the benefit of the staff, while their Chinese colleagues lined their own pockets, the position of *tupan* of the railway having long been regarded as "the biggest financial plum in Manchuria."[30] Badham-

[28] Chen to Henderson, London, August 27, 1929, FO 371/13954–62.

[29] Meyers to MacMurray, No. 186, Mukden, February 7, 1929, FRUS 1929, II, 189; Hanson to MacMurray, No. 1869, Harbin, December 31, 1928, FRUS 1929, II, 187–88; Magruder to US Legation in China, Report No. 7675, Peking, July 26, 1929, FRUS 1929, II, 251; Lampson to Henderson, No. 930.

[30] The profitability of the CER had declined also because of featherbedding. Since 22,000 out of the 28,000 railway officials employed in 1929 were Soviet citizens, most of the salary funds went into Russian pockets. The income of the railway, which had risen from 11 million rubles in 1924 to close to 20 million in 1926, fell to under 10 million in 1927 and to under 5 million in 1928, even

Thornhill reported that *Tupan* Lü, who was suspected of having embezzled some company funds together with Emshanov, had accused his Soviet colleagues of subversion and had obtained permission to raid their premises after learning that his own activities were about to be investigated by a special commission named by Chang Hsüeh-liang, so that he could remove all papers and persons that might have incriminated himself.[31]

Consul General B. G. Tours also attributed the immediate responsibility for the Russo-Chinese crisis to Lü, who had been moved to "rash and hasty action" to further his own ends, but he noted that Mukden shared "a modicum of blame" for leaving Lü in a position where he could take such action and for failing to intervene when he had done so.[32]

Mukden did not intervene, because it favored a strong policy toward USSR, and there is evidence that Lü's actions also had the consent of Nanking, even though the Chinese government disclaimed them after they had boomeranged. As the American consul observed, the "feebleness" of Soviet action, "limited to protests," in response to the Chinese raids on the Soviet embassy and consulates, the abuse and expulsion of Soviet consular officers and the seizure of CER property, "had made the Chinese believe that any move, no matter how drastic, they made would also be met with only protests on the part of Moscow."[33]

---

though Canadian and American experts calculated that the CER could be made to bring an annual profit of 50 million gold rubles. (Otto Mossdorf, "Der mandschurische Konflikt des Jahres 1929," 50–63.)

[31] Badham-Thornhill to Lampson, Report VIII, "Secret," Peiping, August 13, 1929, enclosure in No. 1, Lampson to Henderson, No. 1180(130/107A), Peking, August 18, 1929, FO 371/13955–632.

[32] Tours to Lampson, Mukden, August 2, 1929, FO 371/13954–632.

[33] Hanson to MacMurray, No. 1991.

Nanking's approval of a strong policy by Mukden may have had an ulterior motive. Hostilities with the Soviet Union in Manchuria stood to weaken Chang Hsüeh-liang, of whose loyalty the central government was not certain. By prodding Chang into a collision with the USSR, Chiang Kai-shek may also have sought to forestall a rumored coalition between Chang and General Feng Yü-hsiang against him.[34]

On July 13 Karakhan handed to Hsia a strong protest for communication to both Mukden and Nanking. The Soviet government branded Lü's demand that Emshanov surrender the management of the railway to a person designated by him as "unlawful" and in "flagrant violation" of the Peking and Mukden agreements of 1924. It labeled the seizure of the railway, the closing down of the various Soviet establishments, and the arrest of Soviet citizens as "a most manifest and a most flagrant violation of the direct and incontestable provisions of the treaties existing between the USSR and China." It cited articles and points of the agreements to document the fact that Lü's acts, "sanctioned by the Chinese Government," had been illegal and constituted "in substance the seizure of the Chinese Eastern Railway and an attempt at unilateral abolition of existing treaties." At the same time it pointed to the movement of Manchurian troops toward the Soviet border, and asserted that Mukden planned to send units of White Russians—"White Guards" as it called them—into Soviet territory. The Soviet government made "the most decisive protest" against the "glaring violation of the treaties existing between the USSR and China" and directed the attention of Mukden and Nanking "to the extraordinary seriousness

---

[34] Kapitsa, 195.

of the position which has already been created by these acts."

Reciting the voluntary relinquishment by the Soviet Union of concessions and extraterritorial rights still held by other powers, the Soviet government reiterated its support of "the struggle that the Chinese people had been making for the abolition of the unequal treaties and for the restoration of the sovereignty of China." But it pointed out that the Chinese had "the full possibility, provided by the treaties, to present any complaint or demand of it to the government of the USSR in a lawful manner." Regretting that the Chinese authorities had mistaken its policy of settling all issues peaceably as a manifestation of weakness, the Soviet government warned that it had at its disposal "sufficient means, requisite for guarding the lawful rights of the peoples of the USSR from any and all violent encroachments."

The Soviet government reiterated its willingness to solve "the whole complex of questions connected with the Chinese Eastern Railway" by peaceful negotiation and proposed the convening of a conference for that purpose, provided the Chinese immediately freed all Soviet citizens under arrest, halted the persecution of Soviet citizens and all encroachment on their rights and the rights of Soviet institutions, and revoked all unilateral acts in regard to the CER. It threatened that the rejection of its proposal would have "serious consequences" and concluded with the ultimatum that if no satisfactory reply was received within three days, it would be "obliged to resort to other means of defending the lawful rights of the USSR."[35]

Once again the Soviet warning went unheeded. The

[35] FRUS 1929, II, 201–206; DVP, XII, 380–86; *North China Standard,* July 16, 1929; *Sino-Russian Crisis,* 35–39.

local Chinese authorities, in the words of the American consul, "had hypnotized themselves into the belief that the Soviet authorities would never go beyond verbal action." On July 15 General Chang Ching-hui, the civil administrator of the special area, ordered the surrender of the railway's many libraries with their hundreds of thousands of valuable books to the Chinese Educational Administration, the incorporation of the railway's land office at Harbin into the Chinese Land Administration, and the nationalization of the railway's twelve slaughterhouses and two disinfection stations, while Assistant General Manager Fan closed down the railway's departments of steamship affairs and labor rationalization.[36] The dismissal and deportation of thousands of Soviet employees proceeded apace.[37]

The Chinese government replied to the Soviet note on July 16. Its answer had been delayed by the fact that it had taken Hsia apparently a whole day to translate the lengthy Russian note into Chinese—his telegram containing the text was dated the fourteenth—and it had taken Nanking in turn another two days to decipher Hsia's telegram. The reply, in Chinese, was dispatched on the sixteenth; it was handed to Karakhan, translated into Russian, the following day.

The reply professed that the Chinese government and the Chinese people "according to their traditional sense of world brotherhood" had always endeavored to meet the Soviet government and the Soviet people "with a spirit of equality and mutual assistance," but

---

[36] Hanson to MacMurray, No. 1991.

[37] MacMurray to Stimson, No 575, Peking, July 16, 1929, FRUS 1929, II, 206–207; No. 584, July 18, 1929, FRUS 1929, II, 208. Reports from the Security Service (OGPU) offices of the Transbaikal Railway and the Far Eastern region described in detail where the arrested Soviet citizens were being kept and how they were being mistreated. See documents 284, 285, 287, 291, 303, 304, 313, 315, and 322 in USSR, Academy of Sciences, *Pogranichnye voiska SSSR*.

that the repeated discovery in recent years in China of organized propaganda and other activities seeking to incite the Chinese people against their government and social structure had forced Chinese authorities to take measures necessary for the maintenance of public order. The search of the Soviet consulate in Harbin and the steps taken in regard to the CER by the officials of the Three Eastern Provinces had been directed toward this end and had been executed with care so as to "localize the incident."

The Chinese government asserted that it had been informed repeatedly by the local authorities of the Three Eastern Provinces that the general manager of the CER and important Soviet colleagues had never really abided by the provisional agreement of 1924. It accused the Soviet officials of committing such a mass of illegal acts that it was impossible to list them, thereby preventing their Chinese colleagues from carrying out the agreement, which they themselves had violated to boot by spreading secret propaganda. The local authorities, it insisted, thus "could not but take the given measures in regard to the CER." "It is clear and understood," the Chinese government proclaimed, "that the responsibility for the violation of the Sino-Soviet agreement does not lie on our side."

Nanking asserted that the Soviets had arrested and imprisoned without cause no less than a thousand Chinese emigrants and traders, while many more Chinese citizens in the USSR were "squashed" by Soviet restrictions and were unable to earn a living. In contrast, Soviet emigrants and traders living in China, as well as Soviet commercial establishments had enjoyed the Chinese government's "hospitality and generosity" and had all been granted great conveniences. The Chinese government reiterated that the recent arrests of Soviet citizens and the closure of Soviet establishments had been carried out merely to put a stop to hostile propaganda and to maintain public order and tranquility. It promised that if the Soviet government would free all Chinese citizens arrested by the state political authorities and provide them with the possibility of returning to their fatherland (excepting those against whom cases were pending and for whose stay in the Soviet Union the Chinese embassy and consulates would vouch) and if all Chinese citizens, traders and organizations would be guaranteed due protection, it would take corresponding action toward all the closed Soviet establishments (and free the arrested Soviet citizens). The reply voiced the hope that the Soviet government would "consciously rectify its past improper actions" and respect Chinese sovereignty and laws "and not make proposals contrary to the facts."

The Chinese government expressed its intention to have Chu Shao-yang, its minister to Finland, stop at Harbin on his way back to his post and investigate everything. "All matters pertaining to Sino-Soviet relations and relations concerning the CER could be settled in good time and jointly with the People's Commissariat of Foreign Affairs of the Union of Soviet Socialist Republics in accordance with justice and law."[38]

The Soviet answer, written to Hsia the same day, on July 17,[39] branded the Chinese reply as "unsat-

[38] DVP, XII, 390–92. Differences in tone may be found in the English translations published in *The Sino-Russian Crisis* (pp. 28–29) and in FRUS (1929, II, 210). The *Peking Leader* of July 25, 1929, rendered the clause "Although it does not consider the following as a condition" as "The National Government does not entertain, in the least, any desire of making counterproposals." (Lampson to Henderson, No. 1094, Peking, July 28, 1929, FO 371/13954–632.) It can be assumed, however, that the Soviet government considered only the Russian version.

[39] Lampson and the British War Office Weekly Intelligence Summary for July

isfactory in content and hypocritic in tone." It noted that the Chinese government instead of reversing the actions of the *tupan* had sought to justify them and instead of agreeing to the immediate convocation of a conference to regulate all controversial questions had ignored the matter, "rejecting thereby the proposal of the USSR for a conference and destroying the possibility of regulating the dispute by agreement of the two sides." Moscow contended that it was "false and hypocritic" to cite propaganda as the cause of the unlawful actions, "for the Chinese authorities possess in their territory sufficient means to prevent and to stop such activity had it actually taken place, without seizing the Chinese Eastern Railway and severing the treaty relations existing between China and the USSR." The real motivation of the Chinese authorities, it argued, could be found in the recently published statement of Chiang Kai-shek: "Our steps, designed to take the Chinese Eastern Railway into our hands, contain nothing unusual. . . . We want first to take the Chinese Eastern Railway into our hands, then to take up the discussion of the other questions."

Asserting that the means for the amicable regulation of the controversies and disputes, "caused by the Chinese authorities and aggravated by the note of the Chinese Government of July 17," had been exhausted, the Soviet government announced the recall of all Soviet diplomatic, consular and commercial representatives from China; the recall of all CER officials, appointed by the USSR; the suspension of all railway communication between the two countries; and the expulsion of the diplomatic and consular representa-

---

24, 1929, reported that it was delivered the following day. (FO 371/13932–611.) It was published in *Izvestiia* on the 18th.

tives of the Chinese Republic from the USSR. The Soviet government pinned "the entire responsibility for the consequences" of these actions on Nanking, while declaring that it reserved for itself "all rights arising from the Peking and Mukden agreements of 1924."[40]

On July 19 the Chinese government issued a manifesto in which it presented its side of the conflict to the other powers. It was a broadside attack against Soviet use of diplomatic, consular and commercial offices for the dissemination of Communist propaganda and repeated the charge that the raid on the consulate at Harbin had broken up a meeting of the Comintern. "During the search at the consulate," the manifesto asserted, "documents were found disclosing Soviet plots for the destruction of the political unity of China, for the organization of a corps of assassins to be active in Nanking, Mukden and other important centers, and for the organization of a secret army to destroy the Chinese Eastern Railway." Viewing the "remedial measures" taken by China as "entirely within the realm of necessity," the Chinese government bemoaned that the government of the USSR "failed to realize its mistakes," had suddenly presented a note "embodying conditions contrary to the facts of the case," and had demanded a reply within a specified period of time. Asserting that the Chinese government "in accordance with its traditional and consistent policy of forbearance" had in its reply set the record straight in the hope that the Soviet government would bethink itself, it charged Moscow with continuing to ignore the facts in its second note, which, it alleged, contained "nothing but empty phrases designed to mis-

[40] Karakhan to Hsia, July 17, 1929, DVP, XII, 388–90; FO 371/13954–632; FRUS 1929, II, 212–14.

lead the world." It adduced the fact that the reply of July 17 had made no mention of China's proposal of dispatching a representative for negotiation as "sufficient proof of the customary evasion of Soviet Russia in its international dealings as well as of its aggressive aspirations towards China and its determination to violate the Agreement."

The manifesto insisted that the CER incident constituted "the culmination of the violation by the Soviet Government of the Agreement of 1924" and was only partly concerned with the railway itself. The basic issue, it reiterated, was "Communist propaganda, and the attempts to overthrow the Chinese Government and to disturb the peace in Manchuria." Announcing that the documents seized in the raid on the Harbin consulate were being made public in order to substantiate the charges of Soviet subversion,[41] the manifesto expressed the earnest hope that the governments and peoples of the various powers would take note of Nanking's exposure of the Soviet plots against China. It proclaimed China's devotion to the maintenance of peace, but warned: "the right of self-defense is an undeniable right, and should the Soviet Government flagrantly violate it, the responsibility for the breach of peace must rest entirely upon the Soviet Union and not upon China."[42]

[41] The Shanghai press began publishing them on July 22; the *Peking and Tientsin Times* printed them between July 25 and August 2.

[42] Wu to Stimson, undated, received by the Department of State on July 23, 1929, FRUS 1929, II, 228–31. A slightly different wording is given in *The Sino-Russian Crisis,* pp. 25–27. In a communication to the signatories of the Kellogg Pact a month later, the Nationalist government asserted that the Chinese note of July 17 had been "couched in all sincerity," while the Soviet government, in its response on the 18th, "chose to persist in its arrogant attitude and employ misrepresentation for whitewashing the actual facts." It labeled the measures taken by the Soviet government as "a gross violation of the Sino-Soviet agreement, a contemptuous disregard for international good faith, a wilful juggling of the actual facts, a misrepresentation of the true intent contained in China's reply, and a calculated design to bring about the . . . severance of international com-

Through-traffic via Pogranichnaia Station had been discontinued on July 14; the trans-Siberian express from Harbin was halted at the border on July 17. Soviet officials and civilians left Mukden and Harbin within the next few days. The Soviet consul general at Harbin also packed his belongings but delayed his departure. The Soviet Far Eastern Bank (Dalbank) transferred its funds to New York. On July 20 Nanking announced its decision to break off relations with the Soviet Union.[43]

There followed a war of nerves as Russian troop movements and fire power demonstrations along the frontier gave rise to rumors of a Soviet invasion. At Pogranichnaia (Suifenho) and Manchuli the Red Army trained powerful search-lights across the border while Soviet airplanes maneuvered in the sky; at Blagoveshchensk the Russians engaged in heavy artillery practice. As the Chinese authorities, in spite of sending some reinforcements to the frontier, made no serious preparations to meet a Soviet attack, panic spread among the inhabitants of the Manchurian border towns, which had been razed by Russian armies in 1900. Although the Chinese military replied to the Soviet gunnery practice disdainfully with the blares of a brass band, it was apparent to Western observers that the "Kirin braves," to whom the defense of the frontier was entrusted, "had no stomach for the fight

munication," and contended that "the responsibility for such a situation should be shouldered entirely by the Soviet Government." ("A Communication of the Nationalist Government of the Republic of China to the Signatories of the Treaty for the Renunciation of War," in Chen to Henderson, London, August 27, 1929, FO 371/13954–632.) The British minister, on the other hand, sympathized with the Russian position. He called the Chinese reply, which made no mention of the *status quo ante,* "characteristic in its evasion of realities." (Lampson to Henderson, No. 930.)

[43] Lampson to Henderson, No. 930; MacMurray to Stimson, No. 599, Peking, July 19, 1929, and No. 601, July 20, FRUS, 1929, II, 219; No. 621, July 24, FRUS 1929, II, 233–34.

when the Harbin scaremongers prophesied bloody war." The British consul general predicted that in the event of hostilities, "the Manchurian Mars" would prove to be "a god of straw."[44]

On July 22 Tsai Yun-sheng, the commissioner of foreign affairs of the Mukden government at Harbin, called on Consul General Mel'nikov and proposed an agreement whereby the arrested Soviet laborers would be released; the government of the USSR would appoint the general manager and the assistant general manager of the CER; the conflict on the CER would be solved by a conference of representatives of both governments; and the Soviet government could make the statement that it did not recognize the order prevailing after the conflict and that it did not prejudice the impending negotiations. Chang Hsüeh-liang promised to apply for the consent of the Nationalist government if the Soviet Union agreed with the above proposal.[45]

Mel'nikov did not have the authority to discuss the proposal, but agreed to communicate it to Moscow.[46] On July 23 Mel'nikov and Tsai secretly traveled to Changchun, where they conferred the following day with General Chang Tso-hsiang, the governor of Kirin, and Li Shao-keng, assistant general manager of the CER. Governor Chang, whose province bordered unto the USSR and stood to suffer from war between the two countries, made certain propositions to Mel'nikov, presumably "independently of Nanking and, perhaps, Mukden as a whole."[47] Upon his return to Harbin,

[44] Tours to Lampson, No. 49, Mukden, July 24, 1929, FO 371/13954–632; Memorandum by Johnson, Washington, July 19, 1929, FRUS.1929, II, 218.

[45] Karakhan to Chang Hsüeh-liang, August 1, 1929, DVP, XII, 426–27; FRUS 1929, II, 265.

[46] Karakhan to Chang Hsüeh-liang, August 1, 1929; FRUS 1929, II, 266.

[47] Hanson to MacMurray, No. 1991, Harbin, August 16, 1929, FRUS 1929, II, 282.

Mel'nikov received Moscow's answer to Chang Hsüeh-liang's proposal and on the afternoon of the twenty-fifth handed it to Tsai for transmission to Mukden, then boarded a special train and with the remaining Soviet officials headed for the Russian border.[48]

In its reply the Soviet government declared that after the "high-handed actions" on the part of the Chinese CER officials, it could not "treat with confidence" the proposal advanced by Commissioner of Foreign Affairs Tsai in the name of the Mukden government. It would, however, adopt a "favorable attitude" toward the proposal, should it be made directly by the Nanking government or the Mukden government to the Soviet government and should the provision that the Soviet government could make the statement that it did not recognize the order prevailing after the conflict and that it did not prejudice the impending negotiations be changed to read: "Both sides agree that the situation which has formed itself on the Chinese Eastern Railway after the conflict is bound to be altered in conformity with the Peking and Mukden agreements of 1924."[49]

Tsai carried the Russian reply to Mukden, then traveled with an answer to the reply to Manchuli Station. On August 1 he handed to Mel'nikov a letter from Chang Hsüeh-liang to Karakhan, dated July 29, 1929. Declaring that the CER was "a joint commercial enterprise belonging to both countries and regulated by the Peking and Mukden agreements of 1924," Chang proposed the convening of a conference on the CER question. The situation currently existing on the

[48] Lampson to Henderson, No. 930; Karakhan to Chang Hsüeh-liang, August 1, 1929, FRUS 1929, II, 266.
[49] Karakhan to Chang Hsüeh-liang, August 1, 1929, DVP, XII, 427; FRUS 1929, II, 266.

railway was to be regarded as "temporary, subject to readjustment after the conference on the basis of the Peking and Mukden agreements." The citizens of each country arrested by the other were to be released, Soviet citizens to be deported to the USSR.[50]

Informed of the text of the letter by telegraph, Karakhan cabled to Chang the same day that his proposal of July 29 differed "essentially" from that made in his name by Tsai on the twenty-second. Firstly, it omitted altogether the provision that the Soviet government appoint the general manager and the assistant general manager of the CER immediately; secondly, instead of the formula suggested by the Soviet government that the situation created on the CER after the conflict should be changed in conformity with the Peking agreement and the Mukden agreement his letter proposed "the legalization of the prevailing situation on the Chinese Eastern Railway, brought about by the forcible seizure of the railway, which is an obvious violation of the Peking agreement and the Mukden agreement." Karakhan asserted that the Mukden government was frustrating the negotiation of a settlement by going back on its original proposal. Agreement could be reached only if Mukden accepted the Soviet proposal of July 25. He declared that the situation which had been created was "pregnant with new and serious complications" and that the Mukden and Nanking governments were "wholly and fully" responsible.[51]

The sudden shift in Chinese policy was due to the intervention of the national government, which forbade

[50] Chang Hsüeh-liang to Karakhan, Mukden, July 29, 1929, FRUS 1929, II, 258; DVP, XII, 428; TASS dispatch, dated August 7, 1929, in Lampson to Henderson, No. 1173, Peking, August 17, 1929, FO 371/13954–632.

[51] Karakhan to Chang Hsüeh-liang, Moscow, August 1, 1929, DVP, XII, 426–28; FRUS 1929, II, 267.

the delegates to agree to the reinstatement of Emshanov and Eismont.[52] Misled in part by the judgment of its German military advisers that the Soviet Union could not undertake major operations in Manchuria, Nanking sought to dictate a settlement and announced that Chu Shao-yang, the Chinese minister-designate to Finland, would take charge of the negotiations over the heads of Tsai and Li. But in this, as the British minister put it, "Nanking had reckoned without their host," for when Chu reached Manchuli on August 6, Mel'nikov refused to speak to him on the ground that there were no diplomatic relations between the USSR and his government.[53]

On August 15 Karakhan publicly warned all foreign governments and private individuals and companies that might have business dealings with the CER that "the government of the USSR will not acknowledge a single deal consummated with respect of the road by the Chinese authorities or the personnel appointed by them, nor a single obligation assumed by them in the name of this road, after the seizure of the Chinese Eastern Railway by the Chinese authorities."[54]

While Mel'nikov refused to meet with a representative of the Nanking government, Moscow voiced its willingness to negotiate with the latter indirectly,

[52] There is some evidence also that Chang Hsüeh-liang was losing interest in the controversy. Tours reported on August 2 that while Chang's advisers were pressing upon him the establishment of a commission of inquiry into the administration of the railway so that charges against the ousted Russian management could be substantiated upon resumption of the negotiations, "the marshal is already tiring of the Chinese Eastern Railway incident, and now takes a very listless interest in it, preferring for the moment to devote all his attention to 'movie-tone' pictures, which are being demonstrated to him by special agents of the American Fox Company." (Tours to Lampson, No. 50, Mukden, August 2, 1929, FO 371/13954–632.)

[53] Lampson to Henderson, No. 930; MacMurray to Stimson, No. 659, Peking, August 1, 1929, FRUS 1929, II, 263; No. 700, August 13, 1929, FRUS 1929, II, 275–76.

[54] FRUS 1929, II, 277–78.

through the intermediacy of the German Ministry of Foreign Affairs, which had already assumed the protection of the interests of Soviet residents in China and of Chinese residents in the USSR in the absence of diplomatic relations between the two countries. On August 28 Ambassador Herbert von Dirksen handed to Deputy Foreign Commissar Maksim Litvinov the text of a proposed joint Sino-Soviet declaration, which embodied the following Chinese formula for a preliminary settlement of the dispute: (1) Both sides were to declare that they would settle all disputes between them in conformity with the agreement of 1924 and that they would in particular fix the conditions of the purchase of the CER by China in conformity with article 9 of the Peking agreement. Plenipotentiary representatives were to be appointed immediately by both sides to engage in a conference for the resolution of the questions at issue. (2) Both sides were to state that the situation on the CER, which had come about after the conflict, should be changed by the abovementioned conference to conform to the Peking and Mukden agreements of 1924. (3) The Soviet government was to *nominate* a new general manager and a new assistant general manager of the CER; they were to be appointed by the board of directors of the railway. The Soviet government was to instruct railway employees who were citizens of the USSR that they must abide strictly by article 6 of the (Peking) agreement of 1924 (that is, that they must not engage in political propaganda or subversive activities). (4) Both sides were to release immediately all persons arrested in connection with the present incident or after May 1, 1929.[55]

55 DVP, XII, 481–82; FRUS 1929, II, 309–10; *Survey* 1929, 358.

In his reply, given to Dirksen for transmission on August 29, Litvinov agreed to the Chinese draft with two modifications. He struck out "new" before "general manager" in item 3 and inserted "immediately" before "appointed." He expanded the statement that the Soviet government instruct Soviet employees of the railway to observe strictly article 6 of the agreement of 1924 by including a similar commitment on the part of the Chinese government "to instruct its local authorities and their organs" to do likewise.[56] Litvinov's position was flexible to the extent that he expressed willingness to nominate replacements for Emshanov and Eismont if the Chinese in turn put forth a new president of the board of directors, but he insisted that this must be done simultaneously with the signing of the joint declaration, before formal negotiations concerning the resolution of the various issues could be opened.[57]

In a note, dated September 9 and handed to the Soviet government through the German embassy in Moscow on September 11, the Chinese government agreed to the insertion of the word "immediately," but rejected the demand that the appointment of a new Soviet general manager and a new Soviet assistant general manager be a precondition for the signing of the joint declaration. In a supplementary statement, dated September 11 and transmitted on the thirteenth, Nanking took a step backward and spoke only of a new Soviet assistant general manager.[58]

The Soviet government replied in a verbal note, handed to the German embassy on September 17, that

[56] DVP, XII, 482; FRUS, 1929, II, 310.
[57] *Izvestiia*, August 31, 1929; FRUS 1929, II, 310–11; DVP, XII, 481–83; *Survey* 1929, 358–59; Kapitsa, 208–209.
[58] DVP, XII, 508–509; Kapitsa, 215.

it had introduced merely the most minor and absolutely necessary changes and clarifications in the text of the proposed joint declaration. It stated that these had been derived from the second paragraph of Nanking's own draft affirming the Mukden and Peking agreements and constituted the most elementary prior conditions for the work of the conference. The Soviet government asserted that the Chinese, in their notes of September 9 and 11, had gone back on their own proposal and thus were thwarting the settlement of the conflict by means of an agreement. Declaring that in view of Nanking's rejection of the basic conditions for the signing of the joint declaration and the conduct of the negotiations, the question as to where the negotiations were to take place had lost meaning, it warned again that "the responsibility for the further development of the conflict rests fully on the Nanking Government."[59]

The Soviet government had pointed out to the Nanking and Mukden governments in declarations made on August 19 and September 9[60] that a dangerous situation was being created by "the systematic provocative attacks on the territory of the USSR on the part of armed White Guard detachments and Chinese units." On September 25 the Soviet government listed some thirty new frontier incidents that allegedly had occurred since its protest of September 9 and contended that they proved the unwillingness of Nanking and Mukden to take preventative measures. Reiterating that the Nanking and Mukden governments were fully responsible for the damages done to the Soviet border zone and for the consequences that might follow, the Soviet government warned that the Soviet military command would be forced "to take all neces-

[59] DVP, XII, 507–508.
[60] The latter was transmitted through German channels.

sary measures for coping with the above-mentioned phenomena and for averting their recurrence."[61]

The Nanking government did not respond to the Soviet note of September 25 until November 14.[62] When it finally did, it denied categorically the truth of the Soviet accusations and proposed the immediate formation of a mixed commission, including citizens of a neutral country, to investigate the matter and to determine responsibility for the serious border situation. It suggested that the expansion of the conflict be averted by the immediate, simultaneous withdrawal of the armed forces of both sides thirty English miles from the frontier. As evidence of "the purity of its motives," Nanking declared its willingness to submit the whole question to arbitration by a neutral and impartial party, acceptable to both sides.[63]

The Chinese note was sent by way of Berlin. By the time that Dirksen conveyed it to Litvinov two weeks later, on November 29,[64] the whole situation had changed.[65]

[61] DVP, XII, 517–21.

[62] The Soviet note had been handed to the German embassy on September 25. It is not clear when it was transmitted to Nanking.

[63] DVP, XII, 597.

[64] Litvinov to Dirksen, November 29, 1929, DVP, XII, 596.

[65] It is unlikely that the prompt transmittal of the note would have altered the course of events, for the Soviets insisted, as had their tsarist predecessors in 1900, that the Sino-Russian conflict must be settled directly by the two parties concerned.

3

Red Russians versus White Chinese

The Manchurian Campaign

As attempts to negotiate via Berlin failed, both sides settled down to wear out each other's patience.[1] Border incidents became frequent. The Chinese catalogued a series of Soviet attacks, whose blows seemed directed primarily at Chinese morale,[2] while the USSR recorded an equally long list of Chinese and White Russian incursions.[3]

Mutual recriminations escalated along with the fighting. The Soviets charged the Chinese with foster-

[1] Lampson to Henderson, No. 930.
[2] Lamb to Lampson, No. 87, Harbin, August 19, 1929, FO 371/13954–632; No. 89, August 22, 1929, FO 371/13955–632; Christopher, 112–22.
[3] Statement of Soviet government to Nanking and Mukden governments, September 9, 1929, DVP, XII, 493–96. For Soviet intelligence concerning the concentration of Chinese troops, see documents 279, 280, 308 and 322 in *Pogranichnye voiska SSSR.* Some of the military men, among the many White Russian emigrés in Manchuria, had entered the services of Chinese war lords to sustain themselves by plying the only trade they knew. (See Petr Balakshin, *Final v Kitae,* I, 265–67, 280–81.) Others, who had settled in the border region, had organized themselves into White partisan forces to defend themselves both against Red raiders and Chinese soldiers who seized from the settlements whatever food and fodder they required. (C. F. Garstin to Lampson, No. 52, Harbin, October 9, 1930, FO 371/14701–639.)

ing the White Russian raids; the Chinese and White Russians accused the Red Army of committing atrocities. The allegations of both sides were exaggerated. Mukden had little control over the areas from which the White Russian raids were launched, and neutral investigators found no evidence of Soviet atrocities. Yet there was an element of truth in the charges. White Russian bands did invade their fatherland, whether for genuine political motives or to wreak vengeance or for plunder. Red partisan raiders in turn sought to liquidate the White Russians and to eradicate their bases of operations. The Soviets did harass the Chinese by minor raids along the frontiers, by shelling the eastern and western ends of the railway, and by broadcasting warnings of bigger raids to come in an attempt to shake their recalcitrance.[4]

Upon the expiration of their ultimatum, the Soviets impeded Chinese navigation on the Amur River by seizing two Chinese merchant steamers. They also tried to halt the operations of the CER. Many railway employees who had become Soviet citizens resigned and left their posts, while Communist agitators sought to persuade their colleagues to do likewise. But the railway administration managed to retain the service of those who were more interested in their jobs than in politics and filled vacancies with White Russians and Chinese, who kept the trains running.[5]

Isolated Soviet forays, such as the bombardment of the Chinese garrison at Suifeng, were recorded as early as July 19, following the recall of Russian diplomatic representatives. Serious military operations were not mounted, however, until the formation of

---

[4] Lampson to Henderson, No. 930; *Survey* 1929, 359–62.
[5] Hanson to Stimson. Harbin, July 21, 1929, FRUS 1929, II, 221; Lampson to Henderson, No. 930.

a special Far Eastern Army under the command of General Vasilii Bliukher (Blücher), erstwhile military adviser of the Kuomintang, and N. E. Donenko, a member of the Revolutionary Military Council.

In mid-August the Soviets struck at Chinese entrenchments near Chalainor, defended chiefly by Mongols and Chinese mercenaries, as well as some regular cavalry supported by guns.[6] The Chinese, "either by design or fluke," fled some 400 yards to the rear, where well posted machine guns forced the Russians to withdraw with heavy losses.[7]

In mid-October nine Soviet naval vessels, supported by land and air forces, pushed up the Amur River to the confluence of the Sungari. On the morning of October 12 they scattered a Chinese flotilla of seven river gunboats, confiscated from Germany at the end of the First World War, sinking two or three of them, and the next day captured T'ungchiang, formerly known as Lahasusu.[8] As the Chinese troops fled in complete disorder toward Fuchin, Soviet cavalry and infantry gave chase, killing many with shrapnel fired by the light artillery. Total Chinese casualties were close to 1,000 dead or wounded.

The Chinese soldiers who reached Fuchin plundered all the stores there and killed civilians who got in their way. The Red Army carried off Chinese military stores and supplies, including large quantities of foodstuffs, but did not touch the civilian population or its property. In fact, at a public meeting on October 16, it invited

---

[6] Vladimir Kulagin and Nikolai Iakovlev, *Podvig Osoboi Dal'nevostochnoi*, 127; Tang, 218–23; Christopher, 112–13. The formation of the Far Eastern Army had been decreed by the Revolutionary Military Council of the USSR only some ten days before; it is not clear whether the Chalainor raid was a product of the new command.

[7] Badham-Thornhill to Lampson, Peking, September 24, 1929, "Secret," FO 376/13955.

[8] Lampson to Henderson, No. 930; Wu, 207.

any Chinese to enlist in the Red Army and go with it to Khabarovsk.[9]

On November 17 Soviet military pressure exploded in a vigorous but limited invasion of Manchuria.[10] The Russians were afraid that they might eventually be outnumbered almost three to one in the border region and had decided to annihilate the enemy forces before they were fully assembled.

The Transbaikal Group of the Special Far Eastern Army, under the command of Stepan Vostretsov, was concentrated in the area of the stations Dauriia and Borzia and of the settlement Abagaituevskii. It consisted of the Thirty-fifth and Thirty-sixth Rifle Divisions, the Fifth Detached Kuban Cavalry Brigade, the Twenty-sixth Light Bomber Group, the Eighteenth Corps Artillery Division, the Eighteenth Corps Combat Engineer Battalion, the First Railway Company, the Detached Buryat-Mongol Cavalry Division, and three armored trains. The Twenty-first Perm Rifle Division and a company of MS-1 tanks stood in reserve at Chita. However, the units had not been put on a war footing and had only their minimal peacetime strength—between 50 and 80 infantrymen per company and not more than 1,000 combatants (500 active

[9] Memorandum by Vice Consul T. L. Lilliestrom, dated Harbin, October 28, 1929, transmitted by Hanson to Assistant Secretary of State Johnson on October 29, FRUS 1929, II, 337–38.

[10] *Survey* 1929, 362–63; Beloff, I, 73. According to Soviet historians the strike was preventive, to forestall an invasion of the Russian Far East by the militant forces of the Mukden regime. It is difficult to say to what extent fear of a Chinese attack was genuine, to what extent it was a pretext for Soviet action and a means of inflaming the fighting spirit of the Russian soldiers. Soviet strategists observed later that the Chinese emphasized "passive defense." (Kulagin and Iakovlev, 126.) It is not clear whether this evaluation came as the result of the campaign or had been held before. When Bliukher ordered the attack, he commanded: "To respond to a blow with a double-blow, to a shell with a hundred shells. Let the Chinese generals know that we do not begin the shooting but end it." A young Red Army soldier, recalling the night before the attack wrote: "The enemy wants to cross our border. We must . . . forestall the strike that is being prepared." (N. Lipman, *Zapiski krasnoarmeitsa dal'nevostochnika*, 115–20.)

bayonets) per regiment. Thus at the beginning of military operations the Transbaikal Group numbered 6,033 infantrymen and 1,599 cavalrymen, armed with 166 light machine guns, 331 heavy machine guns, 88 artillery pieces, 9 tanks and 32 airplanes.[11]

On the eve of the attack, the Political Section of the Eighteenth Infantry Corps issued to the commanders of the units a directive for the "political insurance" of the military operations. "The success of this operation," the directive asserted, "will have a completely exceptional political significance in that it will demoralize the Chinese forces in all sectors, change the feeling of the poorest part of the Chinese population in our favor, and will create a completely positive public opinion for the hastening of the settlement of the protracted conflict by peaceful means." It would at the same time be "a new and striking demonstration of the superiority of the Red Army over its opponents."[12]

To secure the goodwill of the Chinese populace, the Soviets renounced any territorial ambitions. The objectives of the Manchurian campaign, the directive noted, were limited to the defeat of the opposing armies, the smashing of all military installations and fortifications, and the destruction of prisons and police stations and the freeing of all inmates. Other buildings were not to be damaged. Particular care was to be taken, the directive stressed, not to destroy hospitals,

[11] Kulagin and Iakovlev, 121–22; N. P. Suntsov, A. I. Teleshenko, and M. P. Khvostikov, *Krasnoznamennyi Dal'nevostochnyi*, 120. According to American sources, Bliukher had 100,000 men under his command. (FRUS 1929, II, 274.) They do not state how many of these men were utilized in the attack. Chinese and Soviet sources agree that over 60,000 Manchurian troops defended the border regions in Heilungkiang and Kirin. (T'ien Hsiao-sheng, *Chung O chan shih*, I, 75; Chi Wang, "Young Marshal Chang Hsueh-liang and Manchuria: 1928–1931," 150; Kulagin and Iakovlev, 137.)

[12] Kulagin and Iakovlev, 123.

schools and other cultural institutions, as well as national shrines. To give substance to the slogan "The Red Army is the friend of the working people of China," the directive enjoined the commanders to treat "all layers of the population and especially the working people" correctly and not to abuse them. They were to "forbid strictly the appropriation by military personnel of even the smallest things as well as any purchases on enemy territory."

While Western and Chinese military experts believed that the morale of the Red Army was low, the soldiers appeared self-assured, for the Political Section deemed it necessary to warn against overconfidence—against the attitude prevalent in the Russo-Japanese War of 1904–1905 that the little enemy soldiers could be defeated by throwing hats on top of them.[13] The enthusiasm of the Soviet troops was whipped up by protest meetings against the bombardment of Russian territory by the Chinese artillery and by the allegation that the Chinese were about to invade the USSR. "The White Chinese[14] are preparing a blow," a political instructor asserted and using the same language as Bliukher declared: "We must be prepared to ward it off and to answer the blow with a double blow."[15]

In haranguing the troops, the political agitators met separately with the members of the Communist Party and of the Komsomol, the Communist Youth Organization, exhorting them: "Communists and Komsomols are in front everywhere. In battle too they must be first!" The companies of the Red Army actually challenged each other to "Socialist competition in battle."[16]

[13] *Ibid.*, 124–25.
[14] *"Belokitaitsy."*
[15] Kulagin and Iakovlev, 128.
[16] Lipman, 115–22.

As he lay in the cold, silent night, waiting for the signal to attack, a young Russian soldier reflected: "Several hours remain until morning. One must rest before the battle. The severe frost does not let one close one's eyes. Thousands of thoughts turn over in one's head. Somewhere gnaws a dark fear, but consciousness rejects fear. The moon, the cold, bright Manchurian moon is indifferent to everything. It shines for them and for us. Dawn comes stealing up like a cat. Time drags on slowly, agonizingly. But lo, it will soon be dawn. And the class hatred will come to a boil, will seethe, and with fire and steel will sow death in the land of the enemies. They will not trample under their feet the land of the Soviets!"[17]

Songs taught the soldiers by the political agitators stressed the defensive nature of the campaign:

V'iutsia rel'sy vdaleke
I v kolechko v'etsia dym
My svoiu K-V zh. d.
Nikomu ne otdadim.

The rails wind in the distance,
And the smoke curls in a ring.
We shall not cede our CER
To anyone.[18]

. . . .

My dralis' i budem drat'sia,
Khot' ne khochem voevat'.
My zastavim Chana sdat'sia
I prava nashi priznat'.

We have fought and will fight
Though we do not want to war.
We shall force Chiang to surrender
And recognize our rights.[19]

---

[17] *Ibid.*
[18] *Ibid.*, 40.
[19] *Ibid.*, 125.

Many of the songs ridiculed the Chinese:

Chan Kai-shi vsegda voiuet,
No naprasno zhdet pobed;
On voiuet, kak torguiet,
S pereryvom na obed.

Chiang Kai-shek is always warring,
But vainly waits for victories;
He fights as he trades,
With a break for dinner.[20]

The Soviet offensive on the Transbaikal front was directed against two fortified regions, centered about Manchuli and Chalainor. There the Chinese had constructed miles of effective antitank ditches and a network of strongpoints, fire trenches, communication trenches, and partially covered shelters. Their machine guns, mortars, and cannons were in emplacements, covered by one or two rows of rails or logs and up to five feet of sand, hardened by the cold. (The temperature in mid-November reached −4° Fahrenheit.)[21]

The offensive was planned in two stages. On the morning of November 17 the Soviet forces were to sweep past Manchuli and capture the Chinese forces at Chalainor in a surprise attack by infantry from the front and by cavalry from the rear. Then they were to wheel around and take the westward facing fortifications at Manchuli by an assault from the east.

The emphasis was on the element of surprise,[22] and every precaution was taken to hide the assembly of troops and the taking up of advance positions on the Chinese side of the border. The soldiers were forbidden

[20] *Ibid.*, 82.
[21] Kulagin and Iakovlev, 124–26.
[22] The element of surprise was to be a key factor in Soviet strategy in Manchuria again in 1945. For an account of that campaign, see G. A. Lensen, *The Strange Neutrality*, 156–73.

to talk or smoke, and the wheels of carts and guns, shells, and the metal links of horses' harnesses were wrapped or bound to deaden all sound. As the advance units stole across the border during the night of November 16–17, they had orders not to shoot but to silence any opposition with their bayonets. They managed to advance across the frozen Argun River to the Chinese defense lines unobserved.

When the Red Army attacked at dawn, the Chinese were caught completely off guard, and the first line of trenches was overrun in a matter of minutes. At the same time the cavalry brigade, which had made its way to the rear of Chalainor, cut the railway line, preventing either the retreat of the Chinese forces to Hailar or their reinforcement from there. Trapped, the defenders offered fierce resistance in spite of heavy casualties—almost the entire Chinese Fourteenth Regiment was killed—and prevented the capture of the city that day. But on November 18 a coordinated assault of the regiments of the Thirty-sixth Rifle Division from the southeast and of the Thirty-fifth Rifle Division from the northeast, supported by tanks, overwhelmed the defenders before reinforcements, sighted by Soviet air reconnaissance east of Ts'okang Station, could come to their support. Chinese soldiers who sought to flee rather than surrender were overtaken by the Kuban cavalry brigade and cut down.[23]

Merrily the Kuban Cossacks sang:

Pokazala svoiu pryt'
Nasha kavaleriia
Chan Kai-shi nochei ne spit—
Stala dizenteriia.

---

[23] Kulagin and Iakovlev, 131–32.

Our cavalry
Has shown its speed
Chiang Kai-shek does not sleep at night—
Dysentery has set in.

.   .   .   .

Metko b'iut vintovki nashi,
Khorosho svistiat klinki.
Ekh, i vsypali my kashi
Vam, burzhuiskie synki.

Our rifles hit accurately,
Our blades whistle well.
What a shellacking we have given
You sons of bourgeoisie.[24]

When the fighting stopped, the populace hastened from Chalainor to the Chinese soldiers who lay strewn about the countryside and knocked out their gold teeth and fillings.[25] As the Russian troops entered the city, they found it in shambles. Everything had been broken; not one window remained intact. The streets were littered with weapons and equipment, torn-down shutters and sundry objects, discarded by the fleeing, plundering Chinese troops.[26]

On November 19 the Soviet forces turned back toward Manchuli, which had been bypassed but blockaded, and attacked the fortified positions in their path, south and southwest of Chalainor. There was no longer any question of a surprise attack, so that a preliminary artillery barrage was possible and tanks noisily spearheaded the assault. The Chinese lines were taken after an hour and a half of heavy fighting.[27]

The eastward thrust from the Transbaikal region had

[24] Lipman, 125.
[25] Kulagin and Iakovlev, 133–34.
[26] Lipman, 115–22.
[27] Kulagin and Iakovlev, 132–33.

been synchronized with a southwestward drive from the Maritime region. On November 17 a composite group of the Special Far Eastern Army, under the command of A. Ia. Lapin and Commissar A. A. Gusev, advanced toward Mishan-fu, while Soviet planes bombed Chinese airfields, railway stations and artillery emplacements. The composite group consisted of the First Pacific Rifle Division, commanded by A. I. Cherepanov, the Ninth Detached Cavalry Brigade, led by D. A. Vainerkh, and an air group, composed of the Fifth Fighter Group and the Fortieth Bomber Group, under E. P. Karklin. The composite group had a total strength of 2,800 infantrymen, 960 cavalrymen, 36 guns, 131 heavy machine guns and 25 aircraft. Facing it stood the First Mukden Cavalry Division and the Forty-second Infantry Division, with a total strength of about 4,000 cavalrymen, 1,500 infantrymen, 6 guns, 24 bomb throwing devices, and 24 machine guns.

The Soviet cavalry was particularly effective in the roadless terrain, as the Chinese were trapped in a cul-de-sac of swamplands—the swampy valleys of the Muren' River in the west and north, and the swampy plain bordering Lake Hanka in the east. Hundreds of Chinese soldiers were killed by Russian riflemen as they plunged panic-stricken into the Muren' River to elude the saber-wielding cavalry.[28]

On the morning of November 20, after a night march of almost eight miles, the forces of Vostretsov surrounded Manchuli and demanded the surrender of its garrison. When the local *tupan* and a representative of the Japanese consulate sought to begin negotiations, Vostretsov gave the ultimatum that the "White

[28] Suntsov, 118–19; Kulagin and Iakovlev, 137.

Chinese'' command must send a bearer of a flag of truce within two hours. Then, without waiting for the truce envoy or the expiration of the two hour time limit, Vostretsov brazenly rode into the city with several of his commanders in two automobiles, his troops following behind. The Chinese soldiers were too busy looting the shops and houses to interfere.

Although General Liang Chung-chia, the commander of the Northwestern Front, and his staff were captured in Manchuli without a shot, isolated Chinese units outside the city offered stubborn, if futile, resistance. Told that Communists behaved like beasts, many of the soldiers in these units committed suicide rather than surrender.

Chinese casualties exceeded 1,500 dead and 8,000 captured, plus 1,000 wounded. The Red Army lost only 123 dead and 605 wounded. It captured practically all of the Chinese artillery, two armored trains, and a large collection of war materials and military supplies.[29]

A large Chinese host remained intact in the east, at Hailar. During the battle for the Manchuli-Chalainor region, General Hu Yu-k'un, who commanded the Chinese Eleventh Army, had planned to send the First Infantry and Third Cavalry Divisions and an Artillery Division by way of Ts'okang Station as reinforcements. Bliukher had learned of this when a communication from Hu to the Chinese defenders had mistakenly been dropped into Soviet hands by a Chinese plane. Bliukher now called upon the officers and men of the First Infantry and Third Cavalry Divisions to surrender as General Liang had done and save their lives. Not receiving any reply, Bliukher ordered Vostretsov

[29] Kulagin and Iakovlev, 143–44, 150, 152.

to advance along the railway and take Hailar, some 95 miles away.

When the advance units of the Thirty-sixth Division entered Hailar in the early hours of November 27, they found that the Chinese troops had retreated eastward, to the Khingan Mountain range, leaving in their wake the corpses of Russian railway personnel and train passengers whom they had robbed and killed. On November 28 Soviet planes, operating from Hailar, began bombing military installations in and around Pokotu (Bukhedu), east of the Khingan Mountains, where the Chinese had set up their headquarters. Panic-stricken, Chinese troops fled further east, toward Tsitsihar, plundering the countryside.[30] Only at Fularki (Fulaerchi), 10 miles west of Tsitsihar, was the Chinese command able to halt them, after General Wan Fu-lin, who held the bridge over the Nonni River, shot down several hundred of them. Hordes of demoralized soldiers and civilian refugees were deflected south, toward Taonan, to prevent their entry into Harbin.[31]

The young commander and commissar of the Fifth Detached Kuban Cavalry Brigade, Konstantin Rokossovskii, who was to gain world fame during the Second World War as a marshal of the Soviet Union, evaluated the Chinese foot soldier as "hardy, modest, stubborn in defense, warmly clad, and very poorly trained."[32] Like Russian officers who had fought in Manchuria during the Boxer disturbances at the turn of the century, he noted that the Chinese shot without taking

[30] *Ibid,* 155–59; H. W. Kinney to Sir John Pratt, Dairen, February 13, 1930, FO 371/14700; A. E. Eastes to Lampson, No. 154, Harbin, December 2, 1929, "Confidential," FO 371/14700–639.

[31] Badham-Thornhill to Lampson, Peking, January 13, 1930, "Secret," FO 371/14700.

[32] Kulagin and Iakovlev, 147.

aim. What now filled many a stout peasant heart with terror, however, were air strikes. As H. W. Kinney, an American employee of the Japanese-owned South Manchurian Railway, wrote to Sir John Pratt, the Chinese troops in Manchuli had become panic-stricken and began to loot the town when Soviet planes had dropped bombs. "The looting Chinese troops sought mainly to obtain civilian clothing, which they donned instead of their uniforms, and many of them appeared in women's clothing, including foreign dresses and bonnets," Kinney related. "When the Russians occupied the town, they rounded up these Chinese soldiers, and took a motion picture of them. The film was first exhibited to the population of Manchouli, whereupon it was sent to Moscow. I had heard reports to the effect that some of the Russian aviators had dropped cabbages and bladders filled with soot, in order to frighten the Chinese troops, but I had not believed these reports until I heard them substantiated by well-informed foreign observers. It seems that while some Chinese troops stood up well under rifle and even artillery fire, the bombing planes invariably drove them into a panic."[33]

The Soviet campaign had seen the skillful coordination of diplomacy, military force, and propaganda by the able troika of Karakhan, Bliukher and Borodin (who had been made head of the TASS news agency). The powerful radio transmitter in Khabarovsk had beamed broadcasts in Russian, Chinese, Japanese, English and Esperanto to China to incite the Mukden authorities against the Nanking government, to under-

[33] Kinney to Pratt, February 13, 1930, FO 371/14700. The Chinese had planes of their own, but Chinese pilots did not dare to challenge the Russians, declaring that their machines were unable to fly for one reason or another. (Secret report on the Manchurian situation by Badham-Thornhill, Peking, January 14, 1930, FO 371/14700–639.)

mine the morale of the Chinese soldiery, and to justify
the Manchurian invasion by accusing the Chinese of
border raids in cooperation with White Russian
forces.[34] So successful were the air attacks, "aided no
doubt by vigorous propaganda, and quite likely also
by money bribes," in demoralizing the Chinese troops,
that the British consul general at Harbin wondered
whether the Soviets were not making a special effort
to demonstrate the "inefficiency of the Chinese
forces" to back their demand for the reinstatement
of at least some Russian railway guards along the
line.[35]

American and British eyewitnesses dwelled
repeatedly on the shameful behavior of the Chinese
troops and, in contrast, the good conduct of the Red
Army, which earned the latter the friendliness of the
populace, which had come to fear its own soldiery.
"Retreat without loot and plunder is the exception,
not the rule in China," Colonel Badham-Thornhill
reflected; "events at Hailar and Pokotu were really
no more than a return to form on the part of troops
from which more was expected."[36]

The consular body, which met in Harbin on November 29 to consider ways and means of protecting
foreign nationals, was unanimous in the view that "the
danger to be feared by foreigners other than White
Russians in the event of the Soviet forces advancing
to the occupation of this town was far less than that
to be apprehended either from deserters from the Chinese ranks or in the event of an outbreak of looting
by the large numbers of Chinese soldiery in and around

[34] Mossdorf, 62.
[35] Eastes to Lampson, No. 154.
[36] Badham-Thornhill to Lampson, Peking, January 13, 1930, "Secret," FO
371/14700.

Harbin." The following day, on November 30, the consular representatives of Germany, Japan, the United States, Great Britain, Italy and Denmark voiced their apprehensions to General Wang, who had moved into the former residence of the Russian vice president of the CER. The Japanese consul made some unflattering comments about "the flexibility of the administration of martial law in China."[37]

The Khabarovsk Protocol

Within forty-eight hours of the Soviet invasion, Chang Hsüeh-liang was ready for peace on Russian terms. On November 19 Commissioner of Foreign Affairs Tsai cabled to the representative of the Foreign Commissariat at Khabarovsk that two former associates of the Soviet consulate at Harbin would set out for the Pogranichnaia-Grodekovo front the following day, and asked that they be met.

On November 21 the two Russians—Kokorin, who had been attached to the German consulate at Harbin to assist Soviet citizens following the break in diplomatic relations between the USSR and China, and Nechaev, a former interpreter of the CER—crossed into Russian territory at Pogranichnaia Station, accompanied by a Chinese colonel. Kokorin transmitted an official declaration by Tsai to the effect that he had been empowered by both the Mukden and Nanking governments to open immediately negotiations for the settlement of the Sino-Soviet conflict, and requested that the Soviet government appoint a representative to meet with him.

Simanovskii, the representative of the Foreign Commissariat at Khabarovsk, conveyed the views of his government the following day, on November 22, and

[37] Eastes to Lampson, No. 154.

the three envoys hastened back to Harbin with the reply. The Soviet government, the telegram stated, favored the peaceful solution of the conflict, but deemed it impossible to enter into negotiations with the Chinese side until the prior conditions, communicated through the German government on August 29,[38] had been carried out, that is, until China agreed to the restoration of the *status quo ante* on the CER on the basis of the Peking and Mukden treaties of 1924; immediately restored the rights of the general manager and assistant general manager of the railway, nominated by the Soviet side in accordance with the Peking and Mukden treaties of 1924; and immediately released all Soviet citizens arrested in connection with the conflict. "The Soviet side declares," the reply ended, "that as soon as the Chinese side will carry out these conditions and the Soviet government will be informed thereof officially and in writing, the Soviet government will free at once all Chinese arrested in connection with the conflict and will participate in a Sino-Soviet conference for the final settlement of all questions at issue."[39]

After studying the telegram which Kokorin had transmitted to Tsai, Chang Hsüeh-liang cabled to the Soviet government on November 26 that "in view of the fact that both sides desire in equal measure to carry out the Russo-Chinese and Mukden agreements of 1924," he agreed in principle to the three prior conditions raised by it. He asked in regard to the second condition that the Soviet government immediately name a general manager and an assistant general man-

---

[38] The same conditions had been embodied in the Soviet notes of July 13 and 25.

[39] DVP, XII, 594–95; Kulagin and Iakovlev, 174; Kapitsa, 223–24; *Survey 1929*, 363.

ager; as for the first and third conditions, he proposed that responsible persons be appointed by both sides to discuss the order and manner in which they were to be realized.[40]

Chang's reply was received by the Foreign Commissariat on November 27. Litvinov answered the same day. Acknowledging Chang's full acceptance of the prior conditions, he "recommended" the reinstatement of Emshanov and Eismont and "immediate and official notification thereof."[41] He proposed that thereupon Chang send a representative to Khabarovsk with official, written credentials to discuss with Simanovskii how to carry out the other conditions and to reach an agreement on questions concerning the time and place for calling a Sino-Soviet conference.[42]

When Dirksen three days later, on November 29, transmitted the central government's note of November 14, Litvinov told him that Chang had already accepted the preliminary conditions necessary for the speedy solution of the conflict by means of direct negotiations and that Nanking's proposals thus could only drag out the conflict and were pointless.[43]

On November 30 Tsai left Harbin as the representative of the Mukden government, accompanied by Li Shao-keng. They reached Nikol'sk-Ussuriisk the following day and entered into negotiations with Simanovskii. On December 3 Tsai and Simanovskii signed a

[40] DVP, XII, 595; *Survey* 1929, p. 364; Tang, 253; Kulagin and Iakovlev, 174. Lampson mistakenly gave the date of Chang's wire as November 24; Kapitsa, as November 25.

[41] Litvinov to Chang Hsüeh-liang, November 27, 1929, DVP, XII, 596.

[42] *Ibid.;* Chargé d'Affaires Perkins to Stimson, Peiping, November 29, 1929, FRUS 1929, II, 362–63; *Survey* 1929, pp. 363–64.

[43] Litvinov to Dirksen, November 29, 1929, DVP, XII, 596–97. Kapitsa's contention that the Nanking proposal was made on the 29th in order to hinder the resolution of the conflict by negotiation between Moscow and Mukden (Kapitsa, 225) is unfair; the proposal had been made before Mukden had agreed to talk.

provisional agreement—a protocol embodying a number of declarations. First Tsai declared that Lü Jung-huan was being dismissed as president of the board of directors of the CER. Then Simanovskii declared that upon Lü's replacement, the Soviet government would be prepared, in line with its note of August 29, to recommend the replacement also of Emshanov and Eismont as general manager and assistant general manager of the CER, though it reserved the right to employ them in other capacities on the railway. Tsai consented to the arrangement orally and pledged that the Mukden government would strictly and fully adhere to the Mukden and Peking agreements of 1924. Simanovskii followed with a similar declaration on behalf of the Soviet government.[44]

Tsai hastened home with the provisional agreement to obtain the approval of the Mukden government. Two days later, on December 5, Chang telegraphed his acceptance.

On December 13 Tsai arrived in Khabarovsk, armed with plenipotentiary powers from both the Mukden and Nanking governments, to conclude a final settlement. As agreed, he gave to Simanovskii a written statement to the effect that Lü had been dismissed as president of the CER on December 7 and that Ho Fu-mian had been appointed acting president until a replacement was named. Simanovskii in turn declared that the Soviet government was nominating Iulii Rudyi as the new general manager and Denisov as the assistant general manager.

---

[44] Nikol'sk-Ussuriiskii protocol, December 3, 1929, DVP, XII, 601–602; Perkins to Stimson, Peiping, December 5, 1929, on the basis of a TASS dispatch from Moscow, dated December 4, FRUS 1929, II, 392–93; Kulagin and Iakovlev, 174–75.

On December 22 Simanovskii and Tsai signed the Khabarovsk Protocol, which provided for the immediate restoration of peace along the Sino-Soviet border, followed by a mutual troop withdrawal. The document affirmed the restoration of the *status quo ante* and left the solution of all disputes that had arisen during the joint administration of the railway to a special Soviet-Chinese conference to be convened in Moscow on January 25, 1930. The following measures were to be put into effect immediately: (1) The board of directors of the CER was to resume its activities on the basis of previous treaties, with the Soviet members of the board entering upon the performance of their duties. Hereafter the Chinese president and the Soviet vice president had to act jointly as provided under point 6 of article 1 of the Soviet-Mukden agreement. (2) The former proportion of Soviet and Chinese citizens heading the various services was to be restored and Soviet citizens who were chiefs and assistant chiefs of the various services were to be reinstated in their rights (or new candidates immediately appointed, should the Soviet side so propose). (3) Orders and instructions for the railway issued on and after July 10, 1929, in the name of the board of directors and of the administration of the CER were to be considered as null and void unless properly confirmed by the lawful board and administration of the railway.[45]

The protocol provided for the immediate release of all Soviet and Chinese citizens arrested in connection with the conflict, including the Soviet citizens who had been seized at the time of the raid on the Harbin consulate. All Soviet workers and employees of the CER who had been dismissed or had resigned on and since July

[45] *Izvestiia*, December 23, 1929, as translated in FRUS 1929, II, 426–29.

10, 1929, and wished to return to their jobs were to be reinstated immediately; full compensation in terms of wages and pensions was to be paid to individuals who chose not to accept reemployment. All former Russian subjects who were not citizens of the USSR and had been hired by the railway during the conflict were to be dismissed at once unconditionally. "White Guard detachments" were to be disarmed by the Chinese and their "organizers and inspirers" deported from the Three Eastern Provinces.[46]

While leaving the question of the resumption of diplomatic and consular relations between the USSR and China to the Moscow conference, the protocol provided for the immediate reopening of the Soviet consulates in the Three Eastern Provinces and of the Chinese consulates in the Russian Far East. The Mukden government guaranteed to the Soviet consulates in Manchuria "all the inviolability and all those privileges which are due to them under international law and custom" and pledged to "refrain from any acts of force which may infringe upon this inviolability and these privileges." The USSR in turn lifted the restrictions which she had placed on the Chinese consulates in the Soviet Far East. The protocol provided for the reopening of both Soviet and Chinese economic institutions and commercial enterprises closed down by the conflict. The question of Sino-Soviet trade in general was left for settlement by the Moscow conference. The final article stated that the Khabarovsk Protocol would go into effect "at the moment of its signature."[47]

[46] DVP, XII, 676. For a translation of the entire protocol, see the *North China Standard*, December 24, 1929. On February 8, 1930, Mel'nikov furnished Tsai with a secret supplement, which listed the White Russians whom the Soviet side was most eager to have removed: Khorvat, Ostroumov, Makarenko, Peshkov, Sakharov, Nechaev, Nazarov, Shil'nikov, and Plotnikov. (Mel'nikov to Tsai, February 8, 1930, DVP, XIII, 84.)

[47] *Izvestiia,* December 23, 1929; DVP, XII, 673–76; FRUS 1929, II, 426–29.

There was agreement among Soviet, Chinese and neutral observers that the Khabarovsk Protocol constituted the complete surrender of China to Russian demands. Yet Professor Tang's characterization of the protocol as "ill-fated" because it remained "conspicuously silent on the subject of Soviet propaganda" and thus provided no guarantee against Soviet interference in Chinese internal affairs through the CER, leaving "Chinese sovereignty and interests continuously at Soviet mercy,"[48] is overdrawn. Sir Miles Lampson reported in July 1930 that in spite of the fact that the terms of the protocol were "a complete capitulation by the Chinese," the Soviets "very wisely did not seek to exploit their victory, but seem to have concentrated on bringing about the return to normal conditions with the least possible friction."[49]

Rudyi and Denisov took up their duties on December 30. A forceful, direct, and self-educated man, Rudyi was respected by the foreign community in Harbin as "a strong and straight forward man" and feared by the Chinese for the "iron hand" he might show. He immediately dismissed the White Russian replacements and rehired the Soviet employees upon their release the following day. On January 6, 1930, Mo Te-hui, former civil governor of Fengtien, took office as the new Chinese president of the CER.[50] Traffic was restored on the eastern line of the CER on January 10, on the western line on January 15; full operations were resumed on January 20. On February

---

[48] Tang, 253.

[49] Lampson to Henderson, No. 930.

[50] Kinney to Pratt, Dairen, February 13, 1930, p. 11; FO 371/14700–639; Lampson to Henderson, No. 930; *Survey* 1929, p. 368. Mo, who was to represent China at the Moscow Conference, had been a member of Chang Tso-lin's government and had been a passenger on the train on which Chang had died. (William Strang to Henderson, Moscow, August 16, 1930, FO 371/14700–639.)

1 the first express departed from Khabarovsk for Moscow.[51]

With the signing of the Khabarovsk Protocol, all Chinese and Russian prisoners had been released and the Soviet troops withdrawn; the last unit had crossed the border on December 25, 1929. During the month that the Red Army had occupied part of Manchuria, Russian sappers had demolished Chinese military installations and emplacements, while Communist Party workers had put up wall posters, blaming the destruction on the desire of the "White Chinese" generals "to trample on Soviet territory."[52]

Soviet propaganda had not been confined to posters. As mentioned, the conduct of the Red Army toward the civilian population had been designed to win friends, and a well organized campaign had been launched by Communist Party agitators to indoctrinate the masses. In the words of a Soviet historian, "Political life seethed in the Chinese cities, occupied by the Red Army."[53]

Every effort had been made to influence the prisoners of war taken to Chita, where they had received food for thought as well as food for the body, as party agitators had striven to give them a new slant on life. The Russian barracks had been decorated with slogans in Chinese, such as "We and the Red Army are brothers," and a wall newspaper had been published under the name *The Red Chinese Soldier*. Within two days, according to one Soviet party worker, 27 prisoners had filed membership applications for the Communist Youth League and 1,240 had petitioned to remain in the USSR.[54]

[51] Kapitsa, 231.
[52] Kulagin and Iakovlev, 158–59.
[53] *Ibid.*, 166.
[54] *Ibid.*, 163–65.

The contention of Chinese historians that Chinese public opinion had been greatly aroused by the signature of the Khabarovsk Protocol[55] is not borne out by the observations of contemporary foreign residents in Manchuria. "One of the most remarkable aspects of Sino-Soviet relations at Harbin since the signing of the Protocol is the absence of any manifestations in the Chinese press or among the students or elsewhere of ill will towards the nation whose armed forces gave the Chinese government and people so sharp a lesson," Consul General C. F. Garstin reported, noting that "such agitation as there has been recently among Chinese students and others has been directed not against Soviet Russia but against the efforts of Chinese officials to check the spread of communist doctrines." "It is interesting," Garstin observed, "to contrast with this attitude the outburst of fury when the Japanese Government sent troops to Tsinan in 1928 to protect their nationals, or the repercussion of the May 30th 1925 incident at Shanghai and of the Wanhsien incident in 1926."[56]

The British Foreign Office's "Annual Report on China" for 1930 noted that with the signing of the Khabarovsk Protocol "conditions on the Chinese Eastern Railway soon returned to normal" and that the Russian and Chinese administrators set to work "in an atmosphere of harmony which, superficially at all

---

[55] *See* Cheng, 157; Wu, 211; and Tang, 258.

[56] Garstin to Lampson, No. 23, Harbin, May 5, 1930, FO 371/14700–639. In fact, there was general merriment as 1,800 Russian men and women with four months' back pay in their pockets congregated on Kitaiskaia Street. "Those were days of great festivity," a Chinese observer recorded. "The western Christmas was followed by the New Year, and the Russian Christmas, which falls on January 7, was close upon the Russian 'old' New Year on January 14. . . . Much vodka was drunk, and much money spent." Tsao Lien-en, "The Settlement of the Sino-Soviet Dispute," 291–92.)

events, continues to prevail." It observed: "The marked restraint and civility with which the returning Soviet officials treated their lately vanquished foes undoubtedly contributed to the smoothness with which the line was again brought into operation; while it at the same time appears to have heightened in Chinese eyes the considerable prestige which the Union of Soviet Socialist Republics had lately won by the display of armed force."[57]

[57] "China, Annual Report, 1930," submitted by Lampson to Henderson from Peitaiho on July 23, 1931, FO 371/15508–659.

4

Attitude of the Powers

The foreign powers had followed the Soviet-Chinese controversy closely. Although French financiers had certain ties with the Russo-Asiatic Bank and the Chinese Eastern Railway and although British firms employed Russians as their agents to purchase produce in Manchuria,[1] the powers had no direct stake in the dispute. Yet indirectly they were involved because they shared Nationalist Chinese fears of Communist subversion, because the resort to force by either side as a means of settling problems thwarted their aspirations for a warless world, and, above all, because Chinese abrogation of the treaty rights of any power constituted a precedent that might eventually be used against them. As the British military attaché, Colonel G. Badham-Thornhill, remarked when the Chinese seized the CER and related installations, although their action had been "ostensibly carried out as a set-off against Russian plans for the use of the railway and its funds for furthering propaganda," it had really been

[1] Tours to Henderson, No. 10, Mukden, September 30, 1929, FO 371/13891–638.

"a part of China's now popular policy of ousting the foreigner wherever he may be found."[2]

The observations of the British, whose special rights and privileges in China were extensive, are of particular interest because of their detail and astuteness. The handwritten minutes, in which Foreign Office officials evaluated the dispatches they received and candidly discussed world affairs, are most revealing.

As early as January 1920, when the Chinese Foreign Office had objected to General Khorvat's assumption of full administrative authority over the Russian population in the CER zone, Sir John Jordan, the British minister to Peking, had reported that the protest "must be considered in conjunction with their whole attitude towards the recovery of rights formerly wrested from them by Russia" and that there was "a strong desire on the part of the Chinese to recover the CER and to prevent it falling into foreign hands."[3] When General Pao had seized the administration of the CER in March of that year, Jordan's successor, Sir Miles Lampson, had remarked: "It seems clear that China is set on forcing an issue over the question of the Chinese Eastern Railway; it is equally certain that in her own interests she should avoid precipitating matters, time being on her side."[4]

Concerned as the powers were about the possibility of hostilities between China and the USSR, the prospect of a Sino-Soviet rapprochement alarmed them even more. Embarrassed by Soviet renunciation of Russian extraterritorial rights in China, they tried to

---

[2] Badham-Thornhill to Lampson, Report VIII, "Secret," dated Peiping, August 13, 1929, enclosed in Lampson to Henderson, No. 1180 (130/107A), Peking, August 18, 1929, "Confidential," FO 371/13955–632.

[3] J. N. Jordan to Earl Curzon, No. 54, Peking, January 31, 1920, FO 371/5310–799.

[4] Lampson to Curzon, No. 117, Peking, March 5, 1920, FO 371/5310–799.

block the Sino-Soviet agreement of 1924, which tacitly acknowledged Soviet ownership of the CER.[5] The Japanese minister in Peking, Yoshizawa Kenkichi, sent identic notes to the director of the Chinese Foreign Office and to the Soviet representative in Peking, making "express reservations" concerning the rights and interests of Japan and her subjects in the CER—"that they shall not be affected in any way either by the clauses relating to the railway contained in the agreement . . . or by the arrangement regarding the said railway to be come to hereafter by virtue of the above-mentioned agreement."[6]

The British saw that China lacked the strength to contain foreign encroachment. Lamenting "how rapidly republican China is drifting to chaos under the disintegrating influence of militarism," a Foreign Office official warned his colleagues that "unless an international scheme for control of army and armament and reconstruction of the fiscal and financial systems is soon introduced and carried through with determination, China will rapidly become a shuttlecock for Soviet intrigue and Japanese militarists, and a great market will be lost to Europe and America."[7]

When Chang Tso-lin bore down on the Soviets in January 1926, a telegram from the British minister in China left the impression that the Russians had been "conspiring with Chang Tso-lin's enemies to create a military diversion in Chang's own territory whilst his troops are threatening Peking" and that Chang's action thus savored of a "defensive offensive." "We do not seem to be immediately concerned and can await

[5] Clubb, *China and Russia*, 207, 210.
[6] Sir Charles E. Eliot to MacDonald, No. 245, Tokyo, July 7, 1924, enclosure, FO 371/10267–760.
[7] FO 371/10951–760, China 1925, p. 127.

events whilst hoping for the success of Wu and Chang," a Foreign Office official commented. A colleague, F. T. A. Ashton-Gwatkin, added that it was clear that Chang had Japanese support and thus was "unlikely to knuckle under." "In that case," he observed, "the Russians will have either to act on their ultimatum or accept a humiliating defeat with loss of much of their position on the Chinese Eastern Railway. The showing up of Russian intrigue, bluff and weakness is all to our advantage."[8]

On January 25 Sir Charles Eliot, the British ambassador in Japan, reported from Tokyo that the British military attaché had learned that the Soviets had sounded out the Japanese, probably through their military attaché in Moscow, about their attitude concerning the possible dispatch of Soviet troops to North Manchuria, and that the Japanese General Staff had voiced strong objections.[9] The Japanese vice minister of foreign affairs told the Soviet ambassador in Tokyo that he sincerely hoped that the USSR and China could settle their differences amicably, because while Japan would remain strictly neutral, it was impossible to predict what might happen in China under existing conditions.[10] On March 24 Sir Ronald Macleay wrote from Peking that the British consul general at Hankow had reported that a Japanese with the rank of consul general and sort of a roving commission in China had given the Chinese Foreign Office an assurance that Japan would support Chang Tso-lin with troops in the event of a Soviet attack. "I should imagine," Macleay stated, "that, although this is doubtless correct, the Japanese Government would scarcely wish to show

[8] FO 371/11666–766, China 1926, pp. 116A–116B.
[9] Eliot to Foreign Office, No. 13, Tokyo, January 25, 1926, FO 371/11666–766.
[10] Eliot to Foreign Office, No. 37, Tokyo, January 29, 1926, FO 371/11666–766.

their hand before the necessity arose, nor to risk precipitating a conflict by promises of support to Chang,
and that therefore Mr. Funatsu may have been speaking on his own authority."[11]

When the halting of traffic on the CER interrupted
the flow of domestic and nternational mail, the foreign
business firms and chambers of commerce prevailed
upon the consular body in Harbin to proffer its
assistance in resolving the controversy. As Karakhan
rejected foreign mediation on the ground that it would
entail "an inadmissible humiliation of China,"[12] the
British consul reported: "The Chinese showed themselves anxious to affect a settlement, and rather tended
to lean upon the consuls for sympathy and support,
but the Russian side held completely aloof, and made
no secret of their view that the matter did not concern
the foreign consuls, but was a purely Russo-Chinese
affair, to be settled by the two parties alone."[13]

The consular body had not taken sides in the dispute,
but had addressed both sides impartially. "It would
be idle to speculate whether the Soviet Government
or Chang, or even both parties simultaneously, deliberately provoked the recent crisis, or whether matters
came to a head without any encouragement," Macleay
wrote from Peking on February 1. "I am . . . inclined
to think that the recent trouble arose from the continu-
ous friction between the Mukden Government and the
Soviet, in which both sides had a certain legitimate
cause for annoyance, but that in this specific instance
the Moscow Government were on the whole justified
in the firm attitude they adopted."[14] "Judged simply

[11] Macleay to Chamberlain, Peking, February 1, 1926, FO 371/11666–766.
[12] Sir R. Hodgson to Chamberlain, No. 104, Moscow, February 9, 1926, FO
371/11666–766.
[13] Porter to Macleay, No. 6, Harbin, February 1, 1926, "Confidential," FO
371/11666–766.
[14] Macleay to Chamberlain, Peking, February 1, 1926, FO 371/11666–766.

as an isolated railway question the Soviet demands seem to be justified by the terms of their treaty of 1924," G. S. Moss (?) commented after reading about Chicherin's ultimatum of January 23.[15] After studying a summary of the Chinese trial of Ostroumov and colleagues, Lampson jotted down in the minutes: "It strikes me as pretty damning and as distinctly useful later if we are accused of being unduly sticky about giving up our extraterritorial jurisdiction at least in *criminal* cases."[16]

"So tension must be less," Ashton-Gwatkin remarked on January 26 upon learning of Ivanov's release, "but it is not clear whether the episode is quite cleared up or whether Chang or the Bolsheviks have scored. They both seem to have been bluffing on poor hands."[17] "It is still not quite clear whether Chang or the Soviet won at the last encounter," Ashton-Gwatkin noted a month later, "but I think it was Chang."[18] Consul Porter shared the view that the Chinese had "scored": "they have made their point, namely, that they will not pay cash to the railway for military transportation, and they have shown that they have the power and the will to arrest and imprison the nominees of the Soviet Government and to take repressive measures against the supposedly all-powerful Bolshevik institutions." At the same time, he felt, Soviet propaganda against foreign imperialism had "recoiled upon her own head" and "the mere threat [of force] must have sufficed to undo the costly propaganda work of years and to have opened the eyes

[15] FO 371/11666–766, China 1926, p. 116.
[16] *Ibid.*, 53.
[17] FO 371/11666–766, China 1926, pp. 121–22.
[18] *Ibid.*, 142.
[19] Porter to Macleay, No. 6.

of all but the most venal Chinese officials to her real policy and objects."[19]

"The Soviets are being forced to give way in every particular," Henry Dobinson (?) commented after reading about Chang Huan-hsiang's rude letter of April 10 to Serebriakov. "This does not surprise us," he remarked, "seeing that the Bolsheviks themselves say that they are too weak to offer resistance in Manchuria." Ashton-Gwatkin added that "the Russians seem meekly to have accepted what is in effect a decisive defeat, as they evidently [feel] that if they do not give way on most points they may lose their railway altogether."[20]

When Karakhan returned to Moscow from Peking in September 1926, the Japanese ambassador and his staff welcomed him at the railway station. Although Ashton-Gwatkin thought that this was "merely Japanese politeness," Toller (?) wondered whether the fact that the Japanese were the only foreigners to welcome Karakhan might not be "a further indication of Japanese-Soviet *rapprochement*."[21]

Soviet reluctance in 1926 to resort to force may have been due partly to the fear that Chang Tso-lin might receive foreign backing,[22] partly to the expectation that a more indirect approach—the overthrow of Chang by supporting General Feng Yü-hsiang on one hand and the Cantonese and Kuomintang forces on the other hand—would prove more effective in the long run. Sir R. Hodgson reported from Moscow that in addition to aiding Chang's enemies, the Soviets were wooing away his friends. He asserted that the Commissariat of Foreign Affairs had adopted "more subtle methods

[20] FO 371/11666–766, China 1926, pp. 222A–222B.
[21] FO 371/11679–766, China 1926, p. 30.
[22] *Ibid.*

for attaining its objective than the double-edged one of dispatching minatory notes" and that two of Chang's leading generals and one high civilian official were now in Soviet pay."[23]

The Japanese ambassador in Moscow made light of Soviet efforts to establish their influence in China. He told his British colleague with irony in his voice that the Russians were "learning by experience what wiser people have learned in times past, that to subsidize one individual or group in China is a poor investment: the recipients will willingly take all that is given, and, except for a wealth of promises, give nothing in return." He predicted that the Bolsheviks would only "burn their fingers."[24] Noting in October 1926 that "the Russians have given very great assistance to the Cantonese armies—with a view presumably to establishing themselves as the permanent advisers and friends of the New China—and perhaps of a new Asia," Ashton-Gwatkin asked: "Will the Chinese do more than use them, and then turn them down?" "No foreign influence, as far as I know, has ever yet succeeded in establishing a *permanent* hold on any Chinese faction," a colleague replied.[25]

In June 1928 the Japanese tried to strengthen their influence by liquidating Chang Tso-lin. Although they sought to hide their involvement in the bombing, the chief Japan experts of the British embassy in Tokyo were agreed that the Japanese were implicated. "I think the evidence against the Japanese, though not sufficient to convict, is very strong indeed," George B. Sansom noted. "On the point of morality, I do

[23] Hodgson to Chamberlain, No. 804, Moscow, November 4, 1926, "Confidential," FO 371/11679–760.

[24] Hodgson to Chamberlain, Moscow, September 6, 1926, "Confidential," FO 371/11679–766.

[25] FO 371/11679–766, China 1926, pp. 26A-26B.

not think that any Japanese statesman of the type of school of General Tanaka [Giichi] would hesitate to use assassination as a political weapon if he thought he could do so without being discovered." Sansom questioned that any "highly placed statesman or official" had initiated the plot, remarking that this would have been unnecessary anyhow. "All he need do would be to abstain from objecting or interfering." "Remarkable" as Ashton-Gwatkin of the Far Eastern Department of the Foreign Office found Japan's apparent involvement in the "barbarous assassination plot," he deemed it "most astonishing of all" that the ultimate object of establishing a thinly veiled Japanese protectorate in Manchuria under Yang had failed, "because the Japanese had not accurately gauged the political forces or the character of the men with whom they had to deal." "The whole story, therefore, if true," he concluded, "show up the Japanese—that is to say, high military officers and perhaps the Prime Minister himself—as not only criminals but blunderers."[26]

As the matter of ridding the CER of Soviet control continued to exercize the minds of the Manchurian authorities, William Henry Donald, who acted as their political adviser, counseled them to seek the acquisition of the railway peacefully by advancing the argument that since the Washington Conference had placed upon China the responsibility of the proper running of the railway, she was entitled to assume the trusteeship of the CER in order to meet this responsibility.[27] "Ingenious" as Donald's citation of the Washington resolutions was regarded in London, the Foreign Office realized that it was not sound judicially.[28] Nor was

[26] Tilley to Chamberlain, No. 113, Tokyo, March 23, 1929, "Secret," FO 371/13889–635.
[27] Tours to Lampson, No. 38, Mukden, June 4, 1929, FO 371/13915–638.
[28] FO 371/13915–638.

it likely, Consul General Tours remarked, that Japan would have accepted Chinese trusteeship of the railway as "adequate for the correlative interests of another Power."[29]

The United States shared British and Japanese apprehensions about developments in Manchuria. In 1900 she had voiced concern about delays in the withdrawal of Russian troops from Manchuria following the Russo-Chinese War; in 1909 she had advanced the Knox scheme for the neutralization of the Russian and Japanese railways in Manchuria; and during the Allied occupation of the Russian Far East she had sent a railway commission to Manchuria. She justified her involvement in the affairs of the CER and of the South Manchurian Railway (SMR) on the grounds that the former was not an independent railway unit physically or economically, but constituted "a link in the one and only direct railway route from Europe, across Siberia, to the Asiatic ports of the Pacific Ocean," while the latter formed "the link between the Trans-Siberian line and the ports and territories of China and Japan." In the words of Stanley K. Hornbeck, chief of the Division of Far Eastern Affairs of the Department of State, "these lines, therefore, no matter who built them or who owns them or who administers them, are not exclusively of Chinese, exclusively of Russian or exclusively of Japanese concern. They were born in and of international politics. They serve not alone the people or the purposes of any one country. They are 'public carriers' in a much broader sense than that which is usually connoted by that expression."[30]

[29] Tours to Lampson, No. 38.
[30] Address of Hornbeck to Williamstown Institute of Politics on August 27, 1929, FO 371/13954–632.

Yet while the Open Door policy, which the United States continued to apply to this region, was partly British in origin, the British did not regard the United States as a dependable ally. Sir Miles Lampson leaned toward collaboration with Japan, with whom Great Britain had a "long and special relationship." He envisioned the possibility of Anglo-Japanese cooperation in such matters as tariff autonomy, extraterritoriality and navigation rights, though he realized that the Japanese might be willing to proceed more quickly in trying to resolve some of the issues than Great Britain might deem prudent, and cautioned that the British "on no account surrender the freedom of action . . . regained with the termination of the Anglo-Japanese Alliance."

Lampson appreciated the need for cooperating with the United States also, but judged Japanese support "practically more important" to Great Britain, "for it is common knowledge that Japan can (and in certain circumstances will) take a much stronger line than America is ever likely to contemplate," and advocated, therefore, cultivation of "the closest relations" with Japan. "The Japanese may be cautious and reserved," Lampson wrote, "but even if one cannot always follow the tortuous paths by which they approach their problems, one can usually make out more or less where they stand. With America this is often not so. However close one's relationship with the American Legation, one never knows with what *fait accompli,* such as their Tariff Treaty of 1928, the State Department may suddenly face an astonished world; and one instinctively discounts in advance any prospect of practical American support in any matter which entails a definite or decided line. In a word, undependable though Japan may be in some respects, America in China is more

so, and her policy more intangible and incho-
ate . . . . "[31]

The American representatives in China concurred
with their British and Japanese colleagues that the
Chinese were largely to blame for the crisis. Consul
Hanson branded the rumored replacement of
Emshanov by a Chinese as being "in direct violation
of the Soviet-Mukden Agreement." He reported that
the Soviet authorities were "angry, but helpless" and
did not expect them to make "more than verbal objections."[32] Although Major John Magruder, the United
States military attaché in Peking, attributed the conflict
to "the insistence of Russia upon hitching a scheme
for the propagation of her political ideas unto a joint
commercial enterprise which had become the expression of Russia's neo-imperialism" as well as to
"China's determination, with her blundering or
devious governmental mechanism, to gain complete
control of a joint enterprise with scant regard for agreements, international practices and the responsibilities
involved,"[33] the American minister to China, John
Van A. MacMurray, reported that "in ousting the Russian staff it was the intention of the Chinese authorities
to obtain possession and control of property and
revenues of the Chinese Eastern Railway" and that
"the subsequent statements made by the Minister for

[31] Lampson to Henderson, Peking, March 16, 1929, "Confidential," FO
371/13890. F. T. A. Ashton-Gwatkin agreed with Lampson's point of view and
after reading the dispatch repeated in the minutes the assertion that the United
States was less dependable than Japan. R. C. Craigie expressed the thought
that the new administration in the United States—the Hoover administration—might prove more dependable and easier to work with than that of President Coolidge. "I hope at all events," he recorded, "that the experiment of
working fairly closely with the new people will be given a good trial." (FO
371/13890)

[32] Hanson to MacMurray, No. 1969, Harbin, July 10, 1929, FRUS 1929, II,
199.

[33] Report No. 7565 of Magruder, Peking, July 26, 1929, FRUS 1929, II, 252.

Foreign Affairs and by the Minister of Railways that dismissing Soviet nationals was a means merely to suppress hostile propaganda, with no intention of prejudicing Russian legal rights in said railway, appear clearly to be a result of the realization that maintaining publicly the position taken is not possible without discrediting the Chinese Government in the world's general opinion."[34]

The assertion by the Soviet historian Mikhail Kapitsa that the decision to seize the CER was made in Peking "with the knowledge of the government of the USA"[35] is unjust. It is true that MacMurray forwarded to Secretary of State Henry L. Stimson a cable from Walter A. Adams, the American consul in Nanking, that he had learned from Kuomintang headquarters that the decision to seize the railway forcibly had been made in Peking, but the cable was dated July 19 and forwarded on the 21st; the information thus had reached Adams and Washington after the fact. When reporting that leaders of the Nanking Chamber of Commerce supported the Chinese government in its attempt to maintain China's rights against the USSR, Adams had put "rights" in quotation marks and had added that "these Chinese do not fully realize [the] gravity of the situation."[36]

Stimson did not rush headlong into the Sino-Soviet dispute. He realized, as he was to tell the Chinese minister to Washington, Dr. C. C. Wu, that in the absence of diplomatic relations between Washington and Moscow any American involvement was likely to be misunderstood by the USSR.[37] When an

[34] MacMurray to Stimson, No. 633, Peking, July 25, 1929, FRUS 1929, II, 246.
[35] Kapitsa, 197.
[36] FRUS 1929, II, 221.
[37] Memorandum by the Secretary of State, Washington, August 15, 1929, FRUS 1929, II, 276–77.

Associated Press dispatch from Tokyo asserted that, in view of the possibility of a tie-up on the CER, the consular body at Harbin was considering mediation to seek a peaceable settlement of the controversy, Stimson instructed MacMurray on July 13: "Whatever precedent may exist for participation by the American Consul at Harbin in representations designed to keep the Chinese Eastern Railway open to traffic, the Department does not deem it expedient that the Consul should participate, unless instructed by the Department, in any attempt to adjust the dispute between Soviet Russia and China in connection with the Chinese Eastern Railway."[38]

Yet Stimson's concern over the possibility of an armed clash between China and the USSR just as the American-sponsored Kellogg-Briand Pact renouncing war as a means of settling disputes was to go into effect, prompted him to send for Wu on July 18 without waiting to see the text of the Soviet note of the preceding day[39] and to impress on him that the issues in the Sino-Soviet dispute seemed to be "eminently justiciable" in nature and "peculiarly fitted for arbitration." When Wu retorted that the Soviets were disseminating propaganda by means of the railway and spoke of Russian incitement of the Communist uprising at Canton, Stimson pointed out that "there was a great difference between a country attempting to protect itself against actions of individuals within its borders by appropriate measures and taking action which seemed to be aimed at another country, Russia." He told Wu that China had acted too hurriedly, "that the seizure of the railway whether rightly or wrongly was

[38] Stimson to MacMurray, Washington, July 13, 1929, FRUS, II, 200.
[39] It reached Washington from Peking on July 19.

not interpreted by public opinion as an attempt to protect China against attacks of individual propagandists but as an attempt to seize property belonging to Russia and in which she had a joint right of management under the agreement of 1924.''[40] When Wu telephoned later to give Stimson the substance of the Chinese note to the Soviet Union, Stimson reiterated that "China should make its position absolutely clear as not intending to go to war and as the first step make clear what was really done with the railway."

At a diplomatic reception the same day Stimson discussed the situation separately with the ambassadors of Japan, Great Britain, France and Italy. All agreed that it was desirable to prevent the outbreak of hostilities between the USSR and China. The Japanese ambassador doubted that there would be any fighting; "neither China nor the Soviet Government was in a position to make war." But the French ambassador was more realistic. He realized that the fact that neither China nor the USSR could afford to make war did not mean that they would not do so.[41]

As the Soviet Union and China broke off diplomatic relations, both sought to justify their policies to the Japanese government, whose position might well affect the outcome of the conflict. On July 19 Ambassador Aleksandr Troianovskii assured Foreign Minister Baron Shidehara Kijuro that although the Soviet Union had found it "utterly useless" to continue diplomatic relations with China, she had no intention at the

[40] Stimson to MacMurray, No. 231, Washington, July 19, 1929, FRUS 1929, II, 215–17; Stimson to MacMurray, No. 236, Washington, July 18, 1929, FRUS, II, 210.

[41] *Ibid.;* Lampson to Henderson, No. 930. On July 25, 1929, George Sansom wrote to his wife Katharine from Tokyo: "I don't like the look of things. Both parties are plainly reluctant to fight, but it's very easy to start a row, and very hard to stop it." (Katharine Sansom, *Sir George Sansom and Japan*, 39.)

moment to resort to war, though war might come about, if the Chinese refused all redress. He explained that the USSR demanded the restoration of the *status quo ante* and would regard any action to safeguard her rights against aggressive measures by China as defensive and as not in conflict with the Kellogg Pact. When Troianovskii equated the status of the CER and the SMR, Shidehara disagreed, asserting that whereas China had equal rights with Russia on the former, she had no rights whatsoever on the latter. He added that the SMR was guarded by Japanese troops who would have to be attacked before Japanese officials could be seized.[42] Yet he did not regard the arrest and expulsion of the Soviet officials as an act of war and expressed the hope that a peaceful settlement would be found.[43]

In response to Shidehara's query how the two sides would continue discussions now that diplomatic relations had been broken off, Troianovskii asked if Japan would be willing to act as intermediary. Shidehara replied that she might, if asked to do so in the interests of peace.[44]

When the Chinese minister presented his case to Shidehara the same day and justified Chinese action on the basis of the discovery of evidence of Communist

[42] When Russia had ceded the South Manchurian Railway (the line between Changchun or Kuanch'engtzu and Port Arthur) to Japan by the Treaty of Portsmouth, the redemption provisions of the Russo-Chinese agreement of 1896 had remained in force, but in 1915 Japan had extracted from China the extension of the railway concession to 2002 and the revocation of China's right to redeem the line after 1939. (Shen, 336.) In July 1928 Chiang Kai-shek had tried to deprive the Japanese of special rights in China, but had backed down when warned by them that they would be "obliged to take such measures as they deemed suitable for safeguarding their rights and interests." (Clubb, *Twentieth Century China*, 160.)

[43] Sir J. Tilley to Henderson, No. 324, Chuzenji, August 1, 1929, FO 371/13954–632.

[44] Tilley, No. 164, Tokyo, July 26, 1929, FO 371/13953–611.

subversion, the Japanese foreign minister asked whether the Chinese had made any attempt to discuss with the Soviets whether or not the documents were genuine before resorting to the forceful measures. Reiterating the hope that the dispute would be settled peaccably, Shidehara again left open the possibility that Japan might serve as a "channel of communication" between the USSR and China,[45] but stated that the question seemed too complicated and delicate for a third power to intervene.[46]

On July 20 Stimson sent for Wu again to impress on him that the United States, "as a sincere friend of China," was concerned over the loss of public support by China. Stimson told Wu, as he summarized in a memorandum, "that he could see for himself that public opinion had now been alienated both by the appearance which had been given that she had deliberately sought to seize this railroad and by the truculent statements which were being given out by her public officials which indicated both a non-peaceful attitude and that the seizure had been deliberate, was justifiable and was a step toward other seizures."[47]

The American minister in China agreed with Stimson's counsel to Wu. In a lengthy dispatch, in which he responded to an account of Stimson's previous meeting with Wu, he recommended additional verbal pressure to restrain China. MacMurray felt that the Chinese, following their "act of aggression" against

[45] The Chinese ambassador in Tokyo had so requested on July 22. (*Survey* 1929, p. 358.)

[46] *Aide mémoire* communicated to British Foreign Office by Japanese ambassador, July 24, 1929, FO 371/13953–61. On July 24 Troianovskii explained to Shidehara that the Soviet government was not willing to accept French mediation, because it did not stipulate restoration of the *status quo ante*. (Lampson to Foreign Office, No. 607, Peking, July 27, 1929, FO 371/13953–611.)

[47] Memorandum by the Secretary of State, Washington, July 22, 1929, FRUS 1929, II, 222–23.

Russian rights on the CER, had now assumed "an air of unconcern regarding the accomplished fact," encouraged in their passive bluff by the complaisance shown by the western powers in connection with previous violations of Chinese obligations and by the belief that the USSR would not retaliate with force for fear of arousing Japanese apprehensions as well as the general antiwar sentiment of the world. Noting that the USSR could not afford being ousted entirely from the CER, "the primary and single dependable link" with Vladivostok and the Maritime region, MacMurray warned that the Chinese, though unprepared for conflict, entertained "so overweening" a belief of their military power, that "in the valor of their ignorance" they might "overplay their hand to create a situation which will prevent either side from withdrawing without hostilities." Since Chiang Kai-shek and other Nationalist officials had linked the Russian phase of "rights recovery" with the general drive to get rid of all unequal treaties, it was necessary, MacMurray observed, "in order to prevent the Chinese from rushing to destruction" to impress on them "the seriousness of disregarding the rights of others." "Extraterritoriality and the Chinese Eastern Railway being interrelated," he wrote, "any tactical success the Chinese might have in dealing with Russia would encourage their forcing upon us the extraterritorial issue."[48]

On July 22 the Chinese minister informed Stimson that his government had no intention of seizing the CER and would not resort to arms except in self-defense.[49] Stimson once again urged on Wu that the

[48] MacMurray to Stimson, No. 611, Peking, July 22, 1929, FRUS 1929, II, 226–28.
[49] Address of Hornbeck, FO 371/13954–632.

Chinese government submit the dispute to "impartial mediation."

In a conversation with the secretary of the German embassy the following day, Stimson solicited German moral support, explaining that the United States was interested solely in preventing war.[50] On July 26 the German government expressed its satisfaction with the measures taken by Washington.

The United States gained the impression that its policy had the support of the other powers. Stanley K. Hornbeck asserted that the British government had indicated its "hearty approval" of the steps taken by the American government and that Italy as well as Germany had communicated their "full accord" with Washington's actions. "The American Government," Hornbeck declared, "thus had assurances of the concurrence of other Powers in the views and hopes which the Secretary of State had expressed on July 18."[51]

Yet when Sir Esme Howard, the British ambassador in Washington, had telegraphed to the Foreign Office on July 18 that Stimson had suggested that the British government also call in the Chinese minister and point out how serious would be the violation of the Kellogg Pact at the very moment when its consummation was about to be celebrated,[52] G. A. Mounsey, the head of the Far Eastern Department, had objected. While he understood that the Americans, "as authors of the Kellogg Pact," deemed it incumbent on them to seek to avert the outbreak of war in the Far East, he warned that "the action they are taking, however, is calculated to lay them open to the criticism of 'taking sides,'

[50] Stimson to MacMurray, No. 245, July 24, 1929, FRUS 1929, II, 233–36.
[51] Address of Hornbeck, August 27, 1929, FO 371/13954–632.
[52] FO 371/13953–611.

as they are making representations to one party only to the dispute, and also of placing one party in the dock without knowing the real facts of the situation." He felt that the action of Aristide Briand, the French foreign minister and co-sponsor of the pact, who had urged a peaceful solution on both the Soviet and Chinese representatives in Paris had been "proper and impartial." Since there was no Soviet representative in London, however, Great Britain was not in a position to make "impartial representations to both sides." Mounsey deemed it "most undesirable" for Great Britain to take "without very good reason and good prospect of some satisfactory result" any action that might offend the Chinese government, with which relations were just improving, or revive its suspicions of Britain's friendly sentiments. "We are not, moreover, intimately concerned in the dispute," he wrote, "and can well afford to leave it to those Powers who are, e.g. Japan, to take what action they consider best calculated to prevent an outbreak of hostilities."[53]

The realization that China had been legally in the wrong made it that much more difficult for the Foreign Office to give advice to China without giving offense. When Hore-Belisha queried in Parliament on July 25 what the attitude of His Majesty's Government was "towards the acquisition by the Soviet government of control of the Chinese Eastern Railway in defiance of the Washington Nine-Power agreement of 1922,"

---

[53] FO 371/13953–611. The assertion by Pauline Tomkins in her excellent study *American-Russian Relations in the Far East* that "the American suggestion that the major powers approach Moscow and Nanking in the sense in which Stimson had discussed the crisis with C. C. Wu was immediately approved by Britain and France" and that "in contrast, Japan dissociated itself from the Stimson policy" (Tompkins, 225) is not borne out by British archival material. The views of the British and Japanese corresponded "very closely indeed." (FO 371/13953–611.)

Toller remarked that Hore-Belisha appeared to be "totally ignorant of the facts." He explained that the technical sub-committee of the Washington Conference had recognized that the status of the CER was still determined by the agreement of 1896; that it was in effect the property of Russia and was being held in trust pending the general recognition of a Russian government. Following the recognition of the Soviet government by Great Britain and the other powers, China had concluded agreements with the USSR, which provided for a dual, Sino-Russian administration of the railway. Since China had now evicted the Soviet personnel, Toller declared, the issue was not "whether the Soviet government shall acquire control, but whether it shall retain the measure of control provided for in these treaties."[54]

Sir Miles Lampson penned a trenchant analysis of the Chinese charges that the Soviets had not lived up to the agreements of 1924 providing for the joint management of the railway and that by retaining effective control of the line, blocking the stipulated revision of the railway statutes, and spreading Communist propaganda, the Soviets had violated the agreements in such a way as to make them null and void. "The facts on which these complaints are based appear to be correct," Lampson wrote, "but the charges that the agreements were thereby violated are not for this reason necessarily justified." He pointed out that the preponderant position of the Russians on the CER had derived directly from the terms of the agreements, and that the clauses providing for equal representation in the employment of personnel had been "expressly qualified" in both agreements by the reservation that

[54] FO 371/13953–611.

due consideration be given to the fitness of applicants. "By the agreements Russia made large concessions from the position which the railway had given her in Northern Manchuria under the Tsarist Government," Lampson wrote, "Russian activities were to be confined to the business operations of the railway, and in these Chinese were to be admitted to a large participation. But the agreements were clearly framed, on the Soviet side, with the intention of securing practical Russian control of the railway for many years to come. China's plea in this respect, therefore, scarcely seems to succeed. To find themselves powerless under the existing system to resist Russian domination of the railway may have been galling, but they do not appear to be justified in pleading that this involved a breach of the agreements either in letter or spirit. Their remedy was to seek a revision of the agreements themselves, and any difficulties they may have anticipated in this respect can scarcely justify their high-handed action in seizing the railway."[55]

Lampson noted that China may have had a better case on the score of Communist propaganda and that "the consistent abuse of the organs of the railway for this purpose might ultimately have justified China in declaring the 1924 agreements inoperative in view of the persistent breaches of the propaganda clauses." But he observed that "if the fear of subversive activities was her real motive, by waiting six weeks after the raid on the Harbin consulate and then without warning proceeding to the expulsion *en masse* of the Soviet Russian employees of the railway, China singularly neglected to take any steps to put herself in the right." It was Lampson's impression that whatever provoca-

---

[55] Lampson to Henderson, July 2, 1930, pp. 5–6.

tions China may have received, "the *coup* was essentially nothing more or less than a spasmodic attempt on her part to acquire by force a valuable property which was not hers by rights."

Lampson realized that the stiff attitude of the Nanking government toward Moscow was dictated in part by domestic considerations. "Clearly, they hoped," he wrote, "by successfully defying Russia and forcing a settlement favorable to China, not only to score a diplomatic victory but to strengthen their claims to authority in the Three Eastern Provinces." Because of its distance, Nanking was "insensible to the very considerable degree of pressure short of an invasion which the Soviet Government were able to bring locally."[56] Besides, it was convinced that the Soviet Union could not risk war because of her internal difficulties and her international isolation.[57]

Shidehara's exchange of views with Troianovskii and the Chinese minister on July 19 had been regarded as private; Shidehara had not wanted to act officially until he knew how the two sides responded to his preliminary soundings. The Chinese minister responded in the name of his government on July 23 that the Soviet Union must give assurance that she would desist from further Communist propaganda; he said that China had agreed to follow Shidehara's "advice" and not invade Soviet territory. When he alluded again to the possibility of Shidehara acting as an intermediary in the controversy with the USSR, Shidehara declared

[56] *Ibid.,* 6–8.

[57] MacMurray to Stimson, Peking, August 1, 1929, FRUS 1929, II, 263. This view was generally shared by Westerners. *See* G. C. Hanson to MacMurray, No. 1876, Harbin, January 9, 1929, FRUS 1929, II, 188–89; Memorandum by Johnson, Washington, July 19, 1929, FRUS, II, 218; Lt. Col. K. J. Martin to Sir W. Erskine, No. 312 (85/5/29), Warsaw, July 25, 1929, "Secret," FO 371/13953–11; Comment by Mounsey, August 26, 1929, FO 371/13954–632.

that he might do so if asked to convey pacific messages, not declarations of this nature. Troianovskii replied on July 25 that a peaceful settlement of the issue depended on the restoration of the *status quo ante*—reinstatement of Emshanov and his colleagues and the release of the prisoners—and the halting of the White Russian activities. In view of the qualified replies, Shidehara concluded that "any intervention from outside must be of a most private kind, both sides being very sensitive." It was his belief that the United States agreed and would take no action for the moment.[58]

Yet on the same day, on July 25, Stimson read an *aide mémoire* to the representatives of Great Britain, France, Japan, Germany and Italy. Realizing that "mediation by any nation or group of nations . . . would have its difficulties and might excite unfounded suspicion," Stimson suggested that "a road of honor out of their difficulties" for the two "sister states" might lie in the convening of an impartial commission of conciliation, with a membership agreeable to both of them to investigate the dispute and make recommendations for its solution. He envisaged that while the commission of conciliation studied the issues, the regular operations of the CER could be restored, "the interests of both Russia and China in said Railway being guarded by the appointment as President and General Manager with full powers, of a prominent national of some neutral country approved by both China and Russia, and by the recognition and continuance in their respective positions as directors under the agreement of May 31, 1924 of the five Russian and the five Chinese appointees."[59]

[58] Tilley to Foreign Office, No. 164, Tokyo, July 26, 1929, FO 371/13953–611.
[59] FRUS 1929, II, 242–44.

The Japanese politely rejected Stimson's proposal on the ground that such intervention was likely to arouse the resentment of both sides. The British regarded it with disfavor for the same reason. Shidehara had reiterated to Sir John Tilley on July 26 that "the important thing for outsiders was to go as quietly as possible—not to try to force mediation on the two parties who were peculiarly sensitive,"[60] and the British foreign secretary had replied on August 6 that he shared the misgivings of the Japanese government "as to the practicability of [the] latest American proposal."[61]

A substitute proposal by the French on August 6 that the Washington Conference powers remind China that they had reserved for themselves by a resolution of the conference the right to insist on the fulfillment of the obligations China had toward the foreign stockholders on the basis of the contracts under which the railway was built also failed to receive Japanese or British support.[62]

The British Foreign Office, ever conscious that diplomacy was the art of the possible, sidestepped also Chinese efforts to draw it into the controversy, declaring that it did not know the rights and wrongs of the case. It did express the hope that "as China had taken the initial step which produced the crisis, she would do all in her power to meet the Soviet Government's requirements for negotiating a solution."[63]

"As to our own attitude," D. MacKillop commented, "we cannot form an opinion on the merits of the case, and should continue to abstain from pres-

[60] Tilley to Henderson, No. 324, Chuzenji, August 1, 1929, FO 371/13954–632.
[61] FO 371/13953–611.
[62] Lampson to Henderson, No. 930; Memorandum by the Secretary of State, Washington, August 26, 1929, FRUS 1929, II, 303.
[63] *Aide mémoire* of Mounsey, August 7, 1929, FO 371/13954–632.

sure on any one of the two parties. We could not mediate unless asked to do so by both parties, and Sir M. Lampson's conclusion that the sound course is to maintain a watchful attitude seems to be right."[64] MacKillop opposed even a study of the strength or weaknesses of the Chinese case, because its conclusion would be "entirely academic." "We have no desire to become involved and fortunately have no major interests to force us to intervene." He went so far as to say, "We can (indeed we must) . . . continue to leave the parties to reach their working agreement and refrain from expressing, (perhaps even from forming, since it would be irrelevant) any opinion on the theoretical rights or wrongs of the case."[65]

Privately, MacKillop considered the Chinese position vis-à-vis the Soviet Union unreasonable. He remarked that they were prepared "to compromise on 100% of what they want"; "their case appears to be entirely *sic volo, sic jubed.*'". But he did not want to get involved, convinced that the two parties concerned must be left alone "to find a practical settlement, based on a mutual recognition of the fact that the Chinese Eastern Railway cannot properly function or be of use to both China and Soviet Russia unless the fervours of Communism on the one hand and Chinese nationalism on the other one are tempered by common sense."[66]

In spite of his reluctance to be drawn into the Sino-Soviet dispute, Shidehara suggested a compromise to the Soviet ambassador and the Chinese minister on August 8 and 9 respectively, though he was careful to convey his idea not as "advice," but as a "personal impression." He proposed that the Soviet government

[64] August 17, 1929, FO 371/13954–632.
[65] September 3, 1929, FO 371/13954–632.
[66] August 26, 1929, FO 371/13954–632.

waive its insistence on the reinstatement of the individuals who had been dismissed from their posts and that the Chinese government agree to appoint other Russian railway officials in their place, thus meeting Chinese objections to the persons concerned, while safeguarding Soviet rights.[67]

When word of Shidehara's action reached London, Ashton-Gwatkin expressed surprise that the Japanese had intervened in this "hornet's nest." "Perhaps Baron Shidehara wants to make a show of activity on coming into power; perhaps he wants to emphasize Japan's interest in the question and her independence of the activities of other powers," he speculated and added: "Japan did not welcome the U.S.'s interference."[68]

On August 20 Shidehara implied to the Chinese minister again that China had a bad case and should agree to the Soviet demand for the appointment of a new director in place of Emshanov.[69] "The Japanese government are going back in some measure towards the original U.S. proposal to bring pressure to bear on the Chinese," MacKillop observed; "but if foreign intervention or mediation is ever going to be invoked," he added, "it seems all the more necessary that the case should not be prejudged. We are now almost alone in not having said anything about the dispute which might embarrass us at a future stage when action on our part might serve some useful purpose, as now it obviously would not."[70]

Meanwhile, on August 15, Stimson had renewed his

[67] Ingram to Lampson, No. 145, August 11, 1929, in Lampson to Foreign Office, No. 651, Peking, August 12, 1929, FO 371/13954–632.

[68] FO 371/13954–632.

[69] "Whether I can claim the credit of giving him this idea I do not know," Sir J. Tilley reported, "but . . . I did suggest it to him [on July 26] and it met with an inarticulate response." (Tilley to Henderson, No. 366, Chuzenji, August 27, 1929, FO 371/13954–632.)

[70] August 22, 1929, FO 371/13954–632.

pressure on the Chinese minister by advising him that "if China could offer to put the railroad 'in escrow' it would put her friends into a better position to defend her."[71] On August 26 he had a lengthy conversation with Sir Esme Howard concerning the history of the Sino-Soviet conflict. They agreed that China had been in the wrong both in her initial action toward the railroad and in her subsequent refusal to make amends and restore the *status quo ante*, but felt that nonetheless these actions would not justify a Soviet attack on China, particularly since the latter had "solemnly sworn" in the Kellogg Pact to resolve controversies by peaceful means. According to Stimson's memorandum of the meeting, Howard suggested that if China could be persuaded to restore the *status quo*, a Soviet invasion of Manchuria would put the USSR "so clearly in the wrong" that sufficient world-wide public support could probably be roused eventually to check Russian military operations by means of a trade embargo.[72] According to Howard's report, the idea had been advanced by Stimson.[73]

"Stimson's appreciation of the merits of the dispute is, as generalities go, fairly accurate; but . . . his projected solution falls to the ground," MacKillop commented upon reading Howard's dispatch. "Interference while China is in her present mood would be calculated to produce a situation without an issue: for we should invite China to take a certain action,

[71] Memorandum by the Secretary of State, Washington, August 15, 1929, FRUS 1929, II, 276–77.

[72] Memorandum by the Secretary of State, Washington, August 26, 1929, FRUS 1929, II, 303. Kapitsa asserts that Stimson and Howard made public their exchange and threatened to arouse world opinion against the USSR and to embargo trade with her. (Kapitsa, 208.) But the memorandum was not published at the time and the discussion of possible economic sanctions was not a threat made to the Soviet Union.

[73] Howard to Foreign Office, No. 389 R, August 26, 1929, FO 371/13954–632.

she would refuse, and we should be publicly committed to the opinion that she was in the wrong. Russia therefore might claim with some force that her offence in opening hostilities was at least palliated by the circumstances."

Mounsey remarked that the anxiety of the American government for the preservation of world peace, especially so soon after the coming into force of the Kellogg Pact, was "perfectly intelligible and worthy of all our sympathy." He felt, however, that in the present case this anxiety was "warping the State Department's judgement and causing them to put forward series of proposals for intervening in the Sino-Soviet dispute which are not at all calculated to achieve that result, and are more likely to accentuate the friction and demonstrate the futility and ineffectiveness of outside intervention."[74]

Howard, therefore, wrote Stimson on August 30 that while his government would be most glad to join in efforts to further the cause of peace, "they consider it a matter of the first importance that only such action should be contemplated as both parties to the dispute would agree to and which would be incapable of interpretation as in any sense prejudging the issue." Since the Chinese government was unwilling to con-

---

[74] FO 371/13954–632. The English regarded the Americans as children when it came to foreign affairs. After commenting on "the naiveté and ignorance in matters to do with foreign affairs, which, among American press correspondents accompanies a certain low cunning," a member of the British embassy in Washington declared in a confidential letter to the foreign secretary: "Of course all Americans rejoice in making international affairs more difficult for themselves by imagining, seeking out, inventing, dark, involved, mysterious, extraordinarily cunning motives, distorted significances, imaginary rules of the game. Their interest of course is a new one, and like in everything else, it becomes an exaggerated and over-intricate one. Again the child and his interest in a game of pretending, the more involved he can make it out to himself and friends to be the better!" (Terence Stone to R. L. Craigie, December 5, 1929, "Private and *Confidential.*" FO 371/13956–611.)

sider the restoration of the *status quo ante* and insisted on undisputed administrative control of the railway, the British government felt that any attempt by the powers to restore the effective management of the railway to Soviet officials "would not only be fruitless and meet with a blank refusal from the Chinese Government, but might also be used by the Soviet Government as excusing or palliating a resort to arms on the grounds that China was condemned in advance as the guilty party in the dispute."[75]

When the Mukden government, informed by Chiang Kai-shek in the latter part of October that further communications with Moscow via Berlin would be fruitless and that he himself could not assist in the resumption of direct negotiations with the USSR, turned to the British legation, the British replied that they could not be of assistance because there were no diplomatic relations between Great Britain and the Soviet Union and because negotiations were taking place by way of Germany.[76]

The Mukden government had approached the British legation through Donald. In reporting that Donald had submitted a proposition of mediation by the British government, Lampson remarked that "Donald, though well intentioned, gets carried away by his desire to play a role in high politics." He noted that "no serious basis for negotiation with Russia" was suggested, but "only a vague proposal that Mukden will take over conduct of negotiations from Nanking," and that a British attempt at mediation would probably end in involving Great Britain "as between Mukden and Nanking." "Whole thing," he telegraphed, "smells

[75] Howard to Stimson, August 30, 1929, FRUS 1929, II, 308.
[76] MacMurray to Secretary of State, No. 934, Peiping, October 29, 1929, FRUS 1929, II, 338–39.

of a typical Chinese domestic intrigue and my advice is that we should not have any concern with it."[77]

Reading Lampson's cable, Toller agreed and added that British relations with the USSR had not yet reached a stage at which Great Britain could intervene, that German susceptibilities must be taken into consideration, and that, at any rate, Great Britain would first have to communicate fully and frankly with the Washington Conference powers. C. W. Orde, who had succeeded Mounsey as head of the Far Eastern Department, questioned whether the Washington powers quite came in, but there was general agreement in the Foreign Office that Great Britain must "keep out of it."[78]

Great Britain also turned her back on the suggestion that she become involved in the question of Soviet atrocities against White Russian refugees. Foreign Office officials believed that Great Britain had no *"locus standi"* to make direct representations to the Soviet government and that if anyone took the matter to the League of Nations, it was China's role to do so, for whether or not the White Russians had become Chinese citizens, they had been under Chinese jurisdiction at the time of their capture. Besides, as MacKillop observed, it was impossible to determine what had really happened. "There is no such thing as final and accepted truth in cases of this nature, only allegations, denials, and counter-allegations."[79]

When the Soviet Union invaded Manchuria and Chinese forces proved unable to halt the Red Army, China on November 26 appealed to the League of

[77] Lampson to Foreign Office, No. 802, Peking, October 9, 1929, FO 371/13954–632.
[78] FO 371/13954–632.
[79] *Ibid.*

Nations and to the Kellogg Pact powers, first of all to the United States.[80] The British were not pleased. Two months earlier, when the Chinese had threatened to turn to the League if the frontier attacks did not cease, MacKillop had expressed the wish that they would not do so, "for this matter is one with which the League seems unfitted to deal."[81]

Prodded by the Chinese appeal and perhaps by the realization that cynics had labeled the conflict "the Soviet-Chinese Kellogg War" to make fun of the fact that the treaty renouncing war had not prevented it,[82] Stimson proposed to the governments of France, Great Britain, Italy, Germany and Japan that they join the United States in addressing identical or similar notes on the same day to the USSR and China to remind them of their obligations under the Kellogg Pact to settle their differences by peaceful means.[83] France and Italy agreed in principle with Stimson's proposal.[84] Germany, on the other hand, declined to join in the American-led démarche on the ground that she was officially protecting the interests of the citizens of the two belligerents. Her decision may have been influenced by the fact that she had concluded a neutrality pact with the Soviet Union in 1926 and her participation might have been regarded by the latter as a violation of the pact.[85] The German ambassador in Washington expressed concern, furthermore, that "China itself might become more intransigent and precipitate further trouble," if she concluded from such declarations that

[80] Mossdorf, 58.

[81] September 16, 1929, FO 371/13954–632.

[82] Mossdorf, 58.

[83] Stimson to Chargé d'Affaires Neville, No. 117, Washington, November 26, 1929, FRUS 1929, II, 350–52.

[84] Chargé Armour to Stimson, No. 535, Paris, November 28, 1929, FRUS 1929, II, 357; FO 371/13956–6473.

[85] Mossdorf, 59.

"the whole world was working in its favor to prevent any further encroachment by Russia."[86] The British went along with Stimson's proposal, but recommended the issuance of one joint statement, presented by Stimson on behalf of the signatory powers.[87] Shidehara, on the other hand, refused to participate in a joint statement, doubting that practical benefits would ensue. He merely offered "on his responsibility [to] tell both the Russians and the Chinese privately that the recent disturbances were attracting the attention of the world and producing a bad impression."[88]

Although Assistant Secretary of State Nelson T. Johnson told the Japanese ambassador on November 29 that the United States had learned that "the Russians had withdrawn from Manchuria and the tension there had relaxed,"[89] and although the British, French, Italian and German governments deemed that it would be wiser to wait and see what would come of the renewed negotiations between the Soviet Union and China,[90] the United States government went ahead with its plans for the issuance of identical or similar

[86] Memorandum by Assistant Secretary of State W. R. Castle, Jr., November 29, 1929, FRUS 1929, II, 363–64.

[87] Ambassador Dawes to Stimson, No. 350, London, November 27, 1929, FRUS 1929, II, 356. Mossdorf states that the British government had shed its reluctance to intervene in the Sino-Soviet conflict and had accepted America's lead following Prime Minister MacDonald's visit to Washington in September-October 1929. (Mossdorf, 60) But as shown above, British unwillingness to become involved in the dispute continued through October and was overcome apparently by the Soviet invasion of Manchuria rather than by American arguments.

[88] Neville to Stimson, No. 111, Tokyo, November 27, 1929, FRUS 1929, II, 355. So long as the Soviets did not entrench themselves in Manchuria, their conflict with the Chinese benefitted Japan. It "softened up" the Manchurian forces and set a precedent for "punitive action" in this region, free from foreign interference.

[89] Memorandum by the Assistant Secretary of State, November 29, 1929, FRUS 1929, II, 364–65.

[90] Ambassador Schurman to State Department, No. 246, Berlin, December 1, 1929, FRUS 1929, II, 369–70.

statements.[91] The text of the American declaration was amplified somewhat. It had stated originally that the United States government hoped that China and Russia "will refrain from measures of hostility and will arrange in the near future to discuss between themselves the issues of which they are at present in controversy."[92] It now declared that it hoped the two powers "will refrain or desist from measures of hostility and will find it possible in the near future to come to an agreement between themselves upon a method of resolving by peaceful means the issues over which they are at present in controversy."[93] Since the United States had no diplomatic relations with the USSR, she could address only China directly. The statement to the Soviet government had to be communicated through the good offices of the French government.

The American statement was cabled to France, Great Britain, Germany, Japan and Italy on November 30 and to all the signatories of the Kellogg Pact two days later. It was transmitted to the governments of China and of the Soviet Union on December 3. The United States reminded China and the USSR of their obligations under the Kellogg Pact to settle any disputes "of whatever nature or whatever origin" by pacific means. "The American Government feels that the respect with which China and Russia will hereafter be held in the good opinion of the world will necessarily in great measure depend upon the way in which they carry out these most sacred promises."[94]

---

[91] Schurman's telegram reached Washington after Stimson's declaration had been dispatched. It is not clear whether the desire of the other governments for a delay was conveyed to Stimson earlier.

[92] FRUS 1929, II, 350–52.

[93] Stimson to Armour, No. 392, November 30, 1929. FRUS 1929, II, 366–67.

[94] *Ibid.;* Stimson to certain diplomatic representatives, No. 1, Washington, December 1, 1929, FRUS 1929, II, 371–73; DVP, XII, 605–606.

However disinterested and noble the invocation of the Kellogg Pact by the United States may have appeared to the American public, the démarche on the very day that Tsai and Simanovskii had signed the provisional agreement looked to the Russians like an attempt to block a Sino-Soviet settlement and actually prolong hostilities.[95] They had no knowledge of Stimson's earlier effort to persuade the Chinese to restore the *status quo ante*, were resentful of continued American nonrecognition of the Soviet regime, and were convinced that the Chinese had seized the railway with Western encouragement. They could not conceive of the Chinese embarking on such a rash venture alone, and believed that the capitalist powers, notwithstanding their professions of peace, wanted to draw the USSR into war with China and Japan.[96] In the words of a song, popular in the Red Army at the time:

Chan Kai-shi za nitku szadi,
Kto-to dergnul za shtany,
Potomu-to etot diadia
Doblvaeisiu voiny.

By a string from behind, someone
Has pulled Chang Kai-shek by the pants;
That's why that uncle
Is seeking war.[97]

Consequently, while the Chinese responded to the American declaration in a polite and conciliatory manner, the Soviets replied with bitter sarcasm and hostility. In a lengthy answer, issued on the same day

[95] Kulagin and Iakovlev, 175, 177. As Pauline Tompkins has noted, "the corresponding wheels of American diplomacy were already turning" before news of the Sino-Soviet talks reached Washington. Word of preliminary discussions was received before the American statement was actually conveyed, but no effort was made to recall it. (Tompkins, 235–36.)

[96] Kapitsa, 197; Vygodskii, 297–98.

[97] Lipman, 82.

on which they had received the foreign notes, the
Soviets pointed out that they, unlike the powers, had
pursued a policy of peace from the moment the USSR
had come into existence and had not engaged in acts
of war except in defense against direct attack or the
"armed intervention of certain powers." Unlike the
powers too, the Soviet Union had voluntarily abandoned her extraterritorial rights, consular jurisdiction
and other privileges in China. Such acts as the violation
by China of the regulations and treaties concluded with
the Soviet Union on the basis of "full equality and
good will" and her seizure of the CER "without any
warning and without previous notification of any claim,
in violation of the existing agreements on the conjoint
administration of the railway" would have been considered by the United States, Great Britain, and
France, if taken against them, as sufficient pretext for
invoking the reservations-they had made when signing
the Kellogg Pact. Yet the Soviet Union had not recognized such reservations then, nor did it invoke them
now. It was the launching of systematic incursions
into the USSR by Chinese forces and "Russian counterrevolutionary bands" that had obliged her to take
countermeasures. The Red Army had acted, therefore,
in absolutely necessary, legitimate defense and not in
violation of any obligations resulting from the Kellogg
Pact, what could not be said of the powers which had
addressed the identical declarations, whose armed
forces were stationed on Chinese territory and in Chinese ports. The Soviet government stated that in view
of the fact that the American declaration had been
forwarded when the Soviet and Mukden governments
had already come to an agreement on a series of terms
and when direct *pourparlers* were in progress, the

démarche constituted unjustified pressure on the talks and could "in no way be considered as a friendly act." It noted that the Kellogg Pact made no provision for the implementation of the pact by an individual state or by a group of states. The Soviet government, in any case, had never agreed that any states "in their own name, or by virtue of a mutual understanding between themselves, should arrogate to themselves such a right." It declared that the Soviet-Manchurian conflict could be settled only by way of direct *pourparlers* between the Soviet Union and China on the basis of terms already accepted by Mukden and known to China, and rejected any intervention in the *pourparlers* or in the conflict." As a crowning touch, the Soviet government expressed "astonishment that the Government of the United States, which, by its own will, does not entertain any official relations with the Government of the Soviet Union, should find it possible to address to [the] latter advice and recommendations."[98]

The sharpness of the Soviet reply threw Stimson on the defensive. In a statement to the press the following day he declared in self-justification that "as far back as the Hague Convention of 1899 the nations of the world agreed that strangers to a dispute, on their own initiative, could make suggestions looking for peace between the states which were at variance and that the exercise of that right is not to be regarded by the parties in conflict as an unfriendly act." In sending the message, Stimson explained, the United States had been motivated not by an unfriendly attitude

---

[98] Armour to Stimson, No. 550, Paris, December 7, 1929, FRUS 1929, II, 404–406. Similar notes were presented to the Soviet and Chinese governments by Italy, France and Great Britain.

toward the Soviet Union but by respect for the Kellogg Pact. He sought to hide the failure of his policy by implying that the declaration of the Soviet government that direct negotiations for the settlement of the dispute with China were underway was due to the mobilization of world public opinion, presumably by him.[99]

Although Stimson had sought to reassure Shidehara that the American action was due solely to his determination "to save the Kellogg-Briand Pact from losing its strength and force" and not to "any desire to intrude into Manchurian affairs,"[100] the Japanese gave a "distinctly cold reception" to the American, British, French and Italian notes to the USSR and China.[101] The British minister in Peking wrote that although Japan had been "obviously the most closely and seriously affected" by the Sino-Soviet dispute in China, she had with "characteristic reserve" given "little or no sign of her feelings, confident no doubt of her ability to protect her position in Manchuria and, it was thought by some, looking on the troubled waters with the feeling of a practiced angler." He believed that "the Japanese Government felt themselves cast for the rôle of honest broker and would have been prepared to intervene had they seen any chance of doing so successfully, and that they resented the readiness of the State Department to rush in where they themselves feared to tread."[102]

The British ambassador in Japan reported that the Japanese regarded the American move as unfair to the Soviet Union and as unduly beneficial to China.

[99] Statement by Stimson to the press, December 4, 1929, FRUS 1929, II, 388–89.
[100] Stimson to Neville, No. 124, Washington, December 5, 1929, FRUS 1929, II, 394.
[101] Tilley to Henderson, No. 533, Tokyo, December 18, 1929, FO 371/14700–639.
[102] Lampson to Henderson, No. 930.

"It is now quite clear," MacKillop commented, "that the sympathies of Japan were with the Soviet Union[103] and, indeed, so long as the latter refrained from any action which Japan might consider provocative, nothing else could reasonably have been expected, since in fighting for the vindication of Russian railway rights in Manchuria the Soviet Union were doing very useful work for Japan. But the attitude of the Japanese Government throughout the dispute and their careful abstention from any action which might embarrass the Soviet Government or prevent them from securing the full benefit of their military superiority is I think a significant one, firstly in that it shows that the Far Eastern policies of Japan and Soviet Russia are, in one highly important respect at least, demonstrably not irreconcilable,[104] and secondly that it shows, or seems to show, an obstinate adherence on the part of Japan to the belief that force, and not world-wide agreements to abstain from the use of force, abstract justice, or world opinion, is the real safeguard of national interests."[105]

The military struggle between the USSR and China had been accompanied by bitter recriminations, the Chinese branding the Soviets "Red imperialists," the Soviets the Chinese "little Napoleons."[106] What mat-

---

[103] As the *Japan Weekly Chronicle* put it half a decade later, looking back at the policy of the USSR in 1929: "Her patience with China was admirable, and her action, when it came, was wonderfully moderate." (*Japan Weekly Chronicle*, March 15, 1934, p. 332) Japan did not wish to see the Soviet Union forced out from the administration of the CER, partly because the railway, which was an artery of Japanese trade, was likely to be run more efficiently by the Russians, partly because her own interests in South Manchuria were the safer, the longer Soviet-Chinese rivalry continued in North Manchuria. (Mossdorf, 60).

[104] "So long as neither encroaches on the other's sphere," Orde inserted in parentheses.

[105] Comments accompanying Tilley to Henderson, No. 533.

[106] For an example of the diatribe of the time, see Dmitrii Lebedev, "Nankinskie napoleonchiki," translated in part in G. A. Lensen (ed.), *Russia's Eastward Expansion*, 148–52.

tered in the final analysis, however, was not the language used or the rights or wrongs of the actions of either side, but the demonstration of Soviet determination to defend Russian interests, if need be by force, of Nationalist inability to put muscle in the drive for recovery of Chinese rights, and of the reluctance of the Western Powers to intervene with more than admonitions. Jubilantly a Soviet author boasted: "Proletarian policy won a brilliant victory in the Far East over the combined forces of counterrevolution. The international position of the USSR has undoubtedly improved in connection with this victory. Soviet foreign policy showed and proved as a matter of fact that it is a policy of peace. The USSR proved that she can indeed defend and win peace." Pointing to the importance of taking advantage of the contradictions that existed among the "imperialists," he declared: "Our policy during the conflict on the Chinese Eastern Railway considered these contradictions and succeeded in exploiting them."[107]

Sir Miles Lampson made some condescending remarks about the Russians and the Chinese in his post-mortem of the dispute. He declared that both sides had "entirely ignored moral considerations from the outset" and remained for the time being "outside the possible scope of any system of international morality based on arbitration of disputes." He asserted, furthermore, that Soviet tactics were "incompatible with the ideas on which our present hopes of world peace are built." Yet he too thought that the outcome of the conflict must be regarded as "a triumph for Soviet diplomacy."

  .   .   . it is impossible [Lampson wrote] not to pay

[107] L. Mad'iar, "Proletarskaia pobeda na Dal'nem Vostoke," 85.

a tribute to the extraordinary skill with which Russia handled the dispute. The restraint, the knowledge of psychology, Chinese and foreign, shown by the Soviet Government, and the manner in which their measures were adapted to the end in view and the means at their disposal were surprising. The situation with which they were faced in July, 1929, was one of which other Powers have had all too common experience—a forcible attack upon rights secured by treaty but which were represented as an infringement of China's sovereignty. An immediate invasion of Manchuria would not only have mobilised the whole opinion of the world against her and possibly provoked the armed intervention of Japan, but as a piece of "imperialist" aggression it would have aroused the violent opposition of Chinese nationalism. If Russia had retaken possession of the railway by force in July (as events showed she could probably have done without difficulty) she would have placed herself in a most awkward position. No further aggression on her part would have been tolerated by Japan, and the offensive would have passed into the hands of the Chinese, who, outraged by the affront to their national self-esteem and knowing that they had nothing more to lose, would have had ample scope to exploit their favorite weapons and paralyse the railway by boycotts, agitations and strikes. Moreover, Russia's chances of political influence in China would have suffered a severe check.

As it was, by November the idea of the violation of Chinese territory had become so familiar that, when the Soviet raids were carried a stage further and assumed the proportions of an invasion, the adverse effect produced abroad was inevitably much diminished and it was generally realised that the chances of the affair developing into anything more than local hostilities were comparatively slight. On the other hand the Chinese in Manchuria, harrassed and demoralised by raids, threats and ever-increasing tension, collapsed, both on the military and the diplomatic front, at the first application of serious pressure and capitulated at once to the Russian demands. Moreover, the predominant feeling after the settlement appears to have been not resentment at defeat but relief at the termination of an intolerable situation and thankfulness to have avoided worse evils. Here again the moderation of the Soviet Government was displayed with excellent effect. . . . .

Apart from this there was something about the Soviet methods, which is hard to define, but which suggests the treatment of China on terms of equality in a way that she has perhaps rarely been treated in the past; and I think this may not have been wholly undeliberate or without its psychological effect. The very unscrupulousness of the Russian tactics may have had something to do with it. There was no suggestion of moral—or, indeed, of overwhelming military—superiority. Both parties were frankly engaged in a dispute over a valuable piece of property, in which each was at pains to make itself as disagreeable as possible to the other. When Russia won, she took possession of her property again with as little fuss as possible, and there the dispute ended, one may almost say with mutual respect on both sides. . . .[108]

---

[108] Lampson to Henderson, No. 930.

5

The Moscow Conference

The Khabarovsk Protocol had provided for the convening of the Moscow Conference on January 25, 1930. On January 11, a fortnight before the scheduled opening, Li Shao-keng asked Simanovskii, who now was in Harbin as acting consul general, for a delay until March 1. Mo Te-hui, he pleaded, had to collect and study materials and must travel to Nanking to obtain instructions, hold a number of preliminary conferences, and obtain wide powers. Simanovskii agreed to convey the request to Moscow, but warned that it would not make a favorable impression in view of persistent delays on the part of Mukden in the carrying out of obligations assumed under the Khabarovsk Protocol regarding the release of all arrested persons, the acceptance of prisoners of war, the restoration of telegraph and telephone communication, and the deportation of White Russian activists.[1]

[1] Simanovskii to Foreign Commissariat, Harbin, January 11, 1930, DVP, XIII, 25. Simanovskii noted in his report that he pursued these matters in daily conversations at Harbin and that the local authorities cooperated by sending messengers to Mukden. He himself had dispatched a courier to Kirin, where Tsai was staying, to transmit the Soviet complaints directly to him.

Karakhan rejected Mo's request for the postponement of the conference until March 1, noting in a cable to Simanovskii on January 15 that Moscow regarded the Chinese move as "a violation of the protocol, which was signed by both sides with the knowledge and agreement of Moscow and Mukden."[2]

The following day, on January 16, apparently before the receipt of Karakhan's reply, Simanovskii telegraphed to the Foreign Commissariat that Tsai Yunsheng[3] requested in the name of Chang Hsüeh-liang and Mo a one month delay in the conference for the reasons already elaborated by Li. While insisting, however, that Mo himself could not depart for Moscow without prior personal consultation with the Nanking government, Tsai stated that in order to avoid giving the impression that the Khabarovsk Protocol was not being carried out, part of the delegation, headed by the diplomatic commissioner of the city of Sakhalian, would set out for Moscow prior to January 25 in order to make technical preparations for the conference.[4]

On January 17 Simanovskii informed Karakhan that he had communicated his reply to Tsai, who had heatedly denied that the proposed delay was an attempt to scuttle the Khabarovsk Protocol. Tsai had agreed to convey to Mo, who lived at his place, Simanovskii's declaration that it would not suffice for only part of the delegation to come and that the plenipotentiaries must depart for Moscow at once—not later than January 18.[5]

In order to acquaint Mukden with Karakhan's reply

[2] Karakhan to Simanovskii, Moscow, January 15, 1930, DVP, XIII, 29.

[3] Tsai must have returned to Harbin by this time.

[4] Simanovskii to Foreign Commissariat, Harbin, January 16, 1930, DVP, XIII, 30.

[5] Simanovskii to Foreign Commissariat, Harbin, January 17, 1930, DVP, XIII, 32–33.

without distortion, Simanovskii handed to Tsai on January 20 a written note reiterating that "the Soviet Government regards the proposal about the postponement of the conference as an attempt on the part of the Central Government of China to delay the matter just as it had delayed it in the month of July, when all questions could have been solved during the negotiations then taking place . . . without the complication of the conflict." Simanovskii added: "The Soviet Government cannot accept these actions of the Central Government at face value, since they undermine the possibilities of a peaceful agreement between the two great countries."[6]

When the Chinese delegation failed to arrive in Moscow as scheduled, Consul General Mel'nikov stated to Tsai in a written note on January 27 that since there had been "no circumstances whatever to delay the normal opening of the work of this conference," it was "exclusively the fault of the Chinese side" that the conference had not been able to begin. Protesting most categorically against such "wholly unwarranted violation of the Khabarovsk Protocol," he declared that the Soviet government insisted on "the speediest possible opening of the conference" and wished to have official notification when the delegates would depart for Moscow. Mel'nikov reminded Tsai that "the violation by the Chinese side of treaties concluded between the USSR and China had in the past inevitably led to serious conflicts, and that the delay in the opening of negotiations, having occurred exclusively through the fault of the Chinese side, can have corresponding repercussions on the course of the pending conference itself."[7]

[6] Note of Simanovskii to Tsai, DVP, XIII, 36–37.
[7] Note of Mel'nikov to Tsai, DVP, XIII, 51.

That month hundreds of White Russian employees who had been dismissed in line with the Khabarovsk agreement stormed into the offices of the railway administration to demand three months severance pay. Ugly scenes occurred as the rebuffed employees gave vent to their anti-Communist feelings and heaped abuse on the heads of Soviet officials.

On February 8 Mel'nikov filed a protest with Tsai in which he reminded the Chinese government of its obligation to arrest and deport White Russian activists from Manchuria. He warned in the name of the Soviet government that if the Mukden authorities did not take appropriate action forthwith, it would be forced to publish this note as well as the secret supplement to the Khabarovsk Protocol listing the White Russians in question. It would also have to give wide circulation to the Chinese government's failure to carry out the obligations it had assumed, which constituted a serious obstacle to the final and full regulation of Soviet-Chinese relations.[8]

When Tsai replied on March 10 that the Manchurian authorities could not find the White Russsians unless furnished full names, Mel'nikov provided the information in a note on March 26.[9] On May 5 the diplomatic commissioner of Kirin province informed Mel'nikov that the authorities in the provinces of Kirin and Heilungkiang and in the city of Harbin had been duly ordered to expel the White Russian organizers and that Ostroumov had already quit Mukden.[10]

[8] Note of Mel'nikov to Tsai, DVP, XIII, 83–85.

[9] Note of Mel'nikov to Tsai, DVP, XIII, 166–67. The White Russians whom the Soviets wanted expelled from Manchuria were identified as Nikolai Pavlovich Sakharov, former general; Ivan Fedorovich Shil'nikov, former general; Pavel Dmitrievich Makarenko, former general; Fedor Dmitrievich Nazarov, former colonel; Vladimir Vladimirovich Plotnikov, former *esaul;* Ivan Aleksandrovich Peshkov; Konstantin Petrovich Nechaev; Boris Vasil'evich Ostroumov; and Dmitrii Leonidovich Khorvat.

[10] Chun Yui(?) to Mel'nikov, May 5, 1930, DVP, XIII, 167. Active counter-

Soviet misgivings that the failure of the Chinese to arrive in Moscow might be due to second thoughts on their part were not without foundation. The Ministry of Foreign Affairs of the Nanking government removed Tsai from his post[11] and on February 8 belatedly denounced the Khabarovsk "minutes," as it called the protocol.[12] The speculation of many observers at the time of the conclusion of the Khabarovsk Protocol that Nanking would "come around and repudiate the pact" on the contention that Tsai had exceeded his powers[13] had materialized.

The statement of the national government noted that Tsai had been authorized to enter into "preliminary negotiations . . . for the settlement of questions arising out of the Chinese Eastern Railway dispute and for the discussion of the question of procedure for holding a formal conference to be held in the future." It asserted that in signing "certain minutes purporting to be a settlement of the dispute," which contained also proposals of a general character concerning relations between the two countries and thus were "outside the scope of his instructions," Tsai had "acted *ulta vires*." "According to international usage

revolutionaries were not the only target of Soviet hostility; all emigrés were regarded as enemies. Among the hundreds of White Russians shipped back to the USSR by the Red Army upon its seizure of Manchuli, Hailar and Chalainor station there were many who had been returned against their will. When Lieutenant General Khorvat, in his capacity as chief of the Russian Emigration in the Far East, appealed to the Danish Minister Henrik de Kauffman, chief of the Diplomatic Corps in Peking, for assistance on April 9, 1930, the Western powers refused to intervene. As C. E. Whitamore of the Far Eastern Department of the British Foreign Office remarked months later—Lampson had not forwarded Khorvat's letter until May 30 and it had reached London finally on August 28—"the Chinese Government will assuredly not take any steps to assist these unfortunate people, but it is obviously their business to do so, not the Diplomatic Body's." (FO 371/14700–639)

[11] Wu, 212.

[12] Consul General C. F. Garstin to Lampson, No. 23, Harbin, May 5, 1930, FO 371/14700–639.

[13] *North China Standard,* Peiping, December 24, 1929.

an arrangement concluded between the delegates of two countries is subject to the approval or ratification of their respective governments."

The statement asserted that the arrangements contained in the "minutes" concerning the railway question had been carried out and normal traffic resumed. It declared that the national government was prepared to send a delegate to the Moscow Conference "for the exclusive purpose of effecting a readjustment of the Chinese Eastern Railway." Should the Soviet government wish to deal with "questions of a general character relating to trade and commerce between the two countries as well as other problems," it should send a delegate to China, where the national government would be willing to enter into negotiations with him.[14]

The Chinese statement was issued in the form of a public declaration; it was not made directly to the Soviet government. Karakhan, therefore, was to refer merely to "rumors" that the Nanking government did not recognize the Khabarovsk Protocol.

On April 12 the diplomatic commissioner informed Mel'nikov that Mo had been provided with plenipotentiary powers and would leave Harbin for Moscow on May 1. Mel'nikov replied on April 19 that the Soviet government had taken cognizance of the information and expressed the hope that there would be no further violation of the Khabarovsk Protocol by additional delays.[15]

The long delay had been due in part to what the British minister called "the obvious unwillingness of the Central Chinese Government to face realities and

[14] Garstin to Lampson, Harbin, May 5, 1930, FO 371/14700–639, pp. 339–40.
[15] Notes of Chun to Mel'nikov and of Mel'nikov to Chun, DVP, XIII, 228.

put themselves in a position where they must treat as the vanquished party."[16] It had also been partly due to Mo's personal reluctance to undertake the responsible and thankless mission. As H. W. Kinney had written in the latter part of March after talking to Soviet and Chinese officials in Mukden, although Mo had returned to that city from Nanking, he "showed no signs of feverish haste to get to Moscow," but planned to proceed to Harbin "mainly to attend to his business as president of the Chinese Eastern Railway" and only upon his return from there would prepare for the Moscow journey. Kinney had added that "Mo has been quite frank in his expression that he is not keen about being the Chinese plenipotentiary, but that he has accepted this post merely as a matter of patriotic duty."[17] The long delay was almost prolonged by the suicide of Mrs. Mo on April 29 out of chagrin that her husband had chosen to take his secondary wife to Moscow rather than her.[18]

In press interviews prior to his departure Mo stated repeatedly that the chief aim of the Chinese delegation would be "to induce the Soviet government to agree to the early redemption by China of the Chinese Eastern Railway on reasonable terms and free of all tramelling conditions after redemption." He denied both personally and through his secretary that the Chinese government had agreed to exceed in the negotiations in Moscow the limits set in its declaration of February 8.[19]

Kinney predicted that although the Russians regarded the redemption of the railway as a "purely

---

[16] Lampson to Henderson, July 2, 1930, p. 11.
[17] FO 371/14700–639.
[18] Garstin to Lampson, No. 23.
[19] *Ibid.*, p. 2.

academic question," the Chinese would concentrate on this issue "to save face," in case they had to give in on the other matters. "Thus they would be able to say that they have arranged for the purchase of the railway and that the other points are of minor importance in so far as they relate merely to a sort of *modus vivendi* until the time when China shall take entire possession of the railway."[20]

On the morning of May 1 Mo left Harbin for Moscow by special train with a staff of 17 persons, including 4 experts and 4 secretaries, and 7 Soviet officials of the CER administration.[21] He took along two truckloads of stores so that his delegation would not have to rely on Russian cooking and would be able to entertain the diplomatic corps in Moscow at sumptuous Chinese banquets.[22]

The Chinese delegation arrived in Moscow on May 9,[23] but showed no haste to enter into negotiations. When Karakhan during his first meeting with Mo eleven days later, on May 20, proposed that Mo that very day set a time for the opening of the conference and determine its agenda, Mo replied that he would come again in a few days with a full list of the experts and consultants on the Chinese side and then would be ready to come to an agreement regarding the date of the first meeting of the conference. Karakhan objected to Mo's idea that the negotiations be begun by the experts and consultants of both sides. He pointed out that since he and Mo were the plenipotentiary representatives for the conduct of the negotia-

[20] FO 371/14700–639.

[21] Garstin to Lampson, No. 23.

[22] William Strang to Foreign Office, No. 466, Moscow, August 16, 1930, FO 371/14700–639.

[23] *Ibid.;* Lampson to Henderson, No. 930.

tions, the negotiations must be begun by them, with the experts of both sides being subsequently used in various commissions to the extent necessary.

Asked concerning his plenary powers, Mo declared that he had received powers only from the national government. When Karakhan inquired whether he had special powers also from the Mukden government, Mo replied in the negative, reiterating that he had been empowered by Nanking to negotiate. To Karakhan's remark that this was a very important communication, since his appointment by the Nanking government to participate in the conference that was being convened on the strength of the Khabarovsk Protocol refuted rumors which had reached the Soviet Union from China to the effect that the Nanking government allegedly did not recognize the Khabarovsk Protocol, Mo responded evasively that the Nanking government attached great importance to the CER question, which formed part of the Khabarovsk Protocol. Karakhan confirmed that the CER question was indeed one of the most important questions before the pending conference.[24]

When several days passed without word from Mo, Karakhan on May 25 sought to prod him into action by sending him a list of experts that were to be included in the Soviet delegation and informed him that he, as the official delegate of the Soviet government, was "ready to open the Soviet-Chinese conference, provided by the Khabarovsk Protocol, any day."[25] Mo responded the following day with a list of the Chinese experts, but avoided setting a date for the convening

[24] Karakhan's memorandum of his conversation with Mo, Moscow, May 20, 1930, DVP, XIII, 282.
[25] Letter of Karakhan to Mo, May 25, 1930, DVP, XIII, 296.

of the conference. "One of these days[26] I would like to talk to you in person, so that the pending Chinese-Soviet conference would take place as soon as possible," he wrote vaguely.[27]

On May 29 Mo met with Karakhan. In the conversation that ensued, the differences in the positions of the Chinese and Soviet governments quickly came to the fore.

"Before we set a date for the opening of the conference, I would like to talk to you in private," Mo stated.

"I shall be completely frank," Karakhan responded. "We must open the conference officially [so that] a record of the proceedings will be duly kept, otherwise we have no guaranties whatsoever that the Chinese government will not spread false propaganda concerning the conference, as happened earlier. I already have word of a telegram, issued by Kuomin, the official agency of the Nanking government, alleging that the conference has already begun, that Litvinov and I have spoken, that speeches were made, issues considered."

"I am ready to open the conference any day," Mo asserted. "But I would like to make a statement about the scope of my plenary powers beforehand. The government has empowered me to negotiate only concerning the CER question, without touching on other questions. I am afraid that if the conference will be opened under such circumstances, these plenary powers may arouse your displeasure, and in order to avoid awkwardness I inform you thereof in advance."

"I don't quite understand the way the matter is put," Karakhan countered. "The conference has been called

[26] "*V odin iz blizhaishikh dnei.*"
[27] Mo to Karakhan, May 26, 1930, DVP, XIII, 296.

in accordance with the Khabarovsk Protocol, and the content of the conference and the questions that it is to consider are spelled out in the Khabarovsk Protocol. As to awkwardness, I suppose that my position can in no way be awkward. Awkwardness can be felt only by the Chinese government in the event that it did not furnish you with sufficient powers."

"My government approaches the question of the solution of the conflict from the point of view of reality and facts," Mo declared. "The government feels that only the CER question is real and concrete. If this question will not be solved, the formulation of all other, secondary questions will be completely fruitless and will only further complicate the conduct of the conference."

"The Soviet government is used to carrying out those agreements which it has signed, and considers that such obligations must be carried out by the other side too," Karakhan remarked. "Permit me to find out in whose name Mr. Tsai signed the Khabarovsk Protocol?"

"He signed it in the name of the Chinese Republic, but had been empowered only to come to an agreement concerning the place and time of the opening of the conference," Mo answered.

"I still do not quite understand," Karakhan persisted. "If both states really sincerely wish to solve all past misunderstandings, they must meet each other with open heart and solve all these questions. How can one in solving one question leave all the other misunderstandings unresolved?"

"I am deeply convinced," Mo retorted, "that if the CER question will be solved satisfactorily, all other questions will also be solved satisfactorily."

"I shall be completely frank with you," Karakhan reiterated. "Its seems to me that you, as well as the Mukden government, are interested in the establishment of normal relations with us [and] really with all sincerity desire to solve all misunderstandings between our states. However, in the more distant regions of China, on the Yangtze, in Nanking, there the government, being far away from us, is not interested in it to that extent. It ties your hands, and you have come to the conference [applying] such brakes as are stronger perhaps than the brakes [made by] Westinghouse. For this very reason I asked you at our first meeting whether you did not have plenary powers from the Mukden government separately. We could come to terms with it more easily, since in Manchuria both sides are equally interested in the establishment of normal relations. Unfortunately you do not have such plenary powers."

"It is my opinion that the establishment of normal, amicable relations between the [central] governments is more advantageous for both sides than the conclusion of such a partial agreement," Mo replied. "An agreement with the [central] government extends to all its parts; an agreement with part of the state, however, cannot be extended to the whole [of the state]."

"I shall send you this very day a copy of my plenary powers, so that you can familiarize yourself with them," Karakhan promised. "I shall ask you likewise to send me a copy of your plenary powers."

"This exchange of plenary powers will be, as I understand, unofficial," Mo observed.

"Of course," Karakhan answered. "The official exchange of plenary powers will take place at the conference; we shall begin it with this. Now, however, we shall exchange copies unofficially in order to inform ourselves mutually and think about [the matter]. But when shall we set the day for the opening of the conference?"

"I am ready always," Mo asserted, "but ask that my declaration be taken into consideration."

"That makes no difference," Karakhan said. "Whatever the decision of the government may be concerning the conference, we must anyway open it officially and exchange statements."

"That is absolutely true," Mo agreed.[28]

On June 8 Karakhan and Mo conferred for two hours. Karakhan told Mo that he did not want him to get the wrong impression from their past conversations that the Soviets insisted on the official opening of the conference as soon as possible or that they were particularly afraid of the false rumors that were being spread throughout the world concerning these negotiations. "We are extremely glad that you feel well in Moscow and are prepared to wait with the opening as long as you deem necessary," he stated and expressed satisfaction that some attempts had been made by Nanking to deny the false stories about the conference.

Asked for his opinion of the plenary powers, a copy of which Mo had sent meanwhile, Karakhan replied that they contravened the Khabarovsk Protocol in their limited scope. "During our first conversation I asked you whether you had plenary powers from the Mukden government," Karakhan told Mo. "This question was not the result of idle curiosity. In our relations with China we have experienced already that an agreement, concluded by the central Chinese government, was rejected by the local authorities. In 1924 I met with

[28] Minutes of the conversation between Karakhan and Mo, DVP, XIII, 299–301.

Marshal Chang Tso-lin and proposed to him to conclude an agreement with us. He told me at the time
that I must go to Peking and confer with the central
government of the Chinese Republic. I went to Peking
and there signed the Soviet-Chinese agreement of 1924.
But the Mukden authorities then refused to recognize
this agreement and I had to send a special delegate
to Mukden, where the Soviet-Mukden agreement was
signed, confirming that the Soviet-Chinese agreement
of 1924 was binding on the Manchurian authorities.
I expect that in your reply to me you will point out
that at that time relations were bad between the central
and Mukden governments, while at present Mukden
fully obeys Nanking, and that thus there could not
arise the situation which had developed in 1924. I take
the liberty, therefore, to point right away to the [civil]
war which is now taking place in China and can lead
to great changes in the existing situation in China. We
do not know what the results of this [civil] war will
be and are not particularly interested in it. It is merely
clear to us that the only strong and stable force in
China is the Mukden group. Considering the fact that
the Mukden authorities at the same time are the only
force in China firmly interested in the establishment
and preservation of good-neighborly relations with us,
we would like that the Mukden authorities would in
one form or another affirm your plenary powers,[29] [that
they] would confirm that those documents which will
be signed here by you as the result of our negotiations will be binding also for the local Mukden
authorities.''[30]

As Karakhan had expected, Mo retorted that the

----

[29] Literally: ''the plenary powers of Mr. Tupan.''
[30] Minutes of the conversation between Karakhan and Mo, June 8, 1930, DVP,
XIII, 324–29.

relations between the central government and Mukden were different now; the very fact that Nanking had selected him as the plenipotentiary was evidence of this. But a discourse by Mo on the subservience of Mukden failed to convince Karakhan. "Speaking privately, I allow myself to express doubt concerning the full and unqualified subordination of the Manchurian government to the national government in Nanking," Karakhan stated. He added that he did not want Mo to negotiate in the name of the Mukden government, merely that he wanted some assurance from Chang Hsüeh-liang, even in the form of a telegram, that he would abide by an agreement signed by Mo.

When Karakhan asked Mo to confirm flatly that the conference would be opened on the basis of the Khabarovsk Protocol, Mo replied obliquely that Nanking's declaration of February 8 fully confirmed that part of the Khabarovsk Protocol which concerned the CER. "Forgive me, but I need a straight answer," Karakhan persisted and recited the pressures and unpleasantnesses to which Tsai had been subjected by Nanking after signing the Khabarovsk Protocol. He pointed out that Chang Hsüeh-liang and other Manchurian officials had assured Consul General Znamenskii that as far as they were concerned, there was no question of the effectiveness of the Khabarovsk Protocol. And it could not be otherwise, he observed, for the document had been signed by both sides. "The Khabarovsk Protocol is not a declaration," he noted. "One can declare whatever one wishes. A unilateral declaration of the Nanking government can in no way concern us." He asserted that the insistence of the Soviet government on the Khabarovsk Protocol as the basis for the conference did not mean that it attached importance to the question of the recognition of the Nanking government and the resumption of diplomatic relations. "The Soviet government is by no means in a hurry to recognize Nanking and under the present circumstances naturally must be still less inclined to force the issue." Moscow demanded acknowledgment of the Khabarovsk Protocol for the simple reason that it existed and that to renounce it would mean to cast doubt on the fate of the new agreement as well.

Mo argued that both the Manchurian and central governments, as well as public opinion in all of China, felt that the stumbling block in the relations between the two states lay in the CER question and that for that reason Nanking wanted this question to be solved first. He expressed the conviction that once this stumbling block was removed satisfactorily, all other questions too would be regulated very quickly. Quoting the Chinese saying, "To reach the top of a mountain one must first pass over its foot, To undertake a long journey one must first have a point of departure," he asserted that the CER question constituted this "foot of the mountain," this "point of departure."

Karakhan retorted dryly that there was no mention of a "foot of the mountain" in the Khabarovsk Protocol. The CER question had not been placed first in terms of Soviet-Chinese relations as a whole in the Khabarovsk Protocol; this was an afterthought. Nor could one act solely on the basis of public opinion, Karakhan stated. Soviet public opinion also was dissatisfied occasionally with treaties concluded by the government, yet the documents signed in a legal way by the representatives of the government did not therefore lose force, but remained binding on both parties.

Mo sought to clarify what Karakhan wanted. Did he mean that if Mo, upon receipt of the confirmation of his plenary powers by Mukden, would begin the conference with the declaration that he recognized the Khabarovsk Protocol as the basis of their negotiations, they would proceed to settle the CER question and that Mo thereupon would request his government to send him plenary powers for the solution of all other questions? Karakhan responded that he was willing to open the conference at any time and to discuss the question of the exchange of plenary powers during the conference itself, but that it would be better if the matter of Mo's powers could be straightened out beforehand. He reiterated that he did not hurry him in the least—Mo could take all the time he needed to communicate with his government or whomever. Meanwhile they could continue their informal talks or open the conference officially, as Mo deemed better.[31]

On June 21 Karakhan specified the scope and form of plenary powers that Mo had to have at the conference, namely that his plenary powers must be officially confirmed by Mukden authorities and that the Nanking government must give him "supplementary plenary powers to discuss and sign also the other questions enumerated in the Khabarovsk Protocol." Since China's "internal order" might make acceptance of such a formulation difficult, however, the Soviet government would be satisfied, Karakhan stated, if Mo received from the Nanking government supplementary powers for the right to solve all economic, political and other questions between the USSR and China. "At the same time, after the opening of the official conference," he told Mo, "you would make a statement that in opening the conference both sides proceed from the recognition of the Khabarovsk Protocol or,

[31] *Ibid.*

if you would find it more convenient, from the recognition of the Soviet-Chinese and Soviet-Mukden agreements of 1924 and the Khabarovsk Protocol."[32]

At Karakhan's request Mo cabled his government at once. On July 4 he informed Karakhan that his instructions had been broadened. "I have the permission of the government," he said, "to make upon the opening of the conference the official declaration that my plenary powers include also the discussion and solution, after the solution of the CER question, also of other questions, to wit: the resumption of diplomatic relations and the establishment of commercial relations between the two states." Karakhan replied that this did not satisfy the proposals he had formulated on June 21. Firstly, no mention was made of the confirmation of Mo's plenary powers by Mukden; secondly, the instructions from the Nanking government to Mo could not, in accordance with customary international practice, be regarded as an official document, for they were addressed to him. "It is essential," Karakhan told Mo, "that your government give you in writing plenary powers for the discussion of the other questions mentioned in the Khabarovsk Protocol in one of the forms which I mentioned to you in our last talk."[33]

On July 6 Mo offered to open the conference with the statement that he was empowered by his government, once the CER question had been discussed, to deal also with other questions, such as the resumption of diplomatic and commercial relations "on the basis of all existing agreements between the USSR and China." But Karakhan continued to insist on specific mention of the Khabarovsk Protocol and reiterated

[32] DVP, XIII, 808, note 112.
[33] DVP, XIII, 808–809, note 112.

that Mo's original instructions need not be changed if Nanking would supplement them by a telegram to the Soviet government declaring that they had been broadened to include other issues. When Mo countered that it was "exceedingly difficult" for him to request from his government two things at once—permission to make the declaration concerning the Khabarovsk Protocol plus the dispatch of the telegram—Karakhan proposed that a telegram alone would do, if the text ran as follows: "In addition to the plenary powers, the chairman of the Central Executive Committee empowers Mr. Mo to conduct negotiations and sign agreements on all questions provided by the Khabarovsk Protocol, signed by the delegates of both sides on December 22, 1929."[34]

Mo threw up his hands and laughed: "Herein lies the main difficulty."

"I wish to repeat," Karakhan replied, "that the Nanking government from the very beginning opposed the peaceful settlement of our conflict. The Nanking government has not recognized the Khabarovsk Protocol, which settled our conflict. The Nanking government now too puts you in a difficult position. I know all this and last time you yourself informed me of the nonrecognition by Nanking of the Khabarovsk Protocol. But it does not follow from this that the Soviet government must change its attitude toward the Khabarovsk Protocol because of such a position of the Nanking government."

Karakhan expressed his appreciation of Mo's sincere efforts to bring their negotiations to a successful con-

---

[34] The minutes of the conversation state "mentioned" (*upomianutykh*), rather than "provided" (*predusmotrennykh*); but this seems to be a clarification made afterwards in response to a question by Mo at the end of the meeting.

clusion, but objected to Mo's attempt to circumvent the problem with a vague opening statement. "Let us assume that your declaration at the conference will be phrased according to this formula," he explained. "In this case the Soviet side will consider that the Khabarovsk Protocol is included in those agreements to which you refer, while the Chinese side will feel that the Khabarovsk Protocol is not included." Endless complications would result. Karakhan opposed also the stipulation that the CER question must be discussed first and reminded Mo that he wished to have a written confirmation by Mukden of his plenary powers. "Desiring in so far as possible to make your difficult position easier," Karakhan told Mo, "we could agree that this confirmation be given in the form of a letter from Marshal Chang Hsüeh-liang to Znamenskii, our consul general in Mukden. The confirmation would be given locally, and in this case you in Moscow would know nothing [thereof]."

Mo spoke at length of the need to deal with the CER question first. Not only had it been the cause of the conflict, but he himself was *tupan* of the CER and was expected by the Chinese public to give primary consideration to the railway question. Karakhan retorted that it would not be practical to sign a railway agreement and then turn to other matters. The conference would determine the order in which various issues would be taken up. Committees would be formed to study different problems simultaneously; the various agreements would be signed at the same time.

Turning back to the text of the proposed telegram at which he had been looking while Karakhan talked, Mo asked: "How is one to interpret the expression 'provided by the Khabarovsk Protocol'? As 'on the basis of the Khabarovsk Protocol' or as 'mentioned by the Khabarovsk Protocol'?''

"That makes no difference," Karakhan replied. "Legally there is no difference here."

"Yes, actually there is no difference whatsoever," Mo admitted. "The difficulty lies in mentioning the very words 'Khabarovsk Protocol.' ''[35]

When Karakhan and Mo met again on July 14, the controversy over Mo's credentials continued. Mo stated that after carefully thinking about the telegram that Karakhan had requested from Nanking, he had come to the conclusion that it would be tantamount to having his former plenary powers changed. It would be "extremely awkward" for him to make such a request, and he asked that Karakhan "abandon the demand that such a telegram be sent." Karakhan responded that Mo's request was contrary to diplomatic practice. He illustrated that foreign ambassadors, upon arrival in the USSR, submitted their credentials, whereupon every statement uttered by them was regarded as made in the name of their government; yet they needed additional written plenary powers to conclude the most insignificant telegraph or postal convention. "You have not transmitted any credentials, are not the ambassador of your government," Karakhan declared. "What's more, you will hand us your plenary powers which deal with only one question [that] of the CER. And that, I must say frankly, is much worse than if you had arrived in Moscow without any plenary powers whatsoever."

Insisting that the Nanking government duly broaden Mo's plenary powers in writing, Karakhan reminded

[35] Minutes of the conversation between Karakhan and Mo, July 6, 1930, DVP, XIII, 384–89.

him of the unpleasant experiences he had had with
the Chinese in the past. In 1924, after he had signed
an agreement with Wang Cheng-t'ing, the Peking government had declared that its foreign minister had not
had the authority to do so, and he had had to renegotiate
the agreement with Wellington Koo, when the latter
took office. Similarly, the Khabarovsk Protocol was
disavowed by the Nanking government, which asserted
that Tsai had exceeded his powers. "I do not want
to say that I do not trust you," Karakhan remarked.
"I am deeply convinced that since you tell me that
your plenary powers have been broadened by the
Nanking government, that this has actually happened.
It is precisely this that forces the Soviet government
to ponder why Nanking does not wish to give a written
confirmation of your plenary powers."

Mo admitted that "theoretically" Karakhan was
"absolutely right," but that his own predicament must
be taken into consideration. He needed the confidence
not only of the Soviet government but also of his own.
In response to his telegram Nanking had made definite
concessions—it had agreed to the discussion of diplomatic and commercial negotiations' in Moscow
despite its declaration of February 8 that they could
be negotiated only in China—with the understanding,
on the basis of his telegram, that the Soviet government
would agree to leaving the text of his old plenary powers unchanged. If he would now have to contradict
himself and demand that his government send a telegram to the Soviet government broadening, in fact
changing, his plenary powers, it would undermine the
confidence his government had in him. He asked,
therefore, again that Karakhan forego his demand, contending that the official oral declaration that he pro-

posed to make at the conference would have the same effect.

Karakhan denied that the Nanking government had made any concessions. The Khabarovsk Protocol, which it had signed, had included these topics. Besides, the Soviets were not proposing to the Chinese anything unusual. He could not conceive of his government refusing to provide him with appropriate written plenary powers if it wanted him to negotiate a particular matter. He noted that the Soviet government was always prepared to write down and sign its declarations, to affix a seal thereunto and, if necessary, to publish them in newspapers. The proposal by the Nanking government to make instead an oral declaration "completely contravened international custom." When Mo asserted that any mention of the Khabarovsk Protocol was unacceptable to his government and that by insisting on the modification of his written powers the opportunity might be missed to negotiate concerning the resumption of diplomatic and commercial relations between their countries, Karakhan retorted: "The Nanking government was to a large degree the initiator of this conflict. It prevented Tsai from settling the conflict when it first began; it delayed in every way the peaceful solution of the conflict; it agreed to its settlement only under pressure from the Mukden government; it rejected the Khabarovsk Protocol, which settled this conflict; and it now is trying in every way to apply brakes to our work and in so doing puts you in an awkward position. Under such circumstances extreme caution is necessary."

Karakhan expressed fear that unless Mo's broadened powers were reduced to writing, the Nanking government later might again disclaim any agreement which they might reach as having been concluded without due authority and that there would be no evidence to refute the charge. Karakhan told Mo that Chang Hsüeh-liang's secretary had come to Znamenskii in Mukden and had told him that Chang had full confidence in Mo and would recognize whatever agreements the latter would make in Moscow in the name of the central government. This too must be put in writing. In 1924 Chang Tso-lin had personally pledged to abide by the agreement that Karakhan would conclude in Peking, then had reversed himself and insisted on a separate agreement.

When Karakhan observed that Mukden, except for a number of points about White Russians and the like, had faithfully lived up to the Khabarovsk Protocol, Mo replied that Nanking was in effect doing the same in spite of its reluctance to confirm so publicly. He said that he did not have the right "even to think" about mention of the Khabarovsk Protocol. Karakhan countered that he too was acting under specific instructions from the Soviet government, which did not deem it possible to abandon the Khabarovsk Protocol and agree to its annulment. "In such a case I lose all hope," Mo declared. "It is absolutely clear to me that in this event you and I shall lose in vain those two or three months, during which we conducted unofficial negotiations. All that will be left for us to do will be to find a way somehow to end our conference."

"It is not so important to open the conference as to conclude it successfully," Karakhan stated. "The successful conclusion of our negotiations will have tremendous significance for the interests of both countries, for the welfare of millions and tens of millions of inhabitants of both states." Hence, he repeated, he was willing to open the conference officially at any time.[36]

Almost three months passed, however, before Mo could tell Karakhan that he had obtained written confirmation of his plenary powers from Mukden as well as a telegram from Nanking broadening his powers.[37] The telegram from the central government, signed by Foreign Minister Wang and addressed to Foreign Commissar Litvinov, a copy of which Mo handed to Karakhan on October 4, stated that Mo was empowered to negotiate and sign documents concerning the CER, commercial relations, and the resumption of diplomatic relations at the forthcoming Sino-Soviet conference and that "the documents signed by him will take effect upon ratification by the Nationalist government."[38]

Yet as Karakhan and Mo discussed what they would say at the official opening of the conference and Mo promised to do his best to bring the talks to a successful conclusion, Karakhan reiterated his doubt of the sincerity of the Chinese government. "I am fully convinced of your sincere desire and the desire of Chang Hsüeh-liang and the Mukden authorities to establish good-neighborly relations with us," Karakhan stated. "Nanking, on the other hand, does not and cannot have this desire." "After all," he explained, "it does not affect absolutely any of Nanking's interests. I shall be quite direct and frank, as I think you want me to

[36] Minutes of the conversation between Karakhan and Mo, July 14, 1930, DVP, XIII, 397–405.

[37] Minutes of the conversation between Karakhan and Mo, October 4, 1930, DVP, XIII, 540. In confirming that Mo spoke for him too, Chang Hsüeh-liang informed Znamenskii through his secretary: "The attitude of the marshal toward the USSR is well known. It was due to his influence that the outlook of the Nationalist government has drawn closer to Moscow's point of view."

[38] DVP, XIII, 819, note 143.

be. Nanking can desire now less than ever the establishment of normal relations with us. The occupation of the Peking-Tientsin region by the Mukden forces can hardly be very desirable for Nanking. Should good-neighborly relations be established between us, this would mean that the Mukden army could operate freely beyond Shanhaikwan. It is, of course, desirable for Nanking that Marshal Chang Hsüeh-liang worry about his rear, that is, that there not be good-neighborly relations with us."

When Mo sought to reassure Karakhan that the Nationalist government, as the central government of all of China, was obligated to act on behalf of the country as a whole, Karakhan retorted: "You think that Nanking will sacrifice the interests of the Nanking clique for the sake of China as a whole? No, the interests of the Nanking clique take precedence for it. However, let's not argue about it. Several months will pass and you will see that my words are based on fact."[39]

On October 7, as the Moscow Conference was about to begin at last, Consul General Znamenskii handed Marshal Chang a stiff note insisting on "the immediate disarmament and dissolution of the existing White Guard bands and the expulsion of their members from the territory of the Three Eastern Provinces; on an end to the anti-Soviet and White Guard organizations operating in Manchuria, the confiscation of their property, and the arrest and expulsion of their leaders and active members, on the dismissal of those White Russians in the Chinese service who are at the same time active members of White Guard organizations; and on the resolute suppression of the anti-Soviet campaign in the White press published in Manchuria."[40]

[39] Minutes of the conversation between Karakhan and Mo, October 4, 1930, DVP, XIII, 540–45.
[40] *Pravda,* October 9, 1930.

The Mukden government replied on the ninth that it was taking measures against Whites engaged in anti-Soviet activity. While stating that White Russians who were serving in the Chinese police force and in other government agencies and were merely seeking to earn a living should not be dismissed without cause, it promised "to keep their activities under careful observation."[41]

On October 11, at 5:20 p.m., the Moscow Conference convened, eight and a half months later than the Khabarovsk Protocol had stipulated. In his opening speech Karakhan referred back to his own declarations of 1919 and 1920, as well as to the Peking and Mukden agreements of 1924, to demonstrate that the policy of the Soviet government "was and is a policy of repudiation of all unfair privileges and those wrested by force from the Chinese people by the Tsarist government."[42] The USSR, he stated, sought friendly relations on the basis of equality and reciprocity. She sympathized with the Chinese people in their struggle for full independence and for the destruction of any and all restraints upon their freedom of development. Asserting that the Khabarovsk Protocol had settled the Sino-Soviet dispute of 1929 and had restored peaceful relations on the frontier and a normal state of affairs on the CER, he called on the Chinese side to join the Soviet Union in recognizing the protocol and the agreements of 1924 as the fundamental documents on which relations between the two countries must be based.

---

[41] *Izvestiia,* October 19, 1930.

[42] The English translation found in the British Foreign Office archives incorrectly states "the unfair privileges wrested by force from the Chinese people." The Russian text reads: *"politika otkaza ot vsekh nespravedlivykh i nasil'stvenno vyrvannykh u kitaiskogo naroda tsarskim pravitel'stvom privilegii."* It does not limit "unfair privileges" to those seized by force.

Mo responded that the Chinese government and the Chinese people had "unswerving faith" in the common desire of the two great peoples of China and the USSR for "peace and brotherhood," but sidestepped the Khabarovsk Protocol issue by stating evasively that "every treaty concluded in a legal manner between China and the USSR is steadfastly observed by China, which constitutes a corresponding international obligation."[43] When Karakhan tried to pin Mo down and asked him for a "clear and unambiguous statement" concerning the Kharaborvsk Protocol, a lengthy but fruitless discussion ensued.[44]

Since Karakhan warned that the next meeting would begin with the consideration of the Khabarovsk Protocol question and that no other issues could be taken up until this matter had been fully clarified,[45] Mo disappeared from Moscow. Rumors spread that he had returned to China, but actually, he had gone to Leningrad and elsewhere sightseeing.

On October 28 Mel'nikov reported from Harbin that

[43] Communiqué of the Foreign Commissariat concerning the opening of the Sino-Soviet conference, October 12, 1930, DVP, XIII, 563–66; Strang to Henderson, No. 606, Moscow, October 13, 1930, enclosure, FO 371/14701–639.

[44] Karakhan to Znamenskii, October 11, 1930, DVP, XIII, 561–62; Izvestiia, October 12, 1930; Strang to Henderson, No. 606. Upon reading the text of the opening statements and of an intemperate Izvestiia editorial, sent by Strang from Moscow, MacKillop remarked that the two sides were not likely to come to grips with the practical questions they had to settle if they could not agree on the starting point. "In fact, however, the situation is not quite so ridiculous as it is in appearance," MacKillop reflected. "The Soviet Government have a shrewd idea that Chang Hsüeh-liang, who is bound to take a more practical view of the necessity of goodish relations between Manchuria and the Union than the theory-maniacs at Nanking, will accept the Habarovsk protocol quite cheerfully, if it is established that the foreign (and other) affairs of Manchuria have nothing in the world to do with Nanking; and they can see (like everybody else) that if they wait a little while Mo Te-hui will either be a Mukden plenipotentiary or a meaningless abstraction. In the former capacity he will no doubt be prepared to start at the Habarovsk protocol and conclude some reasonable arrangement; in the second, as the plenipotentiary of a phantom, it doesn't really matter what he does." (FO 371/14701–639, China 1930, p. 397)

[45] Karakhan to Znamenskii, October 11, 1930, DVP, XIII, 561.

according to all his sources of information, the Chinese had no intention of seriously negotiating with the Soviet Union. Nanking was prepared to break off the conference at any time; Mukden sought to drag it out until peaceful conditions had been reestablished in China or. at least until its own relationship with Nanking had been clarified. "At any rate," Mel'nikov wrote, " the mood of public opinion in Manchuria now is depressed. Everybody awaits a conflict, although perhaps not in the same form as last year, but, at any rate, complications with us are expected."[46]

On October 29 Chang Hsüeh-liang's secretary inquired of Znamenskii what lay behind the demands of the Soviet government regarding the Khabarovsk Protocol—"what formula exactly would suffice for acceptance by the conference and just how to phrase it." Znamenskii reiterated that the position of the Soviet government was "clear and unconditional," namely, that the Khabarovsk Protocol must be recognized in name as well as in fact.[47]

On November 6 Karakhan and Mo discussed informally how to remove further obstacles blocking the progress of the conference. On November 10 Karakhan sent Mo a letter in which he acknowledged that the Chinese government had partially fulfilled the obligations proceeding from the Khabarovsk Protocol by widening the scope of Mo's plenary powers and had generally carried out the provisions of the protocol in regard to the CER as well as the establishment of consular posts and the ensuring of the normal working of Soviet economic organizations. "Consequently," Karakhan wrote, "inasmuch as one can consider the

[46] Mel'nikov to Karakhan, Harbin, October 28, 1930, DVP, XIII, 596–97.
[47] Znamenskii to Foreign Commissariat, Mukden, October 30, 1930, DVP, XIII, 599–600.

basic stipulation of the Khabarovsk Protocol as fulfilled and inasmuch as you declared to me in the conversation on November 6 that there are not and cannot be any doubts of the necessity to preserve on the CER the regime established in accordance with the Peking and Mukden treaties and the Khabarovsk Protocol, the [Soviet] Union Government sees no obstacles to commencing at once at the Soviet-Chinese conference the discussion of concrete questions concerning the CER, commercial and diplomatic relations, etc." He added that until such time as the status of the CER was changed at the conference,[48] be it by mutual agreement to alter the regime of the CER or by redemption of the railway by the Chinese Republic by purchase, the prevailing situation on the CER must not be changed by unilateral action by either side.[49]

But Mo requested in a telegram on November 10 that Karakhan's letter to him not be made public, contending that it did not correctly state what he had said about the CER regime.[50] On November 11 he asked Karakhan in person to think about deleting the paragraph in question.

Karakhan replied at their next unofficial meeting, on November 15, that Mo had stressed during every one of their talks that the Khabarovsk Protocol had in effect been carried out by the Chinese side and that there was no need, therefore, for the Soviets to insist on a formal recognition of the protocol. Now that the

[48] "*Do tekh por, poka na sovetsko-kitaiskoi konferentsii nyneshnee polozhenie na K.V.Zh.D. ne budet izmeneno.*" The English translation of the note sent by Sir E. Ovey from Moscow to the British Foreign Office was incorrect in rendering the clause "while the present position on the Chinese Eastern Railway will not undergo modification by the Sino-Soviet conference."

[49] Karakhan to Mo, November 10, 1930, DVP, XIII, 627–29; Ovey to Henderson, No. 674, November 17, 1930, FO 371/14701–639.

[50] Mo to Karakhan, November 17, 1930, DVP, XIII, 675–76; *Izvestiia*, November 24, 1930.

Soviet government had yielded on the issue, Mo asserted that his letter formed an impediment to the continuation of the conference, even though he had every reason to be proud of his success. Could it be that the Chinese side had raised the Khabarovsk Protocol issue merely as a pretext for wrecking the conference? "Perhaps you simply do not wish to negotiate with us, do not wish to reestablish normal and good-neighborly relations with us?" If so, let Mo say so outright. If not, let them set a date for the continuation of the conference.

When Mo said that Karakhan, with his letter, had put in his path a stone around which it was not in his power to go, Karakhan retorted that the letter was indeed a stone, but one on which the work of the conference must be built. Asserting that Chiang Kai-shek used to say such things as "First we shall take the railway, then we shall talk," he expressed the thought that the "sad conflict" of the preceding year should have taught the Chinese side to know better. Karakhan realized that Mo had told him that he could not talk of the Khabarovsk Protocol, but he pointed out that Mo had in fact done so repeatedly. "I am prepared to admit, " Karakhan declared, "that there is one mistake in my letter, namely the reference to the conversation of November 6. I suppose one should write, 'In accordance with your repeated assertions.' That is the only mistake. Perhaps one should phrase it thus?"

"What are you saying?!" Mo exclaimed. "I ask you to remove one stone from my path, and you offer to put down several more."

Karakhan repeated that the Chinese side had misinterpreted his letter, that it was a great concession on the Soviet side in order to get the conference under way. When Mo agreed not to argue about the matter further, Karakhan told him that he appreciated his difficult position, that he had apparently not gotten the instructions that he would have liked to receive. "We must remember, however," he said, "that our personal difficulties are of secondary importance. What counts is that our negotiations touch the vital interests of peoples, many millions strong."

As Mo left the building, he told the secretary of the Chinese delegation: "I said that he was right, but that one should not have written about it. I have the impression that Oshanin [the secretary of the Soviet delegation] did not translate this." "I did," the Chinese secretary reassured him.[51]

When the Soviets went ahead and published the full text of Karakhan's letter, Mo registered a "strong protest" in a letter dated November 17, insisting that his remarks of November 6 had been misrepresented and that he had repeatedly requested that Karakhan's letter not be made public.[52]

In his reply on November 23, Karakhan added several "stones." "Your statement of November 6, quoted in my letters, is not something new," he wrote, "as it was repeated several times by you in the conversations with me on June 8, June 21, July 4, and October 8." He cited the text of a protocol of a meeting of the board of directors of the administrative council of the CER on January 10, 1930, which made specific reference to the Khabarovsk Protocol and which Mo

---

[51] Minutes of Karakhan's conversation with Mo, November 15, 1930, DVP, XIII, 650–55.

[52] Mo to Karakhan, Moscow, November 17, 1930, DVP, XIII, 675–76; *Izvestiia,* November 24, 1930; Ovey to Henderson, No. 706, Moscow, December 3, 1930, FO 371/14701–639; Kuo Min news release, November 19, 1930, FO 371/15484–659, China 1931, pp. 544–45.

had signed as president of the board. Rejecting Mo's protest as "entirely unfounded," Karakhan declared that the equivocation in Mo's letter of November 17 concerning the "undisputed obligation" not to alter the CER regime by unilateral action, an obligation already undertaken by the Chinese side by the Peking and Mukden treaties and the Khabarovsk Protocol and confirmed by official declarations and documents, could not but arouse "the most serious misgivings." The Soviet government found it necessary, therefore, to repeat to the Chinese government and to the authorities of the Three Eastern Provinces "categorically with special insistence" that under no circumstances could any unilateral action regarding the CER be tolerated, "since precisely such action created in 1929 a serious threat to peace and good-neighborly relations between the USSR and China."[53]

Mo replied in a short note on November 28 that what Karakhan had set forth in his letter, "is the consequence of a misunderstanding, and goes far beyond the matter under discussion." He declared that "the one thing of importance is to continue the sessions of the Sino-Soviet Conference" and proposed that they do so.[54]

Karakhan wrote back on November 30 that he was pleased that Mo was willing to resume the talks and proposed that they meet on December 4.[55] Mo accepted the date.[56]

[53] Karakhan to Mo, November 23, 1930, DVP, XIII, 672–75; FO 371/14701–639, China 1930, pp. 456–59; *North China Daily News,* December 1, 1930.

[54] Mo to Karakhan, November 28, 1930, DVP, XIII, 690; FO 371/14701–639, China 1930, 460.

[55] Karakhan to Mo, November 30, 1930, DVP, XIII, 689; FO 371/14701–639, China 1930, p. 461.

[56] Mo to Karakhan, December 1, 1930, DVP, XIII, 690.

On December 1 Foreign Minister Wang told the British ambassador "quite unofficially and strictly confidentially" that there were two points in the Khabarovsk Protocol which were unacceptable to the Chinese government: (1) the undertaking on the part of the Manchurian authorities to disband the White Guards, for while there may have been bodies of Russian partisans, there existed no organized White Guards who could be disbanded; (2) reference to the expulsion of the Russian legation and consular officials by the Chinese authorities in violation of international procedure and "the implication that, the Manchurian authorities having admitted that they had acted wrongly in the matter, the Russian officials would return." Wang said that Mo had been sent to Moscow to negotiate about the railway, commerce, and the resumption of relations generally. He asserted that it had been the Soviets who had procrastinated in order to see how the political situation in China developed and had opened the negotiations only when they had realized that there was no prospect of a Red Government being formed in China. He told Lampson that Karakhan had "endeavored to make out" that the Khabarovsk Protocol was as binding as the Peking and Mukden Agreements and though Mo had "of course" been unable to agree to this, had written a note to Mo implying that he had done so. "Mr. Mo had tried to telephone to Mr. Karakhan to tell him that he had never agreed to anything of the kind, but Karakhan pretended to be out and published his note."[57]

---

[57] FO 371/15484, China 1930, pp. 542–43. "It will be remembered," a Chinese author remarked, "that the 1924 agreements, while signed by Dr. V. K. W. Koo, were mostly negotiated by Dr. C. T. Wang, the then special commissioner to handle the Russo-Chinese question with Comrade Karakhan, Soviet ambassador to Peking. When the agreements were initialled by Dr. Wang and M.

On December 4 the second official meeting of the Moscow Conference duly took place. At Karakhan's suggestion three commissions were formed: one to deal with problems concerning the CER, another with commerce, and the third with the reestablishment of diplomatic relations. On December 12 Mo wrote Karakhan vaguely that "affairs" required his temporary return to his fatherland and that he had delegated the temporary conduct of the current business to one of the experts of the Chinese delegation.[58] Karakhan responded that the Soviet government fully shared the desire, repeatedly expressed by Mo, really to begin the discussion of the questions for whose study the three commissions had been set up, and would await his rapid return and the resumption of the conference, "as well as the carrying out of all the other obligations assumed by the Chinese side under the Khabarovsk Protocol."[59]

During Mo's farewell visit to Karakhan, the latter emphasized, as had Litvinov when Mo had called on him, that the Soviet Union was deeply concerned about the continued employment of White Russians in the Chinese army and police. She was the more anxious, he said, because the political trial of the group of promi-

---

Karakhan they were rejected by the Peking Cabinet, with Dr. Koo as Foreign Minister. Thereupon Commissioner Wang resigned and Dr. Koo resumed negotiations with M. Karakhan. Final agreements were soon signed by the Foreign Minister, which differed little from those initialled by the retiring commissioner. What an irony of fate that to-day Wang, as the Nationalist Foreign Minister, should be accusing the Soviet of the violation of the agreements signed by his political rival, with Koo rumoured to be carrying on independent negotiations with Moscow from Mukden behind the back of Nanking, while Karakhan is again matching wits with both Koo and Wang in defending the Soviet's interests in the Chinese Eastern which he himself categorically renounced by his famous declaration of exactly ten years ago!" (Wang Ching-chun, "The Dispute between Russia and China," 172–73.)

[58] Mo to Karakhan, December 12, 1930, DVP, XIII, 729.
[59] Karakhan to Mo, December 15, 1930, DVP, XIII, 728–29.

nent engineers and technicians in Moscow in November-December had revealed that even the "official circles" of several powers were preparing an attack against the USSR and intended to make use of the White Russians in this.

Asked by Mo what message he had for the Chinese government, Karakhan said that he had no special wishes. He did want to point out that it had taken them almost eight months to remove the obstacles for getting the conference under way and that now that they had finally been removed and fruitful talks could be begun, Mo was leaving to obtain instructions from his government. "The Soviet government considers the Chinese side responsible for this new delay in the work of the conference," Karakhan declared.

Mo responded that since the scope of the questions to be discussed at the conference had been broadened, the Chinese were not yet fully ready for negotiation. The purpose of his trip was to hasten their preparation and to speed up the successful conclusion of the work of the conference. Karakhan pointed out that the questions to be discussed were not new. They had been raised as far back as 1924 and there had been ample time to study them.

Mo rejoined that in view of the exceptionally long frontier which China and the USSR shared, the resolution of all disputes and the establishment of friendly relations between them were absolutely inevitable, but that this would take time.

Karakhan again voiced doubt that the Nationalist government was genuinely interested in improving Soviet-Chinese relations and pointed to the reluctance of the Chinese authorities of the CER to go along with the budget cuts proposed by the Russians because of the world economic crisis. He alleged that the railway had to support all kinds of unnecessary Chinese organs, which must be dissolved or taken over by the Chinese.

After some debate about the ratio of Soviet and Chinese citizens employed on the railway—Mo contended that there were twice as many Soviets as Chinese, Karakhan that the number was about equal—Mo asked whether Karakhan had received his letter about Chinese redemption of the railway. Karakhan replied that he had, but that he had not yet discussed it with his colleagues because Mo's impending departure forced them to interrupt their work anyhow. "Your letter is formulated very briefly and unclearly, and I cannot quite understand the principles set in this letter," Karakhan stated. "I fear that if the redemption of the railway were carried out on the basis of these principles, the Soviet government in such case would not only have to surrender the railway to China for free, but would have to add money for China to take the railway." Mo said that he did not know the exact figures involved, but quoted "approximately 225 million" as a rough estimate of the worth of the CER.

"That is cheaper than [if it were sold] for scrap!" Karakhan exclaimed.

"I fear that the redemption figure has been translated incorrectly. I think it comes to two billion," Chang, the secretary of the Chinese delegation, interjected and began to work out the sum in Arabic numerals.

"If two billion, there is nothing for us to discuss," Karakhan said lightly. "Let us have two billion and take the railway."

"No, it really comes to 200 million," Chang responded, his calculation completed.

"I repeat," Karakhan objected, "it would come to more if one sold the railway for scrap."

"This figure expresses roughly the value of the property of the railway," Mo declared. "The principles on which these calculations are based and which are set forth in my letters are as follows: Let us take, for example, the Harbin bridge. When it was built, it cost so-and-so much. Now, after deducting amortization, [it costs] so-and-so much."

"This principle is not quite correct," Karakhan argued. "Imagine, for example, my left arm. How much does it cost? If one were to cut it off and put it on the table, it wouldn't be worth a penny, because one would have to bury it in the ground and have no use for it. But when it is connected with my body, legs and head, when it forms part of an organism, it is a completely different matter. The railway constitutes an intricate organism. If you pile up the sum of its inventory—the tracks, ties, buildings, parts of bridges, etc.—you will still not get the value of the railway. The railway, as a single entity, as a working organism, has far greater value. This, one must take into consideration." He paused a moment, then said, "Oh well. Where are you thinking of getting the money?"

"We thought of floating a loan and collecting the necessary sum by issuing bonds of a domestic loan," Mo explained.

"But would you be able to raise the necessary sum of money by such means?" Karakhan queried.

"It is probable that it will be possible to raise such a sum over a certain period of time, say, three or five years," Mo replied. "At any rate, we shall not resort to assistance from a third [power] in this respect. We feel strongly that the railway must be redeemed with Chinese money."

"This is, of course, true," Karakhan concurred. "The railway must be redeemed with Chinese money;

however, you will hardly collect so much money in China."

"I think it will be possible to collect the necessary sum with the railway itself as security," Mo answered.

"But how will China be able to mortgage the railway until she is its owner?" Karakhan protested. "In order to mortgage the railway, one must first redeem it."

"About this, I hope, we can come to an understanding," Mo stated. "Perhaps the Soviet government will agree to give us a loan for this purpose."

"Oh, we don't have money ourselves!" Karakhan laughed. "No. I think that rather than talk of a loan, which we cannot give you anyway, it will be better for us to turn at once to the solution of disputes concerning the railway and its position."[60]

As Mo returned to China, he was met at the frontier on December 28 by the chief Chinese officials of the CER and boarded the train for Harbin, where he was to stay for several days to undergo medical treatment for rheumatism before proceeding to Tientsin to see Marshal Chang Hsüeh-liang and then to Nanking to consult with his government. While the train was still in Manchuli station, Mo granted an interview to local Chinese and Japanese correspondents. Though he said that he had been given leave provisionally for a month and a half and that the date for his return to the USSR had not been fixed, he was careful not to utter anything that might endanger the talks. Asked whether the Soviet government was sincere in its attitude towards the Moscow Conference, he replied cautiously: "Both sides have had as their primary object to reach some mutually beneficial agreement, and they both hope to be able to do so." When the newspapermen wanted

[60] Karakhan's record of his meeting with Mo, December 18, 1930, DVP, XIII, 736–42.

to know what Mo thought of conditions in Russia, where he had been for eight months, Mo responded that while the people appeared to be "not very affluent," they were making "fierce progress" in industrialization—" 'a thousand *li* [Chinese miles] in one day,' that kind of thing"—and that it was difficult to keep up with them. He declared that if the Five Year Plan would succeed, "the economic position of Soviet Russia in the world will be one of the greatest importance."[61]

Although the period of Mo's leave had been set originally for a month and a half, Mo stayed twice as long. On April 11, 1931, the Moscow Conference was resumed, and twenty-two sessions were held in the subsequent five months. The Soviet draft agreement for the redemption of the railway, transmitted on April 11, declared that "the amount and concrete terms for the redemption of the CER and all property belonging to it, as well as the order of their surrender to the Chinese government, are worked out by a commission, which determines also what the CER actually cost the Russian government and determines a fair redemption price of the railway and its property." It stipulated that the sums owed by the railway to the Soviet and Chinese governments must be taken into account when fixing a fair redemption price, as must be the amounts the governments owed the railway, plus any debits and credits of the company. The Soviet document declared that it was understood that the redemption of the CER, provided in article 9 of the Peking agreement and article 1 of the Mukden agreement, presumed the execution of all the other articles of the agreements.

[61] Resumé of interview appended to dispatch of Garstin to Miles, Harbin, January 5, 1931, FO 371/15484.

Until its redemption, the railway must be administered jointly, as stipulated in the Peking and Mukden agreements.

The Chinese drafts, presented the same day, stated that the amount necessary for redemption, to be calculated by a commission to be formed among the representatives of both sides, was to be worked out on the basis of the sum that the construction of the CER actually cost, minus depreciation due to use and age, and that the lands which were not needed by the railway for its operation, as well as property which had no direct relation to its operation, be recognized as belonging to China and not subject either to appraisal or to payment. The sums which the railway owed to China and the clear profit of the railway were to be deducted from the redemption price.

During the sessions of April 21 and 29 and of May 14 and 24 the Chinese declined to discuss any conditions relating to redemption, arguing that by settlement of the "conditions" governing redemption, the Peking government meant merely the method of determining the redemption cost.

Karakhan responded that the Soviet draft was in line with the Peking and Mukden agreements and that it was not correct to reduce the activity of the railway merely to the transportation of cargo, that "a railway as a commercial undertaking can have—and the CER really has had—a whole string of subsidiary and auxiliary enterprises also of a commercial nature" and that the Peking agreement clearly called for the redemption of both the CER and "all appurtenant properties." Nor were the conditions of redemption confined to the method of calculating the redemption cost. "The conditions of redemption," Karakhan asserted, "by no means are exhausted with the determination of the redemption amount and the methods of its calculation and payment, but embrace the total aggregate of legal and economic questions that arise in connection with the transfer of the railway into Chinese possession."

On June 4 Mo proposed a review of the temporary agreement concerning the administration of the CER. Although Karakhan rejected his contention that the agreement had been concluded for only one year, he expressed willingness to work out new statutes for the railway. On June 21 Karakhan transmitted a long list of problems to be studied by the commission, including the transportation of Chinese troops on credit, the operation of CER schools, clarification of the functions of the president of the CER, measures to be taken to increase the profitability of the railway, and reexamination of the statutes and the contract for the construction and exploitation of the CER and of the conditions governing the existing regime of joint administration.

Subsequent sessions dealt with these issues, but little progress was made. When the Japanese in September 1931 overran Manchuria, where the CER was located, the discussions between the USSR and China lost meaning and were broken off.[62]

*   *   *

As military hostilities between the Soviet Union and China had given way to a war of words, C. E. Whitamore of the Far Eastern Department of the British Foreign Office, had evaluated the exchange of notes between Moscow and Mukden on October 7 and 9, 1930, concerning the activity of White Russian

[62] DVP, XIV, 786–88.

diehards. Remarking that the tone of the Soviet note was so strong as to become "threatening" in places, he observed that the suppression of the White Guards in Manchuria could not be an easy task for Chang Hsüeh-liang even if he wanted to suppress them. "If he fails to do so," Whitamore reflected, "the Soviet authorities may again take drastic action themselves, in which case Chang would have his hands so full in Manchuria that he might have to leave the rest of China to settle its own troubles. This would probably mean a recrudescence of Red activity in the disaffected regions, which is possibly one of the thoughts in the back of the Soviet mind."[63]

"The most interesting feature of this interesting development," MacKillop pondered, "is that the Soviet Government should have addressed a diplomatic note to Chang Hsüeh-liang—and short-circuited Nanking. It obviously suits their book to do so, for Mukden is amenable to pressure whereas Nanking is amenable to nothing, since its fine flights of fancy are curbed by no real administrative responsibilities; and they know that Chang is not averse from accepting the Khabarovsk protocol. The reference to *Mukden* treaty obligations is interesting."

"There is common-sense as well as calculation in this attitude," MacKillop continued, "for it would be grotesque to regard Nanking as having any say in what happens in Manchuria: still this beginning that has been made in the process of recognition of Mukden as a diplomatic entity is of historical interest. The Soviet Government may well also have the other *arrière pensée* mentioned by Whitamore in their minds: a unified China, whether administered by Chang or

[63] October 28, 1930, FO 371/14701–639.

Chiang, is the last thing they want to see—not that there is danger of their seeing it!"[64]

Whitamore found the Mukden note "distinctly conciliatory in matter and tone." He regarded an article in *Izvestiia* commenting on the reply as "hectoring and rather menacing," but admitted that "it is scandalous that Nanking, presumably relying on the fact that they function at a considerable distance from the Sino-Soviet frontier, should be so obstructive regarding the Khabarovsk Protocol."[65]

"I think that the Soviet Government have won rather more than the put trick," MacKillop commented. "They have successfully short-circuited Nanking, for they have not only addressed a diplomatic communication to Mukden, but have received a reply. Both sides ignore Nanking: a development making for a more realistic treatment of the Sino-Soviet issues, since Nanking means nothing at all and Mukden means quite a good deal, and also making for a reasonable settlement since Mukden are bound by material considerations to be reasonable, unlike Nanking whose rhetoric is freed from all unpleasant consequences and may consequently indulge in it ad lib."[66]

Sir Esmond Ovey evaluated the Karakhan note of November 10, 1930, as reflecting "a more friendly atmosphere which should be more helpful to negotiations than the unveiled hostility of previous notes." Whitamore agreed that the note was "much more con-

---

[64] *Ibid.;* "We know very little about the truth or otherwise of these complaints [of White Guard activity]," Orde remarked, "but from what little we have heard I should expect them to have some foundation." (October 30, 1930, FO 371/14701–639.
[65] *Ibid.*
[66] *Ibid.*

ciliatory than previous ones." Orde added: "At any rate the Soviets are no longer breathing fire and slaughter about the railway, 'White Guards,' etc."[67]

When Mo left Moscow, F. K. Roberts of the Northern Department of the British Foreign Office, speculated that his departure may have been due either to Russian attempts to enlarge the scope of the discussions or to "personal pique after M. Karakhan's hectoring tone." MacKillop did not blame Karakhan. "I should imagine," he remarked, "that the longer and the farther Mo Te-hui stays away from any negotiations, the greater their prospect of getting anywhere. His letter [of November 24] is an appalling document."[68]

Henry W. Kinney informed the British Foreign Office that there was talk of replacing Mo with a more experienced diplomat such as Wellington Koo. "It must be remembered," he wrote, "that Mr. Karakhan is one of Russia's most astute diplomats who, when he was in Peking, enjoyed the reputation of being one of the cleverest diplomats in the Far East, whereas Mo Te-hui has had absolutely no experience in such matters, and can hardly be regarded as an adequate match for the Moscow Russian."

Kinney related that the Soviets had greatly strengthened their position in Manchuria since the hostilities in November. The local inhabitants showed no resentment toward them, and Soviet prestige and trade in Manchuria had increased considerably. Kinney judged that the Russians had attained "practically all

[67] FO 371/14701–639, China 1930, p. 445.
[68] FO 371/14701–639, China 1930, p. 451.

their objectives" in Manchuria and now sought merely "formal written instruments" which would give "acknowledgment of conditions which already exist in fact."[69]

The British were skeptical about Chinese allegations that the Soviets were trying to impose Communism in China. As S. G. Harcourt-Smith of the Northern Department of the Foreign Office reflected ironically: "It is interesting to learn that the 'Communist' bandits have been elected to power by the luckless inhabitants of the provinces upon which they prey! It is also satisfactory to know that in most of the areas under 'Communist' control the economic situation is improving!"[70]

The renowned British historian Arnold J. Toynbee, after a personal visit to Mukden and Harbin, concluded that the Soviets had exerted "not more than the minimum of pressure necessary to achieve their diplomatic aim," because while they had been willing to take up arms to attain their objective, "they were anxious at the same time to demonstrate to the world, under the test of severe provocation, that Communists were not as other men are, and that no temptation would induce them to behave like 'Capitalists' and sinners."[71]

By stopping short of a full-scale invasion of Manchuria and by withdrawing promptly (as Tsarist Russia had failed to do in 1900),[72] the Soviet government avoided a collision with Japan. Although Soviet commentators contended that the Western powers wanted another Russo-Japanese War, they admitted

[69] FO 371/15446–815, China 1931, pp. 261A-261H.

[70] June 16, 1930, FO 371/14700–639.

[71] *Survey* 1929, pp. 359–60.

[72] The annexation of North Manchuria had been considered by tsarist Russia even after the Russo-Japanese War. It would have facilitated Russian colonization of the Amur, Ussuri, Sungari and Nonni regions and would have permitted the exclusion of Chinese settlers, who were pouring into Manchuria at a faster rate than Russians into the Russian Far East. (Ventsel', 199.)

that Japan has acted with restraint and had not sec-
onded Western demands for arbitration.[73]

So sympathetic had been Japan's attitude toward
the Soviet Union that some observers went so far as
to speculate that "the course of the Soviet Government
during the conflict over the Chinese Eastern Railway
. . . [had] been shaped by secret negotiations with
Japan, and that the latter country determined the time
and extent of the Soviet military action, designed to
impress the Chinese with the necessity of coming to
terms."[74] But as relations between the USSR and
China improved, Japanese goodwill faded. When the
sale to China of Russian rights in the CER became
the subject of discussion and rumors reached London
that the Soviets were to receive the privilege of import-
ing goods duty-free into Manchuria, a Foreign Office
official remarked that "any such proposal would
undoubtedly arouse Japanese opposition and precipitate a critical situation in Manchuria."[75] The prospects of Soviet economic and political entrenchment
may indeed have contributed to the Japanese decision
to seize control of the region.

While the Japanese had welcomed the Soviet resort
to arms in 1929 to teach the Chinese the lesson that
they could not unilaterally abrogate or violate concession agreements, the might displayed by the Red Army
during the conflict dismayed the Japanese, who from
this time on regarded the USSR as a "definite military
menace."[76]

[73] A. Pevtsov, "Iaponiia i sovetsko-kitaiskii konflikt," 77–82; L. Mad'iar,
"General'naia repetitsiia budushchei voiny." 36–59.
[74] F. W. B. Coleman to State Department, Riga, January 9, 1930, National
Archives, 761.94/419.
[75] June 1931, FO 371/15484–659.
[76] Lengthy resumé of Soviet-Japanese relations by Maxwell M. Hamilton,
October 1933, National Archives, 761.94/646.

The Manchurian Crises

in Soviet Eyes:

A Folio of Cartoons

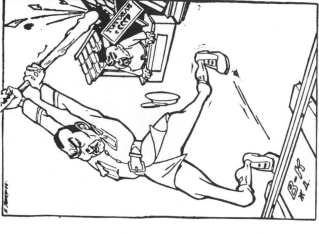

A STICK WITH TWO ENDS

As the Chinese swings way back with his stick in order to strike the Chinese Eastern Railway with all his might, he unwittingly hits the structure behind him, demolishing "Trade with the USSR." (*Izvestiia*, July 24, 1929.)

CHINESE JUGGLERY

The smiling juggler with his left hand shows a poster bearing the mottos "Amicable Relations with the USSR" and "Peaceful Resolution of Conflicts," while with his right hand, behind his back, he shoots at the cashier's window of the Chinese Eastern Railway. (*Izvestiia*, July 18, 1929.)

AN IMPUDENCE THAT
EXCEEDS ALL BOUNDS

Standing with his feet squarely planted on
Russian territory, the Chinese officer
holds up a sign with the inscription: "Help!
Soviet troops are crossing the border!"
(*Izvestiia*, August 29, 1929.)

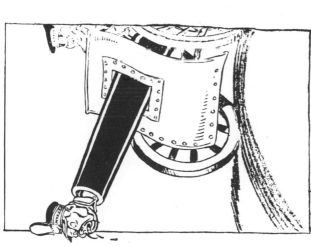

"FRIENDS AND ALLIES"

Nanking is using Mukden as cannon
fodder. (*Izvestiia*, August 23, 1929.)

FOUNDERING OF THE ANTI-SOVIET ADVENTURE

Nanking is going down with the ship as Mukden gets set to jump overboard in an attempt to save itself. (*Izvestiia*, October 29, 1929.)

KEEPING ONE'S HEAD ABOVE WATER

Up to its neck in "the adventure on the CER," Nanking desperately tries to hold itself up by a queue of "lying information about the negotiations with the USSR." (*Izvestiia*, September 21, 1929.)

THE UNIFICATION OF CHINA

The touching "solidarity" of the Chinese generals. (*Izvestiia*, December 18, 1929.)

THE GUARDIANS OF PEACE

The Angels of Peace (the United States, France and Great Britain) sleep contentedly while China attacks the Soviet frontier. They wake up with a start when China proceeds to make an agreement with the USSR. (*Izvestiia*, December 5, 1929.)

THE IMPARTIAL JUDGE

The angelic League of Nations Commission looks into the air while the Japanese army advances under its cloak. (*Izvestiia*, November 29, 1931.)

"STABILITY" IN CHINA

The Nanking and Canton crocodiles devour each other as the bayonets of the Red Army surround them. (*Izvestiia*, May 10, 1931.)

THE WORLD PRESS

The capitalist press, on the left, holds a pen bearing the inscription "Anti-Soviet provocations." The Soviet press, on the right, holds a hammer with the words "The basic purpose of Soviet policy is durable peace and the Second Five-Year Plan." (*Izvestiia*, May 5, 1932.)

JAPAN LOVES
THE WHOLE WORLD

Japan loves the world so much, she wants it all to herself. (*Krokodil*, 1932.)

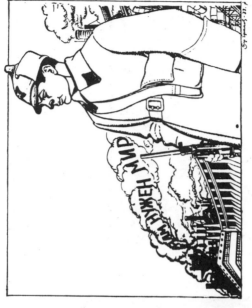

WE NEED PEACE

Although the figure of the Red Army soldier looms large in the foreground, the smoke billowing from Soviet factories spells "We need peace." (*Izvestiia*, February 23, 1933.)

THE SWORD OF DAMOCLES

(*Izvestiia* cartoon, with English word substituted by *Current History* [vol. 40, April 1934, p. 62.])

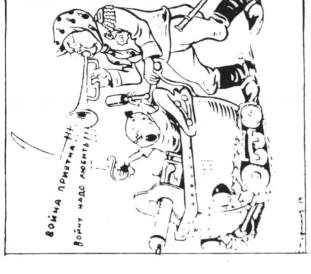

CHILD TRAINING IN JAPAN

The military officer, masquerading as a nanny, plays sentimentally on his bugle, "War is Pleasant," "One Must Love War." (*Izvestiia*, September 4, 1934.)

CRUDE TRICKS

The figure bearing the sign "I am a Soviet employee, an agent of the USSR" and brandishing a pistol and a crowbar with the tag "For the destruction of the CER" is a jack-in-the-box, released by Japan from a box labeled "Information Agency Kokutsu." (*Izvestiia*, September 6, 1934.)

6

The Manchurian Incident

Chang Hsüeh-liang's humiliation at the hands of the Red Army had not dampened his nationalism. On the contrary, it had increased his determination to strengthen China's position in Manchuria. The South Manchurian Railway (SMR) with its industrial enterprises rankled his patriotic feelings no less than had the Chinese Eastern Railway. The fact that the Japanese, who possessed the railway-industrial complex, had assassinated his father, Chang Tso-lin, when he had ceased being useful to them, had not endeared the Japanese to him.[1] In view of his recent defeat by the Russians, Chang Hsüeh-liang could not attempt another railway seizure. Instead, he tried to squeeze the Japanese out gradually by building competitive Chinese railways in Manchuria.

The Japanese regarded Chang's action as illegal, since the government of Manchu China had specifically

---

[1] Clubb, *Twentieth Century China*, 143–44. Although the Japanese had tried to conceal their responsibility for the murder of Chang Tso-lin, Chang Hsüeh-liang had learned the facts from one of the henchmen. (Takehiko Yoshihashi, *Conspiracy at Mukden*, 50.)

promised in 1905 not to infringe on the interests of the SMR in such fashion.[2] Japanese patience was shortened by a Chinese boycott of Japanese goods, even though the boycott had been precipitated by anti-Chinese pogroms in Tokyo and Seoul in the wake of a dispute over the status of Korean residents in Manchuria. The manner in which Japan had industrialized had left her economy overly dependent on foreign trade and the disruption of this trade by the Great Depression had hit Japan harder than any other country. She could not accept the prospect of exclusion from China, her major market.[3] Besides, the Russian show of strength had revived fear of the spread of Communism, and the establishment of a buffer state in Manchuria as a counterpart of the Soviet-dominated Mongolian People's Republic suggested itself to Japanese strategists.[4] Confident that the Great Depression, which had turned the attention of the Western powers inward, precluded military opposition on their part, the Japanese army in Kwantung, the leasehold on the southern tip of the Liaotung Peninsula, took advantage of the killing of one of its officers by Chinese troops and on September 18, 1931, fanned out into Manchuria.[5]

Confronted by civil war—Kuomintang dissidents had formed a rival national government at Canton in May of that year—and with the defeat of Chinese troops by

[2] Dun J. Li, *The Ageless Chinese*, 482–83; Clubb, *Twentieth Century China*, 163–65.

[3] Memorandum of Wellesley, February 6, 1932, FO 371/16146–858.

[4] The Japanese were worried that Manchuria might fall into Soviet hands unless they gained control of it themselves and built up its defenses. (Yoshihashi, 142) Japan's "defensive" measures in Manchuria and Inner Mongolia in turn alarmed the USSR, for they were directed against her, not China. (Testimony of General Tanaka Ryukichi, "Proceedings of the International Military Tribunal for the Far East, Tokyo" [hereafter cited as "IMTFE, 'Proceedings' "], p. 2044; Carl Gilbert Jr., "The Hirota Ministries," 6.)

[5] Li, *Ageless Chinese*, 482–83; Clubb, *Twentieth Century China*, 163–66.

the Red Army fresh in mind, Nanking ordered Chang Hsüeh-liang not to fight back. Resorting to a policy of "nonresistance, noncompromise, and nondirect negotiation," it sought protection from the League of Nations and from the United States, which was not a member of that body.[6]

On September 23 the Council of the League called on the governments of Japan and China to cease hostilities. The United States agreed to follow suit, but although she realized, as Nelson Trusler Johnson, the American minister to China, cabled from Peking, that "the Japanese action in Manchuria constituted an aggressive act . . . apparently long planned and when decided upon most carefully and systematically put into effect" and fell within "any definition of war,"[7] Secretary of State Stimson objected to the contemplated creation by the League of a committee of investigation, lest it inflame the nationalistic spirit of Japan and hamper the efforts of Foreign Minister Shidehara and the other "peacefully disposed members of the Japanese Government" to restore peace.[8] Such a committee of inquiry, Stimson wrote to Hugh Wilson, the American Minister in Switzerland, differed "radically and widely" from an impartial commission such as he himself had suggested at the time of the Sino-Soviet conflict two years earlier, "but even that although much less offensive to national pride than the present

[6] Immanuel C.Y. Hsü, The Rise of Modern China, 646–47.

[7] Johnson to Stimson, No. 615, Peiping, September 22, 1931, "Priority." Typed copies of this and subsequent American dispatches were found among the papers of William R. Castle, Jr., assistant secretary of state, preserved in the Herbert Hoover Presidential Library. Although the name of Peking had been changed by the Nationalist government to "Peiping" in 1928, the British retained the old appellation, a practice followed in this book for the sake of clarity.

[8] Gilbert had reported from Geneva that Sugimura had told him that the Manchurian crisis constituted "a fight to the death between the civil and military authorities in Japan." (Gilbert to Stimson, No. 129, Geneva, September 23, 1931, "Rush.")

suggestion, was opposed by Japan and was not adopted by China and Russia." While assuring Wilson that the American government wished to cooperate with the League of Nations, Stimson remarked: "We feel that the Foreign Minister of Japan together probably with the civilian members of the government are earnestly working to accomplish a peaceful solution, and we are anxious not to make their task more difficult by arousing false national pride."[9]

There was much speculation in Geneva, Washington, and Nanking about the position of the Soviet Union, which like the United States was not a member of the League. A Soviet-Japanese understanding regarding Manchuria was rumored at this time[10] just as it had been rumored in 1929. The American consul general at Nanking reported that the national leaders of China felt that a peaceable solution of the dispute with Japan might be reached through the intervention of the League of Nations or the Kellogg Pact powers, but that if the USSR became involved, "the ordinary methods of peaceful adjustment would have little hope of success, since the present Soviet mentality and methods are in a class by themselves." The Chinese government believed that the Soviets might come in on either side, and feared one prospect as much as the other. It knew what they could do as adversaries;

[9] Stimson to Wilson, No. 23, September 23, 1931, "Triple Priority. Very Urgent. Strictly Confidential." "The principal fear we have as to such an imposed commission is that it would immensely strengthen the nationalist element in Japan and unite Japan behind the military element," Stimson cabled to the American legation in China the next day. Feeling "very strongly" that "a commission could have little success even as a fact finding body if sent to Manchuria without the consent of both the Japanese and Chinese," the State Department had suggested to the League of Nations that "if a commission was to be appointed, there was much more chance of getting the consent of the Japanese if its composition was along the lines of our suggestion to Russia and China two years ago." (Stimson to American Legation Peiping, No. 341, September 24, 1931.)

[10] Prentiss Gilbert to Stimson, No. 129, Geneva, September 23, 1931, "Rush."

it suspected that they could be even more dangerous to it as allies. Disheartened at the reluctance of the League and of the United States to take prompt action to halt Japanese expansion, the Chinese public and especially the highly inflamed student movement might respond to Soviet assistance with such enthusiasm that the government would not be able to cope with Communist subversion.[11]

The Soviet government had too many misgivings about the direction and scope of Japanese expansion to make common cause with Japan. When Ambassador Troianovskii, strongly impressed by the sympathetic attitude that Japan had displayed toward the USSR during the Sino-Soviet dispute, had reported from Tokyo in April, 1930, that the Japanese were desirous of friendly relations with her, Karakhan had evinced considerable skepticism. As he had written in a lengthy letter to Troianovskii on June 13 of that year:

> I fully share your point of view that we are interested in the establishment and maintenance of fully normal, peaceful relations with Japan and that there are no insurmountable obstacles on the way to this. We duly appreciate here the role that Japan played in the Soviet-Chinese conflict, as well as the loyal conduct of the Japanese government at the time of the particular intensification at the beginning of this year of the anti-Soviet campaign in various countries. I am only not quite sure that the Japanese would "gladly go for friendship," if we did not "put pressure" on them, for if the Japanese sincerely sought this friendship (understanding it in a highly qualified and relative sense, as we must always do, when speaking of our relations with a capitalist and imperialist country), they would hardly meet with great obstacles and complications if only they did

[11] September 23, 1931, "Confidential," enclosed in Johnson to Stimson, No. 647, Peiping, September 24, 1931.

not consider that we must pay dearly for the friendship, waiving our very substantial and real interests in the Soviet Far East and give them the possibility of entrenching themselves in the Maritime region. To this we naturally cannot agree, because this would not only fail to strengthen our position in the Far East and secure us from conflicts, but, on the contrary, would whet Japanese appetites and would widen the area of eventual misunderstandings and collisions.[12]

The Japanese occupation of Manchuria constituted a violation of the Treaty of Portsmouth, which had provided for the mutual evacuation of Russian and Japanese troops from that region. The use by the Japanese army of the CER trampled upon Russian economic and strategic interests, and the advance of Japanese forces beyond the CER posed a direct threat to the borders of the USSR. The Soviet Union thus had legitimate grounds for objecting to the Japanese venture.[13] But although the Special Far Eastern Army had not been disbanded upon the defeat of China, it was not ready in 1931 for a test of strength with the Kwantung Army.[14] Moreover, the Soviet government was conscious of its isolation and feared that a collision with Japan might be exploited by the other powers. Hence it responded to the Manchurian Incident with caution,[15] though more actively than was realized in the West.

[12] Karakhan to Troianovskii, June 13, 1930, DVP, XIII, 344.

[13] Kutakov, *Istoriia*, 110; Japan, Foreign Office, O-A Kyoku, *Nisso kosho-shi*, 239.

[14] Harriett L. Moore, *Soviet Far Eastern Policy 1931–1945*, 16. Some Soviet military leaders, including War Commissar Kliment Voroshilov, favored a Soviet counterthrust into Manchuria, but Stalin and the Politburo wished to avoid a confrontation with Japan at this time for fear of inviting Japanese seizure of North Sakhalin, Kamchatka and the Maritime region in the absence as yet of a Soviet navy. (John Erickson, *The Soviet High Command*, 335; Maxim Litvinov, *Notes for a Journal*, 137–38.)

[15] Kutakov, *Istoriia*, 111.

On September 19, 1931, Karakhan summoned Ambassador Hirota Koki and asked him for details concerning the Japanese occupation of Mukden and of military clashes in Manchuria. When Hirota disclosed that he had less information than the Soviet government had obtained through TASS dispatches from Shanghai, Tokyo and other points, Karakhan told him that the Soviet government considered the events in Mukden as of the greatest significance and desired not only more data, but an explanation of the events and the friction, misunderstandings and negotiations that had preceded them. Karakhan pointed out that the events in Mukden could not but alarm the USSR most seriously, because they were taking place near the CER and would affect its operation. He warned that it would be a very serious matter if reports were true that Japanese forces had occupied Kuanch'engtzu, the terminal of the CER.[16]

When two days passed without a reply from Tokyo, Foreign Commissar Litvinov himself summoned the Japanese ambassador. On September 22 Hirota came to his office with Second Secretary Miyakawa Funao. The conversation that ensued was triangular: Litvinov addressed Hirota in English; Hirota replied in Japanese; and Miyakawa translated the response into Russian.

Litvinov declared that developments in Manchuria had aroused world concern. The USSR was particularly alarmed because the events were taking place in a region bordering on the Soviet Union. The USSR had the right to expect that the Japanese government would have kept it informed on its own initiative. It

[16] Karakhan's record of his conversation with Hirota, September 19, 1931, DVP, XIV, 529–30.

had not done so and had not replied to the queries conveyed through Karakhan on the nineteenth. Meanwhile ever more alarming news was being received.

Hirota replied that it was his experience from the fishery talks that telegrams from Moscow to Tokyo took several days. Litvinov remarked that the delay was not due to the telegraph service; he had received a TASS cable from Tokyo dated the same day. He wished the Japanese government would appreciate the degree of Soviet concern and reply promptly.[17]

On September 25 Hirota called on Litvinov with information from his government about the situation in Manchuria. He reported that the number of Japanese troops there was within the 15,000 men limit provided in the railway agreement with China and asserted that most of them had been pulled back by then into the South Manchurian Railway zone. Only a small number had been left at Kirin to forestall a Chinese attack and would be withdrawn as soon as the situation returned to normal.

To Litvinov's surprise Hirota declared that he was glad that no unpleasant questions for the Soviet Union had arisen in connection with the Manchurian Incident, and that it was his ambition, while in Moscow, to resolve any questions, such as for example the fishery question, which might adversely affect Soviet-Japanese relations, and asked for Litvinov's assistance in doing so.

Litvinov replied that the fishery question was not related to the events which had led to their talk.[18] He asserted that Hirota had been in the Soviet Union long enough to know and appreciate the peace-loving

---

[17] Litvinov's record of his conversation with Hirota, September 22, 1931, DVP, XIV, 531–33.

[18] For the fisheries question, see Appendix A.

policy of the Soviet government and its desire to solve all misunderstandings. In the fishery question too, he said, the Soviet government had always sought to accommodate the Japanese government as much as possible, but interested private groups, which were governed exclusively by commercial considerations, frequently put forth unreasonable and unjustified demands. It had been agreed to open diplomatic negotiations to iron out existing disagreements. He for his part was ever ready, of course, to help the ambassador in his ambition to strengthen Soviet-Japanese relations.[19]

The following day, on September 26, Hirota visited Karakhan to confirm that Japanese and Chinese forces had clashed in the vicinity of Kuanch'engtzu. He said that Japanese troops had briefly occupied the barracks in Kuanch'engtzu and the railway station; they had since been withdrawn from the station, and only one platoon remained temporarily in the city to guard against a Chinese attack. He asked that their conversation not be made public.[20]

On October 2 Litvinov had another talk with Hirota and, as he believed in view of Tokyo's silence that his expressions of concern may not have been reported adequately because of Hirota's "poor memory and insufficient knowledge of the English language," had Secretary Miyakawa take down everything he said.

Litvinov declared that the Soviet public was still upset about events in Manchuria, particularly since, at Hirota's request, it had not been informed about their talks. Litvinov remarked that he could not under-

---

[19] Litvinov's record of his conversation with Hirota, September 25, 1931, DVP, XIV, 542–43.

[20] Karakhan's record of his conversation with Hirota, September 26, 1931, DVP, XIV, 548–51.

stand why Hirota did not wish their discussions made public inasmuch as the correspondence between the Japanese government and the League of Nations as well as the correspondence with the American government and Hirota's conversation with the representative of Japan had been published.

Litvinov stated that the Soviet government and the Soviet press continued to receive alarming news from Manchuria. As Hirota himself had admitted, Japanese troops remained outside the railway zone in such places as Kirin. The Soviet government had information that Japanese troops were also at Chengchiatun and Hsinminfu and other places. Hirota had assured him last time that the troops would be withdrawn as soon as conditions returned to normal. That life did not return to normal, he pointed out, seemed not to be the fault of the Chinese alone. The authorities had scattered or ceased to function apparently because of the presence of the Japanese troops. The appearance of new authorities could not be attributed to the desire of the population so much as to the pressure of the occupation forces.

Litvinov expressed particular concern regarding reports of increased White Guard activity in the Japanese occupation zone.[21] He asserted that "the well-

[21] Exaggerated as Soviet fears of White Russian counterrevolutionary activity may have been, it is true that many Russian emigrés in Manchuria were pleased by the Japanese invasion, hoping that the Japanese, unlike the Chinese, would be able to establish order and create conditions favorable for a peaceful existence. As the motorcycles of the Japanese vanguard rattled through the streets of Harbin, the Russian population welcomed them, waving little Japanese flags. Some emigrés advocated cooperation with Japan to free their fatherland from communism. (Balakshin, I, 162–64; An Old Emigrant, "The Truth about the Russian Emigrants in Manchukuo," 81.) Most Whites eschewed such cooperation, however, realizing that Japan might seize Russian territory. (Dorfman, 171.) Besides, their hopes for better treatment by the Japanese were soon dispelled as the Japanese proved no less arrogant and cruel than the Chinese toward the defenseless Caucasians. (O. Leshko, *Russkie v Man'chzhugo*, 9–10 and 98; Harry Carr, *Riding the Tiger*, 105.)

known bandit" Grigorii Semenov, whom the Japanese
had supported during the Siberian Intervention, had
arrived in Mukden immediately after its capture by
the Japanese and had established contact with the
Japanese command; other "bandit leaders" were flock-
ing to that city. Litvinov expressed the apprehension
that Semenov was plotting a Mongol uprising and the
seizure of Hailar. He asserted that "the bandit activity
of White units" had been renewed particularly in the
Barga region, near the western line of the CER. He said
that White Russian bands found shelter at the Changmien (Lumber Company) concession of Japan and that
there was no doubt that the Whites received support
from the Japanese military command. According to
some reports, he stated, they received arms captured
from the Chinese forces. He felt compelled, he
declared, to direct "the most serious attention" of the
Japanese government to this matter, particularly since
it was possible that the Japanese military acted without
its knowledge.

Hirota replied that he knew nothing about the alleged
activity of the White Guards and would inquire about
it at once. When he asked whether he had correctly
understood that the Soviet Union was primarily
interested in the activity of White Guards, Litvinov
retorted that he had said that the USSR was particularly interested in the activity of White Guards,
but she was interested similarly in the whole complex
of questions connected with the recent events in
Manchuria.

Turning to the question of the publication of their
exchange concerning Manchuria, Hirota asserted that
while it was true that Japan's communications with
the League of Nations and the United States had been
made public, the Japanese people had reacted

unfavorably. To release to the press what they had said concerning Manchuria would, he feared, give the impression that there were differences between the Soviet Union and Japan, which was not the case.

Hirota admitted that Japanese forces were in Chiang-chiatun and Hsinminfu, that is to say, outside the railway zone, but he asserted that the Japanese government wished to restore normal conditions as soon as possible. He alleged that bands of runaway Chinese soldiers threatened Japanese residents and expressed the desire for the speedy establishment of strong authority. Hirota said that he got the impression that Litvinov thought that the Japanese interfered with the establishment of such authority. He assured him that his government had instructed its organs not to interfere in internal affairs.

"I replied," Litvinov recorded, "that a vicious circle resulted. The troops were not withdrawn until conditions returned to normal, and conditions apparently could not become normal because of the presence of the occupation troops. The ambassador himself spoke of runaway units of Chinese troops. We know that the Chinese administration also has scattered. It has scattered apparently because of the existence of danger or of a threat, or there would have been no reason for them to flee. In such a way the presence of occupation troops calls forth the abnormal state of affairs."

Litvinov expressed doubt that the arbitrary emergence of new authorities could contribute to normalization. On the contrary, sooner or later a struggle would develop between the new authorities and the old and contribute to the prolongation of the disorders. Hirota was mistaken, Litvinov said, if he thought that the Soviet public was less interested in the Manchurian developments than were the League of Nations and

America. The Soviet public was more restrained, sharing the desire of its government not to complicate the situation, but it could not be indifferent to what happened on the other side of the Manchurian border. He asked that Hirota convey his concern to the Japanese government.[22]

On October 12 Hirota called on Litvinov to give the Japanese version of the origin of the Manchurian Incident and to promise that the Soviet government would be kept informed of further developments in this matter and that the activity of White Russians at the Changmien Lumber Company would be explained. Litvinov thanked Hirota and declared that the policy of the Soviet government was based on the principle of peace.[23]

The following day, on October 13, Hirota reported that the White Russians who were in the Changmien Lumber Company concession area had been there since the Sino-Soviet dispute; they were jobless persons and had nothing to do with politics. It was true that Semenov was at Mukden, but he did not seem engaged in any political movement either. Hirota assured the Soviets that the Japanese military were in no wise connected with the White Russians and did not supply them with arms.[24]

[22] Litvinov's record of his conversation with Hirota, October 2, 1931, DVP, XIV, 559–61.

[23] Nisso kosho-shi, 240.

[24] Nisso Kosho-shi, 248–49. The Japanese did work with White Russian elements following the occupation of Harbin in February 1932. They employed some White Russians as officials in the new state; many of them, after all, had military and administrative experience. The Soviets contended that the white in the five-colored flag of Manchukuo stood for White Russians; the Japanese countered that it symbolized peace. They rebuffed further Soviet inquiries and complaints with the reply that this was an internal matter of the state of Manchukuo and did not concern Japan. When the USSR in 1936 protested that the Japanese military in Manchukuo sent White Russians into Soviet territory to subvert the regime, Japan refuted the charges as unfounded slander. (Nisso kosho-shi, 249–50.)

At the end of September, 1931, Japan had promised to the League of Nations to withdraw her troops into the railway zone and China had pledged to protect Japanese lives and property outside the zone. As the situation had continued to deteriorate, however, the League of Nations and the governments of Great Britain, France and the United States had called on Japan and China in mid-October to carry out their commitments and to exercise "the utmost restraint," but as the American Chargé d'Affaires Edwin L. Neville had realized, foreign mediation was not likely to be accepted: "Direct conversation between the Chinese and Japanese is the only way out, because the Japanese for the present will not welcome interference by any third party."[25]

On October 13 Stimson instructed Prentiss Gilbert, the American consul in Geneva, to propose to Sir Eric Drummond, the secretary-general of the League, "in the strictest confidence" that he consider suggesting *in his own name* "that Chinese and Japanese representatives meet in the presence of friendly observers and, in such presence, at least make the attempt to adjust their differences and come to an agreement." Stimson enjoined upon Drummond "absolute secrecy" regarding the fact that the idea had been his, lest the proposal be received with "initial resentment" by at least one of the disputants.[26] Desirous not to antagonize the Japanese, Stimson instructed Neville to make it clear to Foreign Minister Shidehara that the United States government did not wish either to "sit in judgement" or to suggest the terms of a settlement. Her "sole

---

[25] Stimson to Chargé Neville, No. 192, Washington, October 10, 1931; Memorandum by Stimson, October 10, 1931; and Neville to Stimson, No. 182, October 12, 1931, in FRUS, Japan: 1931–1941, I, 18–22.
[26] Stimson to Gilbert, No. 86, October 13, 1931.

aim" was "to prevent hostilities and encourage settlement through direct negotiations."[27] Stimson authorized Gilbert to participate in League discussions only "as to possible invocation of the Kellogg Pact as a means of mobilizing world opinion against war." While he appreciated the difficulty that the Council as such had in invoking the pact, he felt that individual members of the Council should take the initiative for doing so. The United States could not invoke the pact alone or propose invoking it, Stimson argued, for such a suggestion on her part would inflame Japanese public opinion against her and might postpone the settlement of the issue.[28]

While Stimson expressed irritation at the tendency of most League members to look to the United States for leadership and to involve the United States in the actions of the League, the Western powers were annoyed by Stimson's evasive tactics. In explaining the difficulty of Stimson's position, the British ambassador in Washington was to remind the foreign secretary at the end of the year that "the Secretary of State had placed the United States Government in the forefront of intervention in the Russo-Chinese dispute of 1929, with not very happy results, and the obvious lesson to draw from that experience was that the onus of intervention should be shared with other interveners." He wrote that "confused and irresolute as the attitude of the United States Government may have appeared to those unaccustomed to the limitations under which the Government labours, . . . it cannot be too often recalled that the separation of executive

----

[27] Stimson to Neville, No. 196, October 14, 1931.

[28] Stimson to Gilbert, No. 97, October 16, 1931, "Strictly Confidential—For Guidance," "It would be better not to invoke the Pact at all than to invoke it in this way," Stimson remarked the following day. (Stimson to Gilbert, No. 99, October 17, 1931, "Confidential.")

and legislature under the American system of government engenders great weakness in the executive, which is constantly exposed to subsequent repudiation of its acts by an irresponsible Legislature." The actions of the United States in connection with the Manchurian crisis, he felt, had been consistent so far with "the ineluctable conditions of American policy."[29]

On October 17 the members of the Council of the League who were also signatories of the Kellogg Pact (France, Great Britain, Italy, Germany and Spain) reminded China and Japan in identic telegrams of their obligations under the pact and called on them "to refrain from taking any steps that might endanger the success of the efforts already in progress to secure the settlement by peaceful means of the conflict that has arisen between them."[30]

That day the Council called upon the Japanese government "to begin immediately to proceed progressively with the withdrawal of its troops into the railway zone" and upon the Chinese government "to make such arrangements for taking over the territory thus evacuated as will insure the safety of the lives and property of Japanese nationals there." It recommended that direct negotiations concerning the execution of the above be begun at once between the representatives of the Chinese and Japanese governments and offered "if invited, to nominate one or two persons for this purpose."[31] On October 20 the United States addressed China and Japan along the lines of the identic telegrams sent by the members of the League.[32]

When the Soviet Union did not follow suit, Mo Te-

---

[29] R. C. Lindsay to Simon, No. 2000, Washington, December 31, 1931, "Confidential," FO 371/16141.

[30] Gilbert to Stimson, No. 212, Geneva, October 17, 1931, "Triple Priority."

[31] Gilbert to Stimson, Geneva, October 17, 1931, "Urgent."

[32] Stimson to American Legation in China, No. 388, October 20, 1931.

hui, who was still in Moscow, inquired of Karakhan on October 25 what the position of his government was. Karakhan reminded Mo that when the United States and the other Kellogg Pact powers had addressed the USSR with a declaration of the same nature in 1929, the Soviet government had replied that the Kellogg Pact did not envision for a single state or group of states "the role of guardians of this pact." "On this ground we rejected any intervention of the powers on the basis of the Kellogg Pact," Karakhan stated. "Our attitude toward the rights and obligations flowing from this pact have, of course, not changed since that time."

Karakhan remarked that what mattered was not so much the relationship that the Japanese actions bore to the Kellogg Pact, but the essence of these actions. "And the essence of the events," he said, "consists in the fact that the Japanese, not having obtained what they sought by diplomatic means, have decided to obtain the same by the use of force. This is what counts." "What we now see," he added, "is the usual policy of all imperialist states."

Karakhan noted that in the absence of diplomatic relations between their countries, the Chinese had no right to expect a formal communication from the Soviet government regarding the Sino-Japanese conflict, but he made it plain in response to a question by Mo that he for his part would never have entrusted his fate to the League of Nations.[33]

[33] Karakhan's record of his talk with Mo, October 25, 1931, DVP, XIV, 590–92. The USSR rejected an invitation by the League to join an advisory committee on the ground that since most of the members of the committee did not maintain diplomatic relations with her she would not be able to communicate with them. (Litvinov to Sir Eric Drummond, March 7, 1933, DVP, XVI, 145–47.) But when the League on September 15, 1934, invited the Soviet Union to become a full-fledged member of the League itself, Moscow accepted on the very same day. (Litvinov to Richard Sandler, September 15, 1934, DVP, XVII, 588–91; League of Nations, *Official Journal* 1934, pt. 2, 1392–94.)

On October 28 Hirota called on Karakhan and expressed the concern of his government at rumored Soviet intervention in the Manchurian conflict. Tokyo had information that the Chinese General Chan-shan of Tsitsihar had conferred with a Red Army officer from Blagoveshchensk before leaving Sakhalian two weeks before, that there were Red Army instructors with Ma's forces, and that there was an agreement by which he received Soviet warplanes, pilots and antiaircraft guns.[34] Hirota alleged that Soviet arms were being supplied to Chinese troops in Heilungchiang province. There were rumors, he said, of close collaboration between China and the USSR concerning developments in Manchuria and about the massing of Soviet troops. He warned that the dispatch of Soviet troops to the CER would worsen the atmosphere and acerbate the situation and would compel the Japanese government to take steps for the protection of its residents and of the Taonan-Kokoke railway (the Taonan-Tsitsihar line), which had been built with Japanese money.[35]

The following day, October 29, Karakhan rejected the Japanese allegations as completely unfounded and provocative. The Japanese government could not but know, he said, that the Soviet Union did not support either side in the Manchurian conflict and furnished neither instructors nor arms to any forces in Manchuria. He asserted that the Soviet government adhered to a policy of strict noninterference "not because such a policy might suit or not suit anybody," but "because it respects international treaties, concluded with China, respects the sovereign rights and

[34] A Japanese Foreign Office official had stated without qualification on October 27 that Ma had Russian support. (A. Morgan Young, *Imperial Japan 1926–1938*, 106.)

[35] TASS dispatch, October 30, 1931, in DVP, XIV, 625–27.

independence of other states and considers that a policy of military occupation, even if carried out under the guise of so-called aid, is incompatible with the peaceful policy of the USSR and with the interests of the world in general."[36]

When Japanese newspapers and telegraph agencies continued to carry stories of Soviet aid to Chinese generals, Litvinov summoned Hirota on November 14 and sharply accused "some [Japanese] military circles in Manchuria" of seeking to complicate relations between Japan and the USSR by a systematic, dishonest anti-Soviet campaign. Litvinov added that there was word that the Japanese command planned to cross the CER in the region of Tsitsihar and paralyze its activity, an action that would inflict material loss on the Soviet Union. He reminded Hirota of his promise that events in Manchuria would not adversely affect the interests of the USSR.[37]

On November 19 Hirota returned to Litvinov to declare that it was an "intolerable misunderstanding" to believe that Japanese officers fabricated groundless rumors. He blamed the Chinese for spreading stories of Soviet military aid to bolster the morale of their forces. It was to the Chinese side, he said, that the Soviets should direct their complaint. In view of the strained relations between the Japanese and Chinese

[36] *Ibid.; Nisso kosho-shi,* 240; Kutakov, *Istoriia,* 111. The attitude of the Chinese did not encourage Soviet involvement. "There never was a time during recent years when China could expect to manipulate to better advantage her two equally ambitious and imperialistic neighbors, Japan and Russia, than at the present moment," Samuel H. Chang wrote in the *China Press* on September 17, 1931. "Compared with Japan, Russia is the lesser of two evils, and to be able to play Moscow against Tokyo would not only effectively put a check to the growing menace of Japan, but would also serve as a protection against Moscow's 'Red' Imperialism." (Japanese Archives, S 14, document S 120016, pp. 1140–41.)

[37] TASS dispatch, November 15, 1931, in DVP, XIV, 654–55; *Nisso kosho-shi,* 240; Kutakov, *Istoriia,* 111–12.

forces, Hirota continued, the Japanese government expected a clear statement from the Soviet government that it would not supply the forces of General Ma with weapons or other materials. During the Sino-Soviet conflict of 1929 the Japanese government had adhered to a policy of strict nonintervention and had refused to transport Chinese troops to the vicinity of Manch'zhuriia Station (Manchuli). It now expected a policy of similar nonintervention on the part of the Soviet government.

Hirota declared that Japan had to defend her rights and interests in Manchuria and Mongolia. She tried not to damage Soviet interests and did not plan to paralyze the CER. On the other hand, military clashes along the railway might prove unavoidable, a matter for which the railway must share responsibility for allowing the concentration and transportation of Chinese troops.[38]

Litvinov replied to Hirota the following day, on November 20. He expressed satisfaction that the Japanese government did not lend credence to rumors of Soviet violation of the principles of nonintervention and of Soviet aid to Chinese generals. He took exception, however, to the parallel drawn by Hirota between Japanese nonintervention in the Sino-Soviet conflict of 1929 and the present situation. Litvinov asserted that in 1929, in spite of Chinese violation of Soviet treaty rights, the Soviet government had neither invaded nor contemplated invading Manchuria. Only after Chinese and Russian White Guard units had repeatedly attacked Soviet territory had Soviet troops crossed the Manchurian frontier to defeat and disarm

[38] Press release of the Foreign Commissariat, November 21, 1931, DVP, XIV, 668–70.

the attackers and make further attacks impossible. When they had done so, there had been no question of the occupation, even temporary, of Chinese territory by Soviet troops, nor of the displacement of the old authorities and the establishment of new ones. Nor had there been the slightest possibility of the violation of any legal rights or interests of Japan. As soon as the Soviet troops had achieved their limited objective, they had withdrawn to Soviet territory without Soviet imposition of new conditions or the forced solution of problems not directly related to the above conflict. Furthermore, the South Manchurian Railway, from which the Japanese had barred Chinese troops in 1929, had been completely in Japanese hands and had been guarded by Japanese troops. The Chinese Eastern Railway, on the other hand, was jointly administered by China and Russia and was guarded by Chinese troops. The Soviet Union did not have equal control, and conditions thus were not similar. Nonetheless, she had succeeded on the whole in preserving neutrality. She rejected the contention that the CER must share responsibility for the conflict.[39]

On January 2, 1932, Troianovskii reported that the Japanese were contemplating the inclusion of three White Russians into the government of Manchuria.[40]

[39] *Ibid.*, 670–71; *Nisso kosho-shi*, 241.

[40] In response to a telegraphic query by Troianovskii on January 11, Consul General Slavutskii reported from Harbin that he had no specific knowledge of Japanese plans for using White Russians in the Manchurian government, but that there was the tendency to use White Russians as advisers in various institutions. White Russians would participate in the self-government of Mukden, and the police force in Harbin would be staffed to a large extent by White Russians under Japanese advisers. (Slavutskii to Troianovskii, January 15, 1932, DVP, XV, 27.) The Soviet consul general in Dairen telegraphed to the Foreign Commissariat on January 27 that General Honjo Shigeru, the commander of the Kwantung Army, had promised White Russian representatives, including representatives from Paris, on January 24 to give them aid in reestablishing their influence in Manchuria "at the necessary moment." (Menni to Foreign Commissariat, January 27, 1932, DVP, XV, 66.)

When he queried Premier Inukai Tsuyoshi, who for a month served concurrently as foreign minister, about this on January 12, Inukai responded that such rumors were ridiculous. Troianovskii then inquired whether it was true that General Hsi Ch'ia, who had proclaimed the independence of Kirin Province from Nanking a week after the Japanese invasion of Manchuria and had assumed the governance of the province under the tutelage of the Kwantung Army, was advancing on Harbin, where the loyal forces—the "Old Kirinites" as they were sometimes called in dispatches—had formed a provincial government. Inukai replied that he had no official information, but conceded that Hsi probably wished to subjugate all of Kirin Province. Troianovskii rejected a suggestion by Shiratori Toshio, director of the Information Bureau of the Foreign Office who was interpreting, that the Soviet consul prevail upon the railway guard to submit to Hsi. When Troianovskii complained that the fighting between Chinese generals with the blessing of the Japanese was not order but disorder, Shiratori retorted that sometimes it was necessary to proceed to order through disorder.[41]

On January 27 Japanese officers and men appeared at Kuanch'engtzu Station and demanded space aboard the train to Harbin. When their request was refused on the ground that instructions forbade the transportation of armed persons, they forced their way aboard.[42] A number of railway officials at the station were arrested by the Japanese the same day.[43]

At midnight on January 28 a representative of the

[41] Troianovskii to Foreign Commissariat, January 12, 1932, "Immediately" [*nemedlenno*], DVP, XV, 20–21.
[42] Slavutskii to Foreign Commissariat, January 27, 1932, paraphrased in DVP, XV, 730, note 34.
[43] DVP, XV, 737–38, note 48.

Japanese military mission in Harbin approached Stepan Kuznetsov, vice president of the CER, about the transportation of Japanese troops by the railway. Kuznetsov replied that this was impossible because of the neutrality of the CER, but as the Japanese made it clear that they would move their troops into the railway territory if denied transportation, Consul General Mikhail Slavutskii sought urgent instructions from Moscow.[44]

Karakhan softened his stand. The Japanese military mission was to be told, he telegraphed at once, that the USSR could not on her own allow the transportation of Japanese troops by the CER, since the latter was administered jointly with China and ran through Chinese territory. If the Japanese could secure Chinese approval of the transportation of Japanese troops on the CER, the Soviet side would raise no objections.[45]

The Japanese had no intention of waiting for anyone's permission, however. Two Japanese echelons with full battle equipment occupied Kuanch'engtzu Station that very day. As the station master, on instructions from General Manager Rudyi, would not dispatch trains or service and supply them, the Japanese made preparations to use their own rolling stock.[46]

When the Japanese consul asked Kuznetsov to allow the dispatch of Japanese troops by the CER to Harbin to help their countrymen in that city, Kuznetsov reiterated that he was not in a position to grant such per-

[44] Slavutskii to Foreign Commissariat, January 28, 1932, "Immediately," DVP, XV, 66–67.

[45] Karakhan to Slavutskii, January 28, 1932, "Urgent" [vne ocheredi], DVP, XV, 67.

[46] Reporting that the entry of Japanese and Kirin forces into Harbin was merely a matter of hours, Slavutskii noted that there was panic among the Chinese officials in the city. "They are hiding in private houses" (na chastnykh kvartirakh). (Slavutskii to Foreign Commissariat, January 28, 1932, "Most urgent" [vne vsiakoi ocheredi], DVP, XV, 67–68.)

mission and asserted that Japanese seizure of Kuanch'engtzu Station was an act directed against the Soviet Union. The consul did not argue the point. He merely threatened that if permission for Japanese use of the railway was not granted, the military might seize the trains by force.[47]

On January 29 Hirota told Karakhan that Japanese troops were being dispatched to Harbin for the sole purpose of protecting the tens of thousands of Japanese residents and their property, endangered by the mutiny of Chinese troops in that city. The Japanese government had no intention of violating the interests of the CER. It required its facilities to move its troops, but was prepared to pay for the transportation.

In response to Hirota's assertion that the Japanese government had instructed him to explain the real meaning of the dispatch of Japanese troops to Harbin lest the Soviet government misunderstand its policy, Karakhan replied that it was the manner in which the Japanese authorities had acted in the Harbin area that gave rise to the sort of misunderstanding that Tokyo had asked him to allay. They had approached Kuznetsov for permission to use the railway twelve hours after Japanese troops had actually boarded trains at Kuanch'engtzu and had started north. Karakhan repeated that the CER was a joint enterprise on Chinese territory and that the Soviet government would not object to the transportation of Japanese troops if the Chinese authorities agreed to it, provided the interests of the CER were respected.[48]

On February 1 Consul General Ohashi sharply demanded of Slavutskii that the Soviet railway authorities grant the requested permission for the trans-

[47] DVP, XV, 730.
[48] *Izvestiia,* January 30, 1932, DVP, XV, 70–71; FO 371/16195–680.

portation of Japanese troops without the concurrence of Chinese officials on the ground that the latter had fled. When Slavutskii persisted that the Chinese side existed and that the Russians could not decide for them, Ohashi offered to make the Soviet position "easier" by Japanese seizure of the rolling stock. Slavutskii rejected this "strange proposal" and reiterated that Ohashi must confer with the Chinese.[49]

On February 17 the Soviet officials in Harbin reported that the Japanese insisted on the conclusion of an agreement which would put the protection of the CER in their hands "until the organization of a Chinese guard" and would provide for the transportation of Japanese troops at half fare and of troops and cargo connected with the guarding of the railway free of charge. Although the Japanese had obtained Chinese assent, the Soviet officials planned to refuse on the ground that the guard must remain Chinese and that transportation charges must be at the normal rate.[50]

On February 22 the Japanese military mission in Harbin sought Russian permission to transport troops to Imienp'o and possibly to Pogranichnaia Station, asserting that this would be a temporary measure solely

[49] Slavutskii to Foreign Commissariat, February 1, 1932, DVP, XV, 74–75. Lindley reported that Troianovskii did not believe that the Japanese would seize the CER "and add another quarrel," since they could attain security by building strategic railways. "Japanese would probably install subservient Chinese on the line to which Moscow would not object. If Japanese seized the line Soviet would not fight but would not forget." (Lindley to Foreign Office, No. 66, Tokyo, February 4, 1932.) "The last sentence might have read more correctly 'could not fight,' " a Foreign Office official commented. (FO 371/16195–680.)

[50] Joint telegram of Slavutskii, Kuznetsov and Rudyi to Foreign Commissariat, February 17, 1932, "Immediately," DVP, XV, 114. The telegram was signed "Chetverka" (Foursome). Since January 1931 most basic Soviet documents dispatched from Harbin to Moscow concerning the CER had been sent in the name of four officials—the consul general in Harbin, the general manager, the vice president and the deputy to the vice president of the CER—called "Chetverka" for short. After April 1931 communications were sent in the name of the first three officials only, but the signature "Chetverka" was retained as a matter of tradition. (DVP, XV, 742.)

for the protection of Japanese residents and in no way directed against the USSR.[51] Karakhan instructed the Soviet officials to reply that since the movement of Japanese forces to the Soviet border and an agreement concerning their transportation on the CER were not commercial questions, but deeply political ones touching upon treaties that the USSR had with Japan and China, they could not be decided by the railway administration and had been submitted to Moscow for settlement.[52]

When Slavutskii so informed the Japanese in charge of the consulate on February 25, the latter declared that Japanese troops were set to move in the morning and that there could be trouble [*nepriiatnosti*] if agreement were not reached before then. Slavutskii warned that "one did not react to all trouble in the same way and that trouble did not contribute to the development of [good] relations." The Japanese backed down saying he had meant merely that it would be troublesome if the question remained unresolved much longer.

But the strong line was reasserted by a representative of the military mission who called on Kuznetsov that evening. Hinting that the military command did not like the submission of the matter to Moscow, he threatened that the troops which had arrived from Changchun would probably decide the question on their own. Kuznetsov retorted that he could discuss with him only legal actions and that a disciplined army did not commit any acts without orders from its command.[53]

Meanwhile, on February 24, Karakhan had sum-

[51] Joint telegram of "Chetverka" to Foreign Commissariat, February 22, 1932, "Immediately," DVP, XV, 124.

[52] Karakhan to Slavutskii, Kuznetsov and Rudyi, February 24, 1932, "Most urgent," DVP, XV, 126–27.

[53] Slavutskii to Foreign Commissariat, February 25, 1932, DVP, XV, 134–35.

moned Hirota to inquire whether the Japanese government knew of the demands of the military command in Harbin for the transportation of Japanese forces by the CER to Pogranichnaia as well as of its proposal for the guarding of the railway by Japanese troops and the drastic reduction of transportation and freight charges. He complained also about the alleged activization of White Russians in Manchuria by the Japanese contrary to the assurances that Hirota had given to Litvinov and him, and requested information about the new government that was being formed in Manchuria.[54]

On February 27 Hirota called on Karakhan with an answer from the Japanese government to his queries of the 24th concerning the demands of the Japanese military command in Harbin. The Japanese government declared that it had to move Japanese troops by the eastern line of the CER to the vicinity of Imienp'o and conceivably up to Hailin in order to protect some 20,000 Japanese subjects, including Koreans who had not been able to flee to safety. It requested that the Soviet government permit this as it had permitted the movement of troops to Tsitsihar and Harbin earlier. It assured Moscow that the Japanese command "of course" respected the interests and rights of the USSR in North Manchuria and reiterated that Soviet rights in the CER would not be violated. The Japanese government asserted that it had no knowledge of a proposal by the military command to the railway administration concerning an agreement for the transportation of Japanese troops and that it had requested information from the authorities in Manchuria.

[54] Communiqué of the Karakhan-Hirota talk, published in *Izvestiia* on February 26, 1932, reprinted in DVP, XV, 142–43.

Karakhan gave the desired permission later in the day as an exceptional and temporary measure in view of the unusual circumstances and because the Chinese authorities in Manchuria and the Chinese members of the railway administration had endorsed the request. He noted, however, that the transportation of Japanese troops was contrary to article 7 of the Treaty of Portsmouth (reaffirmed by the Basic Convention of 1925), whereby Russia and Japan had bound themselves to exploit the railways in Manchuria solely for commercial and industrial and not for strategic purposes. The massing of Japanese troops near the Russo-Korean frontier was in violation of article 2 of the same treaty, both sides having agreed to refrain from undertaking any military measures on the Russo-Korean border that might endanger the security of Russian or Korean territory. Karakhan inquired whether the Soviet Union could. count on Japan to abide by the said articles as she herself had done faithfully and demanded an explanation of the alleged troop concentration.[55]

In its reply, handed to Karakhan by Counselor Amau Eiji[56] on March 5, the Japanese government insisted that it had scrupulously observed all the articles of the Treaty of Portsmouth and would continue to do so. It contended that the dispatch of troops to the CER was not "strategic," but constituted a police measure solely for the defense of the lives and property of Japanese residents in that region and that the trans-

---

[55] Press release of the Karakhan-Hirota meeting, first published in *Izvestiia*, February 29, 1932, reprinted in DVP, XV, 147–48; Hirota Koki Denki Kanko-kai (comp.), *Hirota Koki*, 90–91; *Nisso kosho-shi*. 244, 253–57; Kutakov, *Istoriia*, 112.

[56] Two readings of the name are possible: "Amo" (with a long "o") and "Amau." Soviet sources give the name as "Amo," but Japanese Foreign Office officials with whom I discussed the spelling expressed preference for "Amau."

portation of troops by the railway was within its commercial functions. It denied that Japanese forces were being massed at the Soviet-Korean frontier. Troops had been sent to the vicinity of Kanto only to deal with Koreans, hostile to Japan.[57]

The vagueness of the reply did not satisfy Karakhan and he went to see Hirota, who was sick at home, the same day to obtain more specific assurances. But Hirota was equally deft in evading Soviet accusations of Japanese violation of the Treaty of Portsmouth. When Karakhan pointed out that if the Soviet Union was forbidden from having regular troops on the CER for its protection, the same should apply even more to Japan, Hirota retorted that the Japanese troops were not being sent for the protection of the railway, but for the protection of Japanese residents who happened to live along the railway. He denied that the presence of Japanese troops near the Russo-Korean frontier constituted a "massing" of Japanese forces.

Hirota agreed with Karakhan's contention that steps should be taken to improve the atmosphere in which they negotiated. Yet he asserted that the fault lay not in Japanese actions so much as in Soviet press releases. When Karakhan retorted that the Japanese press had had its share of inciting articles, Hirota remarked, "Yes, but in our country one publishes merely personal opinions, in your country one moves troops."

Karakhan admitted that the Soviet Union was strengthening her Far Eastern garrisons, but insisted that that was perfectly natural in view of mounting agitation against her in Japan as well as because of the increase in anti-Soviet activity by White Russians.

After considerable sparring, Hirota agreed with

[57] DVP, XV, 748–49; record of Karakhan's subsequent conversation with Hirota the same day, DVP, XV, 166.

Karakhan that to improve the atmosphere, "it would be necessary to have a sincere exchange of opinions on all questions that have arisen."[58]

On March 15 Karakhan once more visited Hirota, who was still confined at home. Miyakawa, who had just returned from Tokyo, whither he had accompanied Ambassador Yoshizawa Kenkichi when the latter had passed through Moscow en route from Paris to Tokyo to assume the post of foreign minister, presented Karakhan with a vase from Yoshizawa, and Hirota stated that Yoshizawa and others had communicated from Tokyo that they were pleased that Soviet-Japanese relations were friendly and that they wanted to keep them that way. Nonetheless, Karakhan voiced dissatisfaction with the interpretation put by Japan on her obligations under the Treaty of Portsmouth.[59]

As Karakhan pressed for further data about Manchuria, where the new state of Manchukuo had been proclaimed on March 1,[60] Hirota asserted that the information he received was less interesting and detailed than what TASS published. Karakhan rejoined that TASS would be flattered by this statement, but that the ambassador exaggerated, of course. What Karakhan wanted to know were not "outward facts," which were to be found in newspapers, but the meaning and purposes of the establishment of the new state, something known only to the Japanese.

Hirota declared that the government of Manchukuo would adhere to the principles of the Open Door and of Equal Opportunity in its relations with foreign countries; beyond that he had as yet little information, not

---

[58] Karakhan's record of his conversation with Hirota, March 5, 1932, DVP, XV, 162–69.

[59] Karakhan's record of his conversation with Hirota, March 15, 1932, DVP, XV, 178–80.

[60] Foreign Minister Hsieh Chieh-shih to Stimson, Changchun, March 12, 1932.

even whether Japan had recognized the new govern-ment.[61]

When Karakhan discussed the Manchurian situation with Mo Te-hui on March 17, the Chinese envoy expressed the conviction that the Japanese would not expand further. "Japan is not that stupid," he said.

"Sometimes self-interest and greed force an intelligent person to do stupid things," Karakhan observed. "At any rate, developments in Manchuria and China are far from over. They are just getting into full swing."

Karakhan told Mo that it was the policy of the Soviet Union to watch events vigilantly, but not to intervene. "That is the only correct and possible policy now."[62]

On March 19 Hirota told Karakhan that Japan had not yet recognized Manchukuo, but was watching developments closely. He reassured him that Japan would abide by the provisions of the Treaty of Portsmouth, that the Kwantung Army would constrain rather than support White Russians, and that Japanese troops along the Soviet-Korean frontier had no hostile intentions toward the USSR. When Hirota asked about the alleged massing of Soviet troops on the other side of the frontier, Karakhan responded that no such troop concentration was taking place. He added that the Soviet Union would take no military steps that might violate the treaty of Portsmouth.[63]

Karakhan's assurances prompted Hirota to advise his government that Japan had nothing to fear from the Soviet Union and could, to all intents and purposes,

---

[61] Karakhan's record of his conversation with Hirota, March 15, 1932, DVP, XV, 178–80.
[62] Karakhan's record of his conversation with Mo, March 17, 1932, DVP, XV, 181–82.
[63] *Izvestiia*, March 22, 1932, DVP, XV, 199–201.

ignore her in formulating her policy toward Manchuria. The USSR was not likely to intervene.[64]

[64] In informing his British colleague of this, Yoshida Shigeru, the Japanese ambassador to Italy, expressed the view that Hirota's opinion must be based on the fact that "the Soviet Government were incapable of taking effective action rather than that they might not wish to do so." Yoshida, it should be noted, seriously disapproved of his government's policy regarding Manchuria and Shanghai and sought permission to return to Tokyo to explain Western reaction thereto. (Sir R. Graham to Foreign Office, No. 281, Rome, April 9, 1932, FO 371/16163–662) "It is natural that a Japanese living abroad and more conversant with European opinion should have qualms about his Government's policy," MacKillop commented. "We find the converse of Mr. Yoshida's views in Sir F. Lindley's." (FO 371/16163)

7

Trouble Rides the CER Again

While the Soviets had denied use of the Chinese
Eastern Railway to a large party of armed Chinese
police in November 1931 to avoid being accused by
Japan of a breach of neutrality, they had, as seen,
permitted the transportation of Japanese troops in the
conquest of Manchuria.[1] In March 1932 the Soviet
government had agreed to the conveyance of Japanese
troops eastward from Harbin, with the understanding
that they would not advance beyond Harbin.[2] On
October 9 the Soviet government consented to the
transportation of Japanese troops to Manchuli.[3] Upon
the fall of Manchuli in December, it found it difficult
to block the final stages of Japan's suppression of the
insurgents in Northeastern Kirin, led by Generals Li
Tu, Wang Te-lin and Ting Ch'ao, and assented to the

---

[1] Garstin to Ingram, No. 42, "Confidential," Harbin, June 11, 1932, FO
371/16173–665.

[2] Garstin to Ingram, No. 8, Harbin, January 18, 1933, FO 371/17083–760.

[3] Karakhan's record of his conversation with Amau, October 9, 1932, DVP,
XV, 564–66.

use of the CER east of Hailin for military transport purposes.[4]

Yet the Japanese would not pay full fare for their soldiers and did not even meet the reduced payments. By September 1933 the Kwantung Army was millions in arrears—30 million according to Soviet claims, 4 or 5 million according to Japanese estimates—and refused to pay up until a transportation agreement had been concluded.[5]

Since Japanese forces were involved, the Soviets addressed their complaints to Japan as well as to Manchukuo, where they continued to maintain consular representatives. When the Soviet officials in Harbin cabled to the Foreign Secretariat on July 1 that the Japanese navy claimed possession of the Sungari River bank and of the CER wharf and forcibly prevented the transshipment of cargo,[6] Karakhan instructed Consul General Slavutskii and Ambassador Troianovskii on July 5 to take the matter up simultaneously in Harbin and Tokyo. On July 8 Slavutskii filed a written protest with the Manchurian authorities, warning them that they would be held fully responsible for losses suffered by the CER in consequence of the interruption of its operation. The same day Troianovskii asked the Japanese government to take the necessary measures to halt the interference with the normal commercial work of the CER, an interference that was taking place "with the participation and at the initiative of Japanese citizens."[7]

---

[4] The Soviets did, however, let the Chinese flee into Soviet territory. Ting Ch'ao was captured by the Japanese before he reached the frontier. (Garstin to Ingram, No. 8.)

[5] *Nisso kosho-shi,* 246–48.

[6] "Chetverka" to Karakhan, July 1, 1932, "Immediately," DVP, XV, 394–95.

[7] Karakhan to Slavutskii, July 5, 1932, DVP, XV, 399; DVP, XV, 827–28, note 99; declaration of the government of the USSR to the government of Japan, April 16, 1933, DVP, XVI, 241.

On July 15 Vice Minister of Foreign Affairs Arita Hachiro rejected Troianovskii's protest that the interference of Japanese naval authorities with the transshipment of cargo from Soviet vessels at Harbin was contrary to the promise made by Japan to the USSR that the interests of the CER would be respected. He contended that the question was within the jurisdiction of the Manchurian government. Troianovskii retorted that "in such a way one could annul the promise of the Japanese government concerning the Chinese Eastern Railway." He rebuffed Arita's interjection that the promise had been made before the formation of Manchukuo, and declared that the influence of the Japanese government in Manchuria and its responsibility for Manchurian affairs could not be denied.[8]

As the Kwantung Army had overrun Manchuria, dozens of Soviet railway officials and employees had been arrested. When one of them, a man by the name of Vasil'ev, had died in a Harbin jail in the summer of 1932, Consul General Slavutskii had written to Shih Lü-pen, the Harbin representative of the Manchukuoan Foreign Office, to inquire about the cause of death, but had received no reply. In January 1933 the suicide of Engineer A. F. Voronin, who along with some sixty countrymen had been imprisoned and apparently mistreated for the past nine months at Hsinking (formerly Changchun), prompted Slavutskii to send a strong letter to Shih demanding an investigation of the incident and a reply to his query about Vasil'ev's demise.[9]

Shih responded in a letter, dated January 25, that

---

[8] "Chetverka" to Foreign Commissariat, July 1, 1932, "Immediately," DVP, XV, 394–95; Troianovskii's record of his conversation with Arita, July 15, 1932, DVP, XV, 406–408.

[9] Slavutskii to Shih, January 7, 1933, DVP, XVI, 21–23.

Vasil'ev had died of typhoid and that Voronin's suicide had not been the fault of the Manchukuoan authorities. He added verbally that the charges of the mistreatment of the Soviet prisoners were false.[10]

But Slavutskii had appended medical evidence of the maltreatment of Vasil'ev and Voronin to his letters of June 19 and January 7. In a letter, dated February 13, he expressed "deep astonishment" that the Manchukuoan authorities should have ignored these documents. He charged that the majority of the prisoners were kept in irons and deprived of the most elementary sanitary conditions and medical help. He catalogued not only their illnesses, but the tortures to which they were subjected by White Russian inquisitors, notably Martynov, and called for a speedy end to this unjust affair.[11]

As fighting and banditry had spread in Manchuria, the Soviets had withdrawn some of the locomotives and rolling stock to Soviet territory. While the *Japan Weekly Chronicle* recognized that it was not in the interest of the USSR, which shared in the profits of the line, to minimize traffic and that the move "may well have been precautionary, since the line has received less protection from the Manchukuo government than it received in the 'feudal' times of the Mukden Marshals,"[12] the Manchukuoan authorities complained bitterly and in order to prevent any further removal of engines and rolling stock ordered a halt to all freight traffic between the CER and the Transbaikal Railway.

The order was communicated by the Manchukuoan border police to the stationmaster of Man'chzhuriia

[10] DVP, XVI, 802, note 3.
[11] Slavutskii to Shih, February 13, 1933, DVP, XI, 93–95.
[12] *Japan Weekly Chronicle,* hereafter cited as JWC, April 20, 1933, p. 526.

Station on April 7, 1933, and by President Li Shao-keng to Vice President Kuznetsov, on the eighth.[13]

The railway police began enforcing the prohibition on April 9, and on the afternoon of the tenth the representative of the Ministry of Transportation of Manchukuo and the chief of the local railway police demanded of the stationmaster at Manchuli that the rolling stock, which they claimed belonged to the CER, be returned from the Transbaikal Railway. When the stationmaster refused, the railway police itself moved 166 cars, including 21 laden with freight, onto the CER tracks, then drove spikes into the switches so that the Russians could not attempt to return them.[14] Kuznetsov vainly protested to Li in a letter, dated April 10, that these "coercive actions" were in direct violation of the contract for the construction and operation of the CER of 1896, of the statutes of the CER of the same year, and of the Peking and Mukden agreements of 1924.[15]

On April 12 Li demanded in a letter to Kuznetsov (as did the diplomatic representative in Harbin in a note to the Soviet consul general) that the Soviets return within one month 83 locomotives, 194 passenger cars, and 3,200 freight cars, allegedly removed by them.[16] In another letter on April 18 Li informed Kuznetsov that the switches connecting the Chinese Eastern and Transbaikal Railways had been closed by order of the Ministry of Transportation in order to protect the property of the CER and halt direct communication without the reloading of goods. International trains traveling between Europe and Asia would be allowed

[13] DVP, XVI, 829–30, note 107; *Izvestiia,* April 24, 1933.
[14] DVP, XVI, 830, note 108.
[15] DVP, XVI, 829–30, note 107; *Izvestiia,* April 24, 1933.
[16] *Izvestiia,* April 14, 16 and 24, 1933; JWC, May 11, 1933.

to continue unhindered. "The Soviets seem to forget," Li asserted according to a press summary, "that the CER being a purely commercial enterprise, it is liable to all the obligations under the sovereignty of Manchukuo."[17]

In retaliation for the severance of traffic between Manchuria and the USSR, the Soviets obstructed the passage of a Japanese military freight train from Manchuli to the Hailar line and hindered the advance of an east-bound international train.[18]

Japanese gendarmes of the frontier detachment at Pogranichnaia Station (Suifenho) in turn detained a train for Vladivostok and uncoupled 4 empty freight cars and 18 empty tank cars belonging to the Ussuri Railway, claiming that there was no written sanction for the through-transit of railway cars from the Maritime Province into Manchuria and vice-versa.[19] They also attempted to prevent the departure of two locomotives and fired upon another locomotive belonging to the Ussuri Railway depot as it set out from Pogranichnaia to Grodekovo.[20] Meanwhile Japanese troops occupied the office of the transit wharf at Harbin, raised the Japanese flag over the building, and posted a guard.[21]

On April 8 Karakhan had complained to Counselor Sako that some Japanese circles were seeking to impair the economic interests of his country on the railway

---

[17] *Izvestiia*, April 24, 1933; JWC, May 4, 1933, p. 602.

[18] JWC, April 20, 1933, pp. 533–34; May 4, 1933, p. 602.

[19] Garstin to Lampson, No. 39, Harbin, April 11, 1933, FO 371/17134. The objection was to through-transit. When Slavutskii demanded on April 24 that cargo destined for the USSR be released, Li responded on May 9 that it was not being detained, merely held for transshipment. Transshipment was begun at Man'chzhuriia Station on May 13. (Karakhan to Slavutskii, April 21, 1933, DVP, XVI, 256; DVP, XVI, 829, note 104.)

[20] JWC, May 4, 1933, p. 613.

[21] *Izvestiia*, April 18, 1933; DVP, XVI, 241–43; JWC, April 27, 1933.

and had declared that "the official representatives of Japan in Manchuria have forgotten or do not know the assurances which the Japanese government made to the USSR."[22] As the situation continued to deteriorate, he summoned Ambassador Ota to his office and in a lengthy declaration on April 16 reminded the Japanese government that it had given repeated assurances at the very outset of the Sino-Japanese conflict and thereafter, both through the Japanese ambassador in Moscow and through the Soviet ambassador in Tokyo, that Soviet rights and interests in general and on the CER in particular would not be violated and that the Japanese military command as well as the Japanese officials in Manchuria had orders to that effect, so that it was clear that "the Japanese government assumed responsibility for everything that might violate the rights and interests of the USSR." Reciting the recent actions of the Manchukuoan authorities and of the Japanese advisers, officials and troops—nonpayment for troop transportation, severance of communication between the CER and the Transbaikal and European railways, seizure of the railway wharf, the mass arrest of Soviet citizens, and the demand for the return of the locomotives and rolling stock—Karakhan accused them of deliberately creating "artificial conflicts" to worsen the situation on the CER.

The eastern line of the CER, he wrote, was in a state of complete disarray as the result of systematic bandit raids on trains and railway facilities, during which Soviet citizens were kidnaped or murdered. He alleged that although the Japanese government, in asking for permission to transport Japanese troops to the eastern line of the CER, had pledged to restore and

[22] Kutakov, *Istoriia*, 125–26.

maintain order, "the situation on the railway was never as grave at the worst times as it is now." The issue of the locomotives was artificial, for the locomotives were Russian and had never belonged to the CER. "Neither the CER, which is the property of the USSR, nor Manchukuo, and least of all the Japanese, can have any claims on these locomotives." As for the railway cars, there had always been an exchange of cars between the CER and the Soviet railways so that it was natural for some CER rolling stock to be in the Soviet Union. He asserted that there was a larger number of cars belonging to Soviet railways in Manchuria. Occasional delays in the return of cars from the USSR had been due to the fact that the CER had for many months been cut off from the Soviet Union both at the eastern and western ends as the result of the hostilities between Chinese and Japanese-Manchukuoan forces.

Karakhan noted that many of the Soviet citizens who had been arrested had been under detention now for over a year without having been brought to trial and were being mistreated and tortured by Japanese gendarmes and officials in the employ of Manchukuo. The Soviet government was compelled, Karakhan declared, "to remind the Japanese government of the assurances that it had given that the interests of the USSR would not be violated and to insist on the adoption of measures which will effectively preserve the rights and interests of the Soviet Union from any encroachment or challenge."[23]

In refutation of the charges levied by Manchukuo and Japan that the USSR had wrongfully removed roll-

---

[23] *Izvestiia*, April 18, 1933; DVP, XVI, 241–43. The translation given in the JWC of April 27, 1933, is marred by a number of mistakes and omissions.

ing stock belonging to the CER, Karakhan handed to Ota an *aide mémoire*,[24] documenting the contention that the 124 locomotives, series "E" (decapod), had been purchased by the Russian government in the United States for the railways in Russia and had been detained on the CER during the Allied Intervention. The *aide mémoire* reiterated that there were if not more, at least as many, Soviet railway cars on the CER as there were CER cars in the Soviet Union, but it promised that a careful check on documents and cars would be made.[25]

On April 20 Kuznetsov replied to Li's letters of April 12 and 18. Noting that his protest of April 10 had remained unanswered, he declared that Li's contention that the CER was a joint enterprise of two states mixed up the question of ownership and administration. "As you know," he wrote, "the CER is the property of the USSR and is merely administered jointly." The position of the Soviet government concerning the rolling stock had been made clear, he noted, in Karakhan's *aide mémoire* to Ota and had been restated in a letter by Slavutskii, dated April 18. He reiterated that the

[24] Although the TASS dispatch, published in *Izvestiia* on April 18, 1933, bears the heading "*Aide mémoire* handed on 15 April of this year by Comrade Karakhan to the Japanese ambassador," an account of the declaration made by Karakhan to Ota on April 16, published on the same page of *Izvestiia*, states that the *aide mémoire* was handed over at the same time. This seems to be correct, because the *aide mémoire* is published in DVP after the declaration of the sixteenth, bearing the same date. (DVP, XVI, 241–46.)

[25] *Izvestiia*, April 18, 1933. The version of the *aide memoire* given in the JWC of April 27 is inaccurate and incomplete. While sympathizing with Soviet complaints of Japanese and Manchukuoan interference with the normal operations of the CER, the JWC did not credit the contention that the locomotives belonged to Russia and had been detained in Manchuria during the Siberian Intervention; "the statement . . . does not sound satisfactory in default of any reason being given as to why they should not have been forwarded into Soviet Russia during the decade when this might have been accomplished." "According to all accounts," the paper observed, " the Soviet has from time to time been in great difficulties for locomotives, and it would hardly have failed to take over its own property from Manchuria before this." (JWC, April 27, 1933, p. 562.)

halting of traffic was a violation of the Peking and Mukden agreements and called on Li to prevail upon the authorities at Manchuli to restore the normal operation of the railway in the interest of both sides.[26]

Li replied in two letters, dated April 20 and 22. He accused the Soviet manager of arbitrary, illegal action in the removal of the rolling stock and questioning the applicability of the contract and statutes of 1896 and even the continued effectiveness of the Treaty of Mukden denied that the CER belonged to the USSR.[27]

Kuznetsov fired back on April 28 that Soviet ownership of the railway had never been questioned by anybody and constituted an "indisputable fact." "Your assertion," he wrote Li, "can be understood only as a direct attempt to violate the existing treaties and first of all the Peking and Mukden treaties with the USSR, concluded in 1924." Reviewing the provisions of the agreements, Kuznetsov asked: "If the USSR, in your opinion, is not the owner of the railway, how could the Chinese side agree to redeem the railway from the USSR?" Asserting that the conflicts and misunderstandings that had arisen on the CER became understandable in the light of the "aggressive aspirations" of the Manchurian side to scuttle the treaties, he warned that by their actions the Manchurian authorities were undermining the international status, on which the joint administration of the railway rested. He reiterated the demand, made in his letters of April 10 and 20, that normal communication

[26] *Izvestiia*, April 24, 1933; Strang to Foreign Office, No. 377 (R), Moscow, May 2, 1933, FO 371/17133–876.

[27] "The Peking and Mukden treaties have been so thoroughly honoured in the breach it is really a moot point whether they are worth referring to now!" a British official remarked upon reading a summary of Kuznetsov's letter of April 20. (FO 371/17133–876)

be restored and the Peking and Mukden treaties be observed, reminding him that the government of Manchukuo had affirmed their obligatory force in a note to the Soviet government on March 12, 1932.[28]

The Manchukuoan authorities publicly dismissed Kuznetsov's stance as "unduly dogmatic." The Mukden and Peking treaties, they felt, had been concluded between the Soviet Union and the old Manchurian regime. The Soviet Union must renegotiate them with Manchukuo, revising provisions that were out of date. Had the Soviet government itself not repudiated unilaterally treaties and agreements when it had come to power?[29]

The Manchukuoan reply to Kuznetsov's protest, transmitted by Morita Nariyuki, director of the Railway Bureau of the Ministry of Communications, on May 5, sought to turn the tables on the USSR and in a review of the history of the management of the CER accused the Soviet side of a number of illegal acts.[30]

With the formation of Manchukuo the once profitable CER had become a losing venture. As the general manager of the railway detailed in a report to the board of directors on May 7, since the beginning of 1932 Manchurian bandits and occasionally mutinous railway guards had killed 56 employees, wounded and disabled 825, and kidnapped 593.[31] They had robbed another 1,000 employees and had damaged or destroyed 50 locomotives, 958 passenger cars, 855 freight cars, and 124 buildings. They had torn up the tracks in 53 places

[28] *Izvestiia,* May 1, 1933.
[29] JWC, May 11, 1933, p. 642.
[30] JWC, May 11, 1933, p. 643.
[31] Most of the prisoners were eventually released, but in such bad physical shape that they were unfit for duty for a considerable period of time.

and had cut communication over 775 times.[32] The railway's losses were multiplied by the resulting spoilage of cargo and by the precautionary measures that had to be adopted—trains had to proceed in daylight, at slower speed, at unscheduled times, and under heavy guard.[33]

The attitude shown by Manchukuoan and Japanese officials convinced the Soviet leaders that Japan would not rest satisfied until she had gained control over the CER, whose management by the USSR was a thorn in the flesh of the Kwantung Army. As it became clear that the League of Nations would not reverse the establishment of Manchukuo and that the CER would constitute for the Soviet Union not only a financial liability, but an increasingly dangerous source of friction with Japan, the Soviet government decided to go ahead with the contemplated sale of the railway.

As Karakhan explained in a letter:

> There are in Japan two tendencies in regard to us. One is the militant one, represented by [General] Araki [Sadao] and a significant part of the military, which is for war with us, which prepares war, which therefore does not want to conclude a [nonaggression] pact, which seeks any causes for conflict, sharpening and inflating any sort of misunderstandings that arise between us in Manchuria, and most probably, sharpening and inflating the conflicts, wishes to enter into them and, perhaps, without the ruling circles fully realizing it, get into an

---

[32] One is reminded of the conditions which led to the Russian occupation of Manchuria in 1900. See Lensen, *The Russo-Chinese War.*

[33] *Izvestiia,* May 12, 1933; Kutakov, *Istoriia,* 124–26. Rudyi complained that neither the police nor the railway guards dared to oppose the *hunghutze* (Manchurian bandits), who learned about the movement of trains and about protective measures by tapping the telegraph lines. The losses did not include the illegal occupation of over 100,000 square meters of railway buildings by Manchukuoan and Japanese officials, alleged to have taken place between 1930 and 1934. (Prosecution document 2146, IMTFE, "Proceedings," 7743.)

armed conflict with us and in such a way present Japan as a whole with a *fait accompli*. The other line is the line of peace with us, represented by part of the government and apparently by [Premier] Saito [Makoto] himself and by a number of influential industrial and financial circles, navy ministry circles, and very likely by a significant part of the diplomatic representatives. The struggle between the two tendencies is waged with alternate success now for one, now for the other line, which is tangibly reflected in the measures and actions of the Japanese authorities in Manchuria. Our proposal concerning the sale of the CER knocks the advocates of war from their position.

While the Soviet government regarded its offer to sell the CER as "a factor which impedes the realization of the militant plans of the Japanese military," it realized that there was the danger that some Japanese would interpret this as a sign of weakness on the part of the USSR and become more intractable on other issues. It was necessary, Karakhan warned, to make it absolutely clear to the Japanese that "the CER and questions connected with Manchuria, i. e. problems outside our territory, were one thing, their claims concerning questions inside the territory of the USSR, another thing."[34]

Soviet willingness to sell the CER, after having fought over its possession in 1929, puzzled many observers. Explanations ranged from the assertion that it was a humiliating confession of weakness[35] to speculation that it was a scheme on the part of Stalin to acerbate Japanese-American antagonism. Some even thought that the Soviets planned to collect the purchase price

[34] Karakhan to Konstantin Iuren'ev, May 17, 1933, DVP, XVI, 297–99.
[35] Strang to Foreign Office, No. 399, Moscow, May 13, 1933, FO 371/17133–876.

and then take the railway by force.[36] The Japanese army, evaluating the question from a strategic point of view, concluded that the USSR was willing to sell the railway because she realized that she would not be able to defend it in the event of war with Japan.[37] One of the more astute observations was made by the *Japan Weekly Chronicle* when it pointed out that the situation of the CER had changed with the creation of Manchukuo not only in that the Japanese could exert greater military pressure than China, but that the Japanese could bring to the railway more efficient management than could the Chinese.[38] While this made the Japanese more eager to obtain direct control of the railway, it made the Russians less apprehensive in some respects about selling the railway, whose services they would continue to use.

On March 18, 1932, the Japanese industrialist Yamamoto Jotaro, who was president of the South Manchurian Railway Company, had suggested to Troianovskii the amalgamation of the two railways into one corporation, in which Japanese, Manchukuoan and Soviet representatives would participate as share holders.[39] On April 15 Troianovskii had proposed to Yoshizawa unofficial, secret talks with private persons concerning the solution of Soviet-Japanese problems in general and of the CER question in particular. In mid-May he had actually begun a series of conferences with Fujiwara Ginjiro, president of the gigantic Oji Paper Manufacturing Company, with whom he was

---

[36] Gilbert, 55–57; G. Z. Bessedovsky, *Revelations of a Soviet Diplomat*, 176; "Documents Relating to the Negotiations Between Japan and the USSR Concerning Transfer of the Manchurian Railway," January 1934, Japanese Archives, reel WT 42, IPS document 1642, p. 68.
[37] Gilbert, 59 and 296.
[38] JWC, May 11, 1933, p. 269.
[39] DVP, XV, 790–91, note 229.

personally acquainted.[40] But the question of the out-right sale of the CER to Manchukuo seems to have been raised first by Hirota during a meeting with Karakhan on August 29, 1932. Stating that he knew about the Sino-Soviet negotiations on the subject, Hirota expressed the presumption that they could be continued with Manchukuo. He declared that one must, for the sake of lasting peace in the Far East, solve those questions which demanded solution and asked whether the USSR would not sell the CER to Japan.[41] Karakhan replied on September 6 of that year that the most influential members of the Soviet government regarded the sale of the railway as possible in principle.[42]

The conversations between Troianovskii and Fuji-wara foundered on the question of the rate of exchange. While Troianovskii gave 250 million yen as his personal estimate of the CER's value,[43] Fujiwara said that the Japanese did not know what amount to offer in view of the fall in the exchange rate of the yen.[44]

On April 24, 1933, Ota told Karakhan that the CER question required a political solution.[45] Karakhan responded that the USSR would be willing to sell the railway to Japan.[46]

---

[40] During his first meeting with Troianovskii, Fujiwara said that he met with him at the suggestion of the minister of war; subsequently he asserted that the military were not interested in the question, but on October 14 he stated that the military had definitely decided to begin the negotiations for the sale of the CER through him. Foreign Minister Uchida suggested to Troianovskii on November 19 that Fujiwara was the man with whom the sale of the CER should be negotiated. (*Nisso kosho-shi*, 294–95; Kutakov, *Istoriia*, 126–27.)

[41] DVP, XV, 794, note 245.

[42] Karakhan's record of his conversation with Hirota, September 6, 1932, DVP, XV, 510–11.

[43] *Nisso kosho-shi*, 294–95.

[44] DVP, XV, 790–91, note 229.

[45] DVP, XVI, 831–32, note 114.

[46] *Nisso kosho-shi*, 294–95; *Hirota Koki*, 139.

On May 2 Litvinov made an oral protest to Ota against Japanese incitement of the Manchurian authorities against the USSR. He asserted that the Soviet government had "authentic and absolutely reliable" documentary evidence that Consul General Morishima had recommended the arrest of top Soviet CER officials. Litvinov agreed that the CER question required a "political solution." Noting that in mentioning a political solution Ota must have meant the sale of the railway, Litvinov reiterated that the Soviet government was prepared to sell the railway in order to remove the source of friction and in order to forestall possible hostilities between their countries. He proposed that negotiations be begun on the subject.[47]

Ota asserted that the idea of a political solution of the CER question had not been initiated by him, but by Karakhan. He eventually agreed, however, that it was inconsequential who had brought the matter up first. There was a conflict on the CER which must be settled.

In response to Litvinov's protest, Ota stated that the situation, not the policy of his government, had changed. The assurances of the Japanese government referred to the external situation of the CER. The current dispute between the USSR and Manchukuo, on the other hand, concerned the internal situation of the CER. Remarking that he had no detailed information

[47] DVP, XVI, 831–32, note 114; *Nisso kosho-shi*, 294–95; Kutakov, *Istoriia*, 126–27. According to Japanese sources the desire to improve relations with Japan was only one of the reasons given by Litvinov for Soviet willingness to part with the railway. He also stated allegedly that the USSR had lost interest in the management of the CER because of her inability to operate it on a paying basis. According to Japanese sources Litvinov made it clear that the Soviet asking price was negotiable and held out the possibility of leasing the railway. He remarked that the sale of the railway to Manchukuo would be interpreted by some as Soviet recognition of the state of Manchukuo but that his government was prepared to sell the railway in spite of this either to Japan or to Manchukuo; she was under no constraint by the League of Nations. (*Nisso kosho-shi*, 295)

about the activities either of the Japanese advisers or of Morishima, he asserted that the deeds of the former did not concern Japan, as they were in the employ of Manchukuo. Morishima's actions, if the allegations were true, would be contrary to the instructions issued both by the Foreign Office and the military authorities to their officials in Manchukuo not to give advice in violation of international law and of the interests of third powers. He reiterated that the Japanese government "heartily and sincerely respects the mutual relations [with the USSR] and wishes to improve them."

Litvinov warned Ota that the division of disputes into those that concerned Japan and those that concerned Manchukuo fooled no one; Ota knew what was being said in Geneva and elsewhere of the role of the Manchukuoan government. "If we seek a political solution of the question, we must also reason politically and not formalistically," Litvinov stated and expressed hope that the Japanese government would not repeat its formalistic references to the exclusive competence of Manchukuo to the problems he had raised.[48]

When Konstantin Iuren'ev, who had succeeded Troianovskii as the Soviet ambassador in March, elaborated in mid-May on his country's willingness to sell or lease the CER to Japan or Manchukuo, Foreign Minister Uchida Kosai replied that Japan had not yet come to a decision on this matter, but that she would reply as soon as a policy had been formulated.[49]

[48] Litvinov's record of his conversation with Ota, May 2, 1933, DVP, XVI, 279–81.
[49] JWC, May 18, 1933, p. 684. According to French sources Iuren'ev met with Uchida on May 14. News of Soviet willingness to sell the CER to Manchukuo scuttled Sino-Soviet talks concerning a nonaggression pact and a treaty of commerce. (Minister Wilden to Foreign Minister Paul-Boncour, telegram No. 187, Peking, May 17, 1933, Document Diplomatiḋues Français [hereafter cited as DDF]. First Series, vol. 1, p. 285.)

On May 23 the Japanese cabinet decided to purchase the CER if it could be done at an acceptable price, because in Soviet hands it was a channel for Communist propaganda as well as an artery of economic influence. Although purchase of the railway by Japan directly would have strengthened the latter's hold over northern Manchuria, the cabinet decided to let Manchukuo acquire the railway to bolster her apparent independence, with Japan acting ostensibly as go-between in the negotiations.[50]

In its long-awaited reply to Karakhan's declaration of April 16, transmitted by Ota on May 26, the Japanese government insisted that it had remained true to its pledges. "Both the Japanese army and the Japanese authorities in Manchuria, despite various difficulties in clearing the North Manchurian districts of bandits, have taken all possible care not to damage the interests of the CER." In spite of Litvinov's admonitions to Ota, the Japanese government contended that it had no relation whatsoever to cases which belonged "entirely within the jurisdiction of the government of Manchukuo" and rejected all responsibility for the actions of Japanese advisers and officials on the ground that they had entered the employ of Manchukuo "of their own volition" and were acting "completely under the instructions and control of the government of Manchukuo." The Japanese government wrote that the occupation of the transit wharf in Harbin had been the result of a minor dispute unrelated to the CER and that the question of payment for the transportation of Japanese troops was under negotiation, with agreement in sight. It pointed out that Japanese and Manchukuoan citizens had been among the victims

---

[50] *Nisso kosho-shi*, 296; *Hirota Koki*, 139.

of the bandit raids in what it called a "temporary situation." The government denied that the question of the locomotives had been artificially created by the Japanese authorities and accused the Soviet side of "artificially attributing facts." It asserted that traffic had been restored on the western line of the CER in December and on the eastern line in January; the failure to return the railway cars thus could not be attributed to the blocking of the line. The Japanese government alleged that the many Soviet citizens who had been arrested in April and May 1932 had been involved in incidents "directly or indirectly" aimed at the Japanese army, such as the wrecking of troop trains or the demolition of bridges, and that the cooperation of Japanese gendarmes with the Manchukuoan authorities in their apprehension and occasionally in their interrogation had been "completely natural" under the circumstances. It denied that there had been a single instance when Japanese gendarmes had subjected the Soviet prisoners to torture. The Japanese government declared that disputes concerning the exploitation of the CER must be settled directly between Soviet and Manchukuoan officials. It admitted its own serious interest in the matter, in view of Japan's military pact with Manchukuo and the fact that "the maintenance of peaceful relations between the USSR and Manchukuo is the most important foundation for general peace in the Far East."[51]

Karakhan told Ota on this occasion that it was known that there had been a meeting in the Japanese embassy in Hsinking at which it had been decided to interrupt communication between the Ussuri Railway and the CER at the end of May. He called upon the Japanese

---

[51] *Izvestiia*, June 1, 1933; *Moscow Daily News*, June 3, 1933.

government to take urgent steps to forestall what was evidently an attempt to acerbate the situation and impede the negotiations that were taking place between the two governments for the purpose of removing conflicts and misunderstandings.

Ota expressed doubt about the veracity of Karakhan's information but agreed to communicate the matter to his government. He said that he hoped that the Soviet Union would soon receive an answer to its offer to sell the CER.[52]

On May 29 Ota conveyed the Japanese reply. The imperial government wrote that it had given careful consideration to Litvinov's "sincere offer" to sell the railway and that it was pleased that the proposal had been made out of a desire to maintain and strengthen friendly relations with Japan. It sought to minimize the value of the CER by asserting that the economic significance of the railway had decreased greatly since the establishment of Manchukuo due to the construction of competing lines and pretended to favor a basic solution of the CER question merely in the "general interests of peace in the Far East." The Japanese government communicated that it had exchanged views with Manchukuo, the party most directly interested in the CER, and that Manchukuo proposed to redeem the railway if acceptable conditions could be negotiated. "The Imperial Government has no objections to it."

Japan advised the USSR to take the matter up directly with Manchukuo, but expressed willingness to act as intermediary. If the Soviet Union would accept Tokyo as the meeting place, Manchukuo was prepared to start negotiations at once. The Japanese government warned, however, that while negotiations

[52] Karakhan to Iuren'ev, May 27, 1933, DVP, XVI, 315–16.

could thus be initiated, their rupture would have harmful consequences for the relations between the three countries. In order to arrive at a radical solution of the problem, as suggested by the Soviet government, it was absolutely essential, therefore, to settle the matter "from beginning to end politically, from the point of view of the general state of affairs" and not get bogged down in questions of a technical character.[53]

When the government of Manchukuo the next day, on May 30, accused the Soviet railway authorities of continuing to remove rolling stock into Russian territory in violation of the CER-Ussuri Railway agreement and announced the suspension of traffic between the two lines at Pogranichnaia the following afternoon "in order to effect by forcible means what protests and other diplomatic means have failed to achieve," Ambassador Iuren'ev immediately hastened to Vice Minister of Foreign Affairs Shigemitsu Mamoru to ask for Japan's good offices in settling the dispute amicably. Though Shigemitsu declared that this was a local issue in which Japan was not concerned, he agreed to assist in the amicable solution of the conflict, remarking at the same time that the Soviet government should consider the return of the locomotives.

Direct service was nonetheless suspended on May 31. While Li Shao-keng charged that Soviet removal of the rolling stock had obstructed communication in Manchuria and thus had constituted a violation of the sovereignty of Manchukuo, Kuznetsov protested to Li on June 1 that the "blockade" amounted to unilateral abrogation by Manchukuo of the Soviet-Manchukuoan transit agreement. On June 2 the Soviet consul general in Harbin made a similar verbal protest

---

[53] *Izvestiia*, June 4, 1933. See also *Nisso kosho-shi*, 296–97 and JWC, June 15, 1933, p. 8.

at the Harbin office of the Manchukuoan Foreign Ministry to Sugihara, who was in charge in the absence of Shih Lü-pen, the Manchukuoan representative to Harbin.[54]

On May 31 Deputy Commissar of Foreign Affairs Sokol'nikov communicated to Ambassador Ota the Soviet answer to the Japanese reply of May 26.[55] Taking note of the Japanese government's affirmation of its former assurances that it would respect the rights and interests of the USSR in North Manchuria and would not permit the violation of the interests of the USSR on the CER as the result of its actions in Manchuria, the Soviet government asserted that these assurances precluded the possibility of the Japanese government waiving its responsibility for the violation of Soviet interests in Manchuria by the Manchurian authorities under the formal pretext that these matters were solely within the jurisdiction of Manchukuo. It expressed regret that the Japanese government had not commented on the locomotive dispute. The Manchukuoan authorities, it alleged, had raised the "utterly illegal and unfounded claims" with the direct collaboration and support of Japanese officials and local Japanese authorities as the pretext for violent, unilateral and unlawful actions injurious to the USSR. The Soviet Union had furnished the Japanese government with exhaustive documentary evidence of her ownership of the locomotives. A correct explanation of the question by the Japanese government to the Manchurian and local Japanese authorities would have put a stop to the attempts to injure the undisputable Soviet interests and would have contributed to the establishment of normal conditions on the railway.

[54] JWC, June 8, 1933, pp. 780–81.
[55] Iuren'ev had talked to Shigemitsu about the note on May 30. (JWC, June 8, 1933, pp. 780–81.)

The Soviet government rejected the explanations given by Japan for the occupation of the transit wharf, the delay in payments for the transportation of Japanese troops, the inadequate protection of the eastern line of the CER, and the mass arrests and torture of Soviet citizens. It called upon the Japanese government to investigate the facts more thoroughly and to halt all actions aimed at injuring the interests of the USSR. Asserting that by its readiness to enter into negotiations concerning the sale of the CER, it had clearly shown its will to do away with the source of conflicts which were impairing the good-neighborly relations between their countries, the Soviet government declared that it expected the Japanese government to do everything in its power to prevent any unilateral and unlawful actions on the part of Manchurian and local Japanese officials regarding the CER in violation of the Peking and Mukden agreements.[56]

On June 3 Sokol'nikov handed Ota a note accepting Japanese mediation in the Soviet-Manchukuoan railway negotiations. Although the Manchurian officials had changed the name of the CER to the North Manchurian Railway (NMR) on June 1 and although the Japanese adopted this appellation, Sokol'nikov and his colleagues continued to use the old name interchangeably.[57] The Soviet government consented that the talks be held in Tokyo and proposed that they be opened on June 25.[58]

The following day, on June 4, Sokol'nikov transmitted to Ota a less pleasant communication—a protest against the forcible disruption of direct communication

[56] *Izvestiia*, June 1, 1933; *Moscow Daily News*, June 3, 1933. The translation of the statement in the JWC of June 8, 1933, is inaccurate and incomplete.

[57] *Nisso kosho-shi*, 297; JWC, June 8, 1933, p. 781; *Izvestiia*, October 9, 1933. To minimize confusion, the old name has been retained in this book except occasionally in direct quotations.

[58] *Izvestiia*, June 4, 1933.

between the CER and the Ussuri Railway. The Soviet note related that a detachment of Manchukuoan police headed by Sato, a Japanese official of the Ministry of Communications of Manchukuo, had appeared at Pogranichnaia and had handed to the stationmaster a letter, signed by Sato and two police officials (one a Manchurian and one a White Russian), ordering him to halt freight traffic. When the stationmaster had returned the letter as unlawful, in that all questions connected with the operation of the railway must be addressed to its administration, the police had arrested him and a number of employees and had forced the workers to block six lines by putting ties across the tracks. On the main line, connecting Pogranichnaia with Grodekovo, a barrier had been erected, which, according to Sato, would be raised only to let through passenger trains.

Reminding the Japanese government that it had informed it on May 26 that such violation of existing treaties and of the special agreement between the CER and the Ussuri Railway had been planned in the Japanese consulate in Hsinking, the Soviet government declared that it had "every reason to expect" that the Japanese government would have prevented the incident. In asking Ota to transmit the protest to his government, Sokol'nikov voiced the hope "that the Japanese government, which shows an interest in the preservation of order and tranquility in Manchuria and has expressed readiness to mediate in the matter of a basic solution of the CER question, will take the necessary measures to restore the situation that has been disturbed."[59]

[59] *Izvestiia*, June 5, 1933. The interruption of freight traffic at Pogranichnaia Station affected not only Soviet interests. The Consular Corps at a meeting in Harbin on July 10 delegated the American, French and English consuls to make a joint representation to Li to permit the passage of the cargo that had been piling up on both sides. (*Izvestiia*, July 14, 1935.)

At a meeting with Uchida on June 6, Iuren'ev repeated the protest, but went on to discuss the sale of the CER and the establishment of a joint frontier committee.[60]

On June 7 agreement was reached at Hsinking on the formation of a Soviet-Manchukuoan commission to deal with railway disputes. The commission was to meet in Harbin, with Li Shao-keng, Morita, and Mori (chief of the North Manchuria Railway Section of the Ministry of Communications of Manchukuo) representing the Manchukuoan side, Kuznetsov and Rudyi, the Soviet side.[61]

On June 8 Ota conveyed the reply of his government to the Soviet note of June 3. It announced that Manchukuo had agreed to the Soviet proposal to begin negotiations on June 25 and requested that the Soviet government inform the Japanese government of the names of the delegates it would send as soon as they were selected.[62]

On June 14 Moscow cabled that Iuren'ev, Kuznetsov, and V. I. Kozlovskii (head of the Far Eastern Department of the Asian Bureau of the Foreign Commissariat) would represent the USSR in the railway talks.[63] Manchukuo appointed Ting Shih-yuan, her minister to Japan, and Ohashi Chuichi, vice minister of foreign affairs.[64] Kozlovskii and Kuznetsov arrived in Japan on June 23,[65] and the informal talks were begun in Tokyo on June 26.[66]

[60] DVP, XVI, 334.
[61] JWC, June 15, 1933, p. 825.
[62] DVP.XVI, 333–34; *Nisso kosho-shi*, 297.
[63] Strang to Foreign Office, No. 29, Moscow, June 14, 1933, FO 371/17134–858.
[64] JWC, June 29, 1933.
[65] *Ibid*.
[66] Preliminary discussions had been held in Harbin between Slavutskii and Ohashi on June 15, while Ting Chien-hsiu, Manchukuoan minister of communications, and a staff of experts had launched an on-the-spot investigation of the railway. (JWC, June 22, 1933, p. 856.)

8

The Tokyo Conference: First Phase

The delegates of the Soviet Union and Manchukuo were introduced to each other formally on the afternoon of June 26, 1933, at the official residence of Vice Minister of Foreign Affairs Shigemitsu. They were feted at a state dinner that evening in the official residence of Foreign Minister Uchida. Negotiations in the form of a full-dress diplomatic conference were begun the next day, on June 27, at Shigemitsu's residence.[1] Iuren'ev, Kozlovskii, and Kuznetsov spoke for the USSR. The Manchukuoan delegates Ohashi and Ting were joined by Shen Juei-lin who represented the president of the CER. Present also were two Japanese "observers" of the negotiations: Nishi Haruhiko, chief of the First Section of the Bureau of European and American Affairs of the Japanese Ministry for Foreign Affairs, and Lieutenant Colonel Suzuki of the War

---

[1] DVP, XVI, note 136. Kutakov, a dispatch from Snow, and the Heibonsha chronology *Kokushi dai-nempyo* also state that the conference was opened on June 26. Tanaka, the semiofficial history of the Japanese Foreign Office, the *Japan Times and Mail*, and *Hirota Koki* date the opening of the conference as the twenty-seventh. Apparently the formalities were begun on the twenty-sixth and the negotiations themselves on the twenty-seventh.

237

Office.[2] Togo Shigenori, director of the Bureau of European and American Affairs, attended the welcoming ceremonies.

Foreign Minister Uchida introduced the delegates, then made an opening speech in Japanese, which was translated into Russian and Chinese. Ting and Iuren'ev followed with addresses in their own tongues, duly translated into Japanese and Russian and into Japanese and Chinese respectively.[3]

Uchida reviewed the history of the CER and the background of the talks. Japan had agreed to play the go-between, he said, because there were no formal diplomatic relations between the USSR and Manchukuo and because the Soviet proposal for the sale of the railway had been addressed originally to her. Though Japan's intermediary role had essentially come to an end with the opening of the face-to-face talks between Soviet and Manchukuoan delegates in Tokyo, Japan would be glad to be of further assistance during the negotiations if the need arose.

Ting thanked Uchida for Japan's mediation. Describing the CER as a relic of tsarist policy, more significant as a source of dispute than of income, he expressed Manchukuo's willingness to purchase it if the terms were reasonable and "pertinent to the actualities of the situation."

Iuren'ev also thanked the Japanese government for its good offices in arranging the conference. It was, he said, because the Soviet government attached special importance to the furtherance of friendly relations with Japan that it had maintained an attitude of strict neutrality and noninterference in the Manchurian affair and had expressed its willingness to achieve a funda-

[2] Snow to Simon, No. 391, Chuzenji, July 7, 1933, FO 371/17134–858.
[3] JWC, June 29, 1933, p. 900; *Nisso kosho-shi*, 297–98.

mental settlement of the CER problem by selling the railway, for the latter had become a source of trouble between the USSR, Japan and Manchukuo, a situation that was being exploited by forces against peace. Iuren'ev declared that while the tsarist government had been guilty of aggressive and imperialist ends in building the railway on foreign territory, the Soviet government was innocent of such aims. The October Revolution had converted the CER from an instrument of imperialist aggression into a purely commercial enterprise, and the Peking and Mukden agreements had given to the owners of the territory through which the railway ran the right to share in the control of the railway and in the profits accruing from it. But the Soviet government, he told the Japanese and Manchukuoans in the same language that Karakhan and Ioffe had used in their negotiations with the Chinese, had to protect its material interests in the railway, which had been constructed with the hard-earned funds of the Russian people. The CER was of great international importance, linking Europe with Asia as well as North Manchuria and the southern districts of Manchuria and the ocean. Its deteriorated condition was due to the present state of affairs in Manchuria and was bound to improve as a matter of course with the development of Manchukuo. Declaring that the Soviet delegation was prepared to confer with the care and sincerity that a fundamental and effectual settlement of the CER question required, Iuren'ev expressed the hope that the Manchukuoan side would show similar sincerity and that the Japanese government would give positive and friendly assistance to bring the negotiations to a successful conclusion.[4]

[4] *Izvestiia*, June 28, 1933; JWC, July 6, 1933, p. 17. The JWC summary is more detailed than the abbreviated original published by *Izvestiia*.

The welcoming ceremonies completed, Uchida, Shigemitsu and Togo withdrew, leaving the Soviet and Manchukuoan delegates to grapple with the CER question in the presence of the Japanese advisers.[5]

It was at the third conference, on July 3, that the two sides presented their widely differing proposals.[6] A lengthy memorandum regarding "the basic principles for the redemption of the Chinese Eastern Railway by Manchukuo," handed by Iuren'ev to the Manchukuoan delegation, defined the object of the sale. For sale was "the CER with all properties belonging to it, including that property of the railway, which was at different times illegally and forcibly seized by the Mukden authorities," to wit:

　　a.　The railway line, the principal track of which is 1,726 kilometers long and which has a total length of 2,544.9 kilometers, including sidings, ballast and firewood track, with a telegraph line of 2,567 kilometers, telephone and water works.

　　b.　The locomotives and cars belonging to the railway.

　　c.　Civilian installations, consisting of track and passenger buildings, warehouses, living quarters, offices, military barracks, etc., with a total area of 1,199,762 square meters.

　　d.　Workshops and depots, including the chief Harbin workshops, the track service workshops, telegraph service workshops, and others.

　　e.　Electric power stations.

　　f.　The telephone station in Harbin.

　　g.　The river fleet, consisting of steamers and non-steam vessels, with the equipped transit wharf at Harbin.

[5] JWC, June 29, 1933, p. 900; *Nisso kosho-shi,* 297–98.
[6] *Nisso kosho-shi,* 297; *Izvestiia,* July 4, 1933.

h. Lands belonging to the railway.

i. Timber concessions.

j. Medical and veterinary-sanitary institutions.

k. Summer homes and sanitoriums.

l. Agricultural undertakings, arboreta, and greenhouses.

m. A saw-mill and drying oil works.

n. An aerated water factory.

o. A wool-washing plant.

p. A printing plant.

q. Water works at Harbin.

r. Automobile transport.

s. Various other buildings, structures, and equipment of the railway.

Specifically excluded from the sale were "various kinds of property of the USSR, not belonging to the CER, but retained on the railway in the years of the intervention or having remained on the railway in the course of the unfinished conventional exchange of cars." Such property, upon inventory by a special commission, was to be returned to the USSR.

The memorandum stressed that the CER, with all the properties appertaining to it, constituted a gigantic economic combine of great international as well as local importance, whose significance would increase with its transfer to Manchukuo. "There are no grounds," it argued, "for confusing the temporary deterioration in the financial position of the railway, caused by the particular conditions created of late which have disrupted its normal operations, with its real economic condition, significance and possibilities of development." From the beginning of the joint Soviet-Chinese management of the CER to 1930 inclusively, receipts had exceeded expenditures by a total of over

140 million gold rubles or by an average of over 20 million gold rubles a year. Even in 1932, when Manchuria had been in the throes of the worldwide depression and of the above-mentioned particular conditions, the railway had shown an excess of 11 million gold rubles in receipts over running expenses. That the CER was not sufficiently profitable for the Soviet government was due entirely to the fact that the railway had had to bear immense unproductive expenditures for the maintenance of police, military guards and governmental establishments and for the free transport of goods and passengers, expenditures which neither the Chinese nor the Manchurian administrators had allowed them to abolish or at least significantly curtail, even though they were alien to the operation of a railway or any other commercial enterprise. By freeing the railway of such unproductive expenses upon taking possession of it, Manchukuó could greatly increase its profitability.

Turning to the cost of redemption, the Soviet memorandum referred to paragraph 2 of article 1 of the Mukden Agreement, which stipulated that "the contracting parties shall determine the actual cost of the CER" in arriving at a "fair price." It asserted that the expenditures for the construction of the railway, the finishing of uncompleted sections, the purchase of rolling stock, the realization of the construction capital, and the payment of interest and amortization during the period of construction, as well as for work done prior to 1932 inclusive for the strengthening and improvement of the railway totalled 411,691,976 gold rubles. This figure did not include 178,579,618 gold rubles lent by the tsarist government to the CER to cover deficits and subsidize its activities during the first years of operation or the immense indebtedness of the railway to the Soviet government for interest accrued on the capital invested in the CER. The Soviet government did not ask for repayment of the actual expenditures. "Guided by the principle of fairness" and taking into account the depreciation of the railway's equipment and a certain decline in its value due to the construction of competing railways, it set the cost of the railway itself at 210 million gold rubles and asked for an additional 40 million gold rubles for the cost of the different properties of the CER, including an immense area of land and the rich timber concession. It thus wanted 250 million gold rubles for the CER and all its appurtenances. This was moderate and equitable indeed, it pointed out, considering the fact that in 1917 the Japanese government itself had been prepared to pay to the former Russian government 20 million gold yen for the small, 103 kilometer stretch of the southern line of the CER from Kuanch'engtzu to Laoshaokou, though it had neither the valuable buildings and undertakings nor the international and economic significance of the CER. At that rate of appraisal, the CER should cost 380 million gold yen or about 370 million gold rubles.

The memorandum stipulated that the CER would go to Manchukuo with all its assets and liabilities so that the Soviet government would not be held liable in the future for any claims against the CER.

As for the method of payment, the Soviet government was prepared to receive half of the above-mentioned sum, or 125 million gold rubles, in goods, delivered in four installments over a period of two years, Manchukuo to issue obligations for their payment, guaranteed by the Japanese State Bank or accepted by a consortium of Japanese banks. One quarter of the monetary half of the payment was to be made immediately in cash; the remainder could be met in obligations of Manchukuo, guaranteed by the Japanese government, redeemable in three years with 4 percent annual interest added.

The memorandum stipulated that in order to safeguard the economic interests of the USSR a special agreement was to be signed at the same time as the general agreement for the sale of the CER providing for the following: unhindered Soviet transit on preferential conditions for goods and passengers between the CER and Soviet railways, with transit goods and luggage exempted from customs duties and all kinds of fees and taxes; direct traffic between Soviet railways and the CER and for the participation of the CER in the direct Europe-Asia traffic to Vladivostok; the allocation to the Ussuri Railway of a definite quota of freight arriving on the CER; and the application of most-favored-nation treatment in regard to tariffs and customs duties to Soviet goods imported on the CER. Another special agreement, signed on the same occasion, was to safeguard the interests of the Soviet employees of the CER by stipulating that they not be replaced at once, but gradually, in small numbers, in the course of not less than two years from Manchukuo's acquisition of the railway, so as to provide them with the possibility of finding work locally or depart for the USSR. When leaving or being discharged, they were to receive a full and immediate settlement in conformity with the regulations of the CER. Their rights to movable and real property in the region of the CER and their right to liquidate it and export it either in kind or monetary equivalent were to be guaranteed, and transportation was to be provided for them and their families and belongings to the chosen point of exit at the expense of the railway.[7]

The memorandum of the Manchukuoan side, entitled "Basic Conditions for a Treaty between Manchukuo and the USSR regarding the Cession of the Latter's Rights on the North Manchurian Railway (formerly the CER)," was much briefer. It offered 50 million yen for all rights possessed by the USSR in the railway and its subsidiary enterprises, the dates and method of payment to be determined in a separate document. A committee for the transfer of the railway was to be appointed by the Soviet and Manchurian governments within a month of the signing of the treaty, the transfer of the railway and its subsidiary enterprises and all other property belonging to the railway to be completed within three months of the signing of the treaty. The Soviet government was to be responsible for all claims by holders of shares and obligations and by other creditors of the railway dating back to the period prior to March 9, 1917, and for all debt obligations of the railway to any third party which arose after March 9, 1917, until the day the treaty came into force and similarly for all claims by third parties connected with the transfer of the railway. The Soviet government was to hand over to Manchukuo simultaneously with the transfer of the railway and its subsidiary enterprises, all the share certificates, bonds, and other documents pertaining to the loan obligations of the railway and all documents bearing on the railway and its enterprises.[8]

Although the Soviet memorandum had noted

[7] *Izvestiia*, July 8, 1933; DVP, XVI, 395–401; enclosure in Strang to Simon, No. 380, Moscow, July 11, 1933, FO 371/17134–858.

[8] *Izvestiia*, July 8, 1933; DVP, XVI, 401; JWC, July 13, 1933.

parenthetically that 1 gold ruble was equivalent to 1.04 gold yen, neither Manchukuo nor Japan calculated in gold yen. The 250 million gold rubles requested by the USSR amounted to 625 million paper yen at the prevailing rate of exchange, while the 50 million yen offered by Manchukuo came to only about 20 million gold rubles.[9]

When the enormous discrepancy in the figures presented by the two sides evoked aspersions in Japan and Manchukuo concerning Soviet sincerity, the *Japan Weekly Chronicle* pointed out that while the continuance of circumstances similar to those which had surrounded the railway for the past twenty-two months might soon make it worth even less than fifty million yen and might compel the Soviet Union to abandon it altogether, 250 million gold rubles constituted a low price if one considered both the actual cost of the railway and its potential value in a well-ordered and developing country. It was about half of what Russia had paid for it. The *Chronicle* remarked, "There is room, therefore, on both sides, to express doubts of the other's sincerity."[10]

Neither side discussed the memoranda at this conference. Time was needed to study them and debate was deferred until the fourth conference, scheduled for the afternoon of July 5. Agreement was reached and made public, however, on the procedure to be followed in regard to the publication of communiqués concerning negotiations. Immediately after each meeting, Ohashi and Iuren'ev were to confer on the gist of the communiqués and, upon securing the approval of their respective delegations, were to have them drawn up by their chief secretaries with consul-

[9] *Izvestiia,* August 18, 1934.
[10] JWC, July 13, 1933.

tation. "All the declarations and documents to be formally laid before the conference may be made public by the party concerned at its own discretion after communicating them to the other party, though it is desirable that there should be previous consultation between the parties as to their publication."[11]

On July 4 the Soviet embassy published the details of the Russian proposal. The action hit Tokyo like a bombshell because the Home Office had forbidden the mentioning of the terms of the sale or purchase. Though the Soviets were within the legal bounds of the agreement on the publication of documents, the Japanese felt that they had violated the spirit of the agreement. Unhappy as they were about the disclosures, they decided at a conference of Foreign Office and Home Office officials and the Manchukuoan delegates on the morning of July 5 that under the circumstances they might as well lift the ban and publish the Manchukuoan proposal as well.[12]

The *Japan Weekly Chronicle* remarked that the Japanese desire to keep the details of the talks secret was unrealistic. They were bound to come out, it wrote, "for there is some diplomacy that cannot be secret forever, and when, from the outset, one side expresses doubts of the sincerity of the other, the other is pretty sure to give reasons for showing that the suspicions were unjust."[13]

When the delegates reconvened on July 5 to discuss their respective proposals, it developed that the fantastic distance between the points from which they had begun their bargaining was increased by differences in assumption regarding the ownership of the CER.[14]

[11] *Ibid.*, p. 44.
[12] *Ibid.*, p. 45.
[13] *Ibid.*, p. 43.
[14] Snow to Simon, No. 391, Chuzenji, July 7, 1933, FO 371/17134–858.

The Soviets insisted that the railway belonged solely to them. They cited not only the Peking and Mukden agreements, but also the report of the technical subcommittee on the CER at the Washington Conference and the proceedings of that conference, which showed that Matsudaira Tsuneo, chief of the European and American Bureau of the Japanese Foreign Office, had told the Chinese delegation at the conference that Russian ownership of the railway was beyond dispute. They pointed out, furthermore, that in the preliminary talks leading to the opening of the current negotiations Japan had not once questioned Russian ownership of the railway.

The Manchukuoan side countered that none of the treaties pertaining to the CER spelled out exclusive Russian ownership of the railway and its properties. Even if original sole Russian ownership of the railway were conceded, it had come to an end with Soviet repudiation in 1917 of all secret treaties, including one which showed that the original justification for the construction of the railway had been to defend China against Japan, and with the Karakhan declarations of 1919 and 1920, which had offered to return the railway to China. Moreover, the railway was under joint Soviet-Chinese control, which proved, the Manchukuoan representatives argued, that exclusive Russian ownership was at most in name, not in fact. As for the contention that the Russian people had expended enormous resources on the railway, Manchukuo could not be expected to reimburse the Soviet Union for the large sums wasted by the tsarist government for strategic and political purposes in the pursuit of its aggressive Far Eastern policy.

The Manchukuoan side asserted that the value of

the railway was insignificant. It claimed that the rails were old and the rolling stock and stations delapidated and that conversion of the line to the standard gauge would be very costly. As for the railway land, most of it had been ceded to Russia by China without payment. The Manchukuoan side contended that it could build a new line, parallel to the CER, for about 130 million yen. Considering depreciation, the CER in its present delapidated state was worth only half of that, or 65 million yen. Since the Soviet Union had but 50 percent of the rights to the railway, her share would be half of that amount, or merely 32½ million yen. Inasmuch as Manchukuo wanted the USSR to assume full responsibility for all claims on the railway by third parties, however, she was willing to pay up to 50 million yen for the CER. The Manchukuoans depicted their offer as very generous, alleging that the Soviets should really surrender this relic of tsarist aggression without compensation.[15]

"The calculation of the price that Manchukuo is willing to pay for the Chinese Eastern Railway is delightful," the *Japan Weekly Chronicle* commented sarcastically, noting that Manchukuo had presumably reckoned on using the CER for tranporting the materials for the above-mentioned parallel line, thus greatly reducing the estimated cost of construction. Relating how Manchukuo had halved this amount and then had "halved the half," adding something "for decency's sake," yet considered that she had "done very generously," the paper reflected: "Of course, at the risk of incurring Russian enmity, it could sit tight and starve the Russians out, getting the line for nothing,

---

[15] JWC, July 13, 1933, pp. 43–44; *Nisso kosho-shi*, 299–300; Kutakov, *Istoriia*, 129.

so perhaps the offer is a generous one, though it may hardly be enough to buy Russia's good will as well as the railway."[16]

The Manchukuoan attitude—the questioning of sole Soviet ownership of the railway and the references to Russian aggression—had visibly upset the Soviets, for the question of ownership had a direct bearing on sale price, not only in determining whether the full amount or only half the amount of the agreed upon cost of the railway would be paid, but in arriving at the cost itself. For example, if part of the railway belonged to China or Manchuria, Manchukuo could challenge, as she did, Russian inclusion in the price of overdue charges for the maintenance and transportation of Chinese and Manchurian troops, police and related cargo.

Tempers had cooled by the time of the fifth conference, on July 14. Iuren'ev calmly declared that it was pointless for the Soviet delegation to enter into a discussion of the unquestionable Soviet sole ownership of the railway, built in its entirety with "the hard earned money of the peoples of the Soviet Union." He insisted that the current negotiations could and must be based only on the Peking and Mukden agreements and the articles of the contract of 1896 stipulated in them. He said that he could not discuss with the Manchukuoans general Soviet policy concerning China and that there was no ground for them to try to cite the Karakhan declarations in opposition to international treaties and agreements binding on Manchukuo. He reminded them that their government had pledged on March 12, 1932, to abide by the Peking and Mukden agreements.

[16] JWC, August 10, 1933, p. 163.

Iuren'ev pointed out that while the Soviet side had carefully documented its appraisal of the railway's cost at 411,019,989 gold rubles, the Manchukuoan side had given no indication how it had arrived at the figure of 226,908,508 gold rubles. The Soviet side could not agree that the CER properties seized by Chang Tso-lin—the railway land, the Sungari River fishing fleet, and the telephone stations—need not be redeemed, since the seizure of someone else's property did not give one legal rights to it. He decried that the government of Manchukuo had inherited from the former Mukden authorities the old arguments used in justifying such illegal acts.

Rejecting Manchukuoan attempts to downgrade the potential importance of the railway, Iuren'ev reiterated that it had been profitable prior to the Manchurian Incident. He refuted the Manchukuoan contention that the Soviet figures were inflated because they included charges for the transportation of Chinese guards and supplies. Iuren'ev insisted that the 40 million gold rubles, charged for this as of January 1, 1932, were still due. He rejected the Manchukuoan contention that the CER was obliged to provide free transportation of guards and supplies in compensation for being exempt from all taxes and levies. The various privileges extended by the Soviet side, particularly the right to share in the profits, constituted adequate compensation. Iuren'ev referred again to the offer once made by the Japanese government for the Kuanch'engtzu-Laoshaokou section of the CER and asked the Manchukuoan delegation to reflect on the fact that its offer for the entire line with all its properties was less in gold yen than what Japan had been willing to pay for the 106 kilometer stretch alone.

Noting that the Soviet asking price for the CER was far below the actual cost of the railway and that the Manchurian delegation itself had admitted that the Soviet method of calculation conformed with treaties and agreements in force, the Soviet side refused to consider the Manchukuoan offer. It asserted that as the result of great expenditures on the maintenance of the railway, the CER and its enterprises were in an excellent state, except for those sections of the eastern line where in consequence of inadequate protection and recent events the railway had suffered and continued to suffer great destruction.

Ohashi denied that the Manchukuoan delegation had agreed with the Soviet method of calculating the cost of the CER. On the contrary, Manchukuo insisted categorically that the price of the CER must be determined on the basis of its present value and that 50 million yen, therefore, was an appropriate price. Disputing Soviet allegations of illegal acts by the former Mukden authorities, Ohashi sharply reminded Iuren'ev (a reminder deleted in the TASS dispatch) that the Soviet authorities had either nationalized foreign property in Russian territory outright or imposed such heavy taxes as to necessitate its disposal. Ohashi taunted the Russians that they would not be willing to sell the railway if it were as valuable as they claimed. He reiterated that Manchukuo could never recognize Soviet claims to sole ownership of the railway and called upon the Soviet side to expedite matters by accepting the Manchukuoan point of view.[17]

On July 17 Iuren'ev proposed to Foreign Minister Uchida that Japan participate directly in the negotiations, since in the final analysis the CER question

[17] *Izvestiia*, July 18, 1933; JWC, July 20, 1933, pp. 76–77 and July 27, p. 107; *Nisso kosho-shi*, 300; Kutakov, *Istoriia*, 129–30.

concerned primarily her and the Soviet Union. But Japan preferred to remain in the background, limiting her presence to the two observers. She would be willing to mediate if necessary, Uchida repeated, but expressed the view that no deadlock had yet been reached and that there was room for further bilateral negotiation.[18] The Japanese did advise the Manchukuoan delegation to make more detailed plans for the negotiations, and the sixth conference was postponed.[19] Rescheduled for July 26, the conference was put off a second time on the plea of illness on the Russian side.[20] To prevent further loss of time Togo proposed that "special" talks be held by Soviet and Manchukuoan delegates without the presence of the Japanese observers. Both sides consented to the holding of informal talks,[21] although Ohashi, "patently manifesting his independence from the [Japanese] Foreign Office," objected to their being called "special." The Soviets agreed to the term "interim talks" (*promezhutochnye soveshchaniia*), even though this did not sound grammatical in Russian.[22]

[18] Kutakov, *Istoriia,* 131; JWC, July 27, 1933, p. 107. Uchida told Harada on August 10 that people were asking him to act as mediator between Manchukuo and the Soviet Union. "I keep refusing, saying, 'I cannot do such a thing.' Manchukuo is going along on its own true strength. Since there is no reason for us to give directions either one way or the other, it cannot be done." ("Saionji-Harada Memoirs," 661.)

[19] Iuren'ev took advantage of the break to go for a brief holiday in Karuizawa, while Kozlovskii went for a visit to Nikko as guest of President Kabayama of the Russian Waters Fisheries Association (Roryo Suisan Kumiai). (JWC, July 27, 1933, p. 107.)

[20] According to the JWC and a report by the British chargé d'affaires, it was Iuren'ev who had allegedly become sick, though Snow cast doubt on Iuren'ev's illness, noting that he paid a call at the Foreign Office the next day. According to a telegram from the Soviet delegation, the conference had been postponed because of the illness of Kuznetsov. Snow wrote that Kuznetsov had retired to the hot springs of Atami, claiming to be suffering from hiccups. (JWC, August 3, 1933; Snow to Simon, No. 453, Chuzenji, July 30, 1933, FO 371/17134–858.)

[21] JWC, August 3, 1933, p. 144. The purpose of the informal talks, according to Soviet sources, was to find a way out of the dilemma created by Manchukuo's position. (DVP, XVI, 837, note 136.)

[22] Soviet delegation to Foreign Commissariat, July 28, 1933, "Immediately," DVP, XVI, 472–73.

At a meeting between Kozlovskii and Ohashi on July 28 for the purpose of reaching final agreement on the informal talks, Kozlovskii proposed that they begin negotiation without waiting for the opening of the postponed conference. Ohashi rejected the idea categorically, stating that he must first make his reply at the conference. He proposed that the conference be held without Kuznetsov, whose illness had prompted its postponement. But to this the Soviets could not agree without permission from Moscow. Ohashi in turn reiterated his refusal to begin direct negotiations with Kozlovskii.[23]

While the British believed that the delays were Russian-made and that the Soviets might have to pay for their "stubborness"—"the Soviet side at the end of the account have to reckon with the Jàpanese military"[24]—a very different picture is obtained from Russian documents. The Soviet delegation, fully conscious of the influence of the Japanese military, attributed the delay to them. "The quarrel between the Foreign Office and the military is being revealed with absolute clarity," the delegation cabled home. "Ohashi is patently working for the prolongation of the negotiations and [their] breakdown and is seeking a ground for impeding the conference." The delegation deemed it necessary to bring pressure through Togo and Hirota and, if the Japanese Foreign Office could not or would not do anything, to call the sixth conference for August 2 in order not to allow the disruption of the negotiations.[25]

The Foreign Commissariat replied on July 31 that

[23] Soviet delegation to Foreign Commissariat, July 28, 1933, "Immediately," DVP, XVI, 472–73.
[24] Snow to Simon, No. 453.
[25] Soviet delegation to Foreign Commissariat, July 28, 1933, DVP, XVI, 472–73.

the delegation's proposal to exert influence through Togo and Hirota was correct. "Agree to the convening of the sixth conference as a last resort."[26]

The imminence of private talks between Ohashi and Kozlovskii aroused optimism in the Japanese press as the sixth conference was expected to open on August 2. Instead, another postponement followed. In a strongly worded announcement, the Foreign Office of Manchukuo stated on August 3 that it would continue to insist, even at the risk of the collapse of the negotiations, that the sovereign rights of Manchukuo must take precedence over any railway regulations or statutes or any agreements concluded between the Soviet Union and China or Mukden. It demanded that "all Communist propaganda vehicles" and "all radical movements" be prohibited in the railway zone, that "all Soviet citizens of marked Communist taint be refused entry into Manchukuo," and that the railway perform whatever "necessary service" the Manchukuoan government might demand.[27]

There had been reports that both sides had agreed informally after conference of July 14 to drop the question of the ownership of the railway and to confine themselves to discussion of its sale price.[28] But no sooner did the sixth conference open on August 4 than Ting announced that Manchukuo continued to contest sole Soviet ownership of the CER. In fact, he went so far as to assert that the entire railway belonged to Manchukuo and that China by the Peking and Mukden agreements of 1924 had ceded to the USSR merely the right to participate in the administration of the railway and that, consequently, the current value and pos-

---

[26] DVP, XVI, 851, note 195.
[27] JWC, August 3, 1933, p. 176; August 10, 1933, p. 176.
[28] JWC, July 20, 1933, p. 77.

sible future yield of the railway be the sole considerations in arriving at a price. The Manchukuoan side denied that the Sungari River fleet and telephone offices belonged to the railway. It claimed that their seizure by the old Mukden authorities had been legal and that they now were Manchukuoan property. Nor did the Manchukuoan side recognize the Harbin Telegraph Office as part of the CER; it contended that it was an ordinary public telephone office. Conceding that the railway's value for Manchukuo might not be as low as originally depicted by the Manchukuoan side, Ting argued that it had lost its importance for the Soviet Union; Litvinov had admitted as much in his memorandum to Ota. In view of this fact and because of the depreciation of the line, the construction of other railways, and Manchukuo's financial position, 50 million yen was all that Manchukuo could pay for the CER.

Iuren'ev refused to get into an argument. He simply confirmed what had been conveyed informally during the recess in the talks—that the Soviet Union was willing to reduce the sale price by one fifth, down to 200 million gold rubles—and expressed the hope that Manchukuo would get down to business and raise her original offer.

Ohashi replied that the Manchukuoan delegation had not been informed of the reduction in price; the information had been conveyed by the Soviets to the Japanese Foreign Office. Anyway, he said, the Manchukuoan offer was already higher than the value of the railway and there was no room for increasing it.

The two sides agreed that the question was too delicate for formal debate. Ohashi and Kozlovskii should work out the terms of sale in private talks, then submit them to the conference for approval.[29]

On August 8 Kozlovskii and Ohashi held their first informal talk at the official residence of the Japanese vice minister of foreign affairs in the presence of several colleagues. Asserting that the points of view of the two sides had been made abundantly clear during the six formal conferences and that they could argue for ten years without reaching agreement if they thrashed out their respective proposals, Ohashi proposed, on the assumption that the success or failure of the negotiations depended on price, that they settle the matter one way or another at once by coming up with their final irreducible figures.

Kozlovskii demurred. He resisted being high-pressured into a quick decision and expressed confidence that a detailed discussion of the Soviet proposal could be fruitful.

Ohashi retorted that further procrastination and polemics would adversely affect Soviet-Manchukuoan-Japanese relations and that a prompt political settlement was necessary. He asked what was meant by payment in gold yen. Surely the USSR did not expect Manchukuo to pay in gold, whose export had been embargoed by most countries? If the market value of 1 gold ruble were taken as being 2½ yen, the Russian asking price of 200 million gold rubles would amount to 500 million yen or more than three times the total annual budget of Manchukuo!

Kozlovskii retorted that if Ohashi did not know what a gold yen was, he ought to go to the Bank of Japan to find out. Ohashi had mentioned the rise in the value

[29] JWC, August 10, 1933, p. 176; *Izvestiia*, August 6 and 8, 1933; Kutakov, *Istoriia*, 130; *Nisso kosho-shi*, 300.

of gold, but actually, Kozlovskii said, the prices of commodities had fallen.

Although Ohashi and Kozlovskii sparred in this vein for seven and a half hours without giving ground, the question of the rate of exchange, indirectly raised by Ohashi, left the situation fluid. By granting to Manchukuo a favorable rate of exchange, the USSR could readily narrow the gap.[30]

When the delegates met for their second informal conversation four days later, on August 12, Kozlovskii did indeed express the willingness of the Soviet government to negotiate on the basis of paper yen against gold rubles, instead of gold yen against gold rubles. It was agreed that the rate of exchange be discussed at the next meeting and that a committee of experts be appointed to work out the terms and conditions of the transfer of the railway.[31]

At the third informal meeting, on August 17, deliberation duly shifted from the question of the cost value of the railway to the determination of a realistic rate of exchange. Ohashi proposed the equation of the two offers by pegging the rate at 25 sen, which, he claimed, corresponded to the real value of the gold ruble as opposed to the official rate of exchange, which was ten times higher.[32] The Soviets took issue with the Manchukuoan calculations, but in almost five hours of discussion failed to modify them.[33] They themselves

[30] JWC, August 17, 1933, p. 208; JTM, August 10, 1933, p. 1.
[31] JWC, August 24, 1933, p. 239.
[32] The Soviet-Japanese fishery rent agreement concluded in 1931 had pegged the exchange rate at 32.5 sen per ruble, but the ratio fixed between the American Insurance Syndicate and the Soviet Government in April of that year came to 25 sen per ruble. The 25 sen rate, proposed by Ohashi, equated the Soviet asking price of 200 million gold rubles with the Manchukuoan offer of 50 million yen. At 32.5 sen per gold ruble, the Soviet asking price would have been 65 million yen or 15 million yen higher than the Manchukuoan offer.
[33] JWC, August 24, 1933, p. 239; DVP, XVI, 837, note 136.

made no specific counterproposal, promising to do so the next time.

At the fourth informal meeting, on August 23, Kozlovskii failed to come up with a concrete plan. He simply rejected Ohashi's proposal of August 17 as not constituting a genuine reply to the Soviet overture; it was merely a rephrasing of the original Manchukuoan offer of 50 million yen.

Ohashi denied the allegation in a hurt tone. He complained that Kozlovskii had not lived up to his promise of producing a specific proposal and warned that if the 25 sen offer was rejected, Manchukuo would have to go by the exchange rate current at Vladivostok, Warsaw and Berlin, namely 2 or 4, at best 10, sen per ruble. He asserted that Manchukuo had gone as high as 25 sen for political reasons and reiterated that the solution of the question must be political.[34]

Kozlovskii suggested that they shelve the question of the exchange rate for the moment and turn to the appointment of a committee of experts to study various issues involved in the transfer of the railway. Although Ohashi had consented to the formation of such a committee at the second informal meeting, he now replied that it would be meaningless to appoint one if no financial agreement could be reached. When Kozlovskii responded that experts from Moscow would arrive in Tokyo on September 4 or 5 to work out an exchange rate based on economic and technical considerations, Ohashi retorted that the question could be settled only politically, not technically. He threatened that Manchukuo might break off the negotiations if the

---

[34] The railway question was regarded as part of a general settlement of outstanding Soviet and Japanese issues, including the fisheries, oil and coal concessions. See Appendix A.

Soviet side did not come up with a concrete proposal at the next meeting.[35]

Kozlovskii reiterated that the 50 million yen figure could not be considered as a serious offer. Soviet willingness to discuss the exchange rate, on the other hand, constituted an offer to revise the price downward. Ohashi's refusal to discuss the subject, Kozlovskii said, could only be interpreted as an attempt to scuttle the conferences.[36]

As neither side budged, the informal talks, like the formal conferences before them, came to a halt.

[35] JWC, August 31, 1933, p. 277; Kutakov, *Istoriia*, 131; *Nisso kosho-shi*, 300.
[36] *Izvestiia*, August 26, 1933.

9

Threatened Seizure of the CER

With the negotiations deadlocked, Manchukuo tried to force the Soviet Union to modify her position by renewed pressure on the CER. For some time the directorate of the railway had been discussing the equalization of the administrative powers of the Soviet general manager and the Manchukuoan assistant general manager of the railway. Suddenly, on August 21, 1933, before any agreement had been reached, the Manchukuoan members of the board of directors ordered Tui Chi-ho, section chief of the management bureau, to examine the railway's service expenses. When the Manchukuoan chief controller of the railway asked the local foreign banks, including the American National City Bank and the Soviet Far Eastern Bank, for information about the railway accounts, the banks rebuffed the request, because according to the established rules such data could be provided only to the board of directors as a whole. Soviet officials charged that the Manchukuoans and their Japanese advisers, who were familiar with the statutes, had sought to create a situation which would leave the impression that the railway was in a state of disorder.[1]

On August 30 President Li Shao-keng announced that the meetings of the board of directors would be discontinued if the USSR did not unconditionally accept Manchukuo's interpretation as to the competencies of the general manager and the assistant general manager of the railway.[2]

In a special report to the railway administration about the mounting number of train wrecks, General Manager Rudyi wrote on September 16 that in the past five days alone there had occurred five cases of damage to the track, three incidents of shooting at trains, two instances of setting fire to railway stations, thirteen attacks on office and railway buildings, and the capture of 150 railway agents.

The same day P. A. Bandura, deputy to the vice president of the CER, handed Li a letter in which he asserted that there had been over 3,000 violations of the rights of the railway in 1930–32 and during the first half of 1933 and that over a third of them had been inflicted by the railway guards themselves. Pleading with. Li to impress on his government the need for effective defense measures, he warned that more was involved than mere financial losses of the company. The preservation of direct communication between Europe and Asia was at stake.[3]

The attempt of the Manchukuoan members of the board of directors to broaden the powers of the chief controller and audit the books of various sections of the CER was blocked by the Soviets, and the audit was limited to the cashier's office of the administration.

[1] JWC, August 31, 1933, p. 276.
[2] JWC, September 7, 1933, p. 298.
[3] *Izvestiia,* September 18, 1933.

The audit had been preceded by allegations in the Harbin press that there were irregularities in the railway accounts, but no such irregularities were found and Li Shao-keng and Morita declared themselves satisfied with the state of the books.[4]

Bandit raids on the railway had increased with the resumption of freight traffic via Pogranichnaia Station.[5] On September 12, for example, some 400 bandits had derailed and looted an international train at Pataohotze, not far from Pogranichnaia, kidnapping 45 Russian and 68 Chinese passengers. (Two Japanese travelers aboard the train escaped capture by hiding in the toilet.)[6] As a result of the raids the activity of the railway was severely curtailed, indeed almost completely halted, on the eastern section.[7]

That month Foreign Minister Uchida, who was nearing 70, had resigned because he was getting hard of hearing and had trouble moving his limbs. He had recommended and obtained as his successor Hirota Koki, who had preceded Ota as ambassador to the Soviet Union. In the words of Shigemitsu, who had agreed to stay on as vice minister of foreign affairs, Hirota was "comparatively young and much is expected of him."[8] When Iuren'ev paid his first visit to him on September 18, Hirota said that he felt that the interim talks should be resumed and that he would discuss this with Ohashi. On September 21 he told Iuren'ev that in his opinion the interim talks which were to be held the next day would deal with preparations for business-like negotiations regarding CER questions that had not yet been touched.[9]

[4] *Izvestiia*, August 26, 1933.
[5] JWC, August 31, 1933, p. 277.
[6] JWC, September 21, 1933, p. 362.
[7] Kutakov, *Istoriia*, 133.
[8] "Saionji-Harada Memoirs," 690–91.
[9] DVP, XVI, 859, note 231.

But that very day, on September 21, Deputy Foreign Commissar Sokol'nikov handed to Ambassador Ota a note, in which the Soviet government declared that it was in possession of reliable information that the Manchukuoan authorities, "at the direction of the Japanese government," planned to carry out within the next few days a number of unilateral changes in the administration of the CER—to make the Soviet general manager virtually dependent on the Manchukuoan assistant general manager and to arrest a number of Soviet employees. Sokol'nikov warned that the Soviet government would regard such measures as an intolerable attempt to seize the railway.

On September 21 Sokol'nikov transmitted a note to Ota in which the Soviet government placed full blame on Japan. "Not Manchukuo, which is powerless and incapable of being responsible for events in Manchuria, but the Japanese Government, which is the actual master in Manchuria, must bear direct responsibility for all the violations of the treaties on the CER, as well as for the seizure of the railway that is being prepared."[10]

Sokol'nikov warned that the Japanese were mistaken if they thought that measures like those contemplated by the Japanese military mission with Japanese officials high in the administration of Manchukuo could contribute to the success of the negotiations. "On the contrary, these measures can only complicate negotiations." He remarked that if the actions signified the decision to seize the CER, it was evident that the Manchukuoan delegation in Tokyo had offered such

[10] *Izvestiia,* September 22, 1933; JWC, September 28, 1933 and October 5, 1933, p. 421; Strang to Foreign Office, No 518, Moscow, September 22, 1933, FO 371/17134–858. I have given preference to the Russian version, but have rendered "Manchurian" as "Manchukuoan."

a paltry sum for the railway in order to scuttle the negotiations.

Iuren'ev transmitted an identic note directly to Hirota the following day, charging bluntly that the steps planned against the Soviets on the CER were for the purpose of "seizing the line and reducing the talks to naught."[11]

Izvestiia commented on September 24 that the statements made by Sokol'nikov and Iuren'ev had exposed Japanese plans for the seizure of the railway. It reiterated the accusation that the Manchukuoan delegation had stalled the negotiations in order to gain time for the contemplated seizure.[12] *Izvestiia* alleged that according to information received by the Soviet government, the first step in the seizure of the railway was to be the arrest of responsible Soviet employees of the railway for carrying out orders issued by the Soviet general manager.[13]

That day the Manchukuoan authorities duly arrested six leading Soviet railway officials: Kalin, chief of the traffic department; Lavrov, chief of the railway repair shops; Kubl', chief of the finance department; Ablov, chief dispatcher; Avramenko, stationmaster of

---

[11] Kutakov, *Istoriia*, 132. S. Harcourt-Smith of the Northern Department of the British Foreign Office regarded the Soviet protest as "rather half hearted." "It seems to grow daily more evident," he observed, "that the Soviet Government are not prepared to resort to extreme measures in defence of their Manchurian interests. Possibly the whole incident has been deliberately provoked by the Japanese in order to force the hand of the Soviet delegate to the CER conference in Tokyo." Orde put a question mark above "half hearted" and added: "The language is quite strong, but there is no threat." (Comments in minutes, September 28, 1933, FO 371/17134–858.)

[12] It was widely believed in Harbin that Ohashi, after rejecting the price asked by the Soviet delegation, had sent instructions home on August 25 to prepare for the arrest of the Soviet officials and the seizure of the CER. (ROSTA dispatch from Khabarovsk, dated September 28, 1933, published in *Izvestiia*, September 30, 1933.)

[13] JWC, September 28, 1933, p. 391.

Man'chzhuriia Station and Katyl', stationmaster of Pogranichnaia Station.[14]

Slavutskii and Bandura protested against this action the same day. When Li replied that the arrests had been ordered by the prosecutor in response to a complaint by the chief controller that funds had been misused by the officials in question, Bandura countered that the correct procedure in the event of any irregularity would have been for the chief controller to inform the board of directors and the revisional committee of the railway of the alleged malpractice, not to approach the prosecutor directly.[15]

On September 26 Bandura wrote to Li protesting against the illegality of the actions of the chief controller of the CER and of the public prosecutor: "The chief controller is not an official of Manchukuo, but merely the employee of a commercial enterprise, governed by the representatives of two governments, and in accordance with the effective statutes and conditions he is not empowered to decide on his own whether or not a criminal abuse of trust has been committed. Thus his approach to the prosecutor as the chief controller is illegal." Bandura pointed out that the fact that the arrest of the senior officials had been followed immediately by Li's request that they be replaced by Manchukuoan citizens was proof that the arrests had been made solely in order to displace the Soviet officials with Manchukuoan ones.[16]

On September 28 Iuren'ev called on Hirota. He had

---

[14] The first four were arrested by Harbin police, the others by Japanese and Manchukuoan border guards. (*Nisso kosho-shi*, 301; Strang to Simon, No. 551, Moscow, October 7, 1933, FO 371/17135–876; *Izvestiia*, September 30, 1933; Kutakov, *Istoriia*, 132.)

[15] Strang to Simon, No. 551, Moscow, October 7, 1933, FO 371/17135–876; *Izvestiia*, September 27, 1933.

[16] DVP, XVI, 860, note 235.

requested the meeting to transmit a communication from his government and went, he thought, on his own initiative. He did not realize that Hirota had summoned him to convey a statement by the Japanese government.[17] Iuren'ev read and then handed to Hirota a note, dated September 26, protesting against the arrest of the Soviet officials on the twenty-fourth. The Soviet government pointed out that it had forewarned the Japanese government several days before, both through its ambassador in Moscow and directly in Tokyo, that such actions were being planned by Japanese and Manchukuoan officials. It asserted that it had "irrefutable evidence" that these measures constituted the beginning of the realization of a plan to seize the CER, a scheme carefully worked out in a series of meetings at the Japanese military mission in Harbin with the participation of responsible Japanese officials in the administration of Manchukuo. The Soviet government warned that it was prepared, if necessary, to publish the documents in its possession. Underlining that Japanese officials had been involved in the formulation of the plan to seize the railway and in the arrest of Soviet officials, the note declared that such actions "cannot but be calculated to [bring about] the rupture of the negotiations regarding the sale of the CER." "The responsibility for the consequences rests fully with the Japanese government."[18]

Hirota remarked that there was more factual data in this statement than in the one Iuren'ev had made on the 22nd, then read a brief reply to the earlier memorandum. Investigation had revealed, the answer

[17] Note of Iuren'ev's conversation with Hirota, recorded by the new Soviet dragoman Mikhail Andreev, DVP, XVI, 546–50; JWC, October 5, 1933, p. 421; Kutakov, *Istoriia*, 132.
[18] *Izvestiia*, September 30, 1933; see also October 10, 1933.

asserted, that the six Soviet employees had been arrested by the Manchukuoan authorities on legal grounds and that the matter was not political in character. The Manchukuoan authorities were in direct touch with the Soviet consul general in Harbin concerning the affair. Hirota added that it was difficult to say how the matter would end, but that he assumed the Manchukuoan authorities would clarify the question conscientiously.

Hirota took issue with the memorandum's contention that Japan was responsible for the Harbin incident. "That is too harsh a statement, ignoring the independence of Manchukuo." The Soviet government, he alleged, had come to the conclusion "*a priori,* without due investigation," and asserted that such accusations only served to impede the negotiations. He, for his part, considered it essential to activate the talks concerning the CER.

Iuren'ev countered that the Harbin incident could not be ignored, for what was happening was that while aimless discussions were being held in Tokyo, the seizure of the CER was being organized in Harbin. So long as the Japanese government allowed the violation of the legal *status quo* on the CER, Hirota's desire that an agreement be reached was merely "platonic." Iuren'ev pointed out that Ohashi had refused to examine essentials at the last informal talk, although Hirota had said that he would do so.

"You are saying that the failure of the negotiations is due to the position of Ohashi, and Ohashi is saying that it is due to the position of the USSR," Hirota remarked. It was his feeling that the solution of basic issues was being help up by technical details.

Iuren'ev reminded Hirota that the latter had told him during their first meeting on his own initiative that businesslike talks must be begun and that the last private talks of the delegation had been organized by the Japanese Foreign Office. He had taken this to mean that the negotiations would receive a fresh start, and now Hirota was saying that they had bogged down over technical points!

Hirota explained that the delegations had not yet come to grips with the basic issues, but still negotiated how to negotiate. The exchange rate was a case in point. While the Soviet side talked about the need of indicating the exchange rate of the yen, it gave no figures; the Manchukuoan side did so.

Iuren'ev replied that this was not a technical question. The Soviet side had invited Manchukuo to make a proposal concerning the exchange rate of the ruble. Manchukuo had suggested 25 sen, which amounted to a repetition of its original offer of 50 million yen. If the Harbin events were designed to force the Soviets into far-reaching concessions, this was "a definite and serious mistake," Iuren'ev declared. "We shall not agree to any ultimatums, and no one will force us by such methods to make any concessions."

Hirota responded that the negotiations had come to a standstill because Manchukuo wished to buy the railway for 50 million yen and the Soviet side, though it had lowered its asking price and had agreed to compute the amount in yen, did not indicate a rate of exchange for the yen. Events in Harbin must not impede the negotiations in Tokyo. Ignoring Iuren'ev's protest that "the center of gravity" of the CER question had shifted to Harbin and that the Japanese government must take steps for the prompt ending of illegal and forcible actions there, Hirota said that "as a third party" he deemed it necessary that the USSR "indicate the rate of exchange of the gold ruble and give the purchase price in yen, not in rubles."

"We do not regard the Japanese government as a

third party," Iuren'ev retorted. He made it clear that the Soviet side had already made a number of concessions and that it was Manchukuo's turn to make new proposals.

Hirota reiterated that the rate of exchange should be proposed by the Soviet side. Did the Soviet side refuse to negotiate?

"The Soviet side does not refuse to negotiate, but it states that it has no new proposals," Iuren'ev declared.

"The Japanese government considers that it would be helpful to arrange a meeting of the Manchukuoan and Soviet delegations, during which one could exchange views," Hirota continued. "There are many questions other than the question of the price concerning which proposals can be made. Japan is not your partner in the negotiations, but I could talk it over with Mr. Ohashi and one might be able to arrange a meeting and set a date, even tomorrow."

"Our financial expert, Comrade Baryshnikov, has fallen ill," Iuren'ev responded. "Besides, we'll be very busy during the next few days. It will not be possible, therefore, to call the meeting together either tomorrow or the day after tomorrow. Moreover, I do not know what we shall talk about at this meeting. It is pointless to repeat the previous meetings." Iuren'ev again referred to the situation at Harbin, implying that it must be settled before negotiations could be resumed. In vain Hirota argued that there was no need to postpone the conference because of Baryshnikov's illness, that the talks were between Kozlovskii and Ohashi, and that the topics for discussion could be suggested by both sides.[19]

[19] Record of Iuren'ev's conversation with Hirota, September 28, 1933, DVP, XVI, 546–50.

The warning that seizure of the railway by means of the arrest of the Soviet officials would impede the negotiations in Tokyo, rather than accelerate them, was repeated the same day in Harbin by Slavutskii to Shih Lü-pen's deputy Shimamura.[20] On September 30 the Soviet delegation responded to a proposal by the Manchukuoan delegation that talks be resumed "under the former conditions" with the declaration that it was pointless and impossible to hold a meeting in the situation created by the Harbin conflict.[21]

In his reply to Bandura's protest, conveyed on September 29, Li had written that the Soviet officials had been summoned by the prosecutor for examination on the basis of a report by the chief controller, accusing them of a criminal abuse of trust. Contending that anybody had the right to approach the prosecutor directly, Li had denied that the incident had been an attempt on the part of Manchukuo to seize the railway. At the same time, however, he had objected to Rudyi's appointment of Soviet replacements for the arrested officials as *ultra vires,* insisting that the positions should have been filled by the Manchukuoan officials next in seniority.[22]

Bandura countered on October 2 that the Soviet employees had been seized at dawn after a search of their homes and were still in prison. "If you call this 'summons for examination,' " he wrote Li, "what do you call arrest?" The officials stood accused of criminal breach of trust, but it had not been specified whose

[20] DVP, XVI, p. 860, note 236.

[21] DVP, XVI, 837–38, note 136.

[22] *Izvestiia,* October 5, 1933; Holman to Foreign Office, No. 1012 (R), Peking, September 30, 1933, FO 371/17135–876; Strang to Simon, No. 55, Moscow, October 7, 1933, FO 371/17135–876. "Still no mention of the charge," Harcourt-Smith remarked upon reading this. "Possibly the 'Manchukuo' authorities have not yet concocted one. In any case it seems clear that they are more interested in the offices than the misdeeds of the detained officials." "Undoubtedly," Orde added. (Comments in minutes, October 2 and 3, 1933, FO 371/17135–876.)

trust they had abused. The trust of the CER? If so, of which organ of the CER—of the administration or of the directorate of the railway? The laws of the state, Bandura lectured, did not recognize breach of trust unless the injured party itself registered a complaint. Nor did they give the right to the chief controller, who was not an officer of the state, to initiate in his capacity as chief controller of the railway prosecution against department chiefs and other employees of the railway for actions committed in connection with their work.

Reiterating that the chief controller and the Manchukuoan authorities both had violated the status of the CER and thus also existing treaties, Bandura repeated the allegation he had made in his letter of September 26 that the real purpose of the arrests had been the replacement of the Soviet department chiefs by Manchukuoan officials as the first step in a concerted effort to seize the railway. He defended the general manager's replacement of the arrested officials by other Soviet citizens as just and in accordance with existing agreements and regulations.[23]

On October 3 Slavutskii rehearsed to Shih Lü-pen how the Soviets interpreted the arrests and the various incidents on the railway. Speaking in a tone that allowed for no argument, he rejected the reply of the Manchukuoan government that the arrests had been made for judicial rather than for political reasons as "absolutely unsatisfactory." Under what articles of law had the officials been arrested? What specific charges had been filed against them?

Shih replied evasively that the investigation was still

<hr>

[23] JWC, October 12, 1933, p. 456, based on Rengo dispatch from Moscow, dated October 4; *Izvestiia,* October 5, 1933; Strang to Simon, No. 551, Moscow, October 7, 1933, FO 371/17135–876.

in progress and that the prosecutor would have to cite the articles of law in question. When he asked what Slavutskii could recommend other than the release of the prisoners, Slavutskii retorted that the only way out of the impasse was "the release of the prisoners and the rejection of adventurist plans."

Slavutskii reported to Moscow that he did not place hope in his representations at Harbin, because Komatsubara, the chief of the Japanese military mission in Harbin, and other local Japanese who had participated in planning the venture would seek to use it for purposes of their own.[24]

When a week and a half passed without a reply to its note of September 26, the Soviet government carried out its threat and on October 9 published the evidence which it had obtained purporting to show Japan's intention, in the name of Manchukuo, to seize the CER by force. The evidence consisted of four documents: three dispatches from General Hishikari Takashi, the Japanese ambassador in Manchukuo, to the Japanese foreign minister, one dated September 4 and two September 9, 1933, and of a report from Morishima, the Japanese consul general in Harbin, to Hishikari, dated September 19.[25]

Hishikari's dispatch of September 4 stated that the various measures taken by Manchukuo regarding the CER since spring were designed to strengthen her bargaining position in Tokyo, although Manchukuo had sought to conceal the connection by stressing that the actions had been purely internal in nature. It related that a determined campaign was being waged to sup-

[24] Slavutskii to Foreign Commissariat, October 3, 1933, signed "Sovkonsul." *DVP*, XVI, 555–56; *Izvestiia,* October 3, 1933; JWC, October 12, 1933, p. 456, based on Rengo dispatches from Moscow, dated October 3 and 6.
[25] Kutakov, *Istoriia,* 133; JWC, October 19, 1933, pp. 492–93.

press the Communist Party and related organizations and that every Soviet employee of the railway was being carefully investigated. In response to a telegram from Ohashi, received on August 25, calling for "active measures" to prod along the stalled negotiations, a conference had been held on September 2 in the State Council of Manchukuo, attended by Japanese heads of departments, Japanese military officers, and representatives of the Japanese embassy (Counselor Tani Masayuki and Hanawa). During the conference the Japanese military had advised against resort to force for the time being, and Tani had warned that careless steps be avoided, since Japan did not deem it possible to create conflicts on the continent until 1935. Tani had observed, furthermore, that joint Soviet-Manchukuoan management of the railway, toward which the measures of the Department of Communications were directed, were in conflict with the objective of purchasing the CER.

In a lengthy dispatch, dated September 9, Hishikari enumerated the measures it had been decided to take to further the negotiations regarding the purchase of the CER: (1) to make use of the controller's section and other organs of the CER to collect data about illegal acts of Soviet railway employees and to arrest them on a small scale, several at a time, contact being maintained between the Department of Justice, the police, and the Department of Railway Administration; (2) the president of the CER was to be instructed by the Ministry of Communications of Manchukuo that henceforth all actions and orders of the general manager of the railway must be approved by the assistant general manager; those not so approved must be declared invalid or must be countermanded by the president; (3) Soviet citizens living in Harbin and in the railway zone must be investigated and Communist organizations, including the railway club and the commercial school in Harbin, must be kept under close surveillance by the police; (4) the Ministry of Finance was to summon officials of Dal'bank (the Soviet Far Eastern Bank) and consumer cooperatives on the railway and make an audit of their books to check their tax payments and "general activity"; (5) the Legal Department, acting jointly with the Department of Railway Administration, was to work out a project to force the private creditors of the railway to present their claims to it, then attach the property of the railway; (6) the Legal Department was to expedite the study of the cases of White Russians, imprisoned since the Sino-Soviet conflict of 1929, and hasten their release; (7) the above actions were to be carried out quickly as internal measures of the Manchukuoan government, giving the outward appearance that they were unrelated to the Tokyo negotiations; (8) close contact was to be maintained throughout with the Japanese military mission in Harbin and through it with the Kwantung Army and the gendarmerie.

In the second dispatch of that date Hishikari communicated some modifications of the above. No mass arrests or seizures of prominent persons were to take place without further deliberation; the implementation of the demand that all orders of the general manager be countermanded by the assistant general manager was to be postponed until an opportune moment; and the presentation of claims by private creditors of the railway was to await further study.

The dispatch from Morishima to Hishikari reported that Japanese officials in Manchukuo—some working for Japanese organizations, others for Manchukuo directly—had met in the building of the Japanese

Military Mission on September 19 to plan the execution of the above measures. They had decided at this meeting to imprison the six Soviet railway officials and had formed an executive committee to coordinate large-scale action following the completion of the investigation by the controller's office. If necessary, force was to be used in effecting the arrest. Time was to be saved by working out the details of the arrests locally.[26]

Izvestiia editorialized that "these documents confirm and expose that aggressive policy toward the CER, which is masked hypocritically with the fiction of the independence of Manchukuo but is dictated from Tokyo and is carried out under the direction of its direct military and diplomatic agents on the spot by the hands of the Japanese police itself and of Japanese officials formally in the employ of Manchukuo." It echoed the warning of the Soviet statements of September 21 and 28 that the Japanese government must bear responsibility for the "Manchurian adventure."[27]

On October 10 Togo told Counselor Nikolai Raivid that the publication of the Hishikari and Morishima telegrams, of which there was no record in the archives of the Foreign Office, was an "unprecedented act in the history of diplomatic relations." He asked whether the Soviet government had considered the consequences of such a step on Soviet-Japanese relations and whether it wished to continue the negotiations concerning the CER.

Raivid replied as instructed by the Foreign Commissariat on October 8, on the eve of the publication of the documents, that the Soviet side had been forced to make them public because of Hirota's reply to Iuren'ev of September 28 and that this could not have

[26] *Izvestiia,* October 9, 1933; DVP, XVI, 560–64.
[27] *Izvestiia,* October 10, 1933.

come as a surprise to the Japanese government, since Iuren'ev had warned it thereof. "The purpose of the publication is to establish before public opinion who is guilty and bears responsibility for the Harbin events, which are aimed at the disruption of the negotiations and the seizure of the railway, and that the Japanese government is the actual master in Manchuria, responsible for what is happening there," Raivid declared. "As for characterizing this act as unprecedented," he added, "what is actually unprecedented is that a state which has normal relations with another tries to violate the legal rights of the latter by force, as is being done in Harbin." The Soviet government still was willing to sell the CER to Manchukuo, but as Zhelezniakov, the secretary of the Soviet delegation, had informed Sugihara, the secretary of the Manchukuoan delegation, on September 30 in response to the latter's proposal the previous day that the delegations meet under the former conditions, negotiations could not be conducted under the pressure of the forcible Harbin acts.

Togo argued that Manchukuo was independent of Japan and that the Soviet Union should have dealt with her directly. When he asserted that the publication of documents which were not in the archives of the Japanese Foreign Office would impair Soviet-Japanese relations, Raivid countered that the worsening atmosphere was no fault of the USSR and that it was due not to the publication of the documents, but to the actions of the Japanese in Harbin. "The Soviet government addressed the one, whom it regards as the master of Manchuria," Raivid stated.

Togo questioned the authenticity of the documents and demanded "objective proof." Raivid replied that he could not discuss the nature of the documents, since his government had declared that it was in possession of accurate documents. If the Japanese government desired further details, it should approach the Foreign Commissariat through the Japanese ambassador. Raivid rebuffed Togo's efforts to separate the Harbin events from the CER negotiations and reiterated that the former must be resolved before the latter could be resumed fruitfully. Though neither Raivid nor Togo gave ground, their exchange took place in a friendly tone.[28]

The publication of the documents did not have the desired effect. It did not bring the pressure of world opinion to bear on the Japanese government. On the contrary, whatever public outrage was stirred up by the documents was turned against the USSR, as "highly indignant" Foreign Office officials and army officers declared that the documents were forgeries and that their publication constituted an act of "bad faith" on the part of the Soviet Union. Instead of softening the Japanese position, the publication of the documents hardened it. There was talk of Japan's washing her hands of the Soviet-Manchukuoan negotiations.[29]

The Japanese did not accuse the TASS correspondent or the Soviet government of having fabricated the documents. A Foreign Office official suggested

---

[28] Iuren'ev to Foreign Commissariat, October 10, 1933, signed "Polpred," DVP, XVI, 568–70; DVP, XVI, 861–62, note 241. On October 19 Rink told his British colleague that the Japanese army was furious at the position in which it had been placed by the Soviet publication of the secret Japanese documents. "If the authenticity of the documents is denied, it will be difficult for the military to seize the railway as already planned. If the genuineness is not denied, they are put in the invidious position of having their plans exposed." (James to Snow, Report No. 34, Tokyo, October 21, 1933, "Secret," FO 371/17152–858.)

[29] JWC, October 19, 1933, pp. 492–93. The Soviet delegation got a different impression; it reported, as will be seen below, that the publication of the documents "caused an undoubted increase in the opposition of the moderate circles to the military."

that the Soviets had been entrapped by unscrupulous persons who sold forged diplomatic documents to agents of various governments.[30] He likened the Japanese documents to the celebrated Zinov'ev letter, the publication of which by the English press in 1924 had led to the rupture of Anglo-Russian trade relations even though the Soviet government had denied its authenticity.[31]

It is not clear whether or not the above documents were authentic. On one hand, they seemed to lack "the characteristics of Japanese official style and ways of thinking."[32] On the other hand, the Soviets had definitely obtained *some* genuine documents, the Foreign Office denying their loss and consequently the authenticity to avoid a scandal.[33] "The documents may be forgeries," a British official reflected, "but at least it is clear that the Soviet had foreknowledge

[30] Harcourt-Smith agreed: "It looks as if the Japanese, for once, are sincere in their denials of authenticity." (Comments in minutes, dated October 16, accompanying Strang to Foreign Office, No. 563, Moscow, October 10, 1933, FO 371/17135–876.)

[31] JWC, October 19, 1933, p. 492. The letter, alleged to have been written by Grigorii Zinov'ev, chairman of the executive committee of the Comintern, to the British Communists, urging the overthrow of their government by force, was published by the Conservatives in a successful bid to unseat the Labor government. What makes the reference to the Zinov'ev letter particularly intriguing is that the letter had not only been a forgery but may have been planted by Stalin's secret police to topple Zinov'ev. (Donald W. Treadgold, *Twentieth Century Russia* [Chicago: Rand McNally, 1959], p. 237; Ruth Fischer, *Stalin and German Communism* [Cambridge: Harvard University Press, 1948], pp. 458–63.) One wonders whether the Japanese documents, if forged, had been concocted by Japanese swindlers for monetary gain or whether they had been produced by militarists for the purpose of bringing negotiations with the USSR to a halt.

[32] Comment by Harcourt-Smith, October 16, 1933, accompanying Strang to Foreign Office, No. 563, Moscow, October 10, 1933, FO 371/17135–876.

[33] Baron Harada recalled a conversation he had had with Lt. Col. Suzuki on October 15: "He spoke of an affair that was in dispute, the incident of the secret documents stolen by the Russians, that is, the telegram of September 4th from Tani [counselor of the Japanese embassy in Manchukuo] and the telegram to Manchukuo from Vice Consul Ohashi, which had been seized by the Russians. To say that they had been stolen was a grave matter, so with considerable indignation each newspaper was informed that the secret documents had been located." ("Saionji-Harada Memoirs," 716.)

of the intended arrests which were actually carried out. There is no reason to doubt the readiness of the Japanese to resort to such methods.''[34]

On October 24 Slavutskii wrote a lengthy letter to Shih Lü-pen complaining that his many oral and written appeals for protection of Soviet citizens in Harbin and along the entire CER line from harrassment by White Russian police officials in the employ of Manchukuo and the railway had remained without result. Listing the many arrests of Soviet citizens that had been made, Slavutskii objected in particular to the "obvious and deliberate mockery" of Soviet citizens by White Russian officials, who, for example, gave permission for the holding of a dance at the railway meeting hall at Tsitsihar Station, but without music; or who allowed the playing of athletic games, but without athletic costumes. Slavutskii noted that he had not been informed whether any measures had been taken by the police to investigate the intrusion into the Soviet consulate grounds by two armed White Russians, or whether any disciplinary measures had been taken against the police officials who had detained one of the Soviet trade officers in an attempt to make him into a secret police informant. He had reported these incidents to Shih in August of the preceding year. Contending that in view of the strict police censorship in Harbin the Manchurian authorities were responsible for the many slanderous stories published daily in the local newspapers about the USSR and her representatives in Manchuria, Slavutskii asked that the government of Manchukuo immediately take effective measures to provide for the normal life of Soviet citizens in Manchuria.[35]

[34] Orde, October 17, 1933, commenting on Strang to Foreign Office, No. 563, Moscow, October 10, 1933, FO 371/17135–876.
[35] Slavutskii to Shih Lü-pen, October 24, 1933, DVP, XVI, 579–82.

When Iuren'ev called on Hirota on November 6 to protest the violation of Soviet airspace by a number of Japanese planes, Hirota took the opportunity to rebuke Iuren'ev for the publication of the secret documents. "Such actions are very disagreeable," he scolded. "Previously you mentioned to me that you had some documentary proof in hand. Didn't I say to you that I would like to see it? Also I told you: 'Negotiate with Manchukuo concerning the North Manchurian Project.' In spite of this you published a memorandum several days later and failed to show me the documentary proof. Why did you publish such a thing?"

Hirota said that the most important issue now was the CER question and that a general improvement in the atmosphere between their countries was necessary. Noting that the transfer of the American fleet from the Pacific to the Atlantic had considerably alleviated tension between the United States and Japan, Hirota urged the Soviet Union to improve Soviet-Japanese relations by pulling back some of her forces from the Manchukuoan border.

Iuren'ev replied that the situation was different. The USSR bordered on Manchukuo, and the reduction of armaments in border areas could not be effected so easily. Besides, certain influential circles in Japan were openly preparing for war with the USSR.

Iuren'ev concurred that the speedy solution of the CER question was desirable, but remarked that Japan must first restore normal conditions in Manchuria. If such actions as the arrest of Soviet railway employees would cease, the Soviet government would be willing to resume the negotiations for the sale of the CER. Iuren'ev stated that the Soviet Union wished to live in friendship with Japan and had offered to conclude a nonaggression pact with her; she would be glad if

Japan would be ready to sign one now. But he warned: "We shall not sell the railway for next to nothing, and we are not afraid of Manchurian threats to seize the railway."

Taken aback, Hirota insisted that the Soviet Union exaggerated Japan's preparation for war. The Soviet Union and Japan must understand each other and normalize their relations. He reiterated that Japan had nothing to do with the arrests and asserted that if the USSR were truly interested in selling the railway, she would not harp on such "irrelevant incidents." When he contended that it would be difficult for him to do anything about the arrests, that his position was "very delicate," Iuren'ev replied that he understood this. The Soviet side might refrain from publicizing Hirota's concessions in this regard.[36]

On November 7 the Soviet consulate general in Harbin gave a reception, at which Slavutskii and Komatsubara, the chief of the Japanese military mission, agreed to meet to discuss the situation that had arisen.

On November 9 Komatsubara called on Slavutskii, as arranged, and they talked for about four hours. Komatsubara revived the question of the locomotives, and Slavutskii reiterated the demand that the arrested Soviet officials be released. When Komatsubara mentioned the rights of the Manchurian side, Slavutskii retorted that he could talk about the Manchurian side somewhere on the North Pole, but not in Harbin. When he himself talked to Manchurians they frequently re-

---

[36] Saionji-Harada Memoirs," 737–38; Iuren'ev to Foreign Commissariat, November 7, 1933, "Immediately," DVP, XVI, 606–607; JWC, November 16, 1933, p. 602. Snow reported from Tokyo he had learned from a good source that Iuren'ev did not consider that Hirota's suggestion that the USSR withdraw some of her forces from the Manchukuoan border had been intended seriously. (Snow to Simon, No. 652, November 24, 1933, FO 371/17152–858.)

ferred him to Komatsubara. The Soviets had not discussed before who the actual masters of Manchuria
were, but the masters themselves were forcing them
to do so. It was on them that the further steps of the
Russians would depend.

In response to Komatsubara's complaint about the
publication of the documents, Slavutskii asked rhetorically what the Russians should have done when their
treaties and interests were being violated while the
Japanese government was giving categorical assurances that they were being respected. They were forced
to take such a step. When Komatsubara referred to
a speech by Viacheslav Molotov, chairman of the
Council of People's Commissars, in which the latter
had dwelled on the strengthening of the Red Army
and its determination to smash any enemy of the
USSR, Slavutskii assured him that Molotov had talked
also of the continuing desire of the Soviet Union for
good-neighborly relations with Japan. "But the key
to our relations is at the present moment in the hands
of the Japanese government."

Komatsubara admitted that the Japanese had enormous influence in Manchukuo. He insisted, however,
that not everything must be blamed on the Japanese
government. Not all Japanese understood what should
be done, but, he stressed, Japan wanted friendship
with the USSR.

In his record of the conversation, Slavutskii noted
that he had not talked with Komatsubara for a month
and a half. They had met at banquets, but had not
spoken at length as Komatsubara was visibly embarrassed by the situation that had developed. Komatsubara had regarded their long meeting this day as
the renewal of their "intimate friendship," and indeed,

Slavutskii wrote, they had discussed everything "frankly and privately" and as "friends."[37]

On November 10 the Soviet delegation to the Tokyo conference sent an urgent cable to the Foreign Commissariat. The publication of the documents, it asserted, had made a tremendous impression in Japan and had increased the opposition of moderates to the military. Now the Japanese government was trying to spread the false impression that Hirota's appointment had inaugurated a new, peaceful policy toward the USSR and that the Council of Five Ministers (the premier and the ministers of foreign affairs, finance, war and navy) had agreed to Hirota's plan for the amicable settlement of all issues, but that the Soviet government was frustrating this peaceful policy of Japan by a new aggressive course, by preparations for war, and by attempts to enlist the support of the United States against Japan. The Soviet delegation recommended:

> The resolute policy that we are pursuing is unquestionably the only way to sober up the military to a certain extent and to strengthen the opposition of the moderate elements to the policy of challenges and provocations. It is necessary at the same time to expose the double game of the Japanese government and particularly its attempts to don the mask of love of peace while simultaneously continuing and even intensifying the provocations on the CER, which are carefully being hushed up here. We consider it very important that Japanese public opinion learn from the . . . articles and commentaries in our newspapers that [Japan's] adventurist policy and provocation of war have not ceased, that the outrages and provocations on the CER, which thwart the negotiations concerning the sale of the CER and

---

[37] Slavutskii's record of his conversation with Komatsubara, November 9, 1933, DVP, XVI, 618–20.

an improvement in the relations with the USSR, are continuing under the cover of Hirota's empty phrases. We must be firm and must rebuff objections to defense measures on our part. At the same time we should point to the unchangingly peaceful character of our policy. . . .[38]

In a conversation with Iuren'ev on December 14, Hirota broached the subject of the resumption of the railway talks. When Iuren'ev replied that the Soviet side was willing to resume the talks at any time if only the Manchurian side freed the prisoners and restored the *status quo ante* on the CER, Hirota admitted that Manchukuo had committed "a certain error" in regard to the CER. He declared, however, that the cardinal problem was the question of the price of the railway and that the price should be determined at once in yen. Hirota added that if he were sure that the negotiations could be concluded quickly (that the Soviets were serious in their intention to sell the railway), he might be of assistance. Iuren'ev restated that the question of the renewal of the negotiations and of their tempo depended on Hirota.[39]

On December 15 Slavutskii protested to Shih Lü-pen against the attempt by the Manchukuoan authorities "to reduce the rights of the USSR on the CER and unilaterally carry out changes in the administration of the CER with a view toward complete seizure of the railway itself." He complained that since the arrest of the six prominent Soviet railway officials, their Manchurian assistants, the Manchurian assistant general manager, and other Manchukuoan railway offi-

[38] Soviet Delegation (Iuren'ev, Kozlovskii, Kuznetsov) to Foreign Commissariat, November 10, 1933, "Urgent," DVP, XVI, 627–28.
[39] DVP, XVII, 765, note 10; Iuren'ev to Foreign Commissariat, January 8, 1934, DVP, XVII, 33.

cials had stopped obeying the orders of the general manager and of other lawful agents of the railway, declaring them invalid; they had dismissed Soviet citizens and had appointed Manchurians in their place, in spite of the fact that the Soviet citizens had been appointed by the lawful administration of the railway in accordance with existing regulations. In violation of the railway statutes and of the rights belonging to the Soviet general manager, Manchukuoan officials had been acting on their own authority with the assistance of the police.

Slavutskii declared that the Soviet government did not recognize the changes in the administration and management of the CER that were being effected unilaterally by the Manchurian side in violation of the Peking and Mukden treaties and was in no measure bound by them; it reserved the right to demand damages for the losses suffered by the CER as the result of these measures. Asserting that the Soviet side faithfully abided by the Peking and Mukden agreements, Slavutskii expressed the expectation that the Manchurian organs would take measures to restore their observance on the CER.[40]

On December 22 Rudyi wrote to the chief commissary of the Kwantung Army, General Sano, with a copy to Komatsubara, that as of December 1, the Japanese military command had run up a bill of over

[40] *Izvestiia,* December 17, 1933; JWC, December 28, 1933, p. 787. The *Chronicle* sympathized with Slavutskii's complaint against Manchukuoan subversion of the railway administration: "Considering the fact that the Manchukuo Government is negotiating for the purchase of the line, this method of cheapening it is one that commands admiration rather for its astuteness than for its honourableness." (JWC, December 28, 1933, p. 776) When the *Manchuria Daily News* blamed the Soviets for the fact that bandits were attacking trains on the CER at a time when "on every other railway in the country peace has been restored," the *Chronicle* encountered: "On whose shoulders lies the charge of criminal neglect? After all, the duty of the Soviet staff is to manage the line; it is the business of the Manchukuo Government to protect it." (*Ibid.,* p. 779.)

22 million rubles, of which it had paid less than two million. Rudyi realized that the abnormal delay, which caused the railway serious financial difficulties, was probably due to the fact that the Japanese army withheld payment until acceptance of its request for a preferential discount. But Sano had been notified a year ago—in letters of November 29 and December 24, 1932—that a 50 percent discount had been granted by the railway for military transport. Two copies of a temporary agreement to this effect had been sent to him at the time with the request that he sign and return one of the copies. This had not been done. Rudyi requested that the Japanese meet their debt without further delay, discounting the above figure by half.[41]

On January 8, 1934, Iuren'ev called on Hirota and, referring to their conversation of December 14, asked for his good offices in the release of the arrested officials and in the resumption of the railway talks. The Soviet government was prepared, he said, to propose a "new, considerably lowered price" for the CER in paper yen rather than in gold rubles as soon as the Soviet railway officials were freed.

Giving no sign of elation, Hirota noted that the fate of the prisoners was already being discussed between the Soviet consul general in Harbin and the local authorities. Did Iuren'ev want him to advise Manchukuo to release the arrested officials?

When Iuren'ev replied in the affirmative, Hirota remarked that in order to avoid further conflict, it would be best if the Soviet officials quit Manchukuo upon being set free. Hirota stated that although the lowering of the price and its quotation in paper yen would facilitate the negotiations, it was desirable to

[41] *Izvestiia,* December 26, 1933.

be certain that the negotiations would at once bring favorable results, in other words, that the new Soviet figure would approximate that offered by Manchukuo.

Iuren'ev retorted with irritation that he could ask the same question concerning the certainty of the outcome of the negotiations of Hirota, as the success or failure of the talks depended primarily on him and on the Japanese government. He hoped that the Japanese government would do everything to have Manchukuo name a serious price. When Hirota stated that if the "last price" which the Soviet side planned to name would not be low enough, the question might not be resolved, Iuren'ev corrected Hirota that he had in no way qualified the price as "last" or "next to last." It was the price that the Soviet side would name after a series of serious concessions which it had made already.[42]

On January 15 Hirota invited Iuren'ev to the Foreign Office and informed him that he had duly discussed the matter with Manchukuo and that the examination of the prisoners having been completed, they would be set free shortly. Noting that their release would remove the main obstacle to the resumption of negotiations, Hirota asked Iuren'ev to do what he could to expedite matters and facilitate the solution of the exchange rate issue by basing the new Soviet price on paper yen, so that it would be clear how far apart the two sides were.

Iuren'ev thanked Hirota for his intercession and reiterated Soviet willingness to present the reduced asking price in paper yen.[43]

Hirota had told Baron Harada Kumao on January

[42] Iuren'ev to Foreign Commissariat, January 8, 1934, DVP, XVII, 33–34; Nisso kosho-shi, 301; JWC, January 18, 1934, p. 69.

[43] JWC, January 25, 1934, p. 104.

13 that he was eager to solve the CER question. "I'm going to resume negotiations as soon as possible in order to settle the matter."[44] A new hitch developed, however, in connection with the return of the Soviet officials who had been under arrest for five months. Manchukuo wanted to deport them directly to the USSR; the Soviet Union wanted them reinstated in their positions and then "transferred" to Russian territory at some later time. A news dispatch from Harbin described the question as a matter of "face," but the heart of the issue was whether Russians or Manchurians would control the key positions held by the officials before their arrest.[45]

When Iuren'ev called on Hirota again to seek his intercession, the Japanese foreign minister reiterated his willingness to secure the early release of the Soviet officials, but avoided being drawn into the dispute by whom their successors should be named. To Iuren'ev's request for his good offices in halting Manchukuoan agitation for a reduction in railway freight rates, lest ill feeling be generated to the detriment of the talks, Hirota replied that this matter too should be resolved by the Soviet and Manchukuoan sides directly.[46]

On February 14 Iuren'ev repeated to Hirota the desire of his government to reopen the railway negotiations, provided Manchukuo freed the six imprisoned employees and let the Russian side appoint their successors. He did not accept Hirota's counterproposal that the talks be resumed upon the release of the prisoners, the question of their successors being left for negotiation on the spot, although he agreed to communicate the proposal to Moscow.[47]

[44] "Saionji-Harada Memoirs," 780.
[45] JWC, January 25, 1934, p. 104.
[46] *Ibid.*
[47] JWC, February 15, 1934, pp. 212–13.

The following day Komatsubara and Slavutskii compromised that upon the release and departure of the six arrested officials, Rudyi would name in their stead acting chiefs, whose appointment would be confirmed by Li Shao-keng and Bandura. In other words, the Soviet side retained the right of sole nomination, with the Manchukuoan side confirming the nominations.[48] The final agreement concerning the release and replacement of the officials was concluded in Tokyo between Iuren'ev and Hirota on February 19[49] and was initialled on the twenty-second.[50]

The six officials were released and dismissed from their jobs on February 24. They left for the USSR on March 17. Their acting replacements were named on February 24 by Rudyi in an order whose text had been agreed upon beforehand by Iuren'ev and Hirota. The appointments were confirmed by Bandura and Fan Chi-kuan.[51]

[48] DVP, XVII, 765–66, note 11. Japanese sources state more vaguely that "pending the formal appointment of the chiefs of the sections by the Board of Directors of the NMR, the acting chiefs shall be appointed under joint signature of the Manager and the two (Soviet and Manchukuo) Assistant Managers of the NMR." (Japanese Archives, IMT document 391, reel WT 53.)

[49] DVP, XVII, 780, note 64.

[50] Iuren'ev to Foreign Commissariat, February 22, 1934, DVP, XVII, 160; JWC, March 1, 1934, p. 283.

[51] DVP, XVII, 780, note 65.

10

Tokyo Conference: Second Phase

On February 26, 1934, the negotiations for the sale of the Chinese Eastern Railway were resumed after an interruption of half a year. According to Soviet sources, the warnings of the Soviet government, backed by defensive military measures, had made the necessary impression on Japan and had brought about the release of the Soviet officials and thus the renewal of the talks.[1] According to Japanese sources, the Japanese had mediated the freeing of the officials after Ambassador Iuren'ev had told Foreign Minister Hirota on January 8 that the Soviet side was prepared "to change its attitude" and lower the price if the men were released.[2]

Iuren'ev informed Hirota on February 26 that the Soviet government was prepared to sell the CER for 200 million paper yen (about 67½ million gold rubles) plus a discharge allowance for Soviet employees, which, in response to a query of Hirota, he later

---

[1] Kutakov, *Istoriia,* 133.
[2] *Nisso kosho-shi,* 301.

estimated to come to an additional 30 million paper yen. The Soviet government, he said, would be willing to take half of the total sum in goods.[3]

In the second phase of the Tokyo Conference Hirota openly spoke for Manchukuo, having been appointed by the Japanese government as go-between in the talks between the USSR and Manchukuo. Hiorota felt that the Soviets had shunned direct negotiations with Manchukuo partly because they disliked Ohashi, the Manchukuoan vice minister of foreign affairs, as an individual, partly because they feared that the Japanese army might intervene. Besides, Hirota told Harada on March 19, "I believe that they would like to be able to say that the feeling between Japan and Russia has become friendly."[4] To the Soviets, negotiation with Manchukuo alone had seemed futile, since Manchukuo, in their eyes, was but a mouthpiece of Japan. They hailed Hirota's consent to speak in the name of Manchukuo as a diplomatic gain for them in that Japan had now been flushed into the open and could no longer hide behind the Manchukuoan delegation.[5] Yet two months were to pass before the Japanese-Manchukuoan side responded to the new Soviet proposal.

On April 14 Hirota gave a luncheon party for the delegates and for leading Japanese officials at his official residence.[6] The occasion was commemorated by a group photograph in Hirota's garden. When everyone sat down to eat, Hirota suddenly seized the right hands of Iuren'ev and Ting, by whom he was flanked, and brought them together in a symbolic handshake. The

[3] *Izvestiia*, August 18, 1934; Kutakov, *Istoriia*, 133–34.
[4] "Saionji-Harada Memoirs," 833–34.
[5] Kutakov, *Istoriia*, 133–34.
[6] JWC, April 12, 1934, p. 482; April 19, 1934, p. 517.

unexpected gesture provoked general merriment. Hirota himself rocked with laughter.[7]

Iuren'ev reciprocated Japanese hospitality with a luncheon for the conference participants at the Soviet embassy four days later, on April 18.[8]

On April 21 Hirota and Iuren'ev agreed that an informal meeting between the delegates of the USSR and Manchukuo was to be held on April 23, preparatory to the resumption of formal talks. Instructions, which Iuren'ev awaited from Moscow, did not arrive in time, however, and the meeting was postponed for three days.

At the meeting on April 26, Manchukuo was represented by Ohashi, Mori, Sugihara and Uzawa; the Soviet Union, by Kozlovskii, Kuznetsov, and an interpreter. Ohashi presented the new Manchukuoan offer: 100 million paper yen, with the compensation of the dismissed employees to be borne by the seller, that is to say, by the USSR. Manchukuo was to succeed to all the credits and liabilities of the railway as of January 1, 1934, as shown in the ledger transmitted earlier by the Soviets to Hirota.

Manchukuo thus had doubled her offer, while the Soviet Union had halved the asking price in her proposal of February 26. Yet the two sides had started bargaining from such vastly different positions that they were still far apart.[9]

An attempt by Iuren'ev on May 18 to solicit Hirota's good offices in securing Manchukuoan acceptance of

[7] JWC, April 19, 1934, pp. 514, 517.
[8] JWC, April 12, 1934, p. 482.
[9] JWC, May 3, 1934; August 30, 1934, p. 291; Kutakov, *Istoriia,* 134; *Nisso kosho-shi,* 301. Hirota confided to Harada at about this time that the CER question seemed to be developing favorably and that if the Soviet Union was willing to sell the railway, a settlement could probably be reached. ("Saionji-Harada Memoirs," 860.)

the Soviet asking price for the railway failed. Hirota retorted that as an intermediary he could not press Manchukuo alone for concessions. Both sides must compromise. He asked, therefore, that the USSR reduce her demands.[10]

On May 21 the Soviet-Manchukuoan negotiations were resumed, but no progress was registered as both sides clung to their respective proposals. In commenting on the failure to reach an agreement, the Japanese press voiced the suspicion of the military that the USSR was deliberately avoiding a settlement, now that her military preparations in East Asia had been completed, and conveyed their warning that if further negotiations brought no better results, "Manchukuo may be compelled to adopt a resolute attitude in tackling the problem."[11]

On May 25 Iuren'ev informed Hirota that the Soviet side was willing to go down in price by 10 million yen—down to 190 million yen. Hirota said that this was not enough and pressed for a further reduction. When Iuren'ev and Hirota saw each other again on June 4 to discuss various problems, Hirota asked for a reply to his request for a lower figure. Iuren'ev responded that he had not yet received an answer from Moscow, probably because Foreign Commissar Litvinov was away in Geneva.[12] During another meeting, on June 23, Hirota again prodded Iuren'ev to make further concessions. He proposed as a compromise that the Soviet Union sell the CER for the 100 million yen offered by Manchukuo, but that Manchukuo, rather than the USSR, assume the discharge payments of approximately 30 million yen.[13]

[10] JWC, May 24, 1934; Kutakov, *Istoriia*, 134.
[11] JWC, May 24, 1934, p. 694.
[12] Kutakov, *Istoriia*, 134; JWC, June 14, 1934, p. 788; June 21, 1934, p. 829; *Nisso kosho-shi*, 301–302.
[13] *Izvestiia*, August 18, 1934; Kutakov, *Istoriia*, 134.

Five days later, on June 28, Iuren'ev responded that his government was prepared to accept 170 million yen, provided that Manchukuo made the dismissal payments. Hirota was pleased that the Soviets had reduced the amount, but said that the gap was still too wide.[14]

On July 23, after a delay of three more weeks, due in part to the resignation of the Saito government and the formation of a new cabinet, Hirota, who had stayed on as foreign minister, invited Iuren'ev to his office and asked him if the Soviet Union would accept 120 million yen plus discharge payments.[15] Iuren'ev cabled home for instructions, as did Ting, who learned of Hirota's counterproposal only the following day, on July 24.[16]

Predictably Manchukuo accepted Hirota's plan. Foreign Minister Hsieh Chih-shih so stated publicly on July 28.[17] The Soviet side was not satisfied, however, and Iuren'ev presented another set of figures. The USSR, he told Hirota on July 30, would settle for 160 million yen (about 56 million gold rubles). She would be willing to take two thirds, instead of the originally proposed one half, of the amount in goods.

The Japanese welcomed the increase in the proportion of goods to be purchased from Japan. But they did not like the Soviet suggestion that the prices of the goods be fixed as of the date of the conclusion of the negotiations, nor the demand that the monetary portion of the payment for the railway be made in gold.

Both Iuren'ev and Hirota declared their offers to be final. Hirota added the warning that he would aban-

---

[14] JWC, July 12, 1934; Kutakov, *Istoriia*, 134.
[15] *Nisso Kosho-shi*, 302; Kutakov, *Istoriia*, 134.
[16] JWC, August 2, 1934, p. 167.
[17] JWC, August 9, 1934, p. 199.

don his role as intermediary if the Soviet side persisted in its position.[18]

On August 8 the Foreign Ministry of Manchukuo released a statement warning the Soviet Union that she must bear full responsibility for the collapse of the talks if she did not accept Hirota's compromise. It threatened, if no agreement was reached, to treat the railway as a commercial organization under her jurisdiction and to act unilaterally in settling all matters relating to it.[19]

Nonetheless, Iuren'ev reiterated to Hirota on August 10 that the Soviet government could not accept his compromise plan. He did ask Hirota to continue his good offices to bring about a solution, but, true to his word, Hirota refused and told Iuren'ev to conduct further talks directly with the Manchukuoan side.[20]

When Ohashi called on Iuren'ev on the thirteenth, however, Iuren'ev informed him that he would not negotiate with him directly unless he would be willing to pay a higher price. Ohashi retorted that in such a case it was useless for him to remain in Tokyo and that he would leave for Hsinking the following day. Both sides declared (and themselves believed) that the other was unreasonable, insincere, and solely responsible for the breakdown of the talks.

Hirota and Togo concurred with Ohashi's stand. The military felt that his resolve was belated.[21]

[18] Kutakov, *Istoriia*, 134–35; *Nisso kosho-shi*, 302; JWC, August 9, 1934, p. 199; August 30, 1934, p. 291.

[19] JWC, August 16, 1934; DVP, XVII, 815, note 235.

[20] JWC, August 16, 1934, p. 235; August 30, 1934, p. 291; Kutakov, *Istoriia*, p. 135.

[21] *Nisso kosho-shi*, 302–303; Kutakov, *Istoriia*, 135; JWC, August 23, 1934, p. 261 and August 30, 1934, p. 291. It was generally recognized in Japan that the Soviet Union was in a far stronger position now to defend her interests than when the Chinese had tried to seize the railway, and that the Red Army

In accordance with an oral agreement made by Hirota and Iuren'ev on March 5, the specific offers and counteroffers, related above, had not been revealed to the public. But the Soviets had felt for some time that the Japanese had been violating the agreement to confine the release of information about the negotiations to joint communiqués. Iuren'ev had protested to Hirota on March 14, April 24, and June 23 that the tendentious articles in the Japanese press, which hindered the course of the negotiations by giving a false picture of the actual positions of the sides, had been government inspired, and he had warned Hirota that if such articles would continue to be published, the Soviet Union would be forced to set the record straight. When newspapers, upon the collapse of the talks, accused the Soviet side of unwillingness to compromise, the USSR once again appealed to the court of world opinion and on August 18 published a detailed resumé of the protracted bargaining.[22] It revealed how the Soviet side had come down in its asking price from 250 million gold rubles or 625 million yen at the prevailing rate of exchange to 56 million gold rubles or 160 million yen, while the Japanese-Manchukuoan side had raised its offer from 50 million yen to 120 million yen or by only 70 million yen. This was an insignificant increase, it pointed out, considering the fact that the first figure had not constituted a serious offer for the 1,700 kilometers of railway with its rich and varied services, equipment and organizations, which in spite of all the difficulties on the railway still brought con-

---

with its air force would constitute a formidable opponent. (JWC, August 23, 1934.) Yet the Kwantung Army favored a breakdown in the talks, insisting that no more than 120 million yen be offered for the CER. ("Saionji-Harada Memoirs," 973–74.)

[22] DVP, XVII, 817, note 244.

siderable income. There could be no question, *Izvestiia* concluded, which side was uncompromising and aggressive and responsible for the collapse of the negotiations.[23]

The Japanese government on August 22 formally protested the Soviet action, then released its own version of the negotiations. Insisting that it had "left no stone unturned in an earnest endeavor to effect a successful solution of the question," the Japanese government took umbrage at Soviet claims that Hirota's latest proposal had been something like an ultimatum. "That the Japanese Foreign Minister is only a mediator, and as such he is not in a position to present an ultimatum, had been specifically explained by him to the Soviet delegate." Dismissing major concessions of the Soviet side as "nothing other than a confession that the initial prices were based on gross exaggeration," the Japanese government in one breath voiced satisfaction that the Soviet government proposed to preserve peace in the Far East and doubt that it really intended to do so, repeating the allegation current in Japan that "although the USSR professes its desire to negotiate peacefully, it is merely by way of simulation, and that it really tries to delay the parley in the hope of seeing Japan involved in an international 'crisis,' which the Soviet presumes to be imminent." "If the Soviet Government really intends to transfer the railway and desires to do so as soon as possible," the Foreign Office concluded, "it certainly should make proper demonstration of such intention."[24]

In a separate public statement Manchukuo declared that "the Manchukuoan side cannot approve of the

[23] *Izvestiia,* August 18, 1934.
[24] JWC, August 31, 1934, pp. 291–92.

Soviet logic that in selling any goods one must first quote a high price if he expects to get the best of the bargaining.''[25]

The very day that the negotiations were broken off, the arrest of Soviet citizens was renewed. On August 21 Acting Consul General Raivid sent Shih a list of 38 citizens, including chiefs of departments and station-masters, who had been arrested since August 13.[26] He protested that the arrests had been carried out without the presentation of appropriate documents and had been accompanied by the search of the offices and apartments of the prisoners without explanation. The police authorities, he wrote, had not only failed to inform the consulates of the USSR of the reasons for the arrests, but of their very occurrence. He alleged that the prisoners were being mistreated by the police and that the deportation of Soviet citizens from Manchuria to the USSR was continuing without notification of the consulate general. He demanded that Shih provide him with an explanation for the arrest of the 38 citizens and take steps for their release at the earliest possible time and for their humane treatment until then.[27]

The Soviet side regarded the arrests as intentional harrassment, designed to pressure the USSR into accepting the Manchukuoan offer. It said so in TASS press releases on August 18 and 27 and in a strong diplomatic note, handed by Iuren'ev to Hirota on August 22. Berating the Japanese authorities for depriving the railway of its leading personnel under trumped-up charges, the note drew attention to the "astounding" allegations made in an official com-

[25] JWC, September 13, 1934, p. 358.
[26] DVP, XVII, 816, note 242.
[27] Raivid to Shih Lü-pen, August 21, 1934, DVP, XVII, 565–66.

muniqué of the Japanese War Office that the Special Far Eastern Red Army had masterminded the bandit raids on the CER.[28]

The same day, on August 22, Togo told Iuren'ev that the Japanese Foreign Office would file a protest against Soviet violation of the agreement not to publish data concerning the negotiations except by mutual consent. Iuren'ev replied that such a protest would be "mistaken and baseless." He reminded Togo that he had complained many times to Hirota of articles concerning the negotiations in the Japanese press. Dismissing Togo's contention that the arrests on the CER and the breakdown in the negotiations had been a mere "coincidence," Iuren'ev told Togo of the note he had sent to Hirota that day.

When Togo spoke of the need to come to an agreement concerning the CER as soon as possible, Iuren'ev retorted that the Japanese side was solely responsible that the negotiations had to all intents and purposes been broken off. Togo countered that the negotiations had not been broken off[29] and that the departure of "the very restless and impulsive Ohashi" was of no significance; in fact, it might prove beneficial. Togo's warning that further delay in the negotiations might strengthen anti-Soviet sentiment and dangerously impair Soviet-Japanese relations was parried by Iuren'ev with the observation that it was up to those who had heedlessly broken off the talks to think of means of expediting them. As far as "danger" was concerned, the USSR was prepared for any eventualities.

[28] Iuren'ev to Hirota, August 22, 1934, DVP, XVII, 566–68: *Moscow Daily News*, August 25, 1934; *Nisso kosho-shi*, 303; JWC, August 30, 1934, p. 292; September 6, 1934; Kutakov, *Istoriia*, 135–37.

[29] Ohashi himself had denied that his departure constituted a rupture of the negotiations, since Chief Delegate Cheng was remaining in Tokyo. (JWC, August 23, 1934, p. 261; August 30, 1934, p. 291.)

To Togo's assertion that the latest Soviet reduction in the asking price by 10 million yen was not enough, as he had told Raivid at the time,[30] Iuren'ev replied that 10 million was a large sum, but that Hirota was free to make a counterproposal. When Togo asked tentatively how the Soviet side would react to an offer of 130 million yen without discharge pay, Iuren'ev answered that the figure was [too] low, but that he valued the interest and initiative Togo had shown in the matter. "Togo asked that his proposal be submitted to Moscow," Iuren'ev cabled to the Foreign Commissariat. "I did not refuse, but neither did I give a definite reply."[31]

On August 24 Raivid wrote another letter to Shih, protesting against the disruption of normal conditions on the CER. He reminded him that Slavutskii had repeatedly complained about the inadequate guarding of the eastern line of the CER. Yet while the number of attacks on the railway had been increasing, he wrote, guards had been removed from freight trains on the eastern line in May and the mass arrest of Soviet railway employees, which had been taking place since August 13, threatened to leave the railway in a state of complete disorganization. Raivid ridiculed Manchukuoan charges that Soviet railway officials were behind the bandit attacks on the railway, noting that they were being accused in effect of having organized the plundering and kidnaping of themselves and of their own families.[32]

---

[30] In the conversation on August 8 Togo had asserted that by coming down only 10 million yen or one fifth of the difference between the figures proposed by Iuren'ev and Hirota, the Soviet government showed that it did not value the mediation of Hirota, Raivid retorted that the Soviet government did not appraise his mediation in terms of millions of yen. (DVP, XVII, 817, note 245.)

[31] Iuren'ev to Foreign Commissariate, August 22, 1934, DVP, XVII, 568–70.

[32] Raivid to special agent of the Ministry of Foreign Affairs in North Manchuria, August 24, 1934, DVP, XVII, 572–74.

The issue of the protection of the CER was also raised in a letter from Kuznetsov to Li the same day. Noting that all his previous complaints about the "impossible" situation had remained unanswered, Kuznetsov asserted that it was not enough to put guards on passenger trains. The main function of the railway guard, he wrote, was to prevent bandits from entering the CER railway zone and to protect the lives of the workers and employees who maintained the line and could detect and repair damage to the track. This the railway guard was not doing, although it refused to put guards on freight trains on the ground that it needed them for operations against the *hunghutze*. Kuznetsov, like Raivid, refuted "with indignation" the charges levied by Manchukuoan officials against the Soviet railway employees and workers, who had heroically carried out their duties at the risk of their lives. He called upon Li, who had to know better than anyone else "the full absurdity of the wild charges," to prevail upon the Manchurian authorities to cease the repression of Soviet employees and to guard the CER effectively.[33]

On August 22, Ota had proposed to Deputy Foreign Commissar Boris Stomoniakov that they discuss unofficially the undesirable situation on the CER. During the conversation which had ensued that day and was continued on the thirty-first, Ota defended the actions of the authorities in Manchukuo, echoing the charges that the Soviet employees of the CER were connected with the bandits and that the Special Far Eastern Red Army impeded Japanese military transportation in Manchuria. Expressing the fear that the situation might lead to war, Ota said to Stomoniakov: "We diplomats

[33] Kuznetsov to Li, August 24, 1934, DVP, XVII, 574–76.

must think whether one cannot find a way out to remove the existing danger." Stomoniakov replied that he was prepared to do everything in his power to assist Ota in improving Soviet-Japanese relations, but that he could not agree to seek a solution in the direction Ota indicated. He could not accept the accusations levied against the Special Far Eastern Red Army, if for no other reasons that that they were contrary to common sense.[34]

Stomoniakov protested against the torture of imprisoned Soviet citizens by Japanese officials in Manchukuo who were trying to force them to "confess" that they themselves had organized the attacks on the eastern line of the CER. He detailed the case of a female clerk, questioned by the Japanese gendarmerie in Harbin. The interrogators had placed metal rods between her fingers, then had tied up the fingers with a cord so tightly that she had fainted. When she had regained consciousness, they had beaten her in the head and face, had torn out her hair, and had poured water in her mouth and nose in the vain attempt to extort a "confession."[35]

As European and American newspapers echoed the Russian accusations and even Japanese papers waxed critical of the policy of their government, the Foreign Offices of Japan and Manchukuo found it necessary

---

[34] DVP, XVII, 820–21, note 256.

[35] *Moscow Daily News,* September 2, 1934. An account of the above was distributed by the TASS news agency, together with the findings of two doctors who had examined Golovina and another Soviet citizen detained by the Japanese gendarmerie. "The brutalities alleged by 'Tass' seem to be well-supported by evidence," Harcourt-Smith commented. (September 14, 1934, in minutes accompanying Chilston to Simon, No. 438, September 6, 1934, FO 371/18112.) Working with White Russian policemen who had entered their service and sought to prove their loyalty by ferreting out Communists among their countrymen, the Japanese imprisoned and tortured also many emigrés and extracted from some of them false confessions that they were Red agents. (Leshko, 39–59.)

to issue separate denials that the arrests of Soviet employees were related to the negotiations.[36]

In his reply to Iuren'ev's note of August 22, Hirota wrote on September 4 that the arrests of the Soviet citizens had been carried out by Manchukuo "simply in accordance with its jurisdictional powers, owing to conspiracies aimed at the wrecking of military trains." He denied that the War Ministry had issued any official statements concerning the involvement of the Special Far Eastern Red Army in the train incidents. The Japanese government was not responsible for reports that may have been published in private newspapers. Rejecting as "provocative' and completely unfounded accusations that the mounting bandit attacks on the trains were due to "deliberate negligence or actions on the part of Japan and Manchukuo" and that they testified to "an intensification of aggressive attempts on the part of certain Japanese official circles," Hirota reiterated that Soviet citizens were behind the attacks, which differed from ordinary bandit raids in that no attempt was made to rob the trains. Moreover, all the incidents took place on the eastern line of the railway, the majority of trains hit were carrying war materials, and the victims were predominantly Japanese or Manchurians.[37]

Izvestiia ridiculed Japanese and Manchukuoan allegations of Soviet sabotage. A cartoon, entitled "Crude Tricks," depicted a uniformed jack-in-the-box, wearing the sign "I am a Soviet employee, an agent of the USSR," brandishing a pistol and a crowbar with the tag "for the destruction of the CER."

[36] *Nisso kosho-shi,* 303; Kutakov, *Istoriia,* 135–37; JWC, August 23, 1934, p. 262.

[37] Hirota to Iuren'ev, September 4, 1934, Japanese Archives, reel WT 53, IMT document 391, pp. 15–19; *Moscow Daily News,* October 11, 1934; *Izvestiia,* October 10, 1934; DVP, XVII, 568.

He was popping out of a box, labeled "Information Agency Kokutsu," which had been opened by a Japanese sitting behind it.[38]

That day, on September 4, Togo called on Iuren'ev and asked him for an answer to the proposal he had made on August 22. When Iuren'ev refused to make a reply, Togo sought his private opinion. Iuren'ev countered that since Togo had not been empowered officially by Hirota to speak for him, he could not negotiate with him. He confirmed, when Togo asked him directly, that a meeting with Hirota would be more useful.

Togo stated that Adachi, founder of the Kokumin Domei Party, had related to Hirota a conversation he had had with Iuren'ev on August 29. Iuren'ev had allegedly said that Hirota could find the means of resuming the negotiations if he so desired; he could, for example, invite Iuren'ev to his house.[39] When Iuren'ev substantiated this, Togo declared that he would soon receive an invitation for tea from Hirota. Iuren'ev replied he would be glad to come.[40]

Hirota duly invited Iuren'ev to his house on September 6 and there resumed the negotiations with the announcement that Manchukuo was prepared to raise her bid for the CER by 10 million yen, that is, from 120 million to 130 million yen, with the additional sum to be paid in goods. He stated that the government of Manchukuo was prepared to pay approximately one third of the cost of the railway, or 40 million yen,

[38] *Izvestiia,* September 6, 1934.

[39] Adachi, like Togo, had tried to sound out Iuren'ev about a lower figure that would be acceptable to the Soviet side. To his statement that it would be good if the two sides split the 40 million yen difference that separated them, Iuren'ev had answered that no one had made such a proposal, but that should it be put forth, it would be considered like any other business offer. (DVP, XVII, 819, note 253.)

[40] Iuren'ev to Foreign Commissariat, September 4, 1934, DVP, XVII, 582–83.

in cash—10 million upon signature, the rest in four installments over a period of three years. The remaining 90 million yen were to be paid in goods over a period of five years. But Manchukuo objected, he noted, to the inclusion of a gold clause.

Hirota wanted the CER agreement to go into force upon signing, that is to say, without ratification. Manchukuo was to assume immediate and full possession of the railway. The main Soviet officials were to leave upon conclusion of the agreement, the rank-and-file of the employees and workers, in a month or two.

Iuren'ev replied that he was disappointed in Hirota's proposal and that he had no hope that an agreement could be reached soon.[41]

On September 8 Stomoniakov wrote to Iuren'ev a long letter in which he expounded some general thoughts concerning the state of Soviet-Japanese relations. He asserted that "the campaign of blackmail, pressure and threats, unexampled even in the history of Soviet-Japanese relations," which the Japanese had mounted, had as its primary objective the capitulation of the USSR in the CER negotiations, but no doubt intended also to influence the talks about the admission of the Soviet Union to the League of Nations and about the conclusion of an East-European Pact. "The initiators of the campaign—and I think Hirota was the first among them—," Stomoniakov declared, "sought to activate the anti-Soviet elements in the West, persuading them that the position of the USSR is not so very solid, that she is faced with war in the Far East and thus constitutes an unfavorable partner for

---

[41] DVP, XVII, 819–20, note 254. "I believe that this problem will be settled if it is not rushed," Hirota confided to Harada two days later. ("Saionji-Harada Memoirs," 1004–05.)

the League of Nations as well as for the Eastern Pact.''
While the campaign had been initiated by the government as ''a great and courageous maneuver for the
attainment of specific foreign policy objectives,''
Stomoniakov wrote, it had been taken over for a very
different purpose by the ''military-fascist circles'' in
Japan. The latter wished to disrupt the negotiations
concerning the CER, seize the railway, and mobilize
the Japanese public for war with the Soviet Union,
proclaiming that it was the latter who was planning
to attack Japan. Hirota and his colleagues soon could
see that the campaign had not only slipped out of their
hands, but was counterproductive, increasing Soviet
resistance to Japanese demands and winning
worldwide sympathy for the USSR. Stomoniakov
believed that the Soviet communiqué of August 18 concerning the course of the CER negotiations had played
a particular role in the downfall of the Japanese policy,
since it had exposed ''the deceit of the Japanese people
by Hirota and the military,'' who had been trying to
convince everyone of Soviet obstinacy and aggressiveness. Because of the above and ''most probably
as the result of pressure by moderate circles,''
Stomoniakov continued, Hirota and the Japanese government has been forced to seek a way out of the
difficult situation which they themselves had created,
pressed no doubt by the fear, lest the USSR, upon
entry into the League of Nations radically change her
position regarding Manchukuo and consequently also
regarding the CER negotiations. That was perhaps why
Hirota had shown haste in inviting Iuren'ev to his
house and in seeking to ascertain at the very beginning
of their conversation whether the USSR was prepared,
in the event an agreement was reached, to surrender
the CER to Manchukuo immediately.

"It is, of course, theoretically conceivable," Stomoniakov wrote, "that everything that has been happening most recently also constitutes a maneuver, to wit, a maneuver to mask some aggressive plan on the part of Japan. Everything suggests, however, that this is not a maneuver, and that this time Hirota and the Japanese government really want to conclude the negotiations concerning the CER as soon as possible and to attain an agreement which could constitute for them the greatest foreign and domestic political success." He remarked that the USSR remained interested, of course, in liquidating the CER problem in her relations with Japan as soon as possible, provided that her dignity and elementary interests were observed. "We have done everything possible to this end, and it is not impossible that by the time you receive this letter final agreement will have been reached concerning the most important questions regarding the surrender of the CER."[42]

On September 12 Iuren'ev informed Hirota that although the Soviet asking price of 160 million yen was already far below the actual cost of the railway, Moscow was willing to split the difference and sell it for 145 million yen to put an end to the haggling which had been going on for fifteen months. It was willing to discuss the other issues, raised by him on the sixth, after agreement on the price had been reached.

[42] Stomoniakov to Iuren'ev, September 8, 1934, DVP, XVII, 583–86; DVP, XVII, 820, note 255. J. M. K. Vyvyan of the British Foreign Office did not believe that the entry of the USSR into the League that month implied any change in Soviet aims: "Joining the League is merely a logical development of the foreign policy of the five-year plan, which has been authoritatively expressed by Soviet publicists as dictated by the necessity of a 'breathing space' . . . ." But L. Collier remarked, "Nevertheless, policies proclaimed as temporary have sometimes become practically permanent through the logic of facts." (Minutes, October 3, 1934, pertaining to Moscow dispatch No. 476, September 25, 1934, FO 371/18301–880.)

"Make it 140 million yen," Hirota said. "We offered 120 million yen at first, so let's compromise and make it 140 million yen."[43]

As Iuren'ev wired back for instructions once more, Hirota told Harada full of confidence on September 18: "I think that this issue will gradually be settled. If this happens, I believe that the tension in Russo-Japanese relations will be greatly alleviated."[44] At the regular meeting of the Privy Council the following day Hirota reiterated the belief that the railway negotiations would come to a successful end, since the Soviet side was desirous of settlement.[45]

That day, on the nineteenth, Iuren'ev grumblingly accepted the 140 million yen figure (about 48 million dollars) and the provision that the agreement take effect upon signing, on two conditions: that the Soviet administration would be freed of all duties and responsibilities (that is to say, that the discharge payments to Soviet employees would be made by Manchukuo) from the moment that the agreement was published in Moscow, Tokyo and Harbin; and that, in view of a possible rise in the cost of Japanese products, the USSR would have the right to place her orders for the goods that were to constitute two-thirds of the payment for the railway within six months from the day that the agreement was signed, with delivery (at these prices) to be made within two years. Iuren'ev reiterated the Soviet demand that one half of the cash payment

[43] Stomoniakov to Iuren'ev, September 10, 1934, DVP, XVII, 587; *Nisso kosho-shi*, 303-304; Kutakov, *Istoriia*, 137–38; *Izvestiia*, November 1, 1934.

[44] "Saionji-Harada Memoirs," 1015–16. One may discount statements of this sort to a certain extent when made to the Soviets as a diplomatic gesture or when released to the press for public consumption. But when made privately, to colleagues, as above, they can be taken as expressing the true feelings of the Japanese foreign minister.

[45] JWC, September 27, 1934, p. 433.

be made at the time of signing, the other half in four installments over a period of three years, and that the agreement contain a gold clause. "In surrendering things of enormous value on the CER," Iuren'ev told Hirota, "the Soviet government cannot assume the risk of the lowering of the purchase price as the result of a drop in the rate of exchange of the yen." The USSR agreed, he said, that Soviet employees and workers be given four months notice by the Manchurian administration, provided they were allowed three months from the day of dismissal to leave Manchukuo.

Enumerating the concessions made by the Soviet side, including its willingness not to stipulate the goods to be obtained and their purchase price, Iuren'ev said that it had the right to expect that its conditions would be accepted. Hirota replied that it was very nice that the question of the price had been settled. As for the other matters, they were the concern of Manchukuo, and he would have the Manchukuoan delegate come at once to Tokyo and ask him about the opinion of his country. "Perhaps Manchukuo will entrust me with the negotiations," Hirota added. "At any rate, we are interested in the quickest possible liquidation of the disagreements."[46]

Meanwhile the arrest of Soviet railway officials had continued unabated. As Raivid, whose written protests of August 21 and 24 had remained unanswered, complained in another letter to Shih Lü-pen October 4, the number of Soviet citizens arrested since August 13 had risen to 142 by October 1, so that a total of 167 Soviet citizens were imprisoned in North Manchuria.[47]

[46] Record of Iuren'ev's conversation with Hirota, September 19, 1934, DVP, XVII, 601–603; *Nisso kosho-shi*, 304.

[47] Raivid to Shih, No. 011/34, October 4, 1934, DVP, XVII, 622–23; *Nisso kosho-shi*, 303.

On October 5 Iuren'ev handed to Hirota a detailed reply to his note of September 4. Iuren'ev took issue with the allegations, advanced as "proof" of the involvement of Soviet citizens in the destruction of trains, that the majority of the trains wrecked had been carrying war materials and that most of the victims had been Japanese or Manchurians. Of the 22 train wrecks on the eastern line of the CER between January 1 and September 5, 1934, only 1 had been that of a military train, even though 60 military trains had passed along the eastern line during those eight months. True, Japanese military shipments had also been sent on mixed freight trains, but, he pointed out, of the 6,949 carloads of Japanese military supplies and personnel between January 1 and September 1, 1934, there had been damaged only 47 cars according to subsequent Japanese claims, 26 cars according to CER documents drawn up at the time of the incidents. According to the official reports of the CER, a total of only 2 Japanese soldiers were wounded in the 22 train wrecks and the bandit attacks on the railway stations of the eastern line during the past eight months, compared with 9 Soviet railway employees killed, 171 wounded, 43 kidnaped, and 13 robbed. "Thus," Iuren'ev wrote, "the official data completely demolish the Japanese claims and thereby confirm the unjustified and unlawful character of the arrests of the citizens of the USSR."

Iuren'ev asserted that while the Soviet general managers and the Soviet directors had done everything in their power to ensure the safety of traffic on the CER, including its eastern line, and while Soviet employees had risked their lives in preventing train wrecks, including those of Japanese military trains, the Manchurian authorities had not only failed to fulfill their treaty obligations of protecting the line, but they had systematically reduced its protection, especially during the past year, and since May 19 had completely with-drawn guards from freight trains on the eastern line. It was due to this that the number of attacks on the railway had increased and had brought almost complete paralysis of what traffic had remained on the eastern line after the interference of the customs officials and other Manchukuoan authorities.

Iuren'ev disputed Hirota's assertion that the Japa-nese War Ministry had never published a communiqué blaming the Soviet Far Eastern Army for the railway incidents. He remarked that the question of the source of the Shimbun Rengo Telegraph Agency bulletin had lost significance, however, since Hirota himself had "found it possible to repeat in the note [of September 4] the accusations put forward in this communiqué against the Soviet employees of the CER." He ex-pressed "particular amazement" at the allegation made by Hirota in his note that prominent Soviet officials and Soviet publications had been guilty of provocative statements vis-à-vis Japan. While the Soviet govern-ment did not know of a single case "when any, even the smallest, provincial newspaper in the USSR, had come out for war with Japan and for the conquest of territory belonging to Japan or occupied by her," Iuren'ev observed, the "aggressive and bellicose state-ments against the USSR" by leading Japanese news-papers and prominent Japanese officials were common knowledge.

Iuren'ev not only rejected all the charges contained in Hirota's note; he accused the Japanese government of encouraging further arbitrariness on the part of the local authorities in Manchuria by having joined in the charges. Pointing out that the number of Soviet citizens imprisoned in Manchuria had risen from the 22 he had mentioned in his note on August 22 to 167, including

142 CER employees, he protested anew against their seizure and demanded "the immediate release of all the innocently arrested Soviet employees of the CER."[48]

The difficulties which the Soviet Union was experiencing with the Manchukuoan authorities while she was in possession of the CER gave rise to misgivings in Moscow whether Manchukuo, with whom she had no diplomatic relations, would live up to her part of the bargain once the railway had been handed over. The Soviet government, therefore, wanted Japan to guarantee the payments for the purchase of the railway. To be sure, it had reservations about Japanese intentions as well, but it felt that the fishery and oil concessions would give her sufficient leverage to force Japan to live up to her obligations.

In their meeting on October 5, Iuren'ev and Hirota discussed the matter of a guarantee. Hirota declared that the Japanese government could not guarantee the payments of a third country and proposed as an alternative that a Japanese banking syndicate make the cash payments to the USSR on behalf of Manchukuo, with the CER serving as collateral.[49]

As Iuren'ev and Hirota continued their discussions on October 15 and 22, Japanese newspapers voiced concern that the Soviet side might be delaying the negotiation of final terms in the expectation that the unsatisfactory conclusion of the naval talks in London might weaken Japan's bargaining position.[50] Yet Premier Okada had told Harada on October 13 with

---

[48] Iuren'ev to Hirota, October 5, 1934, DVP, XVII, 624–28; *Izvestiia*, October 10, 1934; *Moscow Daily News*, October 11, 1934. Edward Coote characterized Iuren'ev's note as couched in terms of "considerable asperity." (Coote to Simon, No. 506, Moscow, October 12, 1934, FO 371/18112.)

[49] JWC, October 11, 1934, pp. 496–97.

[50] JWC, October 25, 1934, p. 572.

confidence that the greater part of Japan's problems with the Soviet Union would be settled,[51] and Hirota had stated to him on the sixteenth that "the negotiations with Russia are going favorably and the Chinese Eastern Railway problem is cleared up except for two or three incidentals."[52]

At the meeting on October 22 Hirota presented Manchukuo's proposals on the terms of transfer. He elaborated on the alternative to the Soviet demand for the guarantee of the loan by the Japanese government. Hirota offered that a Japanese banking syndicate subscribe to public bonds issued by the Manchurian government, thereby providing a credit in favor of the latter. Payments in connection with the transfer of the railway would be made by the Japanese syndicate to the Soviet representative in Tokyo at the direction of the Manchukuoan government. In the event of disputes about payments, the Japanese government would act as intermediary.

Hirota proposed that payments in kind be completed in three and a half years, rather than two and a half, as demanded by Iuren'ev. He did not see the need for inserting a clause in the agreement providing for the establishment of a committee to fix the prices of goods to be furnished as payment in kind, arguing that these were matters that could be adjusted after the conclusion of the agreement. He concurred that

[51] "Saionji-Harada Memoirs," 1031.

[52] *Ibid.*, 1036. As the sale of the CER neared completion, the Japanese Minister of Railways Uchida Nobuya conferred with Hirota about the replacement of the Soviet employees. It was a task of great magnitude, since some 1,000 senior railway officials and about 6,000 other employees were needed. They agreed to entrust the operation of the railway to the South Manchurian Railway for the time being, but to fill a large portion of the vacancies with Japanese officials and employees then in the service of the Japanese State Railways. Meanwhile the USSR hastened the double-tracking of the Amur Railway, the stretch of Trans-Siberian Railway running along the Amur River, entirely through Russian territory, to Vladivostok. (JWC, October 18, 1934, p. 527.)

Manchukuo should take possession of the railway and its property within a month, but demanded that a new inventory be drawn up by the Soviet Union for this purpose. He took issue with the Soviet demand that the Russian school, libraries, hospitals, and cultural establishments in Harbin remain in Soviet hands, insisting that all buildings except for the consulate general be surrendered to Manchukuo. As for the language in which the agreement was to be drawn up, there were to be copies in Russian, Manchu, and Japanese. The Japanese text, Hirota proposed, was to be regarded as the authoritative one in the event of differences of interpretation.[53]

On October 30 Iuren'ev handed to Hirota a detailed reply to the proposals of the twenty-second. They discussed them at length that day and the following day.[54] The Soviet side agreed to the transfer of the railway rights to Manchukuo immediately upon signature of the agreement, but objected to the proposed order of the transaction, which would have made Manchukuo the owner of the CER while leaving the Soviet side temporarily responsible for its operation. It wanted Manchukuo to take delivery of the railway and its property simultaneously with the signing of the agreement. The USSR saw no basis for the demand that the transfer of the CER occur in accordance with an inventory, inasmuch as it had not been sold for its actual cost, but for an agreed gross price, and since Hirota had been furnished a statement concerning the accounts of the railway, including the obligations which the new owner would have to assume (a supplementary statement up-dating the amount to be prepared). The

<hr />

[53] JWC, November 1, 1934, p. 603; November 8, 1934, p. 638.
[54] JWC, November 8, 1934, p. 638; *Izvestiia*, November 21, 1934.

Soviet Union desired obligations in the form of Manchukuoan public bonds for the portion of the payment that was not to be met at once, but Hirota objected that there was no call for her to possess such bonds till the transfer agreement had been signed.

The Soviet side waived the demand for interest on the amount to be paid in kind, but pressed for the appointment of an arbitration committee under the chairmanship of a national of a third power, appointed by a reputable foreign chamber of commerce such as the Chamber of Commerce of the United States or of Great Britain, in the event disputes arose over purchasing prices.[55]

On November 6 Iuren'ev enumerated the kinds of goods the Soviet Union desired in partial payment for the CER. They included small ships, machines, electrical apparatus, fishing nets, raw silk, silk fabrics, rice and tea from Japan, and wheat and soybeans from Manchukuo. When Iuren'ev reiterated the demand for an arbitration committee on which a third party would sit, Hirota objected, asserting that there would be no way of enforcing the prices fixed by such a body and that the Soviet government ought to trust the Japanese government to arrange for fair prices.

Hirota was displeased with a new proposal concerning the dismissal pay for Soviet railway employees. It had been his impression that the Soviet side would accept installment payments over a period of three years; now it demanded a lump sum settlement. "The Japanese side," the *Japan Weekly Chronicle* reported, "is evincing dissatisfaction at the attitude of the Soviet

[55] JWC, November 8, 1934, p. 638; *Izvestiia,* November 1 and November 21, 1934.

Government which is prone to set forth entirely new proposals as the negotiations progress."[56]

On November 13 Hirota showed Iuren'ev a tentative plan for the settlement of unresolved issues pertaining to the transfer of the CER. After prolonged discussion Iuren'ev consented to the drafting of an additional balance sheet for submission at the time of the signing of the new agreement. Work on such a balance sheet had already been begun at Harbin by Soviet and Manchukuoan officials conjointly. Hirota agreed in the name of Manchukuo that payments in kind be completed within three years; that in the event the exchange rate of the yen fluctuated eight per cent or more in relation to the Swiss franc, a new parity be fixed for cash payments; and that three per cent interest per annum be paid on the balance of the cash payments. But the above was made conditional on Soviet acceptance of the Manchukuoan proposal regarding the methods of cash payments and the guarantee of payments. Iuren'ev rejected the Manchukuoan stand on the guarantee question. Nor could he and Hirota agree on establishment of an arbitration committee.[57]

Izvestiia defended Soviet insistence on a Japanese guarantee of Manchukuoan payments. Noting that the Japanese countered the businesslike arguments of the Soviet side with invocations of "trust" in Manchukuo and with the promise "to mediate" in the event of difficulties concerning payments and that they depicted the Soviet demand for a guarantee as an expression of mistrust, if not a direct insult, vis-à-vis Manchukuo

[56] JWC, November 15, 1934, p. 670. But Hirota was not discouraged. As Harada noted after talking with him on November 27: "He told me that Russia was trying to prolong the negotiations, but that they would eventually be successful." ("Saionji-Harada Memoirs," 1072.)

[57] JWC, November 22, 1934, p. 699.

and Japan, *Izvestiia* remarked: "This position arouses great perplexity in informed Moscow circles, where it is pointed out that it is customary throughout the whole world to give guarantees when concluding such transactions. . . . As regards 'mistrust,' it is quite obvious that the Soviet side would not start demanding a Japanese guarantee if it did not trust the effectiveness of this guarantee. . . ."

Turning to the question of an arbitration committee under the chairmanship of a neutral personage, *Izvestiia* explained that the Japanese counterproposal that the third party be the Japanese minister of foreign affairs or the Japanese minister of commerce had been declined, because Japan could not be regarded as a disinterested "third" party in a dispute between the USSR and Manchukuo. "Japan's rejection of the solution of possible differences between the USSR and Manchukuo by means of the principle of arbitration is the stranger," *Izvestiia* observed, "because Japan herself utilizes this principle in the solution of disputes of an economic nature with other states, as testified by the fact that she is a participant in the international treaty of commercial arbitration."[58]

As noted above, Hirota had expressed vexation that Iuren'ev had altered his position on the discharge payments for railway employees—that he had made a "fresh" proposal. *Izvestiia,* on the other hand, asserted that it was Japanese backtracking on agreements that complicated the negotiations and referred to the self-

[58] "Recent international events have persuaded the Tokyo Government that the rest of the world is not sympathetic, to put it no more bluntly than that, and under these circumstances Japan does not consider that any supposedly neutral arbitration commission would render an impartial decision," the *Chronicle* explained. "It is an unfortunate frame of mind, but there it is. The problem is how to get around it, for Russia is equally entitled to an assurance that there will be no arbitrary interpretation of any of the clauses of the sales treaty." (JWC, December 6, 1934, p. 761.)

same issue as an example of Japanese change of position, claiming that Japan had agreed to a lump sum payment on July 23. It stressed the need to conclude an agreement whose execution would be guaranteed in such a way that no one could turn it "from a weapon of peace into the material for the preparation of new conflicts."[59]

The suspicion that there were elements in Japan and Manchukuo which would seek to sabotage a détente was given substance by the hostile attitude of the local authorities in the CER zone. On October 11 Raivid had vainly protested to Consul General Morishima at Harbin against the seizure by Japanese military units during the past week of buildings belonging to the CER and of the living quarters of Soviet employees.[60]

On November 6 Shih had refuted the charges made by Raivid in his letter of October 4 and in his previous communications, accusing the Soviet side of raising a loud outcry in order to impede the lawful measures taken by the public prosecutor to maintain public safety.[61]

On November 15 Bandura handed to Li a lengthy letter describing how Japanese military officers and men were interfering with the operation of the railway, how they were manhandling railway personnel, stringing telephone lines across the track, and operating armored trains without permission or regard to traffic.[62] On November 26 Raivid informed Shih that his letter of November 6 did not constitute a satisfactory answer to his many written and oral protests concerning the unlawful arrests and outrageous mistreat-

---

[59] *Izvestiia,* November 21, 1934.
[60] *Aide mémoire* of Raivid to Morishima, October 11, 1934, DVP, XVII, 634–35.
[61] DVP, XVII, 623–24.
[62] Bandura to Li, November 15, 1934, DVP, XVII, 675–77.

ment of Soviet citizens in Manchuria. He firmly demanded once more the immediate release of all unlawfully arrested citizens of the USSR, a halt to their mistreatment, and the punishment of those who had tortured them. Placing "all moral and material responsibility" for the damages inflicted on the Soviet citizens on the agencies of the Manchukuoan government, Raivid reserved the right to demand material compensation for every one of the Soviet citizens falsely arrested and tortured and for the families of those who perished during confinement in Manchukuo.[63]

Soviet attempts to settle any questions in Harbin were complicated by the rivalry that existed between the local authorities. The head of the police, the head of the gendarmerie, the chief of staff of the Japanese military mission, and the division commander worked at cross-purposes.[64]

In Tokyo, meanwhile, Iuren'ev visited Hirota on November 26 with new instructions, modifying the Soviet stand on the guarantee question. The USSR dropped the demand for Manchukuoan bonds. Instead, she offered to hold Manchukuoan treasury bills, guaranteed by a Japanese banking syndicate. Hirota in turn transmitted to Iuren'ev a Manchukuoan compromise plan regarding the discharge monies and the retention of buildings by the Soviet side. Nothing concrete was settled at this meeting, however. Hirota and Iuren'ev merely agreed to study each other's proposals.[65]

On November 29 Ambassador Ota, on his way home on furlough with his family for dental treatment as

[63] Raivid to Shih, November 26, 1934, DVP, XVII, 696–99.
[64] Clive to Simon, No. 103, Tokyo, February 19, 1935, FO 371/19347–713.
[65] JWC, December 6, 1934, p. 783.

well as for consultation by his government, was interviewed at Manchuli by a reporter from the Dempo
Tsushin news agency. Ota stated, or was quoted as
having stated, that the Soviet government sincerely
desired to bring the negotiations to an amicable end
and had given in on the matter of a guarantee by the
Japanese government. A mutually acceptable formula
had been found and it was expected, the dispatch noted,
that Ota's return to Tokyo would expedite the conclusion of an agreement. "The whole matter requires a
'political' solution," Ota was said to have explained.
Both sides must meet each other "free from all suspicions." A crisis in Soviet-Japanese relations could
be averted and the Far Eastern policy of the Soviet
Union and the Asian mainland policy of Japan brought
into harmony if Japan refrained from any "positive
action" likely to alarm the USSR.[66]

The news story provoked dismay in Tokyo. The
Manchukuoan delegate Ohashi and Manchukuo's
Finance Minister Hoshino Naoki hastened to the
Foreign Office on the morning of November 30 to com-
plain about the statements attributed to Ota and reiterated their disbelief of Soviet sincerity. Foreign Office
spokesmen admitted that the proposal made by
Iuren'ev on the twenty-sixth was a modification of
the Soviet demand for a Japanese guarantee, but they
expressed doubt that it would lead to the working out
of a formula acceptable to both sides. Moreover, Ota
had left Moscow on the twenty-second and could not
be familiar with the discussions of the twenty-sixth.
Foreign Office officials again called on the Soviet
Union to produce acceptable proposals without further
delay "in sole consideration of the future relations of

[66] JWC, December 6, 1934, p. 783; December 20, 1934, p. 864.

Japan, Manchukuo and herself in Eastern Asia." She should not allow her judgment to be influenced by "idle surmises as to the outcome of the present disarmament talks in London and Japan's future position in international politics."[67]

The *Japan Weekly Chronicle* rallied to Ota's defense in an editorial captioned "Russian Sincerity," noting that in paying tribute to Russian sincerity, Ota had brought "a breath of fresh air" to the protracted negotiations. "There has been altogether too much recrimination over Moscow's attempt to make the best of a bad bargain, and it is not a little significant that Mr. Ota's return to Tokyo is stated to hold out promise of a speedy conclusion of the talks," the *Chronicle* wrote. "There should be little difficulty in reaching agreement if only Mr. Hirota, as intermediary, and the Manchukuo Government, as principal, recognize the fairness of Mr. Ota's assertion." The paper pointed out that it would have been very easy for the Soviet Union to fish in troubled waters in the early days of the Manchurian Incident. That Moscow had made no attempt to do so, "should have convinced observers here that the Soviet Government was this time scrupulously minding its own business."[68]

The embarrassment to the Foreign Office created by Ota's interview emboldened his critics, and there were demands inside and outside the government that advantage be taken of Ota's return to replace him. Rumors began circulating that Ota planned to resign, but Ota denied this in another interview, in which he reiterated his contention that the successful conclusion of the railway talks was absolutely necessary for the improvement of Soviet-Japanese relations.[69]

[67] JWC, December 6, 1934, p. 783.
[68] JWC, December 6, 1934, pp. 761–62.
[69] JWC, December 20, 1934, p. 864.

On December 10 Hirota and Iuren'ev resumed their negotiations. Hirota submitted a new proposal, containing significant concessions. The Japanese government agreed to write an official note, addressed to the Soviet government, in which it would guarantee observance by the Manchukuoan government of the provisions for payment for the railway. Japan consented also on the establishment of an arbitration committee for settling disputes over the prices of goods to be delivered as part-payment, provided the committee was composed of one Japanese, one Manchukuoan and two Soviet nationals. In the event that the committee could not come to an agreement, the Soviet government was to take the matter up on the diplomatic level with the Japanese government in case of a controversy over goods sold by Japanese merchants; with the Manchukuoan government, in case of goods sold by Manchukuoan merchants.

Hirota and Iurev'ev discussed the above, as well as the matter of the discharge allowances, and the transfer of buildings belonging to the railway. Iuren'ev was not able to give a definite reply to Hirota's proposals, however, and sought instructions from Moscow.[70]

On December 24 Morita completed an on-the-spot survey of the actual condition of the CER and headed for Japan. "It is generally expected that with his arrival in Tokyo, the much protracted negotiations will be expedited considerably," the press reported.[71]

Meanwhile, on December 21, Hirota and Iuren'ev had agreed to delegate the working out of the details of an agreement, notably the technical aspects of the guarantee problem, to Togo and Kozlovskii. They did

[70] JWC, December 20, 1934, p. 847.
[71] JWC, January 3, 1935, p. 16.

so in ten sessions, beginning with December 25.[72] By the twenty-seventh, Togo and Kozlovskii were said to have reached "a fair agreement of view" on the guarantee question.[73] "I think that the matter under discussion with Russia will be settled within two or three days," Hirota confided to Harada on the twenty-eighth.[74]

On December 30 Kozlovskii accepted Hirota's proposals of December 10 regarding the makeup of the arbitration committee and Japanese guarantee of Manchukuoan observance of the agreement. Togo made it clear during their discussion that the pledge would stand only when all issues in the negotiations had been settled. Kozlovskii and Togo could not agree, however, on the basis for calculating the discharge allowances of the Soviet railway employees nor on the period of payment.

On January 3, 1935, Kozlovskii and Togo continued their deliberations.[75] A nine and a half hour long conference on the nineteenth still left both sides clinging to their positions, but at last, in the early hours of January 22, after an all night session, agreement was reached on the remaining issues. The terms had yet to be drawn up in final form, the official text to be in English only.[76]

In his customary foreign policy speech at the reopening of the Diet later that day, Hirota declared that negotiations with the USSR were proceeding "in the spirit of good neighborliness." He reported that a compromise had been reached in the railway talks and

[72] *Nisso kosho-shi,* 306; *Hirota Koki,* 141; "Saionji-Harada Memoirs," 1099.
[73] JWC, January 3, 1935, p. 16.
[74] "Saionji-Harada Memoirs," 1101.
[75] JWC, January 10, 1935, p. 40.
[78] JWC, January 31, 1935, p. 146.

voiced the expectation that this would remove the sources of the disputes that had frequently arisen in the past and thus would strengthen friendly relations between Japan, Manchukuo and the USSR. Hirota pledged to redouble his efforts for the peaceful solution of remaining problems between the Soviet Union and Japan. He hoped to do so, he said, with "the sincere cooperation of the Soviet Union." At the same time, Hirota called on the USSR to further mutual trust and confidence by paying special attention to "the question of the establishment of military installations in the Far East, especially along the Soviet-Manchukuoan frontier" in violation of the Treaty of Portsmouth.[77]

The Soviet press confirmed and welcomed the imminence of the successful conclusion of the railway talks and applauded Hirota's promise to work for the reestablishment of normal relations between the two powers. "Normal relations between Japan and the USSR," *Izvestiia* remarked, "constitute one of the cornerstones of peace in the Far East." But it ridiculed Hirota's exhortation that Moscow pay special attention to the military installations along the Soviet-Manchukuoan frontier, remarking sarcastically that he hardly had in mind those constructed on the Manchukuoan side. In view of the fact that the clamor against Soviet military installations was raised by Japanese newspapers which openly advocated war with the USSR, *Izvestiia* expressed regret that Hirota, who must know that Soviet strengthening of the frontier was purely defensive, had added his voice to this issue while pleading for "the sincere cooperation of the Soviet Union."[78]

[77] JWC, January 31, 1935, p. 133; February 7, 1935, p. 176; *Izvestiia*, January 24, 1935.
[78] *Izvestiia*, January 24, 1935.

Japanese business circles were elated that a settlement was in sight. Since only a small portion of the payments in kind were to be made in soybeans and red beans from Manchukuo, Japanese manufacturers stood to sell some 90 million yen worth of products to the Soviet Union over the next three years. The transactions constituted a healthy shot-in-the-arm to Soviet-Japanese trade, which had been declining because of the very long credits demanded by the Soviet trade representatives.[79]

The final agreement for the transfer of the railway was drafted by a committee consisting of Nishi Haruhiko, chief of the First Section of the Bureau of European and Asian Affairs of the Japanese Foreign Office, Ohashi, Kozlovskii, and Kuznetsov. In fifteen sessions, beginning with February 1 and ending on March 5 (not counting talks between Nishi and Kozlovskii about other matters), the committee hammered out a fourteen-article basic agreement for the transfer of the railway, a final protocol, and confidential notes to be signed by the delegates of the USSR and Manchukuo, as well as a seven-article protocol and related notes to be signed by the delegates of the USSR, Manchukuo, and Japan. It also drew up Japan's guarantee of the payment and various other documents.[80]

Meanwhile Soviet citizens held by the Manchukuoan authorities since August of the preceding year on charges of engaging in "Red activities" were quietly released because of "insufficient evidence."[81]

[79] JWC, January 31, 1935, p. 146

[80] *Nisso kosho-shi,* 307; untitled, confidential document in "Manchurian-Japanese Treaties," Japanese Archives, reel TR 4, pp. 92-93; JWC, March 14, 1935, p. 346; JTM, February 3, 1935, p. 2. For the Japanese minutes of the Nishi-Kozlovskii talks see Japanese Archives, reel WT-37, IPS document 1328 (IMT 255)

[81] JWC, February 21, 1935, p. 241; DVP, XVII, 830, note 303.

On March 8 a Foreign Office spokesman announced that the representatives of both sides had come to terms on the sale of the CER and that signature of the agreement was expected to take place on March 22 or 23. The delegates were merely waiting for approval of the final text which they had submitted to their respective governments.[82]

By the basic agreement the USSR was to cede to Manchukuo upon signature all rights concerning the CER, its subsidiary enterprises and properties. The land and buildings occupied by the Soviet consulate general and its officials, and one school and one hospital together with their land were to be leased rent-free and *sine die* to the USSR. The two governments were to renounce mutually in favor of each other the properties, such as locomotives and freight cars, claimed by them in each other's territory, except for the properties of the Transbaikal Railway at Manchuli and of the Ussuri Railway at Suifenho, which were actually occupied and managed by them.

The CER with its enterprises and properties was sold for 140 million paper yen, of which one-third was to be paid in cash (half of that simultaneously with the signing of the agreement), and two-thirds in kind, payments to be completed within three years. (The Manchukuoan government was to pay to Japanese and Manchukuoan merchants for the goods purchased from them by the Soviet trade representative.)

Manchukuo was to be responsible, on the basis of the table of credits and liabilities of the CER submitted by the Soviet delegation in March of 1934 and the supplementary table of credits and liabilities indicating subsequent changes, for the credits and liabilities of

[82] *Izvestiia*, March 9, 1935.

the CER. The USSR was to be responsible for claims of shareholders, bondholders, and creditors of the CER dating back to before March 9, 1917.

Ordinary employees who were citizens of the Soviet Union could be dismissed by the CER after being given three months' notice. The senior members of the administration, on the other hand, were to be dismissed automatically upon the signing of the agreement, the general manager and four other key officials to stay on for one month as advisers to Manchukuo. The chiefs of railway sections, stations, and depots and the chiefs of auxiliary enterprises could be dismissed at any time without previous notice.

A discharge allowance totalling 30 million yen was to be divided among the dismissed employees, part of it to be paid at once, the remainder in four installments over a period of two years. The dismissed and their families and belongings were to receive free transportation home.[83]

The basic agreement provided for the conclusion within three months of an agreement for the facilitation of traffic between the CER (NMR) and the Soviet railway system, and of a separate agreement for the connection of the CER (NMR) and Soviet telegraph lines.

The final protocol, attached to the basic agreement, dealt with the handing over to Manchukuo of the archival records, papers, and documents of the senior Soviet members of the railway administration; the responsibility of the Soviet advisers for their advice; the leasing of the school to the Soviets; jurisdiction over the Soviet hospital; the continuation of the Soviet school maintained by the CER for three months; the liquidation

[83] For a breakdown of the pension payments, see *Nisso kosho-shi,* 313–14.

of the cooperative society of the employees of the CER; and the transitory provisions concerning the telegraphic connection.

The protocol to be exchanged between the delegates of the Soviet Union, Manchukuo, and Japan sought to facilitate the purchase of Manchukuoan and Japanese manufactures in partial payment for the railway by providing for the mediation of disputes by an arbitration commission, composed of citizens of the three countries, and for the settlement of conflicts on the diplomatic level if such arbitration failed.

Japan's guarantee of the payment consisted of two notes, one exchanged between Japan and the USSR, one between Japan and Manchukuo. In the former the Japanese government guaranteed the strict fulfillment by Manchukuo of her obligation to pay 140 million yen to the USSR; in the latter Manchukuo promised to live up to her obligation and not to cause any loss to Japan.[84]

The various documents pertaining to the railway agreement were initialed at the Japanese Foreign Office on March 11. The basic agreement and the final protocol were initialed by the representatives of Manchukuo and the USSR. A protocol relative to the agreement was initialed by Hirota and by the aforementioned representatives. The notes to be exchanged were initialed by Hirota and Iuren'ev.[85] The documents were approved by the Japanese Cabinet unanimously on March 12, then by a plenary session of the Manchukuoan Privy Council in the presence of

---

[84] Japanese Archives, reel WT 53, IMT document 391, pp. 132–38. For the full English text of the agreement and related documents see Japanese Archives, reel TR-4, pp. 42–65, 95–99, 101–106, 111–20. Consult also IPS document 675 on reel SP 171 and IPS document 1328 on reel WT-37, plus Japan, National Diet Library, *Nisso kokko chosa mondai kiso shiryo-shu,* 167–80.

[85] Japanese Archives, IMT document 391, pp. 20–22.

Emperor Kangtse (Henry P'u-yi) on the nineteenth and by a plenary session of the Japanese Privy Council in the presence of Emperor Hirohito (Showa Tenno) on the twentieth.[86] Formal signature took place on Saturday, March 23, at Hirota's official residence, twenty-one months after the commencement of the negotiations.

According to the published schedule, the Japanese officials assembled at Hirota's official residence at 8:30 in the morning. They included in addition to Hirota himself: Shigemitsu, Togo, Nishi, Kurusu Saburo (chief of the Foreign Trade Bureau), Kuwajima Shukei (chief of the Asian Bureau), Kuriyama Shigeru (chief of the Treaties Bureau), and Amau Eiji (director of the Information Bureau). The Soviets—Iuren'ev, Kozlovskii and staff—arrived at 9 A.M.; the Manchukuoan officials—Ting, Ohashi, Wu Tse-sheng and staff —came shortly thereafter.[87]

At 9:30 sharp the proceedings were opened with the formal examination of the plenipotentiary status of the respective delegates. Thereupon the basic agreement for the transfer of the CER was signed by the Manchukuoan and Soviet delegations, and Ting festively handed Iuren'ev a check for 23,300,000 yen as the first installment of the cash payments and Manchukuoan treasury bonds for the remainder. Then the Soviet-Manchukuoan-Japanese protocol and the final Soviet-Manchukuoan protocol were signed by the officials concerned, as were the notes exchanged between Japan and Manchukuo and between Japan and the USSR.[88]

[86] *Izvestiia,* March 14, 1935; JWC, March 28, 1935, p. 411; JTM, March 21, 1935, p. 1.

[87] JWC, March 28, 1935, p. 411; JTM, March 24, 1935, p. 1.

[88] JWC, March 28, 1935, p. 410. The sale of the CER to Manchukuo constituted *de facto* recognition of the latter. As Troianovskii had explained to a European

With the signing of the various documents completed, Hirota made a brief speech in Japanese. He declared that the agreement marked a new epoch in the relations between the USSR and Manchukuo. It insured the steady growth of mutual cordiality between them, and it brightened in consequence the outlook of East Asian international relations in general. Hirota attributed the successful outcome of the negotiations both to the "firm determination" of the Soviet government to settle the CER question once and for all and to the "fine spirit of conciliation" shown by the Manchukuoan side. He did not deem it surprising, in view of the historical importance of the agreement, that the negotiations should have lasted for almost two years and should have been beset with difficulties. He was convinced, he said, that with the same conciliatory and cooperative spirit all other issues pending between their countries could be solved amicably and satisfactorily.[89]

Iuren'ev concurred with Hirota's high appreciation of the agreement's importance. He asserted that its signing should bring "genuine satisfaction to every lover of peace throughout the world." Agreeing that Japan and Manchukuo had displayed a spirit of conciliation and cooperation during the talks, Iuren'ev

---

colleague earlier, the USSR had not signed the Nine Power Treaty and thus had made no commitment to respect the territorial integrity of China. The British, who did not share the American proclivity to moralize, understood how the Soviets could regard the Japanese as guilty of imperialist aggression, yet at the same conclude an agreement with them and Manchukuo to secure their own economic interests. The USSR believed, Pratt remarked, that "Japan . . . is digging her own grave in Manchuria and the more the Nanking Government is weakened and discredited the more likely is Communism to spread in China." (Minutes, October 31, 1932, FO 371/16180–867; IMTFE, "Proceedings," 19702; Ovey to Simon, No. 263, Moscow, May 23, 1932, "Confidential," FO 371/16171–665; Garstin to Ingram, No. 42, Harbin, June 11, 1932, "Confidential," FO 371/16173–665.)

[89] Japanese Archives, reel WT 53, IMT document 391, pp. 113–14.

thanked Hirota on behalf of the entire Soviet delegation for his positive contribution to the success of the negotiations. He expressed confidence that the Japanese government would secure the strict fulfillment of the obligations under the agreement and would further show its good will by solving the questions pending between the Soviet Union and Japan.[90]

Ting echoed the theme that the agreement was "a definite contribution towards the peace of the Orient." He remarked that the transfer of the railway not only laid the basis for good-neighborly relations between the Soviet Union and Manchukuo, but promised to accelerate the economic development of North Manchuria.[91]

Soviet and Manchukuoan officials in Harbin meanwhile had gathered in the banquet hall of the CER directorate. As soon as a radio-telephone message from Tokyo announced the successful signing of the agreement, Minister of Communications Ting Chenhsiu and Bandura shook hands and congratulated each other. After brief speeches by Ting and Bandura, everyone drank a toast in celebration of the occasion.

Then, at the office of the general manager, Rudyi gave his last instructions, telling the Soviet employees to cooperate with the Manchukuoan officials in the amicable transfer of the railway. He was followed by his Japanese successor, Sawara, who picked up the phone and directed the new stationmasters to begin the transfer of the railway at once.

A note from the newly established Harbin Railway Bureau to the People's Commissariat of Communications, dispatched that morning, announced that the Harbin Railway Bureau was undertaking the junction

[90] *Ibid.*, 117–18.
[91] *Ibid.*, 120–21.

of the CER (NMR) and the Siberian Railways. A statement issued at Dairen proclaimed formal assumption
of the administration and operation of the CER (NMR)
by the South Manchurian Railway Company.

There was another celebration at 10 A.M. at Hsinking, at the official residence of Foreign Minister Hsieh
Chieh-shih, attended by all the staff officers of the
Kwantung Army and by high government officials.
General Minami Jiro, commander-in-chief of the
Kwantung Army and concurrently Japanese ambassador to Manchukuo, issued an announcement in which
he reiterated that the transfer of the railway eliminated
one of the major causes of dispute in the Far East
and thus brightened the prospects of peace in that
region.[92]

As soon as word of the signing of the agreement
reached Moscow that day, Foreign Commissar Litvinov sent a telegram to Hirota thanking him for his
productive participation. "I feel sure," he wired, "that
we will continue our further fruitful cooperation for
the elimination of any cause for conflicts and misunderstandings between our countries and for the strengthening of really friendly relations between them in the
interest of our nations and of general peace."[93]

In a telegram, dated March 25, Hirota reciprocated
the feeling of satisfaction at the successful completion
of the negotiations and in turn thanked Litvinov for
his "steadfast and untiring efforts" in finding a solution.

"The Agreement," Hirota cabled, "will promote
cordial relations between the USSR and Manchukuo,
and a foundation has been laid by this Agreement for
further development of friendly relations between

[92] JWC, March 28, 1935, pp. 410–11.
[93] Japanese Archives, reel WT 53, IMT documented 391, pp. 123–24.

Japan, the USSR, and Manchukuo. I firmly believe that the same spirit of conciliation and cooperation demonstrated in the present negotiations will insure amicable settlement of other pending questions, thereby further strengthening the basis of peace in East Asia.''[94]

[94] *Ibid.*, 125.

11

The Nonaggression Pact Question

The Soviet Union had sold the Chinese Eastern Railway to decrease the chances of being drawn into war with Japan as she had been drawn into war with China. She had taken other measures to reinforce her security: she had restored diplomatic relations with China, had attained recognition by the United States and had joined the League of Nations. Yet the most direct step—the conclusion of a nonaggression pact with Japan—had eluded her diplomacy.

The idea of a nonaggression pact was not new. Ever fearful, in consequence of the Allied intervention during the Russian civil war, of a joint capitalist effort to stamp out communism, the USSR had been seeking to conclude nonaggression pacts with all her neighbors. She had first approached Japan on this subject in August 1926, when Chargé d'Affaires Grigorii Besedovskii had proposed to Vice Minister of Foreign Affairs Debuchi Katsuji the conclusion between their countries of either a neutrality pact or a nonaggression pact along the lines of the Soviet-German treaty of April

335

of the same year, but Debuchi had shelved the matter until "an appropriate occasion in the future."[1] On January 14, 1927, Debuchi had questioned the use of such a pact, observing to Besedovskii that if relations were friendly, no pact was needed, and if they were not friendly, no pact would help.[2]

When Ambassador Valerian Dovgalevskii had reiterated to Foreign Minister Tanaka Giichi that summer the desire of his government to negotiate a nonaggression pact, Tanaka had responded that while the two countries must adhere to the spirit of nonaggression in order to develop economic relations, the time was not ripe for a political treaty such as a nonaggression pact. Dovgalevskii's argument that the conclusion of a nonaggression pact between the two states would greatly ease tensions in Asia had gone unheeded.[3]

Japan and the USSR had approached the matter from different points of view. Ambassador Tanaka Tokichi had told Karakhan in October 1927 that the Japanese public would react unfavorably to the conclusion of a nonaggression pact with the Soviet Union prior to the solution of outstanding economic problems between their countries. Karakhan had rebutted that the signature of a nonaggression pact would contribute to the settlement of the economic problems and of itself would allay the misgivings of the population in Russian Asia and dissipate the suspicions of Soviet and Japanese officials in China of each other. An attempt by Ambassador Troianovskii in March 1928 to discuss a nonaggression pact had been rebuffed by

[1] DVP, IX, 735–36, note 88; *Hirota koki*, 94–95. For the text of the Soviet-German Neutrality Pact, see DVP, IX, 250–52.

[2] *Nisso kosho-shi*, 282.

[3] DVP, X, 626–28, note 17; *Hirota Koki*, 95.

Foreign Minister Tanaka with the old argument that economic differences must be resolved before a nonaggression pact could be concluded.[4]

The Japanese invasion of Manchuria increased the Soviet Union's desire for a nonaggression pact with Japan. When Yoshizawa, who had concluded the Basic Convention of 1925 and had earned Soviet respect as a man interested in improving Russo-Japanese relations, stopped in Moscow at the end of December 1931, on his way from Paris to Tokyo, Foreign Commissar Litvinov informed him that the USSR had concluded nonaggression or neutrality pacts with Germany, Lithuania, Turkey, Persia and Afghanistan, had initiated a pact with France and was negotiating or about to begin negotiating such pacts with Poland, Finland, Estonia, Latvia and Rumania. She would soon be bound by nonaggression pacts with all her neighbors except Japan, a "queer situation." Calling for the filling of this "gap," Litvinov contended that the conclusion of a nonaggression pact between their countries would lay to rest speculations in Western Europe and the United States about the future of Russo-Japanese relations.[5]

Yoshizawa replied that he had not been in touch with his government since his appointment as foreign minister and could not yet speak on its behalf. He took pride, he said, in the role he had played in the establishment of diplomatic relations between Japan and the USSR; personally, he favored the preservation and strengthening of amicable relations between their countries and was pleased that Litvinov was similarly

---

[4] *Nisso kosho-shi,* 282–85; Kutakov, *Istoriia,* 71–80.
[5] Litvinov's record of his conversation with Yoshizawa, December 31, 1931, DVP, XIV, 746–48; IMTFE, 7714–15; Hirai Tomoyoshi, "Manshujihen to Nisso kankei," 106–107.

inclined.[6] Promising to discuss the issue in Tokyo, Yoshizawa left the Russians with the impression that an answer of some sort would be forthcoming.[7]

A fortnight later, on January 12, 1932, Troianovskii asked Inukai what he thought of the conclusion of a nonaggression pact between their countries. This was two days before Yoshizawa was to take over as foreign minister and Inukai responded that he himself had not yet studied the matter.[8]

When Minister of Agriculture Yamamoto Teijiro told Troianovskii on February 10 that the Japanese government desired a political and economic rapprochement with the USSR and that he could obtain Premier Inukai's assent for a private exchange of opinions with him, Troianovskii observed that the USSR had made a step toward a rapprochement with Japan when she had proposed the conclusion of a nonaggression pact, but that no reply had been received.[9]

Troianovskii saw Foreign Minister Yoshizawa on February 29, but found him "poorly informed as in the past." Yoshizawa told Troianovskii that the Japanese government was in no hurry to conclude a nonaggression pact, since the Kellogg pact performed a similar function; it wanted the fishery and concession questions solved first. Troianovskii vainly argued these issues had nothing to do with the treaty, "since the Japanese government, of course, did not plan to solve these questions by aggression."[10]

Troianovskii brought up the nonaggression pact

---

[6] IMTFE, "Proceedings," 22678; Litvinov's record of his talk with Yoshizawa, December 31, 1931, DVP, XIV, 746.

[7] *Nisso kosho-shi*, 286; Kutakov, *Istoriia*, 114.

[8] Troianovskii to Foreign Commissariat, January 12, 1932, "Immediately," DVP, XV, 20–21; *Hirota Koki*, 96–97.

[9] DVP, XV, 790, note 229.

[10] Troianovskii to Foreign Commissariat, February 29, 1932, "Immediately," DVP, XV, 149.

issue again a week later in a conversation with Vice Minister of Foreign Affairs Nagai Matsuzo, as the latter sought to assure him that neither the Japanese government nor the Japanese military wished to worsen relations with the USSR. Troianovskii told him that he personally did not believe that the Japanese wanted to go to war with the Russians, since it would bring them nothing but casualties and destruction, yet their silence concerning a nonaggression pact looked to the Soviet government like a sign of aggressive intent. When Nagai responded that the absence of aggressive intentions made a pact superfluous, Troianovskii remarked that their presence made a pact impossible and that in such a case they could never sign a pact. He stated that he could not understand why the Japanese government would not translate its assurances of friendship into a treaty.[11]

On March 16 Litvinov, while attending the Geneva Disarmament Conference, spoke to Ambassador Matsudaira Tsuneo about the need for a nonaggression pact. Matsudaira gave the curious reply that since both countries had already assured each other informally that neither planned to attack the other, all that a nonaggression pact would do would be to arouse the suspicion of the other powers.[12]

That day Admiral Kato, a member of the Supreme War Council and a director of the Nippon-Soviet Society, confided to Troianovskii that the silence of the Japanese government regarding the proposed nonaggression pact was due to a split in the Japanese

[11] Troianovskii to Foreign Commissariat, March 7, 1932, "Immediately," DVP, XV, 173. Troianovskii had tried to confer directly with the military, notably with General Araki, the minister of war, but had not been able to arrange it as yet. (Troianovskii to Foreign Commissariat, February 29, 1932, "Urgent," DVP, XV, 149.)
[12] *Nisso kosho-shi*, 287.

leadership. One faction favored a rapprochement with the USSR, the other faction a break in relations; the former was more numerous, the latter more active. The opponents of the USSR, Troianovskii reported, feared the growth of Soviet power as the result of the Five Year Plan and inveighed against the Third International, "a specter that frightens many."[13]

Troianovskii tried to reassure Kato about the Third International in another private conversation on April 8 by contending that the Comintern and the Soviet government were not one and the same and that the ideas of Communism spread independently of the Comintern, Bolshevism having been victorious in Russia when no Comintern had existed. Kato did not argue the point and expressed the desire for friendly relations with the USSR.[14]

In June the president of the Japanese Fisheries Association told Troianovskii that the Saito government had a different attitude toward a nonaggression pact with the Soviet Union than Inukai, but that there were still some basic problems. "He hinted," Troianovskii telegraphed, "that the conclusion of a pact with us would force [Japan] to conclude pacts with others, and this is impossible."[15]

On July 26 and 27 the *Japan Advertiser* carried a translation of an article by Araki, originally published in April in the military journal *Kaikosha,* in which he spoke of Outer Mongolia and Eastern Siberia as

[13] Troianovskii to Foreign Commissariat, March 17, 1932, DVP, XV, 180–81; Troianovskii to Foreign Commissariat, January 26, 1932, "Immediately," DVP, XV, 63. For a lengthy Japanese article on the menace of the Comintern, see Hayashi Nobuo, "Rono Rokoku sekka senden no shinso to waga taisaku." Anna Marie Anderson Clayberg discusses the worldwide activity of Communist and Communist-infiltrated organizations in opposition to Japanese aggression. ("Soviet Policy Toward Japan, 1923–1941," 152–213.)

[14] DVP, XV, 751, note 90.

[15] Troianovskii to Foreign Commissariat, June 14, 1932, "Immediately," DVP, XV, 360.

obstacles in the path of Japan's "national mission" to spread Japanese morality throughout Asia and the rest of the world. Troianovskii hastened to Uchida Kosai, who had just become foreign minister, and referred to the article. When Uchida said that the Japanese government had no aggressive intentions, Troianovskii declared that "the government, perhaps, does not have them, but the minister of war does" and that "in view of the atmosphere that prevailed a nonaggression pact was necessary." But Uchida retorted that "the Japanese cannot become accustomed to the idea that such a pact is necessary."[16] As Hirota had explained, when the subject had been broached in Moscow the preceding day, since the Treaty of Portsmouth had stipulated in detail what actions both sides must shun, no other agreement was needed.[17]

When Hirota returned to Japan in the fall, he advised Uchida that serious consideration be given to a nonaggression pact with the USSR, but the foreign minister demurred,[18] even though Japanese journalists, who had been antagonistic to the idea of such a pact at the beginning of the year, had begun writing in support of it following a number of meetings between Troianovskii and Araki and some favorable comments by Hirota and Ohashi, the vice minister of foreign affairs of Manchukuo.[19]

[16] DVP, XV, 787, note 212; Lindley to Foreign Office, No. 339 (R), Tokyo, September 2, 1932, "Confidential," FO 371/16246–680; Kutakov, *Istoriia*, 115–17.

[17] Kutakov, *Istoriia*, 115–17. Counselor Amau told Strang that "the treaty relations between the Soviet Union and Japan already in some respects went beyond the terms of the usual pacts of nonaggression, in that by the Treaty of Portsmouth both parties bound themselves not to concentrate troops on each other's borders." He did think, though he did not deem it practical, that there might be sense in a nonaggression pact that stipulated that the USSR would not attack Manchukuo and that Japan would not attack the Mongolian People's Republic. (Strang to Simon, No. 491, Moscow, September 5, 1932, "Confidential," FO 371/16178–665.)

[18] *Hirota Koki*, 97.

[19] Lindley to Simon, No. 590, Tokyo, November 9, 1932, FO 371/16246–680. For discussion of a nonaggression pact between Japan, the USSR, and

On November 3 Litvinov, who was back in Moscow, showed Counselor Amau a TASS dispatch which asserted that Hirota's newly selected successor, Ambassador Ota Tamekichi, had expressed doubt about the need for such a pact. He reminded Amau that while there had been many statements in the Japanese press favoring or opposing the conclusion of a nonaggression pact, no official reply had yet been received by the Soviet government to its proposal.

Amau replied that the dissension in Japan, which delayed an answer, was not so much over the objectives of a nonaggression pact as over the form of the agreement. The conclusion of pacts and treaties required the approval of the Privy Council and was a complicated procedure; the controversy at the time of the ratification of the Kellogg Pact had led to the fall of the cabinet. "Amau said that one must differentiate between the conclusion of a pact and of an agreement, which need not be in the form of a pact," Litvinov noted in his record of the talk.[20]

When Matsuoka Yosuke, who headed the Japanese delegation to the disarmament conference, stopped over in Moscow for several days en route to Geneva, Litvinov and Karakhan reiterated to him on November 4 their desire for a nonaggression pact.[21] Although Matsuoka's request for an interview with Stalin, made in advance of his visit, was not granted on the grounds that Stalin rarely received foreign representatives and that Matsuoka had arrived on the eve of the Soviet

---

Manchukuo, see Komuro Makoto, "Nichi-Ro-Man no fushinryaku joyaku ron." There was talk also of a Japanese-Soviet-German alliance against the Anglo-Saxon powers. (Hirai, 109.)

[20] Litvinov's record of his talk with Amau, November 3, 1932, DVP, XV, 595–97; *Hirota Koki*, 97.

[21] *Nisso kosho-shi*, 287; Japan, Foreign Office (comp.), *Nihon gaiko nempyo*, II, 72; Ovey to Simon, No. 633, Moscow, November 8, 1932, FO 371/16246–680.

Union's greatest holiday, the anniversary of the Communist Revolution on November 7, when everyone was busy,[22] and although Matsuoka emphasized publicly the informal nature of the views exchanged between him and the Soviet officials, his talks with Litvinov and Karakhan further stimulated speculation in the press concerning the conclusion of a nonaggression pact.[23]

Karl Radek, the leading commentator on foreign affairs in the Soviet press, with whom Matsuoka met on November 6, proposed Soviet recognition of the state of Manchukuo in exchange for Japanese signature of a nonaggression pact with the USSR. The next day, on November 7, he mentioned the possibility of a pact between the Soviet Union, Japan and Manchukuo.[24]

On November 9 Karakhan told Amau that Matsuoka had confirmed that there was mounting support in Japan for a nonaggression pact with the Soviet Union. Why did his government show such an indecisive attitude? Eleven months had passed without a reply since Litvinov had proposed the conclusion of a nonaggression pact to Yoshizawa. To Amau's reply that the matter had been complicated by the founding of Manchukuo, Karakhan reiterated Radek's suggestion to Matsuoka that the Soviet Union would be willing to conclude a nonaggression pact with Manchukuo (and thus, as Radek had pointed out, extend recognition) at the same time that a nonaggression pact with Japan was concluded.[25]

[22] Karakhan's record of his talk with Amau, October 27, 1932, DVP, XV, 588–91.

[23] Lindley to Simon, No. 590, Tokyo, November 9, 1932, FO 371/16246–680.

[24] *Nisso kosho-shi*, 287. The possibility of such a pact had also been raised by the Japanese press. (Chargé d'Affaires Adrien de Lens to Foreign Minister Edouard Herriot, no. 415, Tokyo, October 23, 1932, DDF, First Series, vol. 1, p. 556.)

[25] *Nisso kosho-shi*, 287–89; *Hirota Koki*, 97.

The Soviet proposal for a nonaggression pact with Japan had run into determined opposition by Japanese militarists who feared that the conclusion of such a pact might undercut their requests for increased appropriations by removing, or weakening, the specter of the Soviet menace. Moreover, a pact with the USSR might increase American and British alarm about Japanese expansion.[26]

It was on December 13, the very day that the resumption of Soviet relations with China was made public, that the Japanese government pointedly rejected Moscow's proposal for a nonaggression pact. In a "strictly confidential verbal note," handed by Uchida to Troianovskii, it contended that conditions were not ripe for a nonaggression pact and that various problems between the two states must be solved first.[27] Uchida suggested that local arrangements be made meanwhile to forestall incidents that might be precipitated by the proximity of Soviet and Japanese troops; the creation of a Japanese-Manchukuoan-Soviet commission to prevent border incidents might be helpful. When Troianovskii stated that the Japanese reply would make a bad impression in the Soviet Union and would be interpreted as evidence of aggressive intent on the part of Japan, Uchida replied that it should not be made public in order to avoid misunderstanding.

In his telegram to the Foreign Commissariat Troianovskii recommended the opposite, so that the Japanese rejection of a nonaggression pact would receive a public airing.[28] Litvinov agreed, and

[26] Kutakov, *Istoriia,* 116–18.

[27] The problems, General Araki told Troianovskii on January 6, 1933, included the Manchurian, CER and oil questions. (Kutakov, *Istoriia,* 120.)

[28] Troianovskii to Foreign Commissariat, December 13, 1932, "Urgent," DVP, XV, 683; DVP, XVI, 18; IMTFE, "Proceedings," 22682–83.

instructed Troianovskii to reply that since its proposal for a nonaggression pact had been made public and discussed in the world press for a year, the Soviet government did not deem it possible to keep the Japanese answer secret. It would prefer to publish the entire exchange of notes, but if Uchida had strong objections, it would confine itself to printing merely the Japanese answer.[29]

Amau, who saw Karakhan on December 27, spoke up against the publication of the Japanese reply on the ground that it would make a bad impression. He asserted that the Japanese government had not yet made up its mind—it had merely postponed a decision until a more suitable time. Karakhan retorted that the Japanese government had had a year to consider the matter and that the USSR could not but regard the reply as a rejection of the Soviet proposal, garbed in diplomatic language. When Amau repeated that the publication of the Japanese answer would make a bad impression and adversely affect relations between the two countries, Karakhan observed that it was the answer itself and not its publication that made the bad impression. A bad thing could not be made better by hiding its existence.[30]

On January 4, 1933, Troianovskii handed to Uchida Moscow's response to his rejection of the proposal for a nonaggression pact. The Soviet government agreed in its note that there were problems between the two states that needed to be worked out, but it contended that to make the solution of these problems a precondition for the conclusion of a nonaggression pact would be counter to the very idea of a nonaggres-

[29] Litvinov to Troianovskii, December 27, 1932, DVP, XV, 705.
[30] Karakhan's record of his talk with Amau, December 27, 1932, DVP, XV, 705–708.

sion pact, which provided for the solution of problems by peaceful means. It saw no problems between the USSR and Japan that could not be settled peacefully and in proposing the conclusion of a nonaggression pact had not ignored the Kellogg-Briand Pact but had wished to strengthen and broaden it by applying it specifically to the Soviet-Japanese situation. The Soviet government deemed it unrealistic on the part of Japan to hold that nonaggression pacts should be concluded only between states that had no disputes of any sort, for such a situation was hardly possible, particularly among neighboring states, in view of the economic and political interrelationship of peoples in modern times. It observed that "the settlement of existing disputes is no guarantee against the occurrence of new disputes in the future, especially when the policy of some state is geared toward aggression and the spread of a foreign sphere of influence."

Uchida objected to this phrase. He protested that it was a "false accusation" of Japan. But Troianovskii refused to reword the verbal note, stating that this sentence did not necessarily refer to Japan.[31]

Troianovskii reiterated the decision of the Soviet government to make the note public when he met with Uchida again the following day. He so informed also Vice Minister of Foreign Affairs Arita on January 6 and 11.[32]

[31] Note of the Soviet government, January 4, 1933, DVP, XVI, 16–18; *Nisso kosho-shi*, 289–90; Kutakov, *Istoriia*, 119; USSR, Academy of Sciences, Institut Istorii, *Istoriia vneshnei politiki SSSR*, I, 271; prosecution document 2371, IMTFE, "Proceedings," pp. 7719–20; see also pp. 22684–85; *Pravda*, January 17, 1933.

[32] DVP, XVI, 803–804, note 9. P. Broad of the Northern Department of the British Foreign Office did not regard the Soviet decision to publish the correspondence as a wise move "even if they have abandoned all hope of attaining the pact." "I do not believe the Japanese have given up the idea of a pact ultimately," V. A. L. Mallet of the Far Eastern Department observed, "but they probably consider the present moment, as soon after the Sino-Soviet *rap-*

When Uchida related at a cabinet meeting on January 13 that the USSR intended to publish the correspondence, Finance Minister Takahashi asked why Uchida had not concluded a nonaggression pact.

"The Army was very concerned, because they thought that it might facilitate the spreading of Communist propaganda," Uchida replied.

"If we had such a treaty, then we could really protest," Takahashi countered. "You can consider that the treaty and Communist propaganda are two separate problems. I believe that if the treaty had been concluded we would lodge protests. This present [instance of] being dragged along by the Army is very disgusting."

When the war minister said piously that public opinion must be considered, Takahashi burst out: "There is no such thing as public opinion at present. If you say anything unfavorable to the Army, then the Kempei [military police] rattle their swords or point a gun and threaten you. There is no such thing as public opinion. There is nothing so severe as the present suppression of free speech. It is a fact that when a certain newspaper publisher in Kyushu wrote something unfavorable to [about?] the Army, they threatened him by having an airplane circle around [above?] the paper plant and said that they would bomb the plant. This situation of the Kempei following statesmen around as if they were spies is very disgusting. I told a newspaperman, who often comes to my place, that there was hardly any freedom of speech and he agreed with me. He

---

prochement, inappropriate in view of the opposition which such a pact would certainly arouse in certain quarters in Japan. Publication of correspondence would probably knock the whole scheme on the head, at least for many months to come." "The Soviet are apparently piqued," Orde reflected; "but that is not likely to influence Japan." (Comments pertaining to Lindley's telegram No. 6 from Tokyo of January 5, 1933, made in minutes on January 6, FO 371/17151–858.)

deplored the fact that he could not say what he wanted to."

Araki turned red with anger at Takahashi's words and denied that conditions were as Takahashi had described them. They *were*, Takahashi reiterated, and added: "I respect your intentions, but your actions do not accord with them."

No other member of the cabinet saw fit to back Takahashi.[33]

Troianovskii had told the British ambassador, Sir Francis Lindley, during a dinner at the Soviet embassy on January 10 that both Saito and Uchida had been strongly in favor of a nonaggression pact and that even Araki had been brought around to the same point of view in spite of earlier opposition, but that it had been impossible to conclude a pact nonetheless because of the violent opposition of a number of junior officers. "In short," Troianovskii stated (as paraphrased by Lindley), "we have to deal with a Government which does not govern." He told Lindley as he had already informed the German ambassador, Dr. Ernst Arthur Voretzsch, that the Soviet government might publish the correspondence concerning the nonaggression pact in spite of Uchida's objections.[34]

[33] "Saionji-Harada Memoirs," 503–504.

[34] February 2, 1933, FO 371/17151–858. In reporting his conversation with Troianovskii, Lindley wrote that it had come to him "as a somewhat unpleasant surprise to hear that the band of junior officers who had played such a prominent and regrettable part in recent Japanese policy are still sufficiently powerful to block the signature of a diplomatic instrument which does not even directly concern them." He deemed it possible that Araki had falsely given the impression to Troianovskii that he favored the pact and had really used his influence to oppose it. In either case "the predominant influence of the army in the affairs of the country" was evident. (Lindley to Foreign Office, "Confidential," Tokyo, January 13, 1933, No. 19, FO 371/17151–858; Lindley to Simon, No. 34, Tokyo, January 16, 1933, "Confidential," FO 371/17151–858.) R. H. S. Allen agreed with Troianovskii's indictment of the Japanese government as one that failed to govern. "After the murder of Mr. Inukai and the leniency with which his murderers were treated," he remarked, "it is curious that Sir F. Lindley should be surprised at what younger officers can do."

On January 17 the *Japan Times* and such leading Japanese newspapers as the *Jiji Shimpo, Tokyo Nichi Nichi, Hochi* and *Osaka Mainichi* carried a lengthy statement in the form of a paid advertisement by the Shiunso, an ultranationalist society, assailing the idea of a nonaggression pact with the USSR.[35] The statement contended that the Soviet leaders condemned the use of military force merely because they themselves were not in a position at the moment to resort to it with anticipation of success and sought to achieve their objectives instead by diplomatic "finesse," economic pressure, and Communist propaganda. Accusing the USSR of violating the anti-propaganda clause of the Basic Convention of 1925, of showing "lack of fidelity and goodwill" in her policy towards Japan after the Manchurian Incident, of "manipulating" General Su Ping-wen against the Japanese army, and of "carrying on her red invasion in Japan with increasing zeal," it asked rhetorically,"Can anyone think of any obnoxious act comparable to an attempt by one nation to overturn the foundation of another nation with which it is in treaty relations, and to carry on an organized plan of disturbing its social order?" It asserted that the Communist Party of the Soviet Union had recently ordered Japanese Communists "to assume reactionary ultra-patriotism, pointing out that a right-wing upheaval should precede a left-wing revolution," and warned that Japan would greatly suffer from "communists working under the mask of patriotism and posing as reactionaries." Far from soliciting Soviet recognition of Manchukuo, the Shiunso

---

[35] Noting that the Shiunso was "a reactionary society of no great importance," Lindley wondered where it had gotten the money for the expensive advertisement. (Lindley to Simon, No. 59, Tokyo, January 30, 1933, "Confidential," FO 371/17151–858.)

contended that such recognition would be "disastrous," because it would open the doors of Manchuria to red propaganda. It opposed, similarly, possible Soviet economic concessions on Sakhalin and in the Maritime province, even the sale of the CER, as "Russian bait," and argued that instead of considering a nonaggression pact, it would be more appropriate for Japan to discuss the advisability of discontinuing diplomatic relations with the USSR.[36]

That day, on January 17, the Soviet government carried out its plan to mobilize Japanese public opinion in support of the conclusion of a nonaggression pact by publishing the Soviet-Japanese exchange on this subject: summaries of Litvinov's proposal of December 31, 1931, of the Japanese reply of December 13, 1932, and of the Soviet note of January 4, 1933.[37]

On January 19 Arita summoned Troianovskii and expressed the astonishment of his government at the publication of the gist of the notes without its consent. He was annoyed that the phrase concerning an aggressive nation had been left in the note (though it had been deleted from the published summary) and warned that if the text would not be amended, Japan would have to lodge a strong protest. Troianovskii retorted that he had given notice of the intention of his government to publish the note and that Japan could not object to the phrase in question, because Japan was not mentioned and "the Japanese government will not be able to prove that there is not now and will not be a single aggressive country." He was not moved by Arita's argument that anyone who read the note would understand that Japan was meant, and said that he did not

---

[36] JTM, January 17, 1933.
[37] *Izvestiia* and *Pravda*, January 17, 1933.

think that his government would alter the rest of its note.

Troianovskii took the opportunity to protest against the dissemination of "obviously invented anti-Soviet statements" by the Japanese Ministry of War in an official communiqué.[38]

Troianovskii was correct in his supposition that the Soviet government would not modify its note. Irritated by the Japanese objections, Litvinov cabled to him that it was "necessary to reply in an absolutely firm tone, and once and for all to ward off the absurd Japanese pretensions." He instructed Troianovskii to point out that since the Soviet proposal for a nonaggression pact had been made publicly, the Japanese reply should not have been secret. The USSR had warned Japan that she could not hide from the Russian public "such a serious fact in international life as the refusal of a neighboring country to sign a treaty [of non-aggression]" and would publish her reply, but could not do so without publishing also the Japanese note. As attempts to agree on the simultaneous publication of the notes in Tokyo and Moscow had been fruitless she had gone ahead and published the gist of the notes, deleting the phrase to which Uchida had objected. While the USSR thus had tried to be sensitive to Japanese feelings, she could not "write or change her notes at the dictation of another government." She would be willing to have the notes published in full.[39]

That day, on January 20, Ambassador Ota reiterated to Karakhan his government's unhappiness with some of the phrases in the Russian reply and in the unilateral

[38] Troianovskii to Foreign Commissariat, January 19, 1933, DVP, XVI, 41–42; JWC, January 26, 1933, p. 108.

[39] Litvinov to Troianovskii, January 20, 1933, DVP, XVI, 42–43. Troianovskii read Litvinov's communication to Arita in English on January 24. (DVP, XVI, 805, note 17.)

publication of the notes, which, he contended, had created an "unfavorable atmosphere." The consternation of the Japanese government had been increased by the fact that there had been discrepancies in the wording of the English translations of the Russian note which it had received—one prepared apparently by the Soviet embassy in Tokyo and one by the Japanese embassy in Moscow.

Karakhan retorted that what mattered was that Japan had refused to negotiate a nonaggression pact, and dismissed with visible annoyance Ota's contention that the Soviet Union was more interested in publishing the exchange than in signing a pact. He pointed out that Japanese who thought that a nonaggression pact would be solely to the advantage of the USSR were greatly mistaken. "The Soviet Union and Japan need the conclusion of a [nonaggression] pact to the same extent; therefore, we are making the proposal, but have no intention and are taking no steps to force Japan to sign the pact."

When Ota stated that the Japanese government considered the phrase concerning an aggressive nation as insulting, Karakhan replied (as Troianovskii had) that the sentences had been poorly rendered into English; no offense had been intended. His assertion that the sentence could apply to Rumania, which had seized Bessarabia, did not satisfy Ota. "The world press writes that Japan is an aggressive country," Ota declared. "You speak in your note of an aggressive country. The reader of the note will automatically think of Japan."

But Karakhan remained firm that the text could not be changed, particularly because two weeks had passed since the transmission of the note, and when Ota said that the Japanese government then might have to return it, retorted that this too was impossible by this time.[40]

As Ota belabored the subject when they continued their lengthy exchange the following afternoon, on January 21, Karakhan gave up the pretense that the phrase was not directed at Japan. Noting that Japan alone was responsible for the delicate and tense situation in the Far East, he declared: "No one has the right to expect that we shall close [our] eyes to the events which are happening near our borders and shall regard the situation as just as calm as it was before September 18, 1931." Whatever unfavorable atmosphere had been created in the Far East, Karakhan observed, had not been due to the Soviet note, which had supported a nonaggression pact, but due to Japanese rejection of such a pact. Surely Japan must understand the Soviet Union's systematic strengthening of her frontiers.[41]

At the reopening of the Diet on January 21, Count Uchida made a foreign policy speech in which he stressed the need for amicable relations with the USSR. "Fortunately," he said, "the Soviet Union Government ever since the beginning of the Manchuria Incident has maintained an attitude so cautious that nothing unpleasant has occurred to mar its relations with Japan. This is a matter for congratulation for the mutual relationship among Japan, Manchukuo and the Soviet Union."

Uchida noted the apprehensions of General Araki, without mentioning him by name, that the restoration of diplomatic relations between the USSR and China

---

[40] Karakhan's record of his conversation with Ota, April 20, 1933, DVP, XVI, 43–50.

[41] DVP, XVI, 805–806, note 18.

might strengthen Communist propaganda, and agreed that Japan must be on guard against the spread of Communism in the Yangtze valley and South China. He said that the principles of a nonaggression pact between the Soviet Union and Japan were embodied in the Basic Convention and in the Kellogg Pact and had been a living force in the relations between the two countries, but that "in view of the divergent opinions stoutly maintained in different quarters," the Japanese Government had informed the Soviet Union that the time had not yet come for negotiating a nonaggression pact "superimposed upon the treaties now in force." This did not mean, he declared, that Japan had any aggressive designs against the USSR, and expressed the hope that Japan's position was "fully understood and appreciated" by the Soviet government.[42]

In a speech before the third session of the Central Executive Committee on January 23, Molotov said that in view of the League of Nations' failure to take any action in the Far East, the Soviet Union, which had never tied her hopes to the League of Nations and its commissions, had sought to meet the international situation by concluding a nonaggression pact with Japan, but her proposal had been turned down for the moment. "I shall not go into an evaluation of the motives for the Japanese government's rejection of our proposal concerning a nonaggression pact," Molotov stated. "Although we consider this refusal to be temporary, we cannot but take it into account." He damned Araki for the "provocative communications" he had made concerning the Soviet government and the Soviet embassy in China and condemned Uchida for repeating them in his speech, notwithstanding categorical Soviet denials.[43]

[42] JWC, February 2, 1933, p. 155.
[43] *Izvestiia*, February 1, 1933; DVP, XVI, 50–56.

When Ota took issue with Molotov's criticism, asserting in a note to Karakhan on January 28 that Uchida's speech had differed wholly in content and meaning from Araki's communiqué and that, therefore, Molotov had been mistaken in his allegations, Karakhan replied tersely on January 31 that "the Soviet government . . . takes notice of the fact that . . . the Japanese government does not intend to associate itself with the certain communiqué of the Japanese Ministry of War, which drew a categorical denial from the Soviet government. . ."[44]

Troianovskii carried Soviet advocacy of a nonagression pact directly to the Japanese public. At a meeting with the leaders of the Shakai Taishuto (the Social Mass Party) on January 31, he declared that amicable relations between the Soviet Union and Japan were essential for the preservation of world peace. The conclusion of a nonagression pact, he argued, would boost economic relations between their countries, a development from which Japan in particular stood to gain.[45]

During a farewell luncheon several days earlier, on January 27, at the house of George Sansom, the commercial counselor of the British embassy, with whom he was on good terms, Troianovskii had told Sansom, as he had told Lindley, that the objection to a nonaggression pact came from young army officers for purely psychological reasons. They deemed it the duty of the

[44] *Izvestiia*, February 1, 1933; DVP, XVI, 68–69; JWC, February 9, 1933, p. 206; FO 371/17151–858.

[45] Kutakov, *Istoriia*, 119–20; JWC, January 26, 1933. The Shakai Taishuto organized a peace rally to urge the conclusion of a nonaggression pact with the Soviet Union. But every speaker was stopped by the police and no resolution was passed. Recalling that at the time of the Russo-Japanese War the Socialists had been allowed to bring out the antiwar weekly *Heimin Shimbun*, the *Chronicle* wrote: "Their profession of Socialism as well as the liberty they enjoyed to publish (for a time at least) a paper opposing the Government's policy is in marked contrast to what is allowed today, though at the time of the war with Russia the crisis was so grave that some intolerance of dissent could have been understood." (JWC, March 2, 1933, p. 283.)

army to be ready for war at any time against any enemy, and were obsessed with the notion that such a pacifist measure as a nonaggression pact would not only be unbecoming, but would undermine its martial spirit. Araki, many other generals, and most of those who had experienced the hardship of military operations in Manchuria during the winter were in favor of a pact.

Troianovskii remarked that the equipment of the Japanese army had not been up to the requirements of modern warfare the previous year and that the Japanese would have received an unpleasant surprise had they attacked the USSR at that time. The deficiencies had been made good since, but he did not think that there was any danger of war for the next four years, that is, until 1937.[46]

In February the Japanese government belatedly responded to Troianovskii's accusations of January 4. A verbal note, delivered to the counselor of the Soviet embassy by order of Uchida for conveyance to the ambassador, asserted that Troianovskii's note contained "expressions hardly desirable in view of the interests of the friendly relations between both countries." The Japanese government accepted the "explanation," made by Troianovskii subsequently, that the reference to a "certain nation" which was growing by aggression and expansion of her sphere of influence did not imply Japan. "Need it be said," it asked rhetorically, "that following the dictates of her constant feeling of justice, Japan has no designs of armed aggression?" It recalled that it had maintained

---

[46] Lindley to Simon, No. 59, "Confidential," Tokyo, January 30, 1933, FO 371/17151–858. While Troianovskii and Sansom hobnobbed, Mrs. Troianovskii was telling Katharine Sansom about her thirteen year old boy Oleg, who was being educated at an American school in Japan and eventually was to follow the footsteps of his father as ambassador to Japan. (Sansom, 55–56.)

in its verbal note of December 13 that it was clear from the Basic Convention and from everything that had happened since its conclusion that Japan and the USSR were "mutually ready to scrupulously respect the sovereign rights of one another and punctually refrain from any violation of each other's border."

The Japanese government took the opportunity to protest once more against Soviet publication of the details of the negotiations prior to having its acquiescence.[47]

On February 4, at a meeting of the budget commission of the Diet, Representative Matsumoto of the Minscito Party asked how the Japanese public felt about the conclusion of a pact with the Soviet Union. Uchida replied that there were many different opinions on the subject; he was refraining, he said, from expressing his own view. When Matsumoto pressed him, saying that Matsuoka had declared at Geneva that Japanese public opinion favored the conclusion of a Soviet-Japanese pact and that he assumed that the foreign minister's views were in accord with that of his delegate to the League of Nations, Uchida retorted that Matsuoka had not been empowered to make any statements concerning a Soviet-Japanese pact and that anything that he may have said on this topic had been purely an expression of his personal opinion. Matsumoto sharply criticized the lack of unity in public pronouncements, but Uchida merely reiterated his condemnation of Matsuoka for exceeding his instructions.[48]

When Hara Yoshimichi and General Kawai at a com-

[47] IMTFE, "Proceedings," 222688–91.

[48] *Izvestiia*, February 6, 1933. On December 28 Premier Saito had told the Japanese press that he regarded a nonaggression pact with the USSR as necessary, because Soviet-Japanese friendship was essential for the preservation of peace in the Far East. His view was not affected, he said in response to a query, by the improvement of relations between the USSR and China. (*Izvestiia*, January 1, 1933.)

mittee meeting of the Privy Council in March inquired whether the government had any intention of concluding a nonagression pact with the Soviet Union, Uchida clearly said "No."[49]

Uchida warned Konstantin Iuren'ev, Troianovskii's successor, on March 22 not to invite Japan again to sign a nonaggression pact, for he would meet with a flat refusal and relations between their countries would be impaired. Iuren'ev replied that he had no intention of doing so, but that his government stood prepared to sign such an agreement if and when the Japanese changed their mind.

Relating the conversation to the British ambassador at a dinner party on April 5, Uchida remarked that "for all their bluster," the Soviet government was in an "exceedingly weak position." Lindley made no comment, but in his report to the Foreign Office expressed the hope that Uchida's conviction would not lead the military "into taking what they imagine to be a favourable opportunity to embark on a policy of adventure regarding the Soviets."

Premier Saito told Sansom on the same occasion that when Iuren'ev had asked him why the Japanese government was unwilling to sign a nonaggression pact, he had replied that it felt unjustified in doing so because there was an influential body of opinion opposed to it. "Admiral Saito went on to say," Lindley wrote, "that, as a matter of fact, it was useless signing a pact with a Government in which no trust could be placed. He felt, when talking to M. Yureneff, that

---

[49] "The foregoing reply," Harada noted on March 21, "made it evident that during Foreign Minister Uchida's term of office as foreign minister it would be impossible to carry out a policy whereby, in exchange for concluding a nonaggression pact with Russia, Russia would recognize the independence of Manchukuo." ("Saionji-Harada Memoirs," 554.)

any serious agreement would be so unreal that it was dishonest to enter into it."[50] Lindley concluded that the fact that the premier and the foreign minister both had spontaneously raised the question of a nonaggression pact showed that "relations with Russia are occupying a large place in the thoughts of the Japanese Government at the present time."[51]

In a press interview on March 25, Iuren'ev declared that good-neighborly relations between the USSR and Japan were a guarantee of peace in the Far East and elsewhere. He pointed to Soviet neutrality and nonintervention in Manchurian affairs as well as to the proposal for a nonaggression pact as evidence that the USSR was pursuing a policy of peace and friendship and had no aggressive intentions, even though she was fully conscious of her power and ability to defend her interests. He expressed the conviction that the attempts of some elements in Japan to disrupt the good-neighborly relations between their countries would be crowned by failure.[52]

Iuren'ev was less optimistic when he made his customary first call on his British colleague on March 27. Although he professed amusement that all but one of the journalists whom he had addressed had deleted from his statement the passage that the Japanese government had not accepted the Soviet offer of a nonaggression pact, he hinted that he conceived of a Japanese attack on the USSR in the coming spring or summer.

---

[50] These remarks are of particular interest because in his talk with Iuren'ev and in some of his public pronouncements Saito gave the impression of favoring the conclusion of a nonaggression pact. (See Kutakov, *Istoriia*, 121, and *Nisso kosho-shi*, 290.) "A pact would certainly be a sham," a British Foreign Office official remarked. "Anyhow the military clique won't permit the government to sign one." (FO 371/17151–858.)

[51] Lindley to Simon, No. 203, "Confidential," Tokyo, April 6, 1933, FO 371/17151–858.

[52] *Izvestiia*, March 27, 1933.

Yet he would not press the pact upon the Japanese. The Soviet leaders, he said, "were not so poor that they had need to play the role of beggars and were more likely to be successful if they showed no particular eagerness on the subject."[53]

---

[53] Lindley to Simon, No. 183, "Confidential," Tokyo, March 27, 1933, FO 371/17151–858. Troianovskii asked Lindley for his opinion why the Japanese government had refused to sign the pact. Lindley replied that while many influential Japanese favored signature, certain elements in the army opposed it on the grounds that it would increase Communist propaganda, diminish the military spirit of the nation, and restrict the freedom of action of the army. Iuren'ev's retort that the pact would decrease Communist propaganda struck Lindley as naive.

12

The "Inevitability" of War with Japan

Hirota had been correct in advising his government that the USSR would not seek to expell Japan from Manchuria. But while the Soviet Union was unwilling to fight Japan in defense of the rights of China, whose government had broken off relations with her and whose authority over Manchuria she herself had challenged, she insisted that her own rights in that region be respected. As the Kwantung Army contemplated the seizure of the CER and the extension of the Japanese "defense perimeter" into Soviet territory, the "inevitability" of a second Russo-Japanese War became the subject of general debate.

Western observers differed sharply in their analysis of Soviet-Japanese relations. Some wrote of the inevitability of war between the USSR and Japan, others of a tacit agreement between the two powers regarding Manchuria.[1] Not only was there historical

[1] *Istoriia vneshnei politiki*, I, 269–70; DVP, XV, 740, note 55; Tompkins, 249–50; Yakhontoff, 322.

361

precedent for the conflicting views—Russia and Japan had gone to war in 1904 partly over Manchuria; they had arrived at a *modus vivendi* subsequently; and Japan had sympathized with the Soviet actions in 1929—but there were in fact conflicting tendencies in Japanese policy. A number of businessmen favored good relations with the USSR for the sake of economic gain. Political liberals, Social Democrats, Communists, and pacifists also were favorably disposed toward the Soviet Union. Radical rightists and anti-Communist nationalists advocated immediate war with the USSR. "Moderates" advocated war as "self-defense" once the "evil intentions" of the Soviet Union had been demonstrated.[2]

Within the Japanese army itself there was a cleavage of opinion between the Imperial Way Faction, headed by Araki and supported by the younger officers attached to field units, favoring war with the USSR, and the Control Faction, predominantly field grade officers at Army Headquarters in Tokyo, who were more rational and more inclined to compromise. The former opposed the purchase of the CER on the grounds that its retention by the Soviets might provide the excuse for a Russo-Japanese War and that in the event of such a conflict it would fall automatically into Japanese hands.[3]

Although the Soviets themselves were painfully conscious of the possibility of hostilities with Japan, they

[2] Ikuhiko Hata, "Reality and Illusion," 35. Lt. Colonel Kasahara Yukio, the Japanese military attaché in Moscow, was convinced that if Japan wanted to be Great Japan, she would have to fight the Soviet Union eventually. "Considering the capacity of the USSR for national defense and the situation of the other powers," he wrote, "the sooner the Soviet-Japanese war comes, the better for us." (IMTFE, "Proceedings," 23221.) A paper by George B. Bickle, Jr. examines the influence of the "Attack Russia Faction" on Japanese foreign policy. ("Soviet-Japanese Relations 1931–1941," MS, June 1959.)

[3] Hata, 5–18.

regarded the predictions of war in Western newspapers as a deliberate attempt by the capitalist press to incite hostilities between the USSR and Japan. Their suspicions were nourished by the fact that the United States had not yet recognized the Soviet Union and restricted the import of Russian goods. The existence or consideration of similar anti-Soviet legislation in England, France and other countries made the Soviets expect an economic blockade and possibly a new intervention by the Western powers and Japan.[4] The feeling that the conflict of 1929 had been engineered by the Western powers to test Soviet strength was reinforced in the public mind by the "confession" of the defendants at the Menshevik trials in Moscow in March 1931 that a foreign intervention had been planned for 1930 or 1931 at the latest.[5]

To the Soviets the Japanese advance into Manchuria appeared as a thrust towards them. Expecting "the very near future" to reveal Japanese plans concerning the USSR, Ambassador Troianovskii warned in January 1932 that "in military circles thought is given to the occupation of Sakhalin, the Maritime region and Kamchatka."[6]

Western diplomats shared Troianovskii's misgiv-

[4] Molotov's report to the Sixth Congress of Soviets, March 8, 1931, DVP, XIV, 124–59. Ultranationalists in Poland actually contemplated cooperation with Japan to "liberate" Siberia. (Max Beloff, *The Foreign Policy of Soviet Russia 1929–1941*, I, 84.) A number of armchair strategists in Europe and the United States advocated the provocation of another Russo-Japanese War to weaken both countries. (Yakhontoff, 322.) Foreign Commissar Litvinov expressed the conviction that Finland, like Poland, counted in her policy on the possibility of a Soviet conflict in the Far East, "having decided in advance to intervene in the conflict at a given moment." (Litvinov to A. M. Kollontai, October 14, 1934.) Edward E. Brodie reported from Helsingfors that the Finns desired a Soviet-Japanese collision in the expectation that Japan would emerge victorious and that the Finns would be able to wrest the Carelian territory from a weakened USSR. (Brodie, February 23, 1933, National Archives, 761.94/597.)

[5] Molotov's report to the Sixth Congress of Soviets, DVP, XIV, 149.

[6] Troianovskii to Foreign Commissariat, "Immediately," January 7, 1932, DVP, XV, 16.

ings. The United States minister to China confided to his British colleague that he firmly believed that Japan would seek to overtake Russia in North Manchuria and perhaps in the Maritime region and Sakhalin. "I have myself often wondered," Lampson commented in a secret cable to the Foreign Office, "if Japan's present action, under smoke screen of public interest, vis-à-vis China, may not be fundamentally aimed as much at getting ahead of Russia in North Manchuria whilst latter is economically preoccupied as at consolidating Japanese hold on Southern area. Japanese minister admitted to me in Shanghai last December that whilst Japan could naturally not mention at Geneva or Paris her anxieties regarding Russia, they did, in fact, play their part in her policy."[7]

In an "off the record" talk with Japanese newspapermen, Troianovskii declared that it was entirely up to Japan whether or not there would be a conflict between their countries. The Soviet Union did not desire one. He threatened that a military clash would lead to full-scale war with heavy consequences for Japan, as the forces of Japan were no match for those of the entire USSR. In underlining that the Soviet Union had no reason to attack Japan, Troianovskii tried to create a good atmosphere, but as he reported to the Foreign Commissariat, "in so far as the military play the major role, it is still unknown how they will conduct themselves and what they will cook up."[8]

In a lengthy article in *Izvestiia,* the Soviet Union justified the reinforcement of her Far Eastern garrisons by publishing excerpts of documents "originating from representatives of the higher military circles of Japan,"

[7] Lampson to Foreign Office, No. 53, Peking, January 18, 1932, "Secret," FO 371/16141.
[8] Troianovskii to Foreign Commissariat, January 10, 1932, DVP, XV, 19–20.

which called for an invasion of the Soviet Union at the earliest possible time and for the annexation of the Russian Far East. Toeing a narrow path between outrage and accommodation, the USSR, on one hand, proclaimed her determination to defend her territory without threatening anyone else's, and, on the other hand, declared that her sympathy for "the struggle of the Chinese workers and peasants for freedom" did not "in any degree" affect her "unshakable line of strict nonintervention."[9]

Yet war between the USSR and Japan was only narrowly averted in March 1932 when the Chinese General Wang Te-lin, who had taken the field against the Japanese forces in Kirin province, fled to the Soviet border with the (Japanese) Korean Army on his heels. War Minister Araki wanted to attack the USSR and was restrained with difficulty by Admiral Kato.[10]

In a lengthy evaluation of the state of Soviet-Japanese relations at the end of March, Troianovskii wrote that the greatest obstacle to amity between the two countries was posed by the "military-fascist movement" in Japan, but he remarked that since the movement was composed of heterogeneous elements with different sentiments, it was not, and could not be, unanimously hostile toward the USSR. While many

[9] *Izvestiia*, March 4, 1932. The Soviets doubted that the Western powers would take any resolute steps to halt Japanese expansion. When the ambassadors of the United States, Great Britain, France and Italy made separate protests in Tokyo concerning Japanese violation of the International Settlement in Shanghai and the shelling of Western ships by the Chinese because of the proximity of Japanese vessels, Troianovskii reported: "All the démarches were made in an extremely friendly form. Everyone pretended that he made the démarche because the others did so." (Troianovskii to Foreign Commissariat, February 26, 1932, "Immediately," DVP, XV, 144.)

[10] Spil'vanek's record of his conversation with the Japanese journalist Fuse, August 12, 1932, DVP, XV, 465–68. "Of course not only Admiral Kato but a number of persons and groups [in addition to the navy] played their part in this regard," Troianovskii observed. "The work of the embassy in this direction bore fruit." (Troianovskii to Karakhan, August 19, 1932, DVP, XV, 479–81.)

Japanese were impressed by the economic growth of the Soviet Union, "the decisive role" in determining which attitude would prevail would be played "not by questions of sympathy for the building of socialism, but by the correlation between the strength and role of the USSR and by major questions of Japanese foreign policy, at this stage the issue of the Far East. . . ."

The Japanese General Staff, Troianovskii reported, was firmly convinced that neither the United States nor the Soviet Union would or could fight. "It was felt in regard to both America and the USSR that this was the most favorable moment for the Japanese imperialists, since the United States would in the future strengthen her fleet in accordance with the decision of the London Conference, and the USSR, which now was 'impotent,' was gradually increasing her military strength." But the strong resistance put up by the Chinese Nineteenth Route Army near Shanghai and the Soviet military buildup at the Manchurian border had made the situation more difficult for the Japanese. "A military conflict with the USSR will cost enormous casualties and will no doubt arouse China against Japan, even against the will of Chiang Kai-shek, Chang Hsüeh-liang and company," Troianovskii wrote. "All this threatens Japan with catastrophe." Adding to this "the continuing forays of 'bandits' in Manchuria, the worsening of relations with the United States (which, by the way, does everything to avoid war or at least to delay it as much as possible), the difficult financial and economic situation within Japan, along with the ever more widening spread of 'dangerous thought,' " Troianovskii concluded that the most likely development for the present was Japanese entrenchment in Manchuria along the positions which the Japanese imperialists had projected after the failure of the Siberian Intervention. "This does not mean that we have a guarantee that there will be no military conflict. Certainly the danger of one is now very great and became very great when the Japanese 'line of defense' moved close to our borders," Troianovskii wrote. "Some insignificant change in the international situation can easily lead to a state of war, particularly since there will be found any number of people eager to draw us into war. We must, consequently, be on our guard. . . ."[11]

Since the Soviet Union had resorted to force to protect her railway interests in 1929, speculation grew when Manchukuo began violating the same interests whether the Red Army might strike again. In an editorial on April 8, the *Central China Post* expressed the belief that the USSR would explore all diplomatic possibilities before reinvading Manchuria. "When Russia attacked in 1929, it was faced by purely local Chinese troops who occupied the position of pawns for the responsible politicians who were so many hundred of miles away in the south that they might have been of another nation," the paper observed. "Today Russia would have to cause disagreement between Manchukuo and Japan or fight these combined. In the latter case, with Japanese stiffening, it would take more than bags of soot dropped from aeroplanes to cause a rout."[12]

On April 14 Ambassador Lindley reported from Tokyo that while the Soviets seemed "most anxious to avoid becoming embroiled in the Far East" and the Japanese so far had not comtemplated hostilities

[11] Troianovskii to Karakhan, March 31, 1932, DVP, XV, 214–17.

[12] *The Central China Post*, April 8, 1932, clipping sent by Acting Consul General Walter A. Adams at Hankow to Stimson on April 8, 1932, National Archives, 761.94/508.

with them, the "arrogance of the Japanese military is such that if they become convinced that the Russians mean to harass them in Manchuria, they are capable of forcing the issue." Although Lindley thought it most likely that the Soviets would accept "a rebuff coupled with promises of good behaviour in the future," he held out the possibility that "the Soviets, with the strength which they have quietly built up in the Far East, might think the moment was ripe for a great world-revolutionary move," because, as he pointed out, "the temptation to come out as the champions of the toiling millions of China against the militarist Japanese and the imperialist League of Nations, led by Great Britain, must be extraordinarily strong to Bolshevik mentality." While Lindley realized that the above was "mere speculation," he added: "What is not a speculation is that the Japanese General Staff, and wide circles outside the army, are convinced that, sooner or later, there will be a second Russo-Japanese campaign in Manchuria."[13]

P. Broad, a colleague in the Northern Department, questioned Japanese allegations, conveyed by Lindley, that the Soviets were responsible for incidents along the CER and for continued local opposition to Japanese "pacification." "I do not think that the Soviet can fairly be accused of a policy of pinpricks in Manchuria, rather the reverse," Broad wrote. "In their anxiety to avoid trouble they seem to have submitted to a succession of indignities, at Harbin in particular." It was the Japanese who were guilty of such a policy, Broad felt and declared that "if a clash does occur, I think it is they who will be responsible."[14]

[13] Lindley to Simon, No. 205, Tokyo, April 14, 1932, "Confidential," FO 371/16169–662.
[14] May 19, 1932, FO 371/16169–662.

Mackillop agreed. "All existing indications point to the conclusion that, if there *is* a Russo-Japanese conflict, it will be one that the Russians are absolutely unable to avoid."[15]

Sir Victor Wellesley, deputy undersecretary of state for foreign affairs, added that the situation in Japan had become "even more disquieting" since the dispatch had been written and that "the risk of collision with Russia" had increased "very considerably." "The economic and political position is becoming more and more desperate," he wrote, "and it would not surprise me if this were to result in a clash with the Soviets. It may be true that the Soviet Government is anxious to avoid this and will do all in its power to prevent it. But they have got the Red Army to deal with. The latter is nationalistic in outlook and may be less inclined to submit to Japanese aggressiveness."[16]

The Soviet ambassador in Tokyo, who was puzzled and embarrassed by the constant allegations in the Japanese press of Soviet instigation of the recent disorders in North Manchuria, ascribed the invention to Japanese officers and officials in Manchuria rather than to the Japanese government. Telling his British colleague that the Japanese army had two officers attached to the Red Army and that the Red Army in turn had an equal number of officers with Japanese regiments, he said with a smile that the Japanese had recently requested permission to attach additional officers to the Soviet armed forces.[17]

---

[15] *Ibid.*

[16] May 21, 1932, FO 371/16169–662. Wellesley speculated that "a split between the Soviet Government and the Red Army might lead to a military dictatorship at Moscow."

[17] Lindley to Foreign Office, No. 235, Tokyo, April 30, 1932, FO 371/16170–662. Troianosvkii boasted that the Japanese army was copying the Red Army in estab-

Karl Radek, the chief foreign affairs commentator of the Soviet press, told a British member of the League of Nation's Secretariat that while the USSR would not fight for the sake of maintaining her material interests in North Manchuria, lest she appear as an imperialist rival of Japan in the South and endanger the Five-Year Plan which she regarded as more important than anything else, the Soviet government was convinced that the seizure of the CER would be a prelude to the invasion of the USSR. Radek stated that the Soviet Union had spent billions of rubles during the past seven months to prepare for possible war with Japan and that in the event of hostilities long-range bombers based at Vladivostok would raid Japanese naval bases and Tokyo itself.

Radek believed that Japan might court war with the USSR in the expectation of regaining the support of the capitalist powers. He complained bitterly about the absence of diplomatic relations with the United States and about the apparent desire of the Americans "that the Chinese, the Russians or anyone else should fight the Japanese for them."[18]

Foreign Office officials in London doubted that Japan planned to attack the USSR. Pratt expressed the belief that "Japan will have the wisdom to stop short at the Amur River."[19] While Orde thought it possible that Japan might get drawn into war by Soviet encouragement of "insurgent" Chinese in Manchuria,

---

lishing clubs for soldiers and in encouraging instruction in and discussion of political matters among the officers. Amau told Strang that Soviet officers had been attached to the Japanese army and Japanese officers to the Red Army since 1930. (Strang to Simon, No. 491, Moscow, September 5, 1932, "Confidential," FO 371/16178.)
   [18] British Delegation to the League of Nations to Foreign Office, No. 111, April 20, 1932, "Confidential" FO 371/16166-867.
   [19] FO 371-16166-867.

the British ambassador reported from Moscow that the Soviet government's "primary object" was "not to become entangled in any foreign war." He did note, however, that the Russians were "extremely interested in the preservation of the integrity of the Maritime Provinces and their other territories in the Far East" and were "determined to show the Japanese that whatever regime they may temporarily succeed in setting up in Manchuria, there can be no question of Japanese military expansion outside." Should Japan succeed in establishing her hegemony in Manchuria and in temporarily closing that country to Soviet propaganda, Sir Esmond Ovey remarked, "Russia will be able to console herself with the thought that any system of capitalist reactionary repression is more liable eventually to open up a favourable field for the cultivation of the Communist microbe than an unsuccessful attempt to prepare the ground in the face of continued opposition." At any rate, Ovey regarded the Soviet regime as "much more realistic" than the tsarist government had been. He expected that "so far as the Chinese Eastern Railway and Manchuria in general are concerned, they are more likely to be weighed by material considerations than by considerations of mere prestige."[20]

In response to a query from the Treasury Office, whose Export Credit Department wanted to give a long-term credit to Japan, about the prospects of war between Japan and the USSR, H. J. Seymour replied in June that the Foreign Office did not consider that there was serious danger of such a conflict in the immediate future, but that "the conflict between Japa-

[20] Ovey to Simon, No. 263, Moscow, May 30, 1932, "Confidential," FO 371/16171–665.

nese and Russian interests in the Far East may quite well *ultimately* lead to war." The Soviet government, he wrote, had so far shown "a most conciliatory spirit towards Japan's venture in Manchuria, in spite of the anxiety which they have felt in regard to their important interests in that region" and "in their anxiety to avoid trouble" had "submitted to a succession of irritating acts by the Japanese military." On the Japanese side, he pointed out, there were two factions—the militarists, who had "consistently adopted a challenging attitude" toward the Soviets, accusing them of intrigue and subversive activities in Manchuria, and the civilian elements in the government, who did not endorse these charges. He believed that with the recent increase in the influence of the former, the danger of a clash with the USSR had increased, because "a Japanese Government whose guiding ideas are military rather than civilian would not be willing or able to localize or to minimize the effects of such incidents." "The magnitude of the undertaking which a full-dress campaign against the Soviets would represent, especially in Japan's present financial and economic conditions, is such as *should* make even the most fire-eating soldier hesitate," he reasoned, then added "we think and hope that it would, but we cannot be quite sure."[21]

When F. K. Roberts of the Northern Department read a complaint by *Izvestiia* that an article in *Nihon,* a small Japanese newspaper circulating among the reactionary parties and the ex-military class,[22] advocated the immediate seizure of Eastern Siberia on the ground that "if Manchuria means life and death for Japan, then Eastern Siberia means life or death to Manchuria and Mongolia," he concurred that the Japanese argu-

[21] Seymour to S. D. Waley, June 7, 1932, FO 371/16246–680.
[22] Lindley to Foreign Office, No. 380, Tokyo, July 20, 1932, FO 371/16246.

ment was not only "utter nonsense," but "a dangerous doctrine of doubtful validity." While Roberts knew that "responsible Government elements" did not share the feeling of many Japanese, especially the younger officers, that war with the USSR was inevitable or desirable, he admitted that in view of their repeated failures to restrain the firebrands "there is good cause for anxiety at Moscow."[23]

The British consul general in Harbin was struck by "the studiedly moderate attitude of the Soviet government under considerable provocation." He felt that the "extreme lengths of forbearance" to which it went to avoid a conflict with Japan bordered on "pusillanimity." Moscow's consent to the use of the CER by Japanese troops for strategic purposes while proclaiming in the press that it would not yield an inch of Soviet soil, looked to him like the position of one "who seeing a trespasser on his ground and being afraid to attempt to eject him, exclaims in a loud voice that on no account will the intruder be allowed to enter the house." It was his conclusion, after talking to his Soviet and Japanese colleagues and studying the local press, that "the Soviet Government are anxious to avoid an armed conflict with Japan at almost any cost—in fact, that nothing short of an actual invasion of Soviet territory will be deemed to be a *casus belli*."[24]

In seeking to analyze the motives behind Japan's occupation of North Manchuria, British officials disagreed concerning the relative importance of economic and political factors. While Wellesley stressed the economic causes of the undertaking, Lindley argued

[23] *Izvestiia* article dated May 30, 1932; comments made on June 16, 1932, FO 371/16246–680.

[24] Garstin to Ingram, No. 42, Harbin, June 11, 1932, "Confidential," FO 371/16173–665.

that the military action had been "a signal instance of the triumph of political ambition over economic considerations." He contended that for the military party as for most Japanese, Manchuria had represented the political ideal of "a bulwark against Russian and Chinese influence" and that the Japanese had launched their offensive "even at the sacrifice of the great economic interests of Japan in China proper."[25]

The "sudden change for the better" that Troianovskii had perceived in Soviet-Japanese relations once the crisis of March and April had passed, faded by summer as Araki and the young officers who idolized him renewed their clamor for war with the USSR.[26] It mattered little that Troianovskii was on better personal terms with Araki than any Western envoy. (Araki, whose only foreign language was Russian, had spent eight years in Russia as a language officer, military attaché, and officer of the Russian staff during the First World War. He had pleasant recollections of his stay in Russia and seemed to like Russians and Russian customs, drinking tea at home from a samovar.)[27] Araki believed that the fact that the Soviet constitution regarded capitalist and monarchist states as enemies, automatically made Japan an enemy of the USSR.[28]

[25] Lindley to Simon, No. 234, Tokyo, April 28, 1932, "Confidential," FO 371/16170. As an interminable debate threatened to ensue, Vansittart commented: "Novalis affirmed that to philosophise is to generalise; and the older I get the more I mistrust the ancestral pastime, whether applied to nations, sexes, 'or any other adversity,'—including this one." (May 28, 1932, FO 371/16170–662.)
[26] Troianovskii to Karakhan, August 19, 1932, DVP, XV, 479–81.
[27] Grew to Stimson, Tokyo, July 15, 1932, National Archives, 761.93/1466. Improbable as friendly relations between Troianovskii and Araki may seem at first thought, it must be remembered that Troianovskii and his wife were known to be gracious hosts and that Araki enjoyed philosophizing about Communism. As Katharine Sansom wrote about Araki that year, "There's no doubt he is that dangerous creature, a mystic fanatic; but just to meet he oozes charm, and anything less like the spectacular type of fire-eating madman you can't conceive." (Sansom, 53.)
[28] Spil'vanek to Foreign Commissariat, August 12, 1932, DVP, XV, 465–68.

Araki's pronouncements continued to worry Troianovskii increasingly because of the mounting influence of the military. He must have seen imminent danger, for the telegrams in which he conveyed Araki's views were marked *"nemedlenno"* (immediately).

On August 2 Troianovskii cabled that Araki had told a well-known journalist that the differences between the USSR and Japan were differences in principles. In response to the journalist's remark that all other states were seeking compromises and ways for peaceful coexistence, Araki had replied that when principles were involved, compromises and accomodations were impossible. "One cannot accept the situation that Japanese at the trial of Communists act like citizens of the Soviet Union," Araki had declared and, questioned by the journalist whether this meant that Japan would go to war with the USSR, had replied that "war is inevitable sooner or later."[29] When Troianovskii in an attempt to get some reassurance of the peaceful intention of the Japanese government had thereupon asked Matsushima Hajime, the director of the Bureau of European and American Affairs of the Foreign Office, how he would interpret Araki's article in his place, Matsushima had responded with an "uncertain smile."[30]

On August 11, Troianovskii reported that almost everyone who visited the Soviet embassy told of "energetic preparations" in the Japanese Army for war with the USSR. The war plants were working

---

[29] Troianovskii to Foreign Commissariat, August 2, 1932, "Immediately," DVP, XV, 447. Troianovskii was puzzled. "One can almost certainly assume," he wrote, "that Araki knew that this conversation would be conveyed to me. I regard it possible even that Araki wanted that I knew about this talk. At any rate, it must be kept secret." (*Ibid.*, 448.)

[30] *Ibid.*

day and night.[31] Troianovskii repeated that a number of statesmen were speaking out against such a war and that a bitter struggle was in progress between General Araki and Admiral Kato over this issue. He himself was tempted to go and talk directly to Araki, but, he reported, he was being advised against it by persons who feared "a bad impression on the Foreign Office and even a provocation on the part of Araki."[32]

Confirming a week later that Araki and his group had revived their campaign for war with the USSR, Troianovskii called for vigilance on the part of all Soviet agencies that came in contact with the Japanese on Kamchatka, on Sakhalin, in Manchuria, and particularly along the Soviet-Manchurian border. ". . . we must be on guard," he wrote, "and under no circumstances must we be taken unawares."[33]

Western observers were as watchful as Troianovskii

[31] As noted, the Japanese invasion of Manchuria had triggered a buildup of Soviet forces in the Russian Far East. By the end of 1933 Soviet military strength was to be "three or four times as large as before the Manchurian Incident" according to Japanese estimates. The reports of American military attachés in the USSR confirmed "intense military preparations." Although the buildup had come in response to their own advance, the Japanese regarded it as a threat to their security, a view shared by some American observers. Carl Gilbert remarks that "while the official and unofficial world was condemning Japan alone for posing a serious threat to peace and stability in the Far East, the officials on the spot recognized the seriousness of the Soviet buildup and the anxiety which this produced among Japanese leaders." (Gilbert, 16–20.) W. Cameron Forbes, the American ambassador in Tokyo at the time of the outbreak of the Manchurian Incident, on the other hand, lauded the Soviet approach. "The Russians . . . have amassed an army said to be 100,000 strong on the Manchurian frontier and that is having a stronger effect on the evident desire of the Japanese to settle the Shanghai matter quickly than all the protests of the powers and of the League combined. The Russians have made no threats, no protests; just suggested a peace or anti-aggression pact with Japan which Japan has declined, and continue to send troops very quietly to Siberia and let the Japanese find out for themselves that it is happening. (This was exactly the language the Japanese understood—the language of force, without any threats, so that it obviated the need of face-saving on their part. . . .)" (G. A. Lensen, "Japan and Manchuria," 84–85.)

[32] Troianovskii to Foreign Commissariat, August 11, 1932, DVP, XV, 464.

[33] Troianovskii to Foreign Commissariat, August 19, 1932, DVP, XV, 479–81.

for any sign that might indicate a showdown between Japan and the USSR, but at times their imagination got the better of them. Thus Lindley speculated that a large Japanese order for foreign sewing machines might indicate that Japan was about to rupture relations with the Soviet Union.[34] When the Foreign Office requested elucidation, Lindley replied that the placement of such a large order might mean that the War Office planned to sew uniforms.[35] "This is rather absurd of the Tokyo Chancery," Broad remarked. "This is really beyond comment!" he huffed.[36] In another dispatch the same day Lindley reported that Lieutenant Colonel Maruyama of the Imperial General Staff had suggested to the British military attaché that rumors of war between Japan and the USSR had been "put about by Japanese businessmen with a view to 'rigging' the exchange."[37]

In still another dispatch the same day Lindley blamed "irresponsible circles" for recent talk about the imminence of hostilities with the USSR. "The view of this Embassy," he wrote, "has always been . . . that a Russo-Japanese war is an extremely improbable event at the present time for the simple reason that neither country desires it." He added that he had conferred with the vice minister for foreign affairs that morning and that "Mr. Arita stated in the most emphatic manner that he did not see the slightest possibility of war with Russia in the near future."[38]

---

[34] Lindley to Foreign Office, No. 330, Tokyo, August 24, 1932.
[35] Lindley to Foreign Office, No. 337, Tokyo, August 31, 1932.
[36] FO 371/16246–680.
[37] Lindley to Foreign Office, No. 456, Chuzenji, August 31, 1932, FO 371/16246–680.
[38] Lindley to Simon, No. 452, Chuzenji, August 31, 1932, FO 371/16246–680. In forwarding a memorandum by First Secretary W. R. Connor-Green, who had served for nearly a year with the White Russian forces in Siberia after the

While Araki fulminated against the Soviet Union and Uchida rejected the conclusion of a nonagression pact, Admiral Kato reassured Troianovskii on August 30 that Japan desired friendly relations with the USSR and that various individuals "who talked too much" did not matter. Men who counted—Elder Statesman Prince Saionji Kimmochi, Lord Keeper of the Privy Seal Count Makino Nobuaki, and President of the Privy Council Kuratomi Yuzaburo—were for good relations with the USSR, as was Araki himself officially. The Japanese were alarmed, however, Kato explained, by the massing of Soviet troops in Siberia in connection with the Japanese action in Manchuria and were worried about the Communist movement in central China.[39] He advised Troianovskii to meet with Premier Saito "privately" and frankly discuss all questions.[40]

Troianovskii took Kato's advice and visited Saito at his private residence on September 6. He told him about mounting rumors concerning the imminence of war between the Soviet Union and Japan and referred to the articles and speeches of Araki and other militarists. He said that the conclusion of a fishery agreement on August 13 had cleared the atmosphere somewhat, but apparently not enough. "Something broader and concrete must be done." Saito replied that the rumors of war between the Soviet Union and Japan were being spread by American agents and that he wanted

---

end of the First World War, yet was on "particularly friendly terms" with Troianovskii, Lindley wrote the following month that he was "in agreement with his conclusion . . . that Russo-Japanese relations are likely to remain harmonious for some considerable time." (Lindley to Simon, No. 516, September 27, 1932, FO 371/16246–680.)

[39] Fear of the spread of Communism to China had been one reason for Japan's intervention in Siberia in 1918.

[40] Troianovskii to Foreign Commissariat, August 30, 1932, "Immediately," DVP, XV, 498–99.

Troianovskii to discuss various questions with Uchida to remove the basis for the undesirable rumors.[41]

When Troianovskii duly met with Uchida nine days later, on September 15, the foreign minister told him not to pay any attention to the activities of various military men and journalists, for "the military . . . always think of war." Troianovskii replied that military men did not always *advocate* the declaration of war. Besides, the minister of war was not merely a military man, but a member of the cabinet.[42] While warning that the military might find themselves less strong than they thought if they challenged the Soviet Union, Troianovskii declared that war as a test of strength was senseless. There must be serious reasons for war, and there were none. But Uchida refused to discuss the subject. He acted, Troianovskii felt, at the command and out of fear of the military and thus was afraid to say too much about them.

Troianovskii reiterated to Uchida, as he had told Saito, that it was necessary to do "something concrete and big that would dispel all mutual suspicions, would put an end to all rumors, and would calm public opinion in both countries." "If you have in mind a nonagression pact," Uchida replied, "it is meeting with difficulty, on one hand, because Japan and the USSR are signatories of the Kellogg Pact, on the other hand and primarily, because Japan is most afraid of Communist propaganda." Troianovskii expressed surprise at such a formulation of the question. He argued that nowhere had foreign propaganda called forth

[41] Troianovskii's record of his conversation with Saito, September 6, 1932, DVP, XV, 513.

[42] The *Chronicle* called Araki "the most popular figure in the country" and his theories or "Arakism" "Japan's new religion." (JWC, March 16, 1933.)

revolution. To be sure, there had been talk in Russia that the revolution of 1905 had been made with Japanese money, but that was ridiculous. Similarly German propaganda and German money had been credited by some people with the October Revolution, but Uchida himself had been in Russia then and knew well that this was rubbish. And there had been no Comintern at the time. When Uchida said animatedly that he had indeed been amazed how Soviet power had appeared everywhere in the vast territory—"it was just like wild bamboo, which in a few days grows into a whole forest, where there was nothing at first and where no one had planted it"—Troianovskii remarked that the minister had confirmed his words. But Uchida persisted nonetheless that many Japanese were taking the question of Communist propaganda seriously.[43]

On September 20 Troianovskii cabled to the Foreign Commissariat that Araki was very nervous and had lost weight[44] and that he was demanding that a decision be taken concerning war with the Soviet Union. Araki believed, Troianovskii reported, that America and England were "nothing," that the USSR constituted Japan's "main enemy." Araki was dissatisfied with the conclusion of an agreement for the purchase of oil from the Soviet Union; at the same time, he wanted

[43] Troianovskii's record of his conversation with Uchida, September 15, 1932, DVP, XV, 534–35. Asked by the chief of the Japanese Treaty Bureau what it thought of a Soviet-Japanese agreement, the French government replied that such an agreement would be more to the advantage of the USSR than of Japan. (DeLens to Herriot, Nos. 404 and 405, Tokyo, September 13, 1932, and Herriot to deLens, Nos. 253, 254, Paris, September 15, 1932, DDF, vol. 1, pp. 311–12, 330–31.)

[44] "Recently Araki has been suffering from a nervous breakdown and is quite run down," Ozaki told Harada. "The reason for this is that the young officers hurdle the fence and wake the minister up in the middle of the night and ask: 'What happened to the promises you made before you assumed your post as minister?' There are so many who are closing in upon him like this that he is weak from lack of sleep." ("Saionji-Harada Memoirs," 636.)

to know why Troianovskii did not call on him for a frank talk.[45]

Karakhan replied that Troianovskii was not to take the initiative for a meeting with Araki, but that he should agree to one if Araki wanted to see him.[46]

Several days later Troianovskii was visited by two persons who informed him independently of each other that Araki wanted to speak to him and in his name inquired when and where they could meet. Troianovskii replied that he could not see Araki before the seventh because he was not feeling well at the moment; other than that, Araki could decide the time and place.[47]

Troianovskii met with Araki at the latter's invitation on October 7. Araki stated that there were several questions that stood in the way of the establishment of lasting friendly relations and that he had, therefore, not yet made up his mind on the matter. He began by pointing to the difference in governmental structures, but admitted that this was not a realistic question and could be shelved for the time being. Then he queried Troianovskii whether the Soviet Union was supporting the uprising of the Chinese forces against the Japanese in Hulunbuir (Barga).[48] Troianovskii said

[45] DVP, XV, 796, note 258. Araki told the French Admiral Berthelot that so long as the USSR respected her treaties with Japan and abstained from propaganda within and without Japan against Japanese interests and the established order in the empire, she had nothing to fear on the part of Japan. But he regarded the Soviet Union as an "unstable country" and warned that one must keep a sharp eye on her. (*Procès-verbal* of meeting between Araki and Berthelot, September 6, 1932, "Secret," DDF, vol. I, pp. 275–76.)

[46] Karakhan to Troianovskii, September 27, 1932, DVP, XV, 544.

[47] Troianovskii to Foreign Commissariat, October 30, 1932, "Immediately," DVP, XV, 557–58; DVP, XV, 479–81.

[48] The uprising of General Su Ping-wen against the Japanese and Manchukuoan forces at Hulunbuir in September 1932 affected the course of Soviet-Japanese relations as Japan sought and obtained Soviet mediation in the release of local Japanese residents rounded up by Su and their evacuation to the USSR, and as she sought but failed to obtain Soviet surrender or permanent internment of Su's forces when they withdrew into the USSR. (See "Political Report of

No, and promised to convey Araki's wish that the USSR prevail upon the Chinese at Man'chzhuriia Station to release the Japanese trapped there and allow them to return by way of the Soviet Union. When Araki complained that Japanese travelers, particularly military men, received unfriendly treatment in the USSR, Troianovskii retorted that there was no anti-Japanese feeling in the Soviet Union, but that there might be some nervousness in view of the uncertainty of Japan's intentions. He noted that the conclusion of a nonaggression pact would clear up the atmosphere.

Araki responded that if the Hulunbuir affair were resolved, one could talk not only of a nonaggression pact, but of a rapprochement—even of an alliance between the USSR, Japan and Manchukuo. He asked Troianovskii whether he had discussed the matter of a pact with Uchida. Troianovskii answered that there could be no question of an alliance. As for a nonaggression pact, he himself would not raise the issue again. He did not want to be tiresome.

Troianovskii then took the offensive and pointing to Araki's articles and speeches declared that his position was not clear. Araki rejoined that he sometimes talked roughly, but that he had no warlike intentions. He wanted due regard paid to Asia and Japan, with consideration given to their interests and civilization. Asia, he said, wanted to have equal rights with Europe and America. Troianovskii declared that his countrymen would sympathize with this view if it was not based on hostility toward them.[49]

---

the Harbin Consular District for the Quarter ended December 31, 1932," FO 371/17066–768; *Izvestiia,* November 15 and December 24, 1932; documents in DVP, XV, pp. 560–61, 569, 587, 614–18, 636, 656–59, 671–72, 675–79, 682–83; XVI, pp. 23–24, 26–28, 72–73, 133, 195, 208–209; also notes nos. 265, 266, 303, 310 in XV and nos. 324, 342 in XVI.)

[49] Troianovskii to Foreign Commissariat, October 7, 1932, "Immediately," DVP, XV, 562–64.

When Karakhan informed Chargé d' Affaires Amau on October 9 that the Soviet government agreed to the transportation of Japanese troops to Man'chzhuriia Station, he took the opportunity to remind him that the Soviet Union had allowed the Japanese nationals at Man'chzhuriia Station to seek refuge in the USSR, and queried why Araki had not been informed of this and on what grounds he had been led to believe that Japanese travelers were not well received in the Soviet Union. He was concerned, he said, that the military circles were being misled by irresponsible sources, which "strangely" enjoyed greater confidence than the official organs of the Japanese government in the USSR (i.e. the diplomatic service). Amau admitted that there were extreme rightists, hostile to the USSR, who wanted to worsen Soviet-Japanese relations and for this purpose fed false information to the press.[50]

Troianovskii and Araki agreed to continue the conversation, and they met at Araki's private residence a week later, on October 17, but they talked primarily about the Hulunbuir situation, Araki thanking the Soviets for their efforts to save the Japanese at Man'chzhuriia Station.[51]

Soviet efforts to improve relations with Japan were not reciprocated by the Japanese. As the Japanese chargé d'affaires in Moscow put it to the British ambassador: "Soviet-Japanese relations are good, but Japanese-Soviet relations are not so good."[52]

---

[50] Karakhan's record of his conversation with Amau, October 9, 1932, DVP, XV, 564–66. Araki relied for his information about the USSR solely on the network of attachés and military agents that he had in that country. Although these men were diligent and perseverent and wrote much more than their diplomatic and commercial colleagues, their reports were unbalanced and often incorrect, because they evaluated everything exclusively from the military point of view. Thus Araki regarded the Five-Year Plan as a direct threat to Japan. (Spil'vanek to Foreign Commissariat, August 12, 1932, DVP, XV, 465–68.)

[51] DVP, XV, 798, note 267.

[52] Ovey to Stimson, No. 633, Moscow, November 8, 1932, FO 371/16246–680.

Troianovskii made every effort to equalize the situation by reassuring the Japanese public that the USSR wanted peace. In the November issue of the Japanese journal *Chuo Koron,* he attacked the predictions that an armed conflict between the USSR and Japan was inevitable, declaring that "the enemies of Soviet Russia in different countries will have to spend immense energy in dragging Soviet Russia into the vortex of war."[53]

Whatever improvement in Soviet-Japanese relations had occurred in consequence of Soviet mediation in the release of Japanese noncombatants and of Soviet consent to the use of the CER and its facilities by the Japanese expeditionary force to Man'chzhuriia Station was nullified in part by the dispute over the disposition of General Su Ping-wen and his men and by the sudden resumption of diplomatic relations between the USSR and China.[54] Yet while the Japanese military attributed China's quest for Russian and American aid to her loss of hope in help from the League of Nations, the *Japan Weekly Chronicle* observed that "setting apart America, Russia has no desire to make an enemy of Japan" and that the Soviet Union's restoration of diplomatic relations with China did not mean any increase in hostility toward Japan.[55]

When the British Foreign Office learned in January 1933 that the conclusion of a Soviet-Japanese nonaggression pact had been thwarted by the Japanese army, P. Broad commented that while it was "difficult to imagine that war could eventuate in the future," the development tended to confirm the conclusions of

---

[53] Grew to Stimson, Tokyo, November 5, 1932, National Archives, 761.94/580.
[54] "Political Report of the Harbin Consular District for the Quarter ended December 31, 1932," FO 371/17066–768.
[55] JWC, January 5, 1933, p. 18.

the British military attaché that "war is regarded as inevitable sooner or later."[56]

In a speech before the Congress of Collective Farmers in February, Commissar for the Army and Navy Kliment Voroshilov described the state of Soviet-Japanese relations as normal, but complained that "well-known Japanese public figures, particulary military men, were openly speaking of the possibility, sometimes even of the necessity, of war with the Soviet Union." He blamed the Japanese government for paying greater heed to the views of "war-waging imperialists" than to the common sense of the considerable number of Japanese statesmen who desired peace and better economic and other relations with the USSR.

Molotov, in an address to the same congress, alluded to his country's ability to strike back at an aggressor. In the past, interventionists had been able to test Soviet strength unmolested. Now, he warned, an attack on the USSR "cannot end so simply as before."[57]

In his conversation with Iuren'ev on March 27, Lindley expressed doubt that there was danger of war between Japan and the USSR within the next few years. He had heard so much about "inevitable" wars which never, in fact, took place, that he was skeptical that any war was inevitable. Iuren'ev agreed and expressed the belief that if war could be avoided for a few years, it might be avoided completely, implying that by then the Soviet Union would be too strong

[56] Comments in minutes, dated January 13 and 14, 1932, respectively, FO 371/17151–858. The French ambassador deemed a Japanese attack on the USSR "unlikely"; Japan would first have to consolidate her position. But he concurred that Japan's conquest of Manchuria constituted a "grave menace" to the territorial integrity of the Soviet Far East. (Count François Dejean to Foreign Minister Paul-Boncour, No. 22, Moscow, January 19, 1933. DDF, vol. 1, pp. 481–83.)

[57] JWC, March 2, 1933, pp. 306–307.

to be attacked. Iuren'ev did not share Lindley's view that the Japanese must digest what they had swallowed in Manchuria before seizing more. He observed that a serious situation would arise if Japan invaded China proper.[58]

R. H. S. Allen of the Far Eastern Department of the British Foreign Office evaluated the statement made by Karakhan to Ota on April 16 as follows: "The U.S.S.R. obviously don't want a quarrel with Japan just at the moment. The Japanese with their hands full in North China can hardly be anxious for one either; and the present friction will probably blow over."[59] Yet word that the Soviet Military Attaché Ivan Rink, who seemed "particularly well informed," had told his British colleague, Colonel E. A. H. James, that the Japanese, greatly alarmed by the fact that improvements in aircraft had placed Japan's industrial centers within bombing range of Vladivostok, wanted to secure the Maritime Province,[60] prompted Orde to reiterate the belief that war between Japan and the USSR could be postponed, but not avoided altogether. "The Japanese would no doubt dearly like to abolish the danger of air-raids from Vladivostok on Japan and on their communications with Manchuria," Orde wrote. "Will they be content with anything short of possession of Vladivostok? If they would, will the Soviet be prepared to meet them half-way e.g. by demilitarizing the

[58] Lindley to Simon, No. 183, Tokyo, March 27, 1933, "Confidential," FO 371/17151–858.
[59] Comments made in minutes on April 28, 1933, in reference to dispatch No. 204 of Strang to Foreign Office, dated April 20, 1933, FO 371/17133–876. Allen's uncertainty was betrayed by the fact that he had first jotted down that the friction "can hardly fail to blow over," then had crossed out "can hardly fail to" and scribbled "will probably."
[60] James to Lindley, No. 5, Tokyo, March 5, 1933, "Confidential," enclosed in Lindley to Simon, No. 157, Tokyo, March 14, 1933, "Confidential," FO 371/17151–858.

Far Eastern Province? I should expect the answer to both questions to be No, in which case we must look for hostilities sooner or later."[61]

The London *Daily Telegraph* speculated that the Japanese might invade the Maritime Province. The *Japan Weekly Chronicle* commented that it would be extremely difficult for the USSR to defend that region. It added that the Japanese occupation of Jehol had cast a shadow over the future of the Soviet sphere of influence in Outer Mongolia.[62]

Although Lieutenant General Koiso, chief of staff of the Kwantung Army, had publicly threatened vigorous action on the part of Manchukuo when the USSR did not return the disputed locomotives and freight cars,[63] the exchange of notes between Kuznetsov and the Foreign Office of Manchukuo in April and May placed the railway dispute on a diplomatic level. Yet tension continued to mount amid reports that Soviet troops were digging trenches beyond Manchuli.[64] Soviet citizens, it was said, had been told to refrain from any action that might acerbate relations with Manchukuo; they had been warned at the same time, to prepare for any eventuality.[65]

The resignation of Vice Minister of Foreign Affairs Arita in May 1933 drew attention to the split that existed in the Japanese Foreign Office between two rival schools of diplomacy, which Uchida had failed to harmonize or control. One school, led by Shiratori Toshio, director of the Information Bureau, and by

[61] Minutes, April 21, 1933.
[62] JWC, May 4, 1933, pp. 616–17; May 11, 1933, p. 643.
[63] JWC, April 27, 1933, p. 574.
[64] Manchukuoan sources reported that Soviet reservists from the Chita and Irkutsk districts were entrenching themselves in the vicinity of Borzia, sixty-eight miles west of Manchuli.
[65] JWC, May 4, 1933, pp. 616–17; May 11, 1933, p. 643.

Tani Masayuki, director of the Asia Bureau, favored a strong policy with military backing. The other school, identified with Shidehara, advocated a more conciliatory policy. Its adherents included in addition to Arita, Hotta (director of the Bureau of European and American Affairs), Ambassadors Obata and Tanaka (recently retired from the diplomatic service), Matsudaira (ambassador to Great Britain), and Debuchi (ambassador to the United States). Shiratori and Tani had been "the motive forces of Kasumigaseki" for a long time, and the resignation of Arita constituted a victory for the proponents of a hard line.[66]

Major Bratton, the acting military attaché of the American embassy, told his British colleague on July 8 that he believed that the Japanese intended to use the railway dispute as an occasion to force war on the Soviet Union. He also mentioned that he had learned, though he would not reveal his source of information, that the Japanese army had been producing considerable quantities of phosgene gas. Colonel James was skeptical. "American Officers in Tokyo . . . are as a whole, inclined to accept sensational information as true without reasonable skepticism," he reflected. His own thinking was closer to that of the Soviet military attaché, who did not believe that the Japanese would strike in the midst of their army reorganization and did not see evidence of military preparations for immediate conflict.[67] In transmitting the report to London, Chargé d'Affaires Alvan Gascoigne added: "While it cannot be denied that war between Russia and Japan is *a priori* a likelihood within the next few years, my own inclination is to agree with Colonel

---

[66] JWC, May 25, 1933, pp. 704–705.

[67] James to British embassy, Report No. 22, Chuzenji, July 10, 1933, "Secret," FO 371/17151–858.

James that it is improbable that the Japanese will assume this fresh commitment so early as this autumn, and I also share his view that United States military and naval officers in this country are prone to attach undue importance to sensational reports."[68] "The prospect revealed is depressing enough whether war breaks out now or later on," Allen reflected morosely in the minutes.[69]

The tendency of the European press to exaggerate the Soviet menace and the imminence of Soviet-Japanese hostilities was ridiculed by the *Japan Weekly Chronicle*. Quoting a news dispatch from the London *Morning Post* that "two Soviet military aeroplanes flew over USSR territory near the Manchukuo boundary at Manchuli Sunday afternoon," it mocked: "Russian aeroplanes presumably are allowed to fly over Russian territory, but perhaps the *Post,* bringing its religious campaign to a glorious end, is presently to launch a ferocious attack on Sunday aviation. Doubtless my Lord Clive, now on tour, will investigate."[70]

As rumors that Japan would seek a *casus belli* with the Soviet Union that autumn or next spring persisted, Rink reiterated to James that he did not think that the Japanese were courting war, but that the rumors were broadcast by them to facilitate the purchase of the CER on easy terms.[71] "The Japanese are not unaware of the strength of their position or of the fact that this is clearly realised by the Soviets," A. W. G. Randall commented in London. "The rumors, therefore, if deliberately spread by the Japanese, seem to be a part of a tail-twisting process."[72]

[68] Gascoigne to Simon, No. 423, Chuzenji, July 17, 1933, FO 371/17151–858.
[69] August 27, 1933, FO 371/17151–858.
[70] JWC, June 1, 1933, p. 733.
[71] Snow to Foreign Office, No. 352, June 21, 1933, FO 371/17151–858.
[72] Minutes, July 24, 1933, FO 371/17151–858.

A lengthy report from the United States Military Intelligence Division to the Division of Far Eastern Affairs of the Department of State in August stated that "the weakest point strategically in Japan's control of north Manchuria now lies in the Russian ownership of the Chinese Eastern Railway." It described the "more or less disconnected series of incidents" between Japan and the USSR as the building of a case by Japan "to justify a Japanese attack on Russia, if it eventually appears desirable."[73] The report speculated that "the Japanese War Office has undoubtedly decided that a war with Russia is inevitable because Vladivostok and the Priamur District with its minerals, lumber, and fishery resources, Kamchatka with its great fishery resources, and Sakhalin with its great coal and oil resources can only be made completely available to Japan by forcible seizure and must be taken before the Russian Soviet becomes too powerful militarily." The "menace" which the Japanese saw in the Vladivostok airbase to Japan's principal cities and the likelihood of a Russian and Chinese attack on Japan's rear in Manchuria in the event that Japan became entangled in a war with any other great power suggested another thrust into Siberia. "By driving Russia west of Lake Baikal, Japan's defensive position in Asia would become almost impregnable against Russian attack and Russia could be made less able to lead China to attack." The report concluded that in view of the "very real fear" of the Japanese people for their security, "it will not be difficult to give point to Japan's case against Russia by attack." "The case is all prepared and only awaits Japan's need for use."[74]

---

[73] The report recognized the "mass domestic effect" of the incidents, the veracity of which it doubted in a number of cases, "to keep alive a definite patriotic fervor by providing a definite tangible prospective enemy in Russia."

[74] Military Intelligence Division, G-2, Intelligence Branch, Report forwarded

When Iuren'ev called on Saito on September 12, the premier remarked that international relations had grown "very tense and extremely complicated" since their last meeting. "I am convinced that there will be no war between the USSR and Japan, that there must be no war," he volunteered.

"I welcome your declaration that there will be no extreme aggravation of our relations with Japan," Iuren'ev retorted. "Your confidence is a guarantee of the amicable settlement of the questions facing both states."

Saito stated that he personally considered it very important to develop and improve the economic relations between Japan and the USSR and that their policies must be imbued with sincerity. "Your just and prompt measures in connection with the conflict in the north (the slaying of three fishermen) made a very good impression on me and on the entire Japanese nation," he observed. "It is necessary to speak frankly about everything, even about small misunderstandings. If there is something bad, one must mention it outright."

Iuren'ev agreed that there should be sincerity and directness in their relations and that other conflicts should be settled in the same spirit as the incident with the three fishermen, but, he noted, this must be done mutually. Such acts as the seizure of the Soviet steamer *Aleksei Peshkov* made a very grim impression on the Soviets, increasing their uncertainty concerning the stability of their relations with Japan and forcing them to take precautionary measures. "It seems to me," Iuren'ev said, "that all issues between the [two] sides must be solved in a spirit of amicable negotiations.

---

to the Division of Far Eastern Affairs of the State Department on August 14, 1933, National Archives, E/B 761.94/617.

Besides, it is essential to counteract the unfortunately influential elements campaigning for a break with the USSR and for preparation for war.''

"Absolutely correct," Saito chimed in. "It is necessary to strengthen our relations, and first of all in the economic sphere.'' Noting that he was both prime minister of Japan and president of the Nippon-Soviet Society, Saito turned to the Japanese oil concessions on North Sakhalin. He related that Admiral Nakasato, president of the North Sakhalin Oil Company (Kita Karafuto Sekiyu Kabushiki Kaisha) had recently visited him and had asked to negotiate an extension in the term for oil exploration, due to expire in two to three years, so that the company could plan ahead, and for the purchase by the Japanese government of part of the company stock so that the Soviet side could have more confidence in the company. Saito stated that while on the surface the prolongation of Japanese exploration rights was an issue between the Japanese concessionaries and Soviet authorities, it was basically a state matter, concerning the relations between their two countries. He said that Nakasato would shortly call on Iuren'ev, to which the ambassador replied that he would be glad to see him, as always.

"I hope that we shall be able to understand each other and that relations between both countries will stabilize," Saito declared. "Japan is confronted at present with many problems of great international significance."

"Absolutely true," Iuren'ev responded. "In particular, the term for the expiration of the London agreement is drawing near."

Returning to the *Peshkov* incident, Saito promised to instruct the Foreign Office to take measures for its speedy solution. He told Iuren'ev that there were two channels for the regulation of Soviet-Japanese relations: the official one, through the Foreign Office, and the unofficial one, through the Nippon-Soviet Society. Although he himself was too busy for an active role in the society, he advised Iuren'ev to make use of Kurachi and Tanaka, who were directors of the society.[75]

Hirota, who succeeded Uchida as foreign minister, showed moderation in the general aspirations which he expounded to a number of leading Japanese statesmen, including Prince Konoe Fumimaro, president of the House of Peers, Kido Koichi, chief secretary to the lord keeper of the privy seal, and Viscount Okabe Nagakage, one of the directors of the Society for the Maintenance of National Prestige (Kokuikai), at the home of Baron Harada on September 26. "For the next five or six years," Hirota declared, "we must not do anything that will give rise to trouble with foreign nations."[76]

But failure to act in bringing the CER negotiations to a speedy and satisfactory conclusion posed a mounting threat to peace. "There is undoubtedly in the new relations between Manchukuo and Russia, an element of danger," the *Japan Weekly Chronicle* editorialized. "A new State, with foreign advisers possessed of a greater sense of power than of responsibility, is liable to quarrel rather badly with a neighbor which also lacks an urbane diplomatic tradition. There are enough matters to quarrel about very seriously if tact and good will are lacking in the way in which their settlement is approached."[77]

The special correspondent of the London *Times* in

---

[75] Record of Iuren'ev's conversation with Saito, kept by V. V. Zhelezniakov, September 12, 1933, DVP, XVI, 504–507.
[76] "Saionji-Harada Memoirs," 702.
[77] JWC, August 31, 1933, pp. 259–60.

Manchukuo found it difficult to believe that the Japanese sphere of continental interest would not be extended further. "There are ultimately only two factors to check Japan's ambitions in Asia—the state of her finances and the quality of the Red Army."[78]

Asked to give his estimate of the possibility of an armed conflict between Japan and the USSR "within near future or eight months or two years," Ambassador Grew wrote that the Japanese had become "increasingly anxious" since 1929, "when it became apparent that the Russians had effective forces east of Baikal." Although he deemed it "perfectly clear that 'Manchukuo' (i.e. Japan) is determined to acquire possession of the railway by fair means or foul," he doubted that war between Japan and the USSR was imminent, unless set off by "some glaringly provocative incident," a possibility that was always present because "feeling on both sides at the point of contact is tense." Like most foreign observers, Grew thought it "not unlikely" that Japan was determined "to remove the Russian obstruction from the path of her ambitions at an advantageous moment, and that the most advantageous moment, from data at present available, may occur in 1935."[79]

Reviewing the various disputes between the Soviet Union and Japan—the quarrel over the CER, Manchukuoan navigation rights on the Amur, Japanese fishing in Soviet waters, and Japanese refusal to sign a nonaggression pact—the *Japan Weekly Chronicle* in a lead article in mid-October, entitled "Is it Peace?" remarked that the creation of hostile sentiments toward the USSR in Japan by these controversies was "not

[78] London *Times,* September 11, 1933, pp. 11–12.
[79] Grew to Under Secretary of State Phillips, Tokyo, October 6, 1933, FRUS 1933, III, 421–24.

altogether unwelcome" for the Japanese army and navy, which sought Diet approval of enormous military budgets. "If sufficient ill-feeling can be promoted . . . the services will get what they want."[80]

There was evidence that the Japanese military buildup was not for show. As Vice Minister of Foreign Affairs Shigemitsu had gravely informed Baron Harada in early October, "the Army seems determined to attack Russia in 1935, and the Navy the United States in 1936."[81]

Finance Minister Takahashi Korekiyo had confirmed to Harada on October 11 that at the recent Five Minister's Conference, attended by Premier Saito, Foreign Minister Hirota, War Minister Araki, Navy Minister Osumi Mineo, and Takahashi himself, "it was revealed that, according to their respective plans, the army would attack Russia and the navy the United States, hoping meanwhile to keep the goodwill of other nations." Takahashi had warned the ministers of the army and of the navy that their efforts would be in vain if they did not cooperate in drawing up national defense plans.

Takahashi had tried to convey to the ministers of the army and of the navy that the purpose of military preparations was to give strength to Japanese diplomacy, not to start an aggressive war. "It is characteristic of military minds," he complained to Harada, "that a thing has to be either right or left. They run to extremes; they never consider the middle way. At present, even if we are to settle the problem by diplomacy, I think that is is necessary to consider both armaments and diplomacy."[82]

[80] JWC, October 19, 1933, 478–79.
[81] "Saionji-Harada Memoirs," 707.
[82] *Ibid.*, 708–709. "As regards the policy of the Army and Navy vis-à-vis USA," an officer of the Intelligence Division of the British Naval Staff wrote a year

Foreign Minister Hirota had told the war and navy ministers that the Japanese government would go as far as it could by diplomacy. When diplomacy would reach its limits, the government would leave matters for their "disposal."[83]

The Soviet estimate of the situation was laid bare in a letter from the deputy foreign commissar to Iuren'ev, dated October 17. It is a remarkable document that deserves to be quoted at length:

It seems that the Japanese war party is thinking ever more definitely in terms of a preventive war against the Soviet Union. . . . If Japan is preparing for a collision with the United States, if she fears that the United States can knock together a world coalition against Japan, if, furthermore, Japan fears that in the event of a collision with the United States, China will take advantage of the situation to begin fighting, it is natural for the Japanese military under those circumstances to ask therefore, as Araki does, what role the Soviet Union could play should . . . such a collision between Japan and her Pacific rivals materialize. There can be two potential answers to this question concerning the future role of the USSR from the point of view of the Japanese military party: either the establishment of complete peace in the Far East with the Soviet Union, doing away with any uncertainty in Soviet-Japanese relations, or, on the contrary, a preventive war against the USSR in the hope that such a war will result in extensive territorial changes and will hurl back

---

later, "we have no information which would lead us to believe that the Navy wish to be friendly with Russia. We are of opinion that they merely play the American card in preference to the Russian, as it is better propaganda for getting naval needs." (Rear Admiral G. C. Dickens to C. W. Orde, December 19, 1934, "Secret and Confidential," FO 371/18177–713.) "Exactly," Allen agreed on the margin.

[83] "Saionji-Harada Memoirs," 709–10. Premier Saito had not taken part in the exchange between Araki and Hirota but was known to share the views of the foreign minister. (*Izvestiia,* October 15, 1933, on the basis of a dispatch from Tokyo, dated October 11.)

the armed forces of the Soviet Union far from Manchukuo. On the basis of everything we know about the calculations of various groups of Japanese politicians, the military-fascist group is increasingly deliberating about just this sort of dilemma and undoubtedly is leaning toward a preventive war, considering that, if worse comes to worst, only by taking such a course could they possibly attain by means of maximum pressure on us such "pacification" as would allow them to settle to their benefit the questions which interest them even without war on condition that we would withdraw or greatly weaken our armed forces in the Far East. Of particular portent in this respect is one of your conversations, in which the person to whom you talked raised the question of the withdrawal of our units from the Far East. . . .[84]

In the face of such a situation, our policy, while preserving our basic orientation toward peace, cannot be one of concessions to and indulgences of the Japanese military and of glossing over the provocations and outrages that the Japanese government allows itself. We are planning and are carrying out a firm line of rebuff of Japanese importunities, a determined line of every sort of revelation of Japanese provocations, clarifying to the whole country, indeed, to the whole world, the true character of Japanese policy in the Far East toward the Soviet Union. Such a line springs from the realization that if worse comes to worst and the Japanese military really carry out the attempt to attack the Soviet Union, we shall be able to repulse them quite successfully. The situation now is really different from what it was one and a half or two years ago, and we are far from feeling defenseless in the event the enemy tries to feel us out.

If the intention of the Japanese military to wage

---

[84] Iuren'ev had cabled on September 23 that Kurachi, one of the directors of the Nippon-Soviet Society, had stated that in the interest of Soviet-Japanese relations the USSR must withdraw her forces into the interior of the country, whereupon a nonaggression pact could be signed. (DVP, XVI, 862, note 245.)

a preventive war against the USSR is final, concessions on our part could make sense only in case we would be prepared to consider these concessions unavoidable and, on the other hand, would be ready to continue these concessions to the end. Feeding the Japanese beast of prey with small morsels will only increase its appetite and create confidence in its impunity and superiority in strength. There is no point in our supporting such false illusions. By taking a firmer position, we are increasing the chances of peace, are cautioning all those circles in Japan which do not want war, [and] are forcing the proponents of military adventures to adopt a more careful line of conduct. Only if we pursue such a tactic, strengthen our internal buildup, and improve our international position, will we be able perhaps to prevent the attempt to implement the plans of preventive war, inasmuch as the authors of these plans will learn that this is a risky business and that it is better not to begin the solution of the questions of Japanese world policy from this end, that is, from an armed conflict with the USSR. . . .

We nourish no particular hope that Hirota will actually be able to make any changes in the Japanese policy line as it has been executed of late. It could be changed only in the event that the intensification of the internal crisis in Japan led to the victory of those groups of Japanese capitalism, which are speaking up against grand-style imperialistic policy. However, such a solution of the crisis is very unlikely. On the contrary, the whole situation in the world and in Japan indicates that the development of the crisis, so long as it will not be interrupted by a revolutionary upshot, can lead only to an increase in the proportionate weight of the extremist military-fascist and imperialistic groups which will lead Japan along the path of unrestrained military adventures.

As I noted already above, a number of elements

in the Japanese combination can change, the Japanese imperialistic policy will be oriented, perhaps, first of all toward conflict with the United States, rather than with us, [and] the course of events can hasten or, on the contrary, put off the decisive action, but, be that as it may, for the present our line of conduct must be just as sketched above. . . .[85]

The Soviet military attaché had told his British colleague on October 9 that the Japanese military wanted to gain control of the Maritime Province "to keep the Soviets at arm's length and to make the Japan Sea Japanese in fact as well as name." The best hope for peace, he had thought, lay in the difficulty of persuading the Japanese public that "the prizes to be obtained were worth the risks" and the realization by the Japanese General Staff that "any war between the two countries would be long-drawn-out, and, whatever the final outcome, it would leave Japan so weakened that she would be reduced to the position of a third-class power."[86]

Rink believed, and his views were shared by the British and French military attachés, that the thinking of the Japanese army was outmoded in many respects. Japanese armored fighting vehicles and air force were only just passing out of their infancy, and the Japanese General Staff did not appreciate the difficulties it would have to overcome in coordinating the operations of large bodies of tanks, artillery, airplanes and gas

---

[85] Deputy foreign commissar to Iuren'ev, October 17, 1933, DVP, XVI, 573–75.

[86] James to T. M. Snow, Report No. 33, Tokyo, October 9, 1933, "Secret," FO 371/17152–858. "The ultimate elimination of Russia from the Far East is a matter of such vital interest to Japan that it can never be absent from the minds of Japanese statesmen, but I think that their first objective will be Mongolia," Vansittart commented. (Minutes, December 1, 1933, regarding Snow to Simon, No. 584, Tokyo, October 13, 1933, "Very Confidential," FO 371/17152–858.)

units.[87] "The balance of opinion from all sources," Randall remarked in the minutes, "is that the Japanese and Russians envisage war between themselves as a distinct possibility of the future and are both actively preparing for the event, but that the Japanese are on the whole aware of their weakness and therefore unlikely to strike in the immediate future."[88]

When W. R. Connor-Green inquired whether the War Office agreed with his opinion that the Soviet Union was presently in no condition to fight a real war with Japan and would resort merely to rear-guard action for face-saving purposes in the event of a Japanese attack on the Maritime Province, while in two or three years she might be strong enough to make a Japanese attack "too risky to be worth undertaking," Colonel Miles replied, "we feel that, if Vladivostok and the Maritime Province, or indeed any other part of Soviet territory should be attacked, Russia would be likely to put up her maximum resistance; and, in our view, the task of the Japanese would be by no means easy." Noting that Japan would have to improve her railway communications towards the Soviet frontier before she could hope to launch a successful attack against the USSR, Miles expressed the view that, on balance, delay seemed more advantageous to Japan than to the Soviet Union.[89]

Yet some newspapers, like the *Harbin Times,*

---

[87] Comments made by Rink to James on October 19, in James to Snow, Report No. 34, Tokyo, October 21, 1933, "Secret," FO 371/17152–858.

[88] November 25, 1933, minutes regarding Snow to Simon, No. 596, Tokyo, October 25, 1933, "Very Confidential," FO 371/17152.

[89] Connor-Green to Colonel Miles, October 30, 1933, and Miles to Connor-Green, November 2, 1933, "Confidential," FO 371/17151–858. In reviewing the "precautionary measures" taken by the USSR in the Far East in 1932, Miles wrote: "What effect these preparations had on Japanese plans we do not know; but it became apparent that their operations stopped at the Soviet frontier and that Russo-Japanese relations subsequently improved."

remained belligerent. Used to a press which published only what the government wanted published, the Soviets may have attached greater importance to Japanese editorials than they deserved. In view of occasional Japanese censorship, however, the fact that the printing of such wild and aggressive editorials as that of the *Harbin Times* was allowed to continue gave the Soviets reasonable ground for alarm. On October 24, for example, the *Harbin Times* called on the USSR to "forsake her Far Eastern policy and withdraw to the Urals." If instead, the Soviet Union increased her Far Eastern activities, the paper warned, "Japan must take decisive measures with sword in hand and strike a decisive blow at the aggressive actions of the USSR."[90]

Mr. James of the British Chamber of Commerce in Kobe reported in November that since the first of September there had been two times when war with the USSR had been "very imminent." "Each time the Army had got out of hand, and was determined to force its will on the Cabinet, and its way on the people of Japan. But each time there was an upset when it came to gaining the approval of the Emperor." (The Emperor, James wrote, had opposed war on the advice of Prince Saionji through Count Makino.) Now, however, it was certain that there would be no war with the Soviet Union in winter and probably none in spring.[91]

Maxwell M. Hamilton, assistant chief of the Division of Far Eastern Affairs of the United States Department of State, after a tour of Manchuria in November of 1933, saw "a fundamental clash" between Japan

[90] JWC, November 16, 1933, p. 603.
[91] Enclosed in Earl of Lytton to Wellesley, "Very Confidential," FO 371/18180–916.

and the USSR in political and economic aims which was likely to lead to war. "The course of events in Manchuria and in Mongolia," he wrote, "appears to be moving toward a war between Russia and Japan, a war which seems to be destined for 1935 or 1936, although it is possible that it may break out at an earlier date due to the occurrence of some incident which would serve as a lighted match to a fire. For the paper and the wood to make the fire are already gathered." Hamilton did not believe that a resurgence of liberal strength in Japan would prevent war with the USSR; on the contrary, he speculated "the military in Japan may precipitate a war with Russia rather than yield to liberalism."[92]

In a lengthy speech on November 7, on the occasion of the sixteenth anniversary of the October Revolution, Molotov reiterated the desire of the Soviet Union to remain on peaceful terms with Japan, but noted that the systematic violation of agreements concluded with the USSR, and the increasing frankness and impudence of the "ridiculous" plans of some prominent Japanese statesmen for the seizure of Siberia and the Maritime region forced her to be on the alert. In view of the assertion allegedly made by some Japanese that it would be stupid to believe that a declaration of war must precede the opening of hostilities, he warned that in case of an attack on the USSR, the Soviet government would strive for the complete defeat of the adversary.[93]

The Japanese Foreign Office publicly dismissed Molotov's threat, asserting that the USSR was not in a position to wage war. "If the Soviet authorities

[92] National Archives, 761.94/733.
[93] JWC, November 16, 1933, pp. 602–603.

deliberately abuse Japan and exaggerate the strength of the Red Army, as they are now doing, it is because they . . . are seeking to divert the attention of the discontented people to foreign relations.''

Yet the Foreign Office disagreed with those who declared that because the Soviet regime was incompatible with that of Japan, friendly relations between the two countries should be terminated. It favored a peaceful resolution of outstanding problems with the USSR, partly because it believed that given peace, the Communist government might not remain in power much longer, since only about 10 per cent of the population were members of the Communist Party, while a war would strengthen the government's hold over the country by creating domestic confusion which it could exploit.

The Foreign Office contended that there were no outstanding issues between Japan and the USSR serious enough to lead to war and that if the USSR showed sufficient sincerity to bring the CER negotiations to a successful conclusion, ''Soviet Russia's need for concentrating a big force in the Far East will be gone.''[94]

During the Domestic Policy Conference on December 5 another clash occurred between Takahashi and Araki. The finance minister asserted that the anti-Japanese attitude shown by foreign nations was due less to commercial considerations than to the propaganda of the Japanese army and navy that 1935 and 1936 would be critical years and that Japan was on the verge of war with the United States and the Soviet Union. At a time when the United States and European countries were pursuing a policy of peace and made every effort to avoid wars, the prowar

[94] JWC, November 16, 1933, p. 602.

atmosphere of Japan was arousing very bad feelings, which was reflected in trade relations. "For these reasons," he declared, "the military must use prudence in their speech and actions. There will be no such crisis in 1935 and 1936."

Pale with anger, the war minister replied: "That is not true. There will be a crisis. The military have no intention of starting a war today. However, we must make preparations."[95]

In a speech to members of the ultranationalist Imperial Ex-Service Men's Association of the Tohoku district on a parade ground in Sendai a week later, on December 14, Matsuoka Yosuke alluded to the impending crisis and to persons who denied its existence. Dating Japan's "extraordinary times" back to the Paris Peace Conference and subsequent pressures exerted on Japan by the second Five-Year Plan of the USSR and by the agreements made at the Washington and London conferences, Matsuoka depicted the "extraordinary times" as in the process of maturing and foresaw mounting danger for Japan from American and European interference. "When the nation is confronted with such a situation," he proclaimed, "there are some political partisans who are declaring their disbelief in any 'extraordinary times.' Such fellows are traitors and deserve elimination from the soil of this country."[96]

While Foreign Minister Hirota in a talk to a number

---

[95] "Saionji-Harada Memoirs," 755–56.

[96] JWC, December 14, 1933, p. 724. The Japanese regarded not only the First and Second Five-Year Plans as directed against them. They imagined even that the location, if not the creation, of the Jewish autonomous region in 1934 was a Soviet stratagem against Japan! Shigemitsu wrote in his memoirs that "in case the Japanese Army should ever invade Russian territory, a new Jewish State of Birobijan was founded near the military center of Habarovsk, in order to take advantage of Jewish influence over world opinion." (Shigemitsu Mamoru, *Japan and Her Destiny,* 94–95.)

of peers at the office of the Kenkyukai on December 6 reiterated his confidence, on the basis of his personal knowledge of the USSR, that Soviet-Japanese relations could be improved by diplomatic means,[97] Colonel Homma Masaharu, who was close to Araki, told the British military attaché that the Japanese army was convinced that a conflict with the Soviet Union was "inevitable" so long as the Soviet Union retained her political system. There was disagreement only whether it would be better for Japan to go to war before the Russians completed their Five-Year Plan or after the Japanese position in Manchuria had been consolidated.[98]

Randall felt and C. W. Orde agreed that the Japanese government as a whole did not share the military view and seemed "determined to keep the peace all sound and concentrate on the task of settlement with China and consolidation of Manchukuo—a double task likely, one would think, sufficiently to occupy all her energies even beyond the critical year 1936."[99] But Wellesley was not so sure. "I do not personally think," he added, "Japan can stop at Manchuria and that eventually a collision with Russia will be difficult to avoid."[100]

---

[97] JWC, December 14, 1933, p. 727. Hirota told the German Ambassador Herbert von Dirksen on December 18 that Japanese-Soviet relations were "normal" and that there was "no ground for concern" despite the note of protest by the Soviet consul general in Harbin. (Dirksen to Foreign Minister, No. 122, Tokyo, December 19, 1933, *Documents on German Foreign Policy*, Series C, vol. 2, pp. 251–52.)

[98] James to Lindley, No. 42, Tokyo, December 26, 1933, "Confidential," FO 371/18176–776. "Although it is doubtless to British interests that a second war between Japan and Russia should be avoided," Lindley commented, "I cannot help feeling that the conviction of its inevitability, prevailing at army headquarters, which are, at present, so influential in deciding Japanese foreign policy, will be of no little assistance to our diplomacy so long as it persists." (Lindley to Simon, No. 709, Tokyo, December 26, 1933, "Confidential," FO 371/18176–776.)

[99] Comments in minutes, dated Februrary 6 and 7 respectively, regarding Lindley to Simon, No. 709.

[100] Minutes, February 7, 1934.

When word had arrived from E. M. B. Ingram that the Soviet ambassador to Nanking, Dmitrii Bogomolov, regarded "the conversion of Inner Mongolia into the autonomous 'Mongokuo' under the shadow suzerainty of Nanking but dominated by Japan acting through Manchukuo as inevitable" and that the USSR would not intervene because it had little *locus standi* to do so and because she did not want to precipitate a conflict with Japan over Inner Mongolia,[101] Wellesley had expressed agreement with Bogomolov's fears, since Manchuria was not a self-contained region, but the outlet for Mongolia. Without Mongolia Japan's conquest was incomplete. "The Japanese do not intend to cry halt at Manchuria and the collision with Russia seems to be to become more and more probable."[102]

When the German ambassador to Moscow, Rudolf Nadolny, told Litvinov on December 13 that he did not like the situation in the Far East, Litvinov retorted that he did not like it either, but that "some people in Germany seemed to like it." He complained that Germany's great love for Japan had come at the very moment that Soviet relations with Japan had become strained. Nadolny replied that the German rapprochement with Japan was not directed against the USSR, but was based on the withdrawal of both countries from the League of Nations.[103]

A week later Adolf Hitler voiced the apprehension that the Soviet Union, upon defeat by Japan, might seek to regain her lost prestige by attacking Germany.[104] "Herr Hitler is assuming far too much,"

[101] Ingram to Miles, Nanking, October 27, 1933, FO 371/17066–768.

[102] Minutes, December 24, 1933.

[103] Litvinov's record of his conversation with Nadolny, December 13, 1933, DVP, XVI, 740–41.

[104] Sir E. Phipps to Foreign Office, No. 116, Berlin, December 21, 1933, FO 371/17152–858.

Connor-Green remarked. "A Russo-Japanese War is a distinct possibility—nothing more—in about 1936, the year when the pro-war clique in Japanese military circles consider that the position for their country will be as favorable as it ever can be expected to be. But if they engineer an attack, they will get some rude shocks. Russia may get the best of it this time."[105]

In an interview granted to Walter Duranty, Moscow correspondent of the *New York Times,* on Christmas Day, Joseph Stalin reiterated at once Soviet desire for friendly relations with Japan and the apprehension that "the militant faction may push saner policies into the background." "It seems to me that Japan would be unwise to attack us," Stalin said. "Her economic position is not too sound, and she has points of weakness—Korea, Manchuria and China. . . . But good soldiers are not always good economists and do not always appreciate the difference between the force of arms and the force of economic laws."[106]

Stalin's sentiments were echoed by Molotov in a speech at the opening of the All-Union Central Executive Committee session on December 28. Mentioning Japan briefly, Molotov pointed, on one hand, to his government's efforts to improve Soviet-Japanese rela-

[105] Minutes, December 27, 1933. "Is Russia going to attack Germany with Poland and Lithuania between then and no ships worth speaking of in the Baltic? It sounds rather fantastic," Wellesley commented. Vansittart mocked: " 'Mr. Smith, I believe,' said the man in the street, taking off his hat to the Duke of Wellington. 'Sir,' replied the Duke, 'if you believe that, you will believe anything.' " (Minutes, December 29, 1933)

[106] *New York Times,* December 28, 1933; *Izvestiia,* January 4, 1934. "There are still advocates of the necessity of further consolidating Japan's strategic position in the Far East, though the free-spoken days when 'Dr. Baikal' used to orate to patriotic assemblies are gone," the *Chronicle* reflected. "Strategically the Japan Sea is a 'Japanese lake' already, but with a fortified foreign port in its midst it might not always be so. So, partly in dreams and partly in sober earnest, the frontier advances further and further, and it is forgotten that the further it extends the longer it becomes, and therefore the more difficult to defend." (JWC, January 4, 1934, p. 5.)

tions by proposing the conclusion of a nonaggression pact and by agreeing firmly to the sale of the CER and, on the other hand, to Soviet defense preparations to meet possible aggression on the part of "the more reactionary circles of the Japanese military." The latter, he observed, were particularly fearful of Russo-American-Chinese cooperation against Japan.[107]

Foreign Commissar Litvinov went into considerable detail in his report on Soviet foreign policy the following day when he came to the subject of Soviet-Japanese relations. He recalled that "the best good-neighborly relations" had prevailed between the USSR and Japan from the time of the conclusion of the Basic Convention of 1925 until the end of 1931, when Japan had invaded Manchuria. So trustful had the Soviet Union been of Japan until then that she had left her Far Eastern frontier almost defenseless. Although the occupation of Manchuria had constituted a violation of the Treaty of Portsmouth, the USSR had refrained from participating in international actions at the time, partly because she had not believed in the sincerity and consistency of the states taking part in these actions but primarily because she had not sought, and did not now seek, an armed conflict with Japan. All she had wanted to obtain from Japan was the honoring of her commercial interests on the CER, since she had no other interests in Manchuria; yet, contrary to all festive promises and assurances, the representatives of Japan and Manchukuo had disrupted the joint administration of the railway. When the USSR had offered to sell the CER to remove the source of friction, Litvinov continued, it had become evident that Japanese designs were more extensive, that the seizure of the Maritime

[107] DVP, XVI, 780–81; *Izvestiia*, December 29, 1933; JWC, January 4, 1934, p. 21.

Province and the whole Far Eastern region was under consideration. The Soviet government, he said, had no alternative but to strengthen its borders. "But while we took exclusively defensive measures," Litvinov declared, "Japan, as is known, is feverishly preparing for a war which cannot be other than aggressive, since no one has any designs on the security of Japan."

Litvinov realized that there were prudent, influential men in Japan who understood what danger and risk there would be in a war against "such a powerful and energetic giant" as the USSR and who wisely preferred to pay several hundred million yen, which the railway was actually worth, than to spend billions of yen for the increase of the naval budget and on military operations the result of which would be at best questionable for them. But, he observed, she also had more militaristically inclined circles, particularly among the military, "for whom apparently the highest goal in life is war, regardless of what it will bring." Litvinov assured his countrymen that in the event of a clash with Japan the latter stood morally isolated. "In our quarrel with Japan," he stated, "even the capitalist world recognizes that we are right and attributes aggressive intentions exclusively to Japan. It does so, of course, not for the sake of our beautiful eyes, but because it realizes that if it recognizes the actions and policy of Japan as right and thereby strengthens her, tomorrow already these actions and policy will be turned against its own interests too."[108]

Sir Stafford Cripps, one of the leaders of the Labor Party, told Ambassador Ivan Maiskii privately that the British government then in power would sympathize with Japan if the latter attacked the USSR,

[108] *Izvestiia,* December 30, 1933; DVP, XVI. 793–96.

but that it was not likely to support Japan publicly, since this would arouse serious opposition within England. Cripps ruled out British intervention in the event of another Russo-Japanese War, but thought possible British financing of Japanese military orders. At the same time, he expressed confidence that the British proletariat would side with the USSR and that the trade unions would impede the filling of Japanese military orders in England.[109]

Soviet apprehension that the new year might bring hostilities with Japan was reflected in a cartoon in *Izvestiia,* entitled "The Sword of Damocles." Damocles, it will be recalled, had been forced to sit under a sword suspended by a single hair. In the cartoon little New Year lay under a sword held between the teeth of a demon-like samurai. On the sword was the inscription "War."[110]

On January 20, 1934, Sir Francis Lindley filed a comprehensive dispatch regarding the tension between Japan and the USSR, in which he detailed Japanese preparations for war. He enumerated the great increases in Japanese military and naval expenditures, the building of torpedo boats and submarine chasers which would be of great value in countering Soviet submarines, a boost in the intake of army officers, and significant changes in the navy high command, involving the retirement of the older and more conser-

[109] Record of Maiskii's conversation with Cripps, January 9, 1934, DVP, XVII, 34–37. Lord Robert Cecil explained to Maiskii at Professor Lasky's house that the basic principle of British policy in the Far East was not to quarrel with Japan, lest Japan become dangerous to Great Britain and in the event of a conflict with her seize Hongkong, Singapore and Australia. Cecil, like Cripps, was certain that in case of a Japanese-Soviet war Great Britain would not support Japan by military force, but would permit the export of arms to Japan and the floating of Japanese loans in England. (Record of Maiskii's conversation with Cecil, February 5, 1934, DVP, XVII, 110–13.)

[110] *Izvestiia,* January 11, 1934.

vative elements, and their replacement by "the principal exponents of the forward school," notably Admiral Suetsugu, who had been appointed commander-in-chief of the combined fleet. He also mentioned the multiplication of patriotic societies and the indoctrination of the public in line with General Araki's view that modern wars were fought by nations rather than by soldiers alone and that the spirit of the people at home must sustain the troops in the field. Yet the Japanese military improvements, he felt, had been delayed too long and the fleet was not being kept at full strength, the naval program being designed, it seemed, to achieve maximum naval strength between the end of 1935 and the middle of 1936. It was the belief of the British naval attaché, furthermore, that war with the USSR would be unpopular in the navy "principally because of the intense jealousy of the army, which would acquire increased prestige by such a war."

Lindley described some of the Soviet counter-measures as well—the massing of troops east of Chita, the construction of extensive modern defensive positions along the border and at Vladivostok, and the industrialization of the Russian Far East. Observing that it was easier to describe the main features of the disquieting state of affairs than to draw any certain conclusions as to their significance, Lindley weighed the situation:

> On the one hand, we have the bait of Vladivostok, now turned into a bogey which threatens the existence of Japan's centres of population and vital communications with the mainland; and we have the temptation of the Maritime Provinces, with their rich fisheries, a constant source of friction, and the oil of North Saghalien. On the other hand, we have the Soviet counter-measures, which make it probable

that a war would be a serious undertaking; we have
the open unfriendliness of the United States, which
have just recognized the Soviet Government; we
have the isolation of Japan (unless she has come
to some understanding with Germany) and, finally,
we have the eternal question of China. This last
is perhaps the most serious, because a Russo-
Japanese war, even if China refrained from seizing
the opportunity to join the Soviets, could scarcely
fail to increase Communist influence in the Middle
Kingdom enormously. And if China did join in, international incidents likely to involve other Great
Powers in the struggle would be almost sure to occur.
Any sober statesman who, putting aside ethical considerations, calmly considered the pros and cons,
would certainly judge the hazards of an unprovoked
attack on the Soviets in the near future as too alarming to be justified by the chance of success. Unfortunately, sober statesmen, though there are not a
few in this country, have had little to say in the
conduct of Japanese foreign policy since October
1931. They have been overridden by the Military
party, who, placed in the saddle by the disastrous
action of Geneva, are straining every nerve to retain
their hold over the population.

The best hope for peace, Lindley believed, lay in
the division of the military party. "Whilst practically
all the officers regard a war with the Soviets as
inevitable, the younger school consider that the sooner
it comes the better, whereas the older believes that
Japan's preparations should be completed and her position in Manchuria consolidated before a war should
be allowed to break out." "My own feeling," he added,
"is that the more the Japanese look at this adventure
the less they will like it, and that the 'inevitable' war,
like so many other inevitable wars in the past, may

never take place unless it does so before next winter is over."[111]

Lindley's conclusion that the "inevitable" war might never take place if it did not by next winter tallied in substance with information received by the British Foreign Office from other sources. "The danger is not over," Orde remarked in the minutes, "but it seems that if it materializes war will be brought about irresponsibly and not as a deliberate policy."[112] "There are so many imponderable elements in the situation," Wellesley added, "that it would be unwise to say more than that war is possible rather than probable."[113]

On January 21 Ota called on the deputy foreign commissar in Moscow to discuss means of improving Soviet-Japanese relations. Ota said that the speeches of Molotov and Litvinov had aggravated the tense situation, as they had been misunderstood by many in Japan. The deputy foreign commissar replied that the speeches had as their sole purpose the furtherance of peace, and enumerated the steps the Soviet government had taken to assure peace: she had proposed the conclusion of a nonaggression pact, had agreed to a three-power border committee, and had offered to sell the CER. Yet all these proposals, he observed, had been rejected or frustrated by the Japanese authorities and the Soviets were alarmed by the declaration of the Japanese military concerning the need of a preventive war. He referred to the demonstration by some 200 members of the ultranationalist Kenkokukai (National Foundation Society) before the Soviet Embassy the preceding day and to the need

[111] Lindley to Simon, No. 40, Tokyo, January 20, 1934, "Confidential," FO 371/18176–776.
[112] February 24, 1934, FO 371/18176–776.
[113] March 1, 1934, *Ibid.*

to prevent the occurence of similar incidents in the future.[114]

Ota expressed his personal concern over what Stalin might say in his forthcoming speech before the Seventeenth Congress of the Communist Party—his words could worsen or improve the situation. The deputy foreign commissar replied that he had not been informed what Stalin would say and that the People's Commissariat of Foreign Affairs could have no influence on the remarks of the head of the Communist Party at the Congress. He said that it was his personal belief that Stalin's evaluation of the situation would correspond with conditions.

The conversation had been amicable, and the deputy foreign commissar specifically noted in his description thereof that "the reports of some Tokyo newspapers that Ota made a protest concerning the speeches of Molotov and Litvinov are a fabrication."[115]

In a speech at the reopening of the Diet on January 23, Foreign Minister Hirota expressed regret that the attitude of the USSR toward Japan had changed for the worse since 1925. Accusing the Soviet press of exaggerating the deterioration in relations, Hirota asserted that Japan, in spite of the differences between the two states in theory and governmental system, "had always sought to maintain good-neighborly relations with the USSR and had striven to solve all problems by peaceful means." He pointed to Japan's good offices in the CER negotiations as proof of her "sincere intentions."[116]

Karl Radek, *Izvestiia's* foremost analyst of foreign

[114] Raivid filed a formal protest with Togo on January 22. Togo promised that the police would take measures to prevent the repetition of similar incidents.
[115] Deputy foreign commissar to Iuren'ev, January 25, 1934, DVP, XVII, 69–70.
[116] *Izvestiia*, January 24, 1934; JWC, February 1, 1934, p. 137.

affairs, rose to the defense of the Soviet press, noting that in comparison with the stream of words about war with the USSR, published day after day in Japanese newspapers, magazines and novels, Soviet criticism of Japanese policy was "very restrained." Turning to Hirota's complaint that there had been a change in the attitude of the USSR toward Japan, Radek remarked that if Hirota regarded the fact that the Soviet Union did not watch the military preparations against her with folded arms, but openly strengthened her defenses, as a change in the Soviet stand, he had unfortunately failed to understand what position the USSR had taken from the first. "The Soviet Union could not interfere in Japan's seizure of Manchuria," he wrote, "because this would have come down to a struggle over the partition of Manchuria into spheres of influence; the Soviet Union, as an enemy of colonial robbery, could not try to get North Manchuria for herself. She defended in North Manchuria only her economic interests." He pointed out that Soviet unwillingness to fight over Manchuria had never meant that the USSR would not defend her own territory. He recalled Stalin's words at the sixteenth congress of the party: "We do not want one foot of foreign soil. Neither shall we give up one inch of our own soil to anybody."[117]

Dismissing Hirota's assertion that Japan, contrary to Moscow's propaganda, was not establishing new military positions along the Soviet-Manchukuoan border, Radek declared that "this statement proves

---

[117] A literal translation would read: "We do not want one span of foreign soil. Neither shall we give up one *vershok* of our own soil to anybody." ("*Ni odnoi piadi chuzhoi zemli ne khotim. No i svoei zemli, ni odnogo vershka svoei zemli ne otdadim nikomu.*") One span, the distance between the index finger and the thumb, measures about 9 inches; one *vershok* equals about 1¾ inches.

at best that the Japanese minister of foreign affairs knows less than the observers of all other countries who are in Manchuria and in Japan." "Mr. Hirota can say in his defense that his predecessor, Foreign Minister Shidehara, also had learned about the seizure of Mukden from the Japanese newspapers," Radek mocked. "But this [state of] being poorly informed [on the part] of the Japanese ministers, which corresponds to the biblical saying 'the right [hand] knoweth not what the left one doeth,' does not contribute to the stabilization of peace in the Far East."[118]

Yoshizawa Kenkichi, who had negotiated the Basic Convention between the USSR and Japan, was pessimistic about his government's determination to tide over Japan's international crisis by diplomatic means, but he saw no conflict of vital interests between the USSR and Japan that might compel either to resort to arms. Speaking in the House of Peers on January 31, he echoed Hirota's view that the difference in form of government was not a primary consideration; "as Japan is contiguous to Soviet Russia, there must necessarily be friendly relations between the two coun-

---

[118] Karl Radek, "Na Dal'nem Vostoke bez peremen" (No changes in the Far East), *Izvestiia*, January 26, 1934. A. W. G. Randall commented: ". . . the Russians, being incapable of thwarting Japan in Manchuria or China, can safely—perhaps sincerely—proclaim their entirely pacific and purely defensive attitude. In spite of this the Japanese, engaged in 'getting away with' Manchukuo, cannot feel quite secure in that far from easy task while China is not settled and Soviet Russia, on the other flank, makes warlike preparations (from ostensibly defensive motives, but all the same capable of offense if Japan is engaged elsewhere). . . . In this atmosphere of mutual fear and suspicion Japan proceeds to secure herself against all eventualities, and the fact that, by securing herself so, she also puts herself into a potentially offensive position is some justification for Mr. Radek's charges. But there seems to be no doubt that Mr. Hirota has really tried to restrain the militarists, and it seems as if he will continue to do so, unless some catastrophic social change in Japan puts all the cards into the militarists' hands." (Comments in minutes dated February 5, 1934, regarding Lord Chilston to Foreign Office, No. 53, Moscow, January 30, 1934, FO 371/18185–880.)

tries, regardless of the differences in national constitution."[119]

Ultranationalists did not share Yoshizawa's view. Members of the Kenkokukai at a mass meeting on February 3 passed a resolution demanding Soviet demilitarization along the Manchukuoan frontier. Over twenty of them got past the police lines to the Soviet embassy in Tokyo, but were dispersed after a fight without succeeding in their effort to deliver a copy of the resolution to the Russians.[120]

Speaking at the Seventeenth Congress of the Communist Party, Commissar of War Voroshilov ridiculed Japanese objections to Soviet military preparations. So openly and frequently had Japanese military and civilian figures written and spoken in recent years of the need to go to war with the USSR, advocating the conquest of her Maritime Province, the Transbaikal region and even the whole of Siberia, that it would be strange if the Russians made believe they had noticed nothing and regarded their "dear neighbor" as trustingly as before. "It would naturally be more agreeable to our neighbor if our frontiers with Manchukuo were as defenseless as the Chinese frontiers . . . in 1931," Voroshilov remarked sarcastically. "But our amiability does not go so far as to give anybody this pleasure."[121]

Stalin in his long-awaited speech on January 26, mentioned that Japan's war with China, her occupation of Manchuria, withdrawal from the League of Nations, and penetration into North China had acerbated the internal and external crisis which engulfed the capitalist powers and from which bourgeois politicians vainly

[119] JWC, February 8, 1934.
[120] *Ibid.*
[121] JWC, February 15, 1934, pp. 211–12.

sought a way out by means of a new imperialist war. Some, he said, wanted to organize a war against one of the great powers; others against China; still others against an inferior race; others yet against the USSR. "It would be a mistake to think," he added, that only "certain military circles in Japan" desired war with the Soviet Union; some European statesmen had similar plans.

Soviet relations with Japan, Stalin stated, were in need of "serious improvement." He asserted that in spite of Japan's refusal to sign a nonaggression pact, in spite of the arrest of Soviet railway officials, the rupture of negotiations concerning the CER, and the unrestrained campaign in the press by some of the Japanese military for war with the USSR and the seizure of the Maritime region, the Soviet Union would persist in her attempts to improve relations with Japan, because she desired such an improvement. "But not everything depends on us," Stalin declared. "We must, therefore, at the same time take all measures to protect our country from surprises and be prepared to defend her against attack."[122]

During a meeting of the budget committee of the Japanese Diet on January 30, Nagashima Ryuji of the Seiyukai Party observed that Japanese relations with the Soviet Union had taken a turn for the worse since American recognition of the USSR and that Stalin and other Soviet leaders had been using "extreme language" towards Japan.

Hirota replied that it was not unnatural that Soviet fear had been aroused by the extension of Japanese military influence to the Russian frontier as the result of the protocol Japan had concluded with Manchukuo.

[122] Text of speech, DVP, XVII, 73–88.

He viewed the concentration of Soviet troops on the frontier between the USSR and Manchukuo as defensive and felt that his countrymen need not be alarmed thereby. He did favor an agreement to withdraw or limit frontier defense forces rather than "some abstract thing like a nonaggression pact."[123] He admitted that the speeches of Soviet leaders contained some "strange things," but was convinced that Stalin desired friendly relations with Japan.[124]

Not satisfied with Hirota's answer, Nagashima asked the new minister of war, General Hayashi Senjuro, who had replaced Araki a week earlier, whether he regarded the deployment of Soviet troops along the borders as defensive. Hayashi responded that any form of defense was accompanied by preparations for offense. It was impossible, he said, to regard the placement of either Soviet or Japanese forces along the frontier as aggressive in purpose.[125]

[123] In a memorandum handed to President Roosevelt in February 1934, Matsukata Otohiko complained that the Soviets had been cool to Hirota's proposal that the USSR and Japan remove military forces from along their respective sides of the Manchurian-Siberian border line. Stanley K. Hornbeck commented in a memorandum to Cordell Hull that a proposal that both Russia and Japan remove their military forces from along their respective sides of the Manchurian-Siberian border line should contemplate withdrawal of Japanese forces from positions south and east of the southeastern boundary of Manchuria. Instead, the Japanese proposed that the Russians withdraw from positions north of the boundary of Manchuria and the Japanese from positions south of the northern boundary of Manchuria. "Naturally the Russians are 'cool to this proposal' for a withdrawal by them from positions on their own soil in return for a withdrawal by the Japanese from positions not on but far removed from Japanese soil." (Edgar B. Nixon [ed.],*Franklin D. Roosevelt and Foreign Affairs*, I, 655–61.) "Mr. Hirota's remark about 'some abstract thing like a nonagression pact' is interesting," Randall commented in the minutes. "Having refused to conclude a nonaggression pact with the Soviets, the Japanese must minimise the importance of one," Orde remarked. (Comments, dated March 21 and 22 respectively.)

[124] Lindley to Foreign Office, No. 117, Tokyo, February 24, 1934, FO 371/18176–776. When another member of the budget committee asked Hirota on February 5 whether the current strain in relations between the Soviet Union and Japan was not due to the latter's refusal to sign a nonaggression pact, Hirota answered that he was not against a pact as such, but that he wanted outstanding problems between the two states solved first.

[125] JWC, February 8, 1934, p. 167. Araki had tendered his resignation as minister

Ambassador Grew reported on February 8 that there were "reasonable grounds for optimism" that a Russo-Japanese war might be averted. Discerning a slight improvement in the outlook for peace during the past six months, Grew saw a number of major factors working against such a conflict: mounting opposition in the cabinet, in the press, and especially in the Diet to the military and their vast budgetary demands; the resignation of General Araki, who had been an "inflammatory element"; a change in outlook on the part of the middle classes, who in the face of the economic prosperity caused by increasing exports desired a continuation of the *status quo* and dreaded the upsets which a war might bring; the pacific aspirations of the Emperor and of such leading statesmen as Prince Saionji, Count Makino, Baron Hayashi, Foreign Minister Hirota and the premier, who were "personally an influence more peaceful than bellicose"; and the realization by "sane elements" within the army itself of the seriousness of a conflict with the Soviet Union and their questioning whether the end to be attained would justify the risks involved—"whether the game would be worth the candle." Grew regarded American recognition of the USSR as "a restraining influence, probably of greater effect than any other single integral." "Military plans" he explained, "may be regarded as infallible; but the attitude and possible actions of the United States constitute the element of uncertainty and therefore an unknown hazard."

But while Grew was hopeful that the "saner element" in Japan calling for the consolidation of gains

---

of war on January 21 for reasons of health; he had not been well enough to appear at the opening of the Diet the following day. (*Izvestiia,* January 26, 1934.) The American ambassador reported that many viewed Araki's illness as "providential dispensation." (Joseph C. Grew. *Ten Years in Japan,* 118.)

already made before embarking on further military adventures might predominate over those "less amenable to reason," he could not banish the thought that the Japanese army was like "the intensely trained football team which, being convinced of its superiority and dissatisfied with mere practice, desires a game."[126]

The question what result other than a draw would be best for the world should a Russo-Japanese war break out aroused considerable controversy in the British Foreign Office. Randall, in a lengthy memorandum on February 9, held out "little chance of permanent accommodation," between the "two imperialisms" of Japan and the USSR. He saw "no reason to suppose that Japan has given up her ultimate aim of domination of the Asiatic continent, or that Soviet Russia has abandoned the fundamental policy of undermining all *bourgeois* states and using them to spread the Communist idea." Yet he felt that "mutual fear" of each other had improved the behavior of both countries in the international sphere and that "the antagonism between Russia and Japan has been of distinct value to most countries having important dealings with either." "From a detached point of view, therefore, it would seem that this country and Europe as a whole can afford to regard the Russo-Japanese tension without great concern, if not, indeed, with the cynical reflection that such tension may even be serving the interests of their diplomacy."

Although Randall felt that an encounter that ended in a draw might leave outside countries "little, if anything, the worse," he was concerned about a decisive defeat by either side. In view of the Soviet Union's greater size and material and perhaps spiritual

[126] Grew, 117–21.

resources, he regarded that, on balance, "a Russian victory over Japan would probably in the long run have far more serious consequences for Japan than the reverse result would have for Russia." He believed that the Japanese, who had never known defeat in battle might lose faith in their entire social system and in themselves and substitute "a desperate anarchic communism" for their "spartan patriotic discipline." Pointing to the proclivity of the younger generation in Japan for violent action in response to even minor causes of irritation—to make "some desperate attempt to achieve mastery or perish"—he anticipated that "a desperate throw which did not succeed would, if it did not lead to one vast gamble on Japan's entire resources (this bringing about a deliberate waging of war with the United States), be followed by a relapse into utter confusion and impotence." "To the nations that at present resent and fear Japanese self-assertion this might not seem an unwelcome prospect," Randall wrote, "but the gap left in the Far East by the collapse of Japanese authority could not be left empty; it would be filled by someone. China would be incapable of doing so; Russia is the only alternative." With her influence restored in Manchuria and Mongolia and greatly enhanced in Sinkiang and possibly in Tibet, the Soviet Union, Randall feared, would become a serious menace to British interests throughout Asia. "Moscow, more efficient in aggression than in Tsarist times, is to-day physically and morally nearer to being a threat to these interests than Japan, and although the pan-Asiatic ideas now expressed in Japan imply a threat to British rule, yet geographical and psychological factors (among the latter the utter impracticability of whole-hearted Japanese cooperation with China) seem to make such a threat a vain one in comparison with that offered by a Russian triumph."[127]

While Orde agreed that "a Japanese victory would be less harmful than a Russian one"[128] and another official concurred that of the two dangers the Russian was the greater,[129] L. Collier, head of the Northern Department, took issue on the grounds that he did not regard a *complete* victory by the Soviet Union or Japan possible. Arguing that the USSR was relatively weak and interested, for whatever reason, in maintaining the territorial *status quo,* while Japan was relatively strong and interested in overthrowing it, Collier contended that "the Japanese threat to British *commercial* interests is already much greater than any Russian threat could possibly be; while the same must be true of *political* interests if . . . Japanese domination of China, leading ultimately to the destruction of British influence and British commerce in that country, is more probable than Soviet domination."[130]

R. F. Wingram observed that from the European standpoint a "successful defensive" by the USSR was desirable so that she could continue to act as a counterweight to Germany in the East.[131]

"Since tension produces good, or better, behaviour on both sides, it is in our interest that there should be tension but no blows for as long as possible," Sir Robert Vansittart recapitulated. In the event of war "a draw would be the best result", "if that could not be, the choice would be difficult between the two evils."[132]

[127] FO 371/18176–776.
[128] Comment in minutes, February 16, 1934.
[129] Marginal comment in minutes, February 26, 1934.
[130] Minutes, February 16, 1934.
[131] February 19, 1934.
[132] February 22, 1934. Wellesley's brief entry, "All this is very interesting

Meanwhile General Bliukher, the commander of the Special Far Eastern Army, related to the party congress how the Japanese had been turning North Manchuria into a springboard for leaping into the Soviet Far East. During the past two years they had feverishly built over 1,000 kilometers of railway lines, of which not more than 30 to 35 per cent were economically justifiable, 2,200 kilometers of dirt roads, either along the borders or leading toward the Soviet borders, and some 50 airports and air bases in the Mukden-Harbin-Tsitsihar triangle and to the north. But the USSR, he assured the delegates, was ready to defend her borders. Referring to the assertion made by War Minister Hayashi in an interview on February 3 that the Soviets had assembled 300 warplanes in the Far East, Bliukher declared: "We shall not argue with him: perhaps there are less, perhaps there are more. I can only say that if necessary, our party and government will be able to mass so many airplanes that there will certainly be more than the Japanese have." After a moment of loud applause and shouts of "*Pravil'no!*" (Right!), Bliukher added: "But in spite of all the modesty of Mr. Hayashi, I must say nevertheless that the Japanese have in Manchuria 500 planes, although they modestly refrain from saying so." "Comrades," Bliukher warned, "everyone of us understands the purpose of all these measures. They testify, no doubt, to the preparation of the Japanese imperialists for a great war. We understand excellently that the growth of the military budget as well as the growth in produc-

but I am afraid also rather academic and speculative," irritated one of his colleagues. "I rejoice that we should attempt to gaze into the future," he proclaimed. "It is the first necessity of framing a policy, and here we can well imitate Japan whose policy has long been quite definite—a description we should find it difficult to apply to our own in most periods of our history." (Comments in minutes, dated February 20 and 26, 1934, respectively.)

tivity of the war industry of Japan can at any moment be turned against us."

Asserting that the Soviet Union did not wish war—"War, comrades, has not been included in our Second Five-Year Plan," he quipped—Bliukher detailed the economic and military measures that had been taken to strengthen the Russian Far East and warned: "Our borders, as Comrade Voroshilov has said here, are girded with ferro-concrete and are sufficiently solid to withstand the strongest teeth. They will break any imperialist head, which smashes against them gripped with war-fever."[133]

R. H. S. Allen observed on February 23rd that everything seemed to point to the fact that "Japan has missed her moment and that the war, if it comes at all, will not come for some considerable time."[134] None of the civilian elements in Japan wanted war, while the military, "all of whom want the war," were divided over the question of timing, the younger ones favoring immediate hostilities, the older ones insisting on careful preparations. At the moment the older school in the army was in the ascendant and even if Prince Saionji did not succeed in shelving the question of war indefinitely by freeing the government of the military domination, there might not be a war for many years so long as the older officers remained in control. "The only risk—and it must not be minimised—," Allen warned, "is that in the meantime another wholesale murder plot engineered by the younger hotheads might be successful, and might, by depriving Japan

---

[133] *Izvestiia,* February 11, 1934.

[134] General William S. Graves, who had commanded the American expeditionary force in Siberia, felt that Japan's best chance for success had been in the spring of 1932; he doubted that Japan, by mid-1934, could break through the strong Soviet defenses in Siberia. (Hata, 40)

of the few who can exercise restraint and leadership, set her drifting on a path of chaos and adventure."[135]

The exploitation by the Japanese army of minor incidents as a pretext for major hostilities made observers view any Soviet-Japanese incident with nervousness. When Japan filed a strong protest with Moscow concerning the wounding of a Japanese pilot on February 23 during a flight near the Soviet border allegedly in pursuit of bandits, the *Japan Weekly Chronicle* expressed uneasiness over the event in conjunction with reported night flights by Russian machines: "As long as the Japanese planes do their flying by day, and the Russian by night, all may be well, but what happens if this honourable arrangement comes to grief, and Russian and Japanese planes meet on the border—or just over it? There are all the elements of war in this if pilots lose their heads."[136]

As agreement was reached on the release of the Soviet officials and the appointment of their successors and the negotiations for the sale of the CER were about to be resumed, Randall remarked: "Ultimately, it seems that Russia will get money for a wasting asset, and Japan-Manchukuo will get the railway, plus recognition. In this event the danger of a Russo-Japanese conflict might well be postponed for many years."[137] As the fishery dispute also seemed near solution, Randall added the following day, "This give-and-take may end in a definite Russo-Japanese rapprochement."[138]

Iuren'ev, who conducted the negotiations, was less hopeful. He worried about a meeting of division com-

---

[135] Minutes, February 23, 1934, regarding Lytton to Wellesley.

[136] JWC, March 8, 1934, p. 295.

[137] Comment in minutes dated March 27 but apparently written on February 27 (it appears between February entries), regarding Lindley to Foreign Office, No. 37(R), Tokyo, February 23, 1934, FO 371/18176–776.

[138] Minutes, February 28, 1934, regarding above dispatch.

manders that was to take place in Tokyo toward the end of March. Although such meetings were customarily held after the appointment of a new minister of war, a similar meeting of generals had also occurred on the eve of the Manchurian Incident. When Ambassador Grew queried Iuren'ev on March 9 whether he was optimistic that war would be avoided, Iuren'ev replied that it was important to be optimistic. But when Grew stated that most foreign military experts in Tokyo believed that if the Japanese intended to attack the USSR, the spring of 1935 would be the most likely time, Iuren'ev retorted that he deemed this spring more likely, after the conference of the generals. "He seems firmly convinced that the final decision will be taken at this coming meeting of high Japanese military officers," Grew reported.[139]

The prospect of a Soviet-Japanese conflict alarmed the Chinese Minister of Foreign Affairs Wang Ching-wei. He feared, he told the British ambassador to Nanking, Sir A. Cadogan, on March 20 that if Japan should win, China would lose Manchuria outright; if the USSR should win, Manchuria would be Sovietized as a second Kiangsi. Cadogan evaded Wang's inquiry what the attitude of Great Britain and the United States would be in the event that China became unavoidably involved in a Russo-Japanese war, declaring simply that Great Britain regarded "a strong, stable and independent China" as "the keystone of political stability in the Far East." He made it clear at the same time that "on this point of stability of government in China, only the Chinese could help themselves."[140]

[139] Grew, 122-25.

[140] Notes on Cadogan's conversation with Wang, signed by E. Teichman, March 21, 1934, in Cadogan to Foreign Office, No. 27 TS, Nanking, March 23, 1934, FO 371/18147-858. Upon reading the dispatch Vansittart suggested that Cadogan be informed privately of his personal views: "What will suit us best in the Far

The statement made by Amau, head of the Information Bureau of the Japanese Foreign Office on April 17, that China must not avail herself of the military or economic assistance of any country other than Japan[141] was characterized by Ambassador Bullitt in a conversation with Litvinov on the 22nd as the declaration of a Japanese protectorate over all of China. Litvinov agreed and said that this was to be expected. "Inasmuch as Japan had not met [any] obstacles on her aggressive path until now, we, knowing her, were convinced that she would go along this path and farther."[142]

Ambassador Maiskii reported to Deputy Foreign Commissar Nikolai Krestinskii from London on May 11 that the Amau Statement had made Japan "the basic sensation of the political day in England."[143] The Amau Statement, along with all the explanations and amplifications that followed, was regarded as a decision on the part of the military masters of Japan not to attack the USSR, at least during the current year, but to expand south, where the risks were smaller.

Maiskii reiterated his earlier view that the British ruling circles did not want a break with Japan, but, on the contrary, were prepared to do anything possible to remove the existing contradictions between their countries. "British imperialism needs Japan against the

East is that there should be no war between Japan and Russia (but that their reciprocal antipathies should disenable both of them from doing actual harm to our interests, which are peace and the absence of any one sided predominance). If war were to break out—and we now think it improbable, in any predictable future at least—we should be best served by a draw, which is also the most likely result." (May 25, 1934.)

[141] Hugh Borton, *Japan's Modern Century*, 382–83.

[142] DVP, XVII, 794–95, note 138.

[143] In a special report on anti-Japanese feeling in England, sent the same day, Counselor G. A. Astakhov noted that British antagonism had been aroused in part by Japanese refusal to discuss the regulated distribution of textile markets. (DVP, XVII, 796, note 150.)

United States, against the USSR, and finally against China." But while Great Britain wanted Japan to be her ally, she did not want her to be too imprudent or a weight around her neck. During the past year and a half the British had been carefully prodding Japan into a collision with the USSR, Maiskii asserted, and now that the Japanese, having found the Soviets well armed with tanks and airplanes, had lost the taste for adventures in the north and had begun to turn south, they were greatly alarmed. The British still wished to restore their once amicable relations with Japan but were becoming increasingly convinced that to do so they would first have to rap the Japanese military over the knuckles. Yet the relative power position of Great Britain and Japan in the Far East was decisively in favor of the latter and Great Britain could not offer serious opposition alone, nor did she have an ally who would join with her against Japan in the Pacific. Thus it was difficult for the British to take any serious measures against Japan, even if only to teach her a lesson. They could not imitate the strategy the Soviets had applied to Japan during the past year. In the words of Maiskii: "We declared firmly: 'We do not want war but if you stick your pig's snout into our vegetable garden, you'll get it smacked.' We backed our declaration by taking a number of very eloquent measures of a military-political and economic character which forced the Japanese to understand that we would really fight, and fight fiercely, if they should try to attack us. England cannot afford now the luxury of Soviet policy in the Far East, because even if she uttered the same declarations which we had made, the Japanese would not take them seriously, as it would be clear to everyone that there was not enough threatening, real power behind the British declaration."

The British government, Maiskii reported, was therefore playing for time, not only because she needed time to build up her military strength but because she believed that time might bring the economic collapse of Japan or some changes in the international situation which would facilitate the "Christianization" of the Japanese military. There was an unknown factor of crucial importance in the British calculation, however, namely the speed and extent of Japanese agression. "Who will reach the goal first," Maiskii queried, "Japanese or British imperialism?"[144]

During the five-hour long meeting of Iuren'ev and Hirota on June 16 concerning the renewed deadlock in the railway negotiations, there was mention of a number of incidents, such as Soviet firing on Manchukuoan vessels which had allegedly tried to photograph Russian fortifications and the anti-Soviet agitation of Japanese ultranationalists and White Russians. Hirota insisted that there had been unpleasant incidents also in Moscow when he had served there; "such things happen everywhere in the world." He alleged that reports of the imminence of war between their countries had been instigated by Soviet propaganda and, according to accounts in the Japanese press, asked directly whether the USSR desired war with Japan. Taken aback by the undiplomatic query, Iuren'ev was said to have given a simple No for an answer.[145]

"Mr. Hirota can be very direct in his methods!" Harcourt-Smith commented in London. "It seems clear that both sides are, at the moment at any rate, genuinely anxious to keep the peace. They are obvi-

---

[144] Maiskii to Krestinskii, May 11, 1934; DVP, XVII, 327–32.
[145] *Japan Advertiser,* June 18, 1934.

ously not going to fight about the CER, and there is no other important issue outstanding between them. At the same time both sides are frightened of and are busily preparing for war, and are in just the frame of mind likely to provoke 'incidents.' "[146]

"It would have been difficult for the Soviet Ambassador to answer the question about war in any other way on the spur of the moment," Orde observed drily.[147]

But when asked by the British ambassador about the alleged exchange with Hirota, Iuren'ev replied that the press version had been a travesty of their conversation. Seeking to clarify the meaning of a recent speech by Litvinov, Hirota had remarked, "Then I understand Monsieur Litvinov does not want war," and he had responded, "No certainly not, unless you force us into it."

Talking rather freely over vodka and caviar to Lindley's successor, Sir Robert Clive, whom he had known from the days when they had both served in Teheran in 1926, Iuren'ev ascribed the improved outlook for a settlement of the CER question "solely to the fact that the Japanese military leaders now realized that the Soviet forces were very considerable and were prepared to fight if the Japanese decided to force an issue." He assured Clive that the Soviet forces "had no aggressive intentions but were determined to resist to the utmost any aggression on the part of the Japanese."

When Iuren'ev observed that there were people who were saying that the British government would not be sorry to see war break out between the Soviet Union and Japan, Clive remarked that war usually ended

[146] Minutes, July 25, 1934, regarding Clive to Foreign Office, No. 345, Tokyo, June 20, 1934, FO 371/18176.
[147] Minutes, July 26, 1934.

when one or the other side was victorious and asked rhetorically whether Iuren'ev thought that it was in the interest of Great Britain "to provoke a war in order to see a far more powerful Russia or a far more powerful Japan." Clive asserted that "on the principle of 'Live and let live,' the Russian could always get on with the Englishman" and expressed confidence that "as a reasonable man" Iuren'ev "did not believe or encourage his Government in the belief of a Machiavellian policy on the part of His Majesty's Government."[148]

The British consul general in Mukden, P. D. Butler, reported on June 22 that except for the haste with which Japan was constructing strategic railways in Manchuria, there was little evidence that Japan was preparing to launch an aggressive war against the Soviet Union in the near future. Yet while continued Chinese and White Russian reports of imminent hostilities did not deserve credence, the fact that there were many people in Manchukuo "interested in precipitating war between Japan and Soviet Russia" did make for a dangerous situation. "But it is probably reasonable to suppose," he wrote, "that it will require a frontier incident of quite exceptional magnitude to produce a conflict just now if it does not accord with the basic plans of one or other of these Powers."[149]

On July 16, Counselor Tani of the Japanese embassy in Manchukuo told Butler, when the latter visited Hsinking, that popular feeling had changed in Japan since the outbreak of the Manchurian Incident. The Japanese were content with their gains and the vast majority

---

[148] Clive to Simon, No. 367, Tokyo, July 5, 1934, FO 371/18176 776.
[149] P. D. Butler to Cadogan (Peking), No. 131, Mukden, June 22, 1934, enclosed in Butler to Simon, No. 111, Mukden, June 22, 1934, FO 371/18176–776.

of them did not want war. But there was real danger, he alleged, that the Soviets who had assembled a formidable force might be tempted "to use it rather than allow it to rust."

Sato Shoshiro, the second secretary of the Japanese embassy, also expressed conviction that there would be no war between Japan and the USSR, unless the latter attacked. "Not only was Japan not yet ready, but, even when her preparations were complete, she would be defeated, and the Kwantung Army knew this very well. The territory was too vast and the Japanese armies would inevitably get drawn too far into Siberia. The Kwantung Army knew the exact strength of the Soviet forces beyond the frontiers and did not underrate their efficiency."[150]

Although the Soviet Union had some submarines at Vladivostok, she was pinning her faith in the event of a war with Japan primarily on her air force. She was attaching great importance to mechanization, finding Mongolia a suitable region for employing trucks and armored cars.[151] The Japanese, on the other hand, were developing the railway system in such a way as to strike at some point where the Soviets were not predominant in mechanization and aircraft. They believed, as Colonel Shibayama, the Japanese assistant military attaché, told his British colleague, Lieutenant Colonel V. R. Burkhardt, that the two great factors in a war with the USSR were space and time, and that by an intelligent use of these the Soviet Union's

[150] Butler to Cadogan, No. 157, Mukden, July 21, 1934, "Confidential," FO 371/18176–776. Harcourt-Smith was skeptical. "I wonder whether the Kuantung army would really subscribe to Mr. Sato's sentiments?" he commented in the minutes. (August 31, 1934.)

[151] Conversation between Lt. Col. V. R. Burkhardt, the British military attaché in Peking, and his Soviet colleague, Edward Lepin, in Burkhardt to Cadogan, Report VIII, May 5, 1934, "Secret," in Cadogan to Foreign Office, No. 633, May 8, 1934, "Confidential," FO 371/18176–776.

advantage in technical equipment could be neutralized. "As in previous wars," Burkhardt reported, "they will choose the moment for the attack."[152]

On August 2 the Soviet and British military attachés in Japan discussed at length the probable strategy of the Japanese in the event of a second Russo-Japanese War. Rink believed that the weight of the Japanese attack would be thrown against Vladivostok and the Maritime Province, with the main objective of the Japanese Northern Army being the destruction of the Amur Railway behind the Far Eastern Russian armies in order to cut them off completely from their source of supply. He asserted that the Russians had a larger number of mechanized vehicles and airplanes in the Far East than existed in the entire Japanese army and that these would be used at the very outset of hostilities to destroy important railway cities, bridges, and con-centration points. Rink claimed that the Soviet troops in the Far East greatly outnumbered the Japanese forces in Manchuria, and that any Japanese attempt to reinforce their present garrison drastically would be regarded as an act of war by the USSR. While there were no indications that the Japanese were making any preparations for war within the next few months, Rink "did not think that this 'inevitable war' had been relegated to the category of inevitable wars that never took place."[153]

In forwarding James's report, Sir Robert Clive wrote on August 16 that although rumors of war between Japan and the USSR had been in the air for some time past, "it was felt that if Japan was seriously bent on finding an excuse to go to war, she had missed

[152] Burkhardt to Cadogan, Report X, May 30, 1934, "Secret," in Cadogan to Foreign Office, No. 743, May 31, 1934, FO 371/18176–776.
[153] James to Clive, Report No. 15, Chuzenji, August 14, 1934, "Secret," FO 371/18177–713.

her opportunity two years ago." "There is little doubt, however," he added in qualification, "that the Japanese military authorities have an obsession that Osaka and the neighboring industrial district are threatened with danger of an air attack from Vladivostok." Noting that the military were supremely self-confident and had succeeded by intense propaganda in imbuing the Japanese public with a dangerous war spirit and that the army budget estimates were even more prodigious than those of the current year, he saw danger in the belief taking hold that "war is inevitable, and if so the sooner the better." "But in that case Japan would seem to be running an enormous risk," Clive wrote. "She could hardly hope to gain the sympathy of the world for fighting bolshevism when it was clear she had started a war for her own aggrandisement in a spirit of sheer ambition or defiance." He remarked that if it was true that the Soviets had over 150,000 troops in Eastern Siberia and double the mechanized forces and air power of Japan, "it would be rash for the Japanese to expect a repetition of the easy victory of 1904–05. But Clive expected "wiser counsels" to prevail. "It seems most unlikely that Japan, who has been so clever in selecting the psychological moment, would be so unwise as to launch an attack at a moment that would be obviously ill-chosen, while it may be taken for granted that the more sober civilian elements represented in the present Cabinet by the Minister of Foreign Affairs, who is universally trusted, will be absolutely opposed to any rash adventure." In a postscript, dated August 17, Clive added that Iuren'ev had told Grew "that the Russian forces would not this time wait to be attacked, but would immediately take the offensive if Japanese aggression made the prospect of war inevitable."[154]

---

[154] Clive to Simon, No. 443, Chuzenji, August 16, 1934, FO 371/18177–713.

Randall found Rink's assertion that the USSR would look upon any attempt by Japan to send large reinforcements to Manchuria as a *casus belli* particularly noteworthy. "If it has any substance," he reflected, "it means that Moscow has no intention of trusting to the League or even appealing to the Covenant. Perhaps this is a comforting reflection, from some points of view."[155]

"The *military* pros and cons of an early war are evenly balanced," Orde commented. "That being so the civilian arguments against an early war may win the day. But there is always the chance of irresponsible action by subordinate officers which might precipitate matters."[156]

"If common sense or self-interest count for anything," Mounsey added, "the dubious results of going to war, for both parties, seem to afford the strongest argument against such a development."[157]

In a conversation with Clive, Iuren'ev spoke bitterly of the aggressive attitude of the Japanese. Although he did not think that the Japanese government contemplated war at the moment, he regarded the future as very uncertain and reiterated that if war would come, the USSR would fight to the finish.[158] Harcourt-Smith expressed doubt that the Soviet government could even contemplate the possibility of a war over the CER, when merely 3 million pounds divided the two sides. "They have already submitted to so many humiliations from the Japanese," he commented, "that their prestige in Manchuria can hardly be brought lower; and they would, I should have thought, be well advised

[155] Minutes, November 27, 1934.
[156] Minutes, September 29, 1934.
[157] September 28, 1934.
[158] Clive to Foreign Office, No. 211, Tokyo, August 31, 1934, FO 371/18176–776.

to cut their losses and liquidate their Manchurian interests without delay on the best terms obtainable." He speculated that Iuren'ev "was using the bogey of war to discourage any possible incipient tendencies toward an Anglo-Japanese rapprochement." Orde agreed that there was "a certain amount of unreality about the bickering between Japan (and Manchukuo) and the Soviets." "Neither side wants war," he declared, "and the mutual discourtesies are rather superficial."[159]

Lord Chilston, the British ambassador in Moscow, concurred that "the Soviet Union, bent on its work of internal construction, will endure without retaliation anything except direct attack." But while he regarded the Soviet desire for peace with Japan and other countries as "genuine," he thought of it as a temporary policy, "solely to suit their present needs." "When their situation is secure from without and within, when they are in possession of one of the strongest war machines that has ever existed, and when they have more money to spend on furthering the aims and objects of the Comintern," Chilston warned, "then they are likely to return to their original methods and lend their weight to the fostering of revolutionary movements in other countries, not only with words, but with force of arms. These are possibilities which cannot be discounted, however much some of us may believe that Soviet Russia is changing her principles and adopting orthodox means of bringing about that happy state of society which is the aim of most countries."[160]

Commenting on the breakdown in the CER talks, the *Japan Weekly Chronicle* noted that "the Soviet

[159] Comments in minutes, September 1, 1934, FO 371/18176–776.
[160] Chilston to Simon, No. 449, Moscow, September 11, 1934, FO 371/18177–713.

is in a much better position to defend its Far Eastern rights than it was when the Chinese made an attempt to grab the railway." As Julian Grande, who had interviewed members of the Japanese general staff, asserted: "The Japanese General Staff is fully aware of the fact that Soviet Russia is solidly entrenched, that the Red Army is practically trained and equipped, unlike the poor Imperial hordes which Japan managed with difficulty to get the better of in 1904; that the Red Army in Eastern Siberia possesses squadrons of bombing aeroplanes, perfectly capable of turning Japanese coast towns into shambles at twenty-four hours' notice; and finally, that the Red Army and the whole Far Eastern community of Soviet Russia is in charge of a man whom the Japanese authorities—no mean judges—regard as one of the greatest military intelligences of the age. . . . The Japanese General Staff have the highest opinion of General Blücher and are not likely to give way to any sentimental ideas of 'clearing out the Red rabble,' such as is so often advocated in our own cheap Press."[161]

Japanese sources testify to Japanese awareness of mounting Soviet strength. The new premier, Admiral Okada Keisuke, had told Harada on August 16, that it was a fact that Russian defenses in the Far East had increased greatly.[162]

On September 4 Clive reported that Maruyama, the newly appointed Japanese military attaché to London, had asked Colonel James a few days before, "Do you think it is a good moment for Japan to go to war with Russia?" Clive regarded this as a "typical attitude" of the military and warned that Japan might "drift" into war with the USSR. When James had talked at

[161] JWC, August 23, 1934, pp. 255–56.
[162] "Saionji-Harada Memoirs," 972–73.

length to people in the War Office the past week he had gotten "the definite impression that military authorities have made up their minds to war with Soviet as being inevitable before long but are undecided as to when would be the most favourable time."[163]

Orde called this a "sudden revelation," as the strengthening of the Soviet forces in the Far East seemed to have dissuaded the "responsible" Japanese military from the idea of an *early* war. "We cannot want to see a war break out," Orde remarked and wondered whether Great Britain should give the Japanese government "a sermon" concerning the risk of alienating foreign opinion if it fomented war.[164]

"If we are going to do any lecturing," Mounsey observed, "it is only fair to lecture both sides, as we cannot judge which of the parties is being most provocative." At any rate, he thought it " a little premature to lecture either just yet."[165]

The British War Office discounted Maruyama's remarks. It was, in Harcourt-Smith's words, "loath to believe that the Japanese General Staff would commit the folly of going to war with Russia at a moment when the Japanese army is in process of reorganization." It doubted at the same time whether "a timely warning regarding a war of aggression against Russia" would have any favorable effect on the Japanese General Staff if and when it had once chosen to strike against the USSR, or whether it might prove "an irritant rather than a sedative."[166]

Vansittart had divided feelings on the possible effectiveness of British counsel. In view of the risk that

[163] Clive to Foreign Office, No. 213, Tokyo, September 4, 1934, FO 371/18177–713.
[164] Minutes, September 5, 1934.
[165] *Ibid.*
[166] *Ibid.*

the Japanese might take it very much amiss, he felt that "this question of 'to be or not to be' in the matter of advice" must be decided by the Cabinet, "since it is a cardinal point in British policy, only recently laid down and reiterated by the Cabinet, that on account of our own exposed position in the Far East every possible step should be taken to ensure good relations with Japan."[167]

Sir John Simon informed Neville Chamberlain, the acting prime minister, "There are a good many indications of late that the danger of a Russo-Japanese outbreak is increasing and that it is a very formidable fact, but nonetheless I believe on balance the odds are against it—for one thing the Japanese army is not ready."[168]

The War Office wrote on September 19 that no particular significance need be attached to Maruyama's question. "It is typical of Japanese military mentality and of the sort of conversation in which they indulge, even at social functions *pour passer le temps*." After putting itself "in the shoes of the Japanese General Staff" and weighing the arguments for and against an immediate war from the Japanese point of view, the War Office concluded that a choice between the two hinged on whether or not the Japanese army had concluded its reorganization and reequipment and whether sufficient reserves had been stockpiled for industrial mobilization. If Japan was better situated in these respects than the British General Staff thought, she would be wise to strike at once; if the Japanese army was still in the process of "crossing the stream" in these matters, she would be better off to postpone

---

[167] *Ibid.*
[168] Simon to Chamberlain, September 7, 1934, "Personal," FO 371/18177.

hostilities "for at least another year." In either case, "a war between the USSR and Japan—whether it is undertaken forthwith or whether it is postponed—would be a desperate hazard for both sides."[169]

Harcourt-Smith remarked, upon reading the War Office memorandum, that "Russo-Japanese relations, despite their recent détente, still require very careful watching and that the possibility of war breaking out even in mid-winter can no longer be disregarded." On one hand, "the Japanese General Staff no longer appear to doubt the inevitability, or even the desirability of war and . . . are merely undecided as to the most opportune moment for striking against Russia." On the other hand, the assertion attributed to Iuren'ev that the Soviet forces would not wait to be attacked, but would take the offensive if Japanese aggression made war seem inevitable, confirmed that the USSR, "under the growing conviction of military equality, if not superiority" was abandoning its former policy of "almost abject conciliation" for "an almost truculent attitude."[170]

Meanwhile Stomoniakov in his long letter to Iuren'ev on September 18 observed that the unprecedentedly peaceful state of the fishery industry off Kamchatka that year, the establishment of good relations between the Japanese concessionaires on Sakhalin and the local Soviet authorities, and the conclusion of the Sakhalin Agreement [concerning navigation on the rivers constituting the boundary between the USSR and Manchukuo] were all "significant quan-

[169] M. I. 2, "Comments on Telegram No. 213 dated 4.9.34 from H. M. Ambassador, Tokyo, (Russo-Japanese Relations)," September 17, 1934, "Secret," FO 371/18177–713.

[170] September 27, 1934, affixed to above.

tities on the credit side" of Soviet-Japanese relations and would further increase their importance with the settlement of the CER question. "One can expect, therefore, that the successful conclusion of the negotiations concerning the CER will open a new, more tranquil epoch in Soviet-Japanese relations." Stomoniakov realized, of course, that the conclusion of the CER agreement would not remove all dangers from the course of Soviet-Japanese relations. "So long as there is in Japan a strong military party which dreams of expansion on the Asian continent and particularly in our Far East, the Far Eastern problem will remain real and acute for the USSR." Stomoniakov expected the Japanese government to follow the CER agreement up with a proposal for the demilitarization of the Soviet-Manchukuoan border. He deemed it necessary to study the question carefully and to prepare materials and counterarguments in advance to rebuff such a proposal.[171]

Stomoniakov informed Iuren'ev that Ota, who had become very active in the discussion of important issues between the USSR and Japan and reflected the views of the moderate circles of the Japanese bourgeoisie rather than of Hirota, had posed the demilitarization question in a recent conversation.[172] Sto-

---

[171] Stomoniakov to Iuren'ev, September 8, 1934, DVP, XVIII, 583–86.

[172] Ota had told Stomoniakov in their conversation on August 31, that it was his personal opinion that the best way for their countries to solve all issues between them would be to cancel all defense measures and undertake no further ones in the future. Stomoniakov had retorted that neither the Soviet offer of a nonaggression pact nor Soviet concessions in Soviet-Japanese relations had improved the attitude of the Japanese military and nationalistic circles toward the USSR; regarding Soviet tractability as weakness, they had reacted to Soviet yielding with mounting aggressiveness. So long as the Japanese militarists and ultranationalists, who openly clamored for war with the USSR, met no opposition from the government and the moderate elements of the population, Stomoniakov had told Ota, the destruction of defense fortifications would not further peace but precipitate war.

moniakov added that the Japanese journalist [K. K.] Kawakami, who advocated the demilitarization of the Soviet-Manchukuoan frontier in dispatches from Moscow, was living at Ota's home and was being inspired by him.[173]

On September 19 Clive reported that tension between Japan and the USSR had relaxed during the past fortnight, the Japanese military "yielding to reason" as the Soviet Union entered the League of Nations.[174]

Iuren'ev confirmed in a conversation with the British ambassador two months later that the danger of war between Japan and the Soviet Union had passed; at least he did not anticipate war in the near future.[175] He felt (as did Clive) that there might be a serious economic crisis in Japan within the next two years,

[173] Stomoniakov to Iuren'ev, September 8, 1934, DVP, XVII, 583–86; DVP, XVII, 820, note 255. Ota told the British ambassador in Moscow of the "personal suggestion, not on instructions from his government," which he had made to Stomoniakov, "that a mutual withdrawal of troops and defenses to a certain distance on each side of the frontier might be desirable." Asked how his suggestion had been received, Ota replied that it had aroused "no great enthusiasm." He asserted that the many recent conflicts and arrests on the CER were the result of Soviet provocation and that "it was difficult to avoid the impression that the Soviets were preparing for war." (Chilston to Simon, No. 450, Moscow, September 11, 1934, FO 371/18177–713.)

[174] Clive to Foreign Office, No. 216, September 19, 1934, FO 371/18177–713. As the War Office memorandum of September 17 pointed out, a Japanese attack could now be laid before the League by the USSR, and Japan as the aggressor could be subjected, technically at any rate, to international sanctions. A gift of 100,000 yen by the Soviet Society of the Red Cross and the Red Crescent to the Japanese Red Cross on September 25 to render aid to the victims of the disastrous typhoon that had struck Japan that month was a token of improved relations. (*Izvestiia*, October 2, 1934.) Iuren'ev expressed the condolences of his government on September 26, and Hirota the thanks of Japan for the condolences on October 2. (DVP, XVII, 615.)

[175] In a lengthy report concerning Japanese military activity and preparations along the Soviet border (in Manchuria, Korea and on Sakhalin Island), written in December 1934 or thereafter, the administration of the Red Banner Border and Interior Guard of the NKVD of the Far Eastern region wrote that Japanese officers were still telling local inhabitants that war with the USSR was inevitable in the spring of 1935. (USSR, Academy of Sciences, Pogranichnye voiska SSSR, 433–42.)

as the world took measures to curb the intensity of Japanese competition. "Should such a crisis arise, the danger of a fascist movement in Japan could not be overlooked and it might well be that the political crisis of 1935–6, of which the Japanese had talked so much, might turn out to be an internal economic crisis with results which no-one could foresee."[176]

Speculating about the role that the United States might play in the event of a Russo-Japanese War at some later time, Sir Ronald Lindsay, the British ambassador in Washington, expected the United States to remain neutral "at any reasonable cost." American sympathy, he wrote, would undoubtedly be on the side of the Soviets, not because the average American had any regard for the USSR, but because Japan was "far more actively and widely disliked and mistrusted."[177] But Allen wondered whether the American determination not to become involved and not to sell arms to either side would last. Noting that the Foreign Office was thinking not only of a war that might occur in two or three years but equally, in ten or twelve, he asked: "To what extent can we count on the stability of American anti-war, and anti-munition-traffic sentiment? Is it not the case that the Americans are an intensely mercurial people and that what is true now may be profoundly wrong a few years hence?"[178]

Karl Radek also felt that the United States, like Great Britain, could not keep completely isolated from a conflict between Japan and the USSR, which would

---

[176] Clive to Simon, No. 605, Tokyo, November 23, 1934, FO 371/18177–713.
[177] Lindsay to Wellesley, Washington, December 21, 1934, FO 371/19347–713.
[178] January 7, 1935, comment in minutes affixed to above. Craigie thought that there would be "a great deal of talk" in the United States regarding neutrality, but that very little would be done in practice and that the Americans would be "supplying both sides as happily as they have done in the past." (Minutes, January 14, 1935.)

determine the future of East Asia, where she had vital interests. He anticipated that with or without direct intervention by the United States both British and American forces would be tied down in the Pacific and that the resultant isolation of France in Europe would trigger a German advance. "War would inevitably leap from the Pacific Ocean to the Rhine . . . ." It was the realization by the world that peace was indivisible, Radek believed, that had frustrated the attempts of the Japanese military to rally international support for war against the Soviet Union.[179]

The clouds of war had not disseminated, however; they had merely drifted from Siberia to North China, whither the Japanese began their advance in May 1935.[180] When the Soviet Union, following the full-scale invasion of China in 1937, began to supply the Chinese with arms and advisors, the threat of a Russo-Japanese collision came to the fore again. But for the time being, in the autumn of 1934, a ray of peace had broken through the clouds of war.

In reporting on September 19, 1934, that Soviet-Japanese tension had relaxed, Clive had communicated that the negotiations for the sale of the CER were being resumed. Linking the two events, Randall had reiterated the explanation he and Rink had offered the previous year for the exaggeration of the likelihood of war between Japan and the USSR: "As has proved the case more than once before, these war-alarms have clearly been part of the bargaining over the Chinese Eastern Railway."[181]

[179] *Izvestiia*, January 28, 1935.
[180] Hata, 41.
[181] Minutes, September 21, 1934, FO 371/18177–713.

Epilogue

On March 14, 1935, Foreign Minister Litvinov told Japanese newspapermen that the transfer of the railway constituted the solution of one of the most complicated problems in the Far East. He depicted the sale as "one of the greatest manifestations of peacefulness by the Soviet Government" and praised the Manchukuoan-Japanese negotiators for meeting the Russian concessions half-way. Recalling the great difficulties that had to be overcome in the lenghty bargaining process, Litvinov gave thanks to the Japanese foreign minister for his great service. "Mr. Hirota's sojourn in the USSR as Japanese Ambassador," he said, "undoubtedly contributed to the mutual understanding between Soviet and Japanese participants in the negotiations."[1]

Litvinov's interview struck Harcourt-Smith as "perhaps one of the most important pronouncements in Far Eastern affairs made for many months." "It certainly looks as if we are on the eve of seeing a real and, possibly, lasting settlement of Russo-Japanese differences," Harcourt-Smith wrote and reflected: "There may have been a time when such a development could not have been unreservedly welcomed by

[1] JWC, March 21, 1935, p. 376.

446

His Majesty's Government, but our notably improved relations with the USSR would seem to put a different aspect on the problem."[2]

Allen noted that a report from Tokyo in the London *Times* suggested that an entente or détente with the USSR would enable Japan to concentrate on the China problem. "Equally Russia, if Mr. Litvinov's efforts are successful, would be able to devote herself more freely to the German problem which has so suddenly become more acute."[3] "That a Russo-Japanese rapprochement is in the interests of world peace for the moment I have no doubt; but I am less sure that it is in British interests," Wellesley added. "At present there is fortunately no chance of the Russians and Germans coming together, but if Hitler were ever succeeded by someone with the Bismarck outlook of good relations with Russia at any price—the only sound policy from the German point of view—the situation might change overnight and Western Europe might be confronted with a German, Russian, Japanese combination which would be the most formidable thing it has as yet had to encounter. We have reason to bless both Hitler's blindness and bolshevism which makes this impossible at present. Long may they both live!"[4]

On March 24 Hirota reported to the Diet about the successful conclusion of the railway talks and held out hope that further problems between the USSR and Japan could be resolved peacefully.[5] Immediately after the Manchukuoan officials left Hirota's official residence on March 11, following the initialling of the rail-

---

[2] Minutes, March 16, 1935, regarding Chilston to Foreign Office, No. 33(R), Moscow, March 15, 1935, FO 371/19269–736.
[3] Minutes, March 18, 1935.
[4] Minutes, March 19, 1935.
[5] *Izvestiia,* March 26, 1935.

way agreement, Hirota and Iuren'ev and their colleagues had sat down to consider the order in which to tackle the remaining questions.[6]

On April 26 the Pan-Pacific Club sponsored a breakfast at which some 100 leading Japanese businessmen, foreign residents and journalists met with Ambassador Iuren'ev, Commercial Representative Kochetov, Counselor Raivid, and other members of the Soviet embassy to discuss the question of improving Soviet-Japanese relations. Present also were Vice Minister of Foreign Affairs Shigemitsu, Tokugawa Iesato, former president of the House of Peers, and other prominent statesmen.

In a brief welcoming speech, the president of the club, Inoue Tadashiro, former minister of railways and a member of the House of Peers, welcomed the transfer of the Chinese Eastern Railway, "a significant event in the history of diplomatic relations in the Far East," as something that would "facilitate friendship and improve understanding between the USSR and Japan."

Iuren'ev spoke at length about the danger to world peace posed by "the growing aggressive tendencies and growing armament." Asserting that "the deep economic crisis, which has gripped the capitalist countries, and growing political and economic contradictions between them" had strengthened the trend toward war as "a way out of the crisis," he reminded the Japanese of his government's offer to conclude a nonaggression pact with Japan. He reiterated Soviet willingness to discuss the mutual withdrawal of some military forces, including aviation, a certain distance from the border, taking into consideration the geo-

---

[6] JWC, March 21, 1935, p. 377.

graphical features of both sides. Iuren'ev assured the Japanese that the development of Siberia was not directed against them, but was part of the internal development of the USSR. He repeated the expectation that the commercial transactions related to the payments for the CER were but the first step in the expression of economic and cultural relations between the two countries.

Shigemitsu echoed Iuren'ev's sentiments, as did Tokugawa. The latter was particularly enthusiastic. "In recent years," Tokugawa declared, "rumors were spread in Europe and America about the unavoidability of conflict between the USSR and Japan. However, thanks to the farsightedness of the statesmen of both governments the black clouds have disappeared from the horizon and the dawn of peace has ascended in the Far East."[7]

A special "Soviet-Japanese Friendship Number" issued by the *Japan Times and Mail* on May 31 hailed "the common spirit of compromise and cooperation in the common cause of peace in the Far East that both sides had shown in negotiating the sale of the CER. "Surely nothing could add more to the guarantees of the peace and welfare of East Asia," the paper asserted and exclaimed: "Let the authorities concerned be abundantly blessed for the worthy accomplishment they have achieved with such good sense and success, and with such fairness to all."[8]

The friendship number contained the photographs of Foreign Minister Hirota, Ambassador Iuren'ev and Viscount Saito Makoto, president of the Nippon-Soviet Society, between pictures of the Kremlin on the left and Mt. Fuji on the right. In a message, printed on

[7] *Izvestiia*, April 28, 1935.
[8] "How Purchase of CER Line was Negotiated Told," JTM, May 31, 1935.

the same page, Hirota declared that by reason of geographical propinquity Japan and Russia were bound to remain neighbors regardless of differences in national ideals and aspirations. "Happily, despite all sorts of disturbing rumors to the contrary, the two nations have been steadfast in the maintenance of their mutual regard and nothing has affected the solid foundation of their friendship," Hirota stated, pointing to the sale of the CER as an illustration. "The settlement has brought in bolder relief than ever the fact that both Japan and Russia are determined to remain friends and live in peace." He reiterated his conviction that all outstanding problems could now be satisfactorily settled, "bringing Japan and the USSR into that state of close intimacy which the two nations desire and their geographical situation demands."[9]

Iuren'ev, in a message published over his written signature, asserted that the decade which had passed since the conclusion of the Basic Convention in 1925 had shown that with good will and mutual understanding "perfect good neighborly relations" could be maintained between the USSR and Japan. He expressed confidence that whatever questions might arise between them in the future, they would be solved in a friendly and peaceful way.[10]

In an article especially written for the *Japan Times and Mail,* Karl Radek examined the attitude of the average Soviet citizen toward Japan. He contended that the Russo-Japanese War had not aroused public feeling against Japan so much as against the tsarist government, which had been regarded as responsible for the catastrophe. Even during the Siberian Intervention, which had made a deeper impression, resentment

[9] "The Foreign Minister's Message," JTM, May 31, 1935.
[10] JTM, May 31, 1935.

had been aroused against the powers in general rather than against Japan. The great earthquake of 1923 had generated Russian sympathy, and the energy with which the Japanese had rebuilt the ravaged cities had engendered esteem for their organizing and technical abilities.

Radek asserted that the Soviet masses were devoid of the "European" attitude towards Japan, "the attitude based on fear of Japanese arms and an outlook of contempt for the people of Asia." He admitted that it would be insincere for him to deny that the Manchurian Incident and the utterances of some of the military in regard to the Russian Far East had aroused concern in the USSR, but he declared that the Soviet masses had learned that every nation must save itself by its own efforts and that they had no intention "to pick the chestnuts out of the fire for anybody whatsoever." They themselves felt secure, he noted, because their government was strong and well prepared militarily. "They would be glad," Radek proclaimed, "if the treaty with regard to the selling of the CER would be the beginning of good, friendly relations between us and Japan for the mutual benefit of the two countries and to nobody's damage, except perhaps to the damage of those who try to take an advantage of the controversies between the USSR and Japan."[11]

Baron Okura Kimmochi also welcomed the solution of the railway problem as "a matter of great rejoicing" and asserted that it had "swept away the dark shadow that hung over Soviet-Japanese relations . . . since the outbreak of the Manchurian incident." Noting that

[11] "Soviet Masses Hope to See CER Sale Bring Mutual Benefits to Japan and USSR," JTM, May 31, 1935; reprinted in Russian under the heading "Sovetskaia obshchestvennost' i Iaponiia," *Izvestiia*, June 3, 1935.

many other issues remained to be settled—the Soviet-Manchukuoan boundary question, the withdrawal of military forces from the border region, the fishery problem, the North Sakhalin oil problem, and forestry questions—he expressed the fear that even the solution of all these issues would not of themselves suffice to bring about "sincere friendship" between the two powers. "In my opinion," he wrote, "there are two main reasons that stand in the way of the establishment of sincere friendship between the two countries. One is the red propaganda carried on by Soviet Russia; the other is Soviet aggression in Asia." Failing to see the log in Japan's own eye—he claimed that "the 30 million inhabitants of Manchuria could never have been saved except by Japan's benign activities"—Okura voiced apprehension that "now that Soviet Russia has established peace with Japan and Manchukuo in North Manchukuo, she may be ready to carry on more active red propaganda in other parts of China." Nonetheless, he echoed the "sincerest desire" for "a real and unshakable friendship between the two countries" and advocated the sort of collaboration that tsarist Russia and Japan had achieved on the eve of the revolution. In view of his suspicions, Okura advocated the conclusion of an antiwar pact that would prevent ideological as well as military aggression; he proposed that Japan and the USSR "pledge to each other that they will carry on no aggression in any other parts of Asia, and should be prepared to oppose any aggression in Asia by some third power."[12]

Baron Sakatani Yoshiro lauded the "absolute neutral stand" taken by the USSR in the Manchurian affair and her sale of the CER. He declared that the ideas

---

[12] "Soviet-Japanese Peace," JTM, May 31, 1935.

of the Soviet statesmen were fundamentally different from their tsarist predecessors, "clearly proving that the officials of the Moscow Government base their opinions on justice, love of peace, and respect of international friendship."[13]

Viscount Saito Makoto, recent prime minister and concurrently foreign minister, proclaimed that there was "no happier development in international relations than the spirit of accord which marks the intercourse between the USSR and Japan." Asserting that "the world needs both the USSR and Japan," whose people had much to contribute to the economic and cultural progress of the world, Saito wrote that there was no reason why both nations could not work for mutual benefits "on the basis of co-existence and co-prosperity."[14]

In addition to the above-mentioned message of Iuren'ev, the *Japan Times and Mail* carried also a lengthy article by him concerning the "majestic conquests and successes of socialist construction" in the economic field. The ambassador reiterated that the Soviet Union wanted peace; she had made a series of world disarmament proposals and had concluded nonaggression treaties with practically all her neighbors. Reminding the Japanese that his government had offered the conclusion of a nonaggression pact with Japan as well, Iuren'ev stated that it was ready, as Litvinov had declared, "to consider the question of the mutual withdrawal to a certain distance from the frontiers of the armed forces including aviation, taking naturally in consideration the geographical conditions of the respective parties."[15]

[13] "USSR Contributes to World Peace," JTM, May 31, 1935.
[14] "Viscount Saito's Message," JTM, May 31, 1935.
[15] "The Soviet Union," JTM, May 31, 1935.

Baba Hideo in an article on the effect of the sale of the CER on Soviet-Japanese relations felt that the beneficial consequences had been greater than expected. Although he expected "a rough road" ahead in view of the complications that had attended the negotiations, he observed that talk of a conflict between the two powers had been dissipated and that there was even speculation about a Soviet-Japanese alliance. He recalled the saying popular after the Russo-Japanese War: "Yesterday's enemies [are] today's friends."[16]

Yet the Japanese army continued to agitate against the USSR and to accuse her of preparing for a Far Eastern war.[17] As frontier incidents along the Manchukuo-Soviet border recurred in spite of the sale of the CER, the British wondered why the Japanese continued to "bait" the Russians. "Is it a definite policy destined by the Japanese to end in war? Or is it just the stupidity of the swollen headed officers of the Kwantung Army who are so fond of displaying their power, and who cannot resist the temptation to continue a 'positive policy' on the Amur?" Gascoigne asked and himself answered: "I am inclined to think that it is the latter, for we know that neither Russia nor Japan want war at present." Randall concurred that as his department had concluded eighteen months or so ago, when Soviet-Japanese relations had looked very bad, war between the two countries was improbable for a considerable time to come, partly because Japan did not want war while she was reorganizing her army, and the USSR, because of the effect it would have on her internal situation. "But the Japanese mili-

---

[16] "Effect of NMR Sale on Relations Between Japan and the USSR," JTM, May 31, 1935.

[17] JWC, May 2, 1935, pp. 573 and 581; May 23, 1935, p. 667.

tary have lately been more aggressive," he admitted, "and their future actions are not easy to calculate; even the Japanese Foreign Office is sometimes taken by surprise."[18]

If the purpose of the Kwantung pressure along the Soviet-Manchukuoan border was to secure its delimitation and the reduction of the Russian Far Eastern armies, the policy was doomed to failure. "We know that the superiority in numbers which the Russians have on the spot in the Far East would give them a great advantage over the Japanese in the initial stages of a war," Gascoigne observed. "At the present, at any rate, they would hardly fall into such an obvious trap, and throw away the best cards."[19]

* * *

There was a direct link between the Russo-Chinese controversy in Manchuria and the Manchurian Incident in that the failure of the League of Nations and of the United States to come to the effective aid of China in 1929 encouraged Japanese aggression. Some historians have, therefore, damned the Soviet Union, Japan, the League, and the United States alike for contributing to the course of events that were to culminate in the Second World War. It should be noted, however, that the Soviet strike was limited and that the Red Army, unlike the Japanese Army, withdrew voluntarily once it had demonstrated to the Chinese that they could not deprive the USSR of her treaty

[18] July 3, 1935, minutes regarding Chilston to Foreign Office, No. 94 (R), Moscow, July 2, 1935, FO 371/19347–713.

[19] July 8, 1935, minutes regarding Clive to Foreign Office, No. 166, July 6, 1935, FO 371/19347–713. Gilbert argues, on the other hand, that the Soviets by the assembly of an overwhelming number of troops played into the hands of the most radical of the Japanese militarists. "Without the presence of such sizeable Soviet troops formations, the militarists would have been unable to utilize this real or imagined threat as a lever for extracting exorbitant appropriations from the government." (Gilbert, 61.)

rights unilaterally by force.[20] Furthermore, the reluctance of the League of Nations and of the United States to rally effectively to China's side in the 1920s was due less to faintheartedness and lack of principle, than to the feeling that China was legally in the wrong. By the 1930s the Western powers were too weak to stop Japan in her tracks.

While the failure of the League powers and of the United States to shelter China from the Soviet Union in 1929 had signalled to the Japanese that their invasion of Manchuria might go unchecked, the inability of the Western powers to effect a Japanese withdrawal had fostered a Sino-Soviet reconciliation. Although Karakhan had dismissed as counterproductive the idea of an alliance between China and the USSR when it had been broached by China's delegate to the League on his way through Moscow on August 24, 1931, he had informed Mo Te-hui shortly after the Manchurian Incident that the Chinese could be "absolutely confident" that the Soviet Union did not plan "to complicate or make more difficult in any way the already difficult situation that had developed in Manchuria" and that they could, therefore, "freely and without worry" take whatever steps they deemed necessary vis-à-vis the Japanese.[21]

[20] The effectiveness of the policy pursued by the Soviet Union toward China in the 1920s of repaying every blow with a double-blow ensured the adoption of the same policy toward Japan once superior Russian forces had been massed in the late 1930s and again against China in the 1960s and 1970s. The concentration of troops along their borders alarmed the Japanese and the Chinese, who saw it as a threat to their security, but to the Soviets the best insurance against foreign attack was to have vastly superior forces in the field.

[21] Karakhan's record of his conversation with Wang Chia-chen, August 24, 1931, DVP, XIV, 489–93; Karakhan's record of his conversation with Mo, September 23, 1931, DVP, XIV, 533–35. Troianovskii, who had the reputation among his colleagues of being "one of the most pro-Japanese diplomats," believed that Chiang Kai-shek was so strongly under British influence that he would repay any Russian help in the same manner as he had done before and that Soviet-Japanese relations, therefore, should not be endangered for the sake of a rapproche-

China's fear of Japan and her desire for a nonaggression pact with the USSR had provided the latter with leverage for the restoration of diplomatic relations with China.[22] On December 13, 1932, Matsuoka had congratulated Litvinov on the reestablishment of Soviet relations with China and had told him with a straight face that the USSR should be grateful to Japan for having driven China into her arms and that Japan, having accomplished this, now was striving to bring the Soviet Union and the United States closer together. "Matsuoka said all this without blushing," Litvinov cabled in amazement.[23]

The pending sale of the CER to Manchukuo evoked repeated Chinese protests, but as Connor-Green observed, the Soviet embroilment with China over the sale of the railway meant nothing. "Merely a little paper battle."[24] The Chinese contended that the sale constituted a violation of the Sino-Soviet convention

---

ment with China. "He would, however, be willing to endanger Soviet-Japanese relations for the sake of rapprochement with the United States," a European colleague told Ambassador Grew. "It is America that the Soviets consider the big prize."

[22] See Karakhan's record of his conversation with Mo, September 26, 1931, DVP, XIV, 544–48; Karakhan to Litvinov, Moscow, June 29, 1932, "Most urgent," DVP, XV, 392–93; DVP, XV, 401; *Izvestiia*, July 1, 1932; Karakhan to Litvinov, July 4, 1932, DVP, XV, 395. The conclusion of a nonaggression pact with China was delayed by the USSR because the Chinese draft stipulated nonrecognition *de jure* or *de facto* of conditions created by the aggression of a third power in an attempt to block Soviet recognition of Manchukuo and the sale of the CER to the latter. (*Izvestiia*, May 17, 1933.) It was shelved by the Chinese side in 1934 for fear of intensifying Japanese aggression in North China. (DVP, 804–805, note 190.) Litvinov took advantage of the exchange of notes reestablishing diplomatic and consular relations with China on December 12, 1932, to plead indirectly for United States recognition of the USSR, declaring in a press interview that the disturbances in East Asia were due "to no small degree to the fact that normal diplomatic relations were not maintained between all the states bordering on the basin of the Pacific Ocean." (*Izvestiia*, December 13, 1932; Ovey to Simon, No. 718, Moscow, December 13, 1932, FO 371/16228–680.)

[23] Litvinov to Foreign Commissariat, Geneva, December 13, 1932, DVP, XV, 682–83.

[24] Minutes, May 15, 1933, FO 371/17133–876.

of 1924 which stipulated that the railway could be redeemed by China and that its future was to be determined by the governments of the Soviet Union and China "to the exclusion of any third party."[25] The Russians responded that the Peking agreement had derived from the natural and essential assumption that the Chinese government would be able to make use of its rights and carry out its obligations on the CER and that the Soviet government had been forced the very year that the pact had been concluded to sign a special agreement concerning the railway with the autonomous Mukden government, which China had been unable to compel to carry out the obligations of the Peking agreement. "By ratifying the Mukden agreement subsequently," Moscow reasoned, "the Chinese Government recognized that inasmuch as it had not been able to carry out its obligations concerning the CER stipulated by the Peking treaty, the Soviet Government had no alternative but to come to an agreement concerning the CER with Mukden Government, which exercised full *de facto* authority in Manchuria and on the railway." Now due to circumstances beyond Soviet control, Manchukuo had assumed the functions previously carried out on the CER by the Mukden government, and the Chinese government had not protested against the joint administration of the railway by Soviet and Manchukuoan officials. It was the right of the Soviet government—a right and not an obligation—to preserve Soviet ownership of the railway and to continue participating in its administration regardless of circumstances. Nor could the USSR be held responsible for losses suffered

---

[25] JWC, May 18, 1933, p. 684; Strang to Foreign Office, No. 16, May 17, 1933, FO 371/17134–858; JWC, March 21, 1935, p. 377; Behrens to Foreign Office, No. 474, Peking, March 25, 1935, FO 371/19269–736.

by China at the hands of a third power. Besides, the sale of the CER, should it take place, would in no way affect the actual interests of the Chinese government. "If the Northeastern Provinces, which presently form part of Manchukuo, reunite with the Chinese Republic and recognize the sovereignty of the Chinese government, the CER, redeemed by the Manchukuoan Government, will automatically become the property of the Chinese state. If, on the other hand, the reunification of the Manchurian provinces with China will not take place and the sovereignty of China over them will be lost forever, it must be all the same to the Chinese Government whether the CER will belong to the Soviet Government or to the Government of Manchukuo."[26]

In an editorial welcoming the sale of the CER as a means of strengthening peace in East Asia, *Izvestiia* declared: "Any thinking Chinese patriot knows that the USSR would be deeply happy if there were the possibility to hand the railway to a representative of the great Chinese people, friendship with whom the popular masses of the USSR value in particular. But the Chinese people are not masters of the situation in Manchuria, and they would gain nothing if the CER were to become the object of a struggle, which would destroy this Far Eastern route of communication."[27]

In June 1934 Chiang Kai-shek had assured Bogomolov that China regarded the USSR as a good neighbor. "If danger threatens one neighbor, it also threatens the other. Should anything happen, China

[26] Declaration of the government of the USSR to the government of China, June 19, 1933, DVP, XVI, 353–54. When the Chinese government on March 11, 1935, nonetheless formally protested to the Soviet government through its embassy in Nanking against the pending sale of the railway, Moscow dismissed the accusation that the sale of the railway to Manchukuo violated the Sino-Soviet treaty of 1924 with the rejoinder that the Chinese had destroyed the treaty by their willful actions in 1929. (Gilbert, 57.)

[27] *Izvestiia,* March 24, 1935.

will always sympathize with the USSR and do everything possible to show her friendship."[28] In October of that year he had sent Professor Ch'en Li-fu to Moscow as his personal envoy to sound out Stomoniakov in a "confidential and unofficial" conversation whether the USSR would be willing to effect a rapprochement with China, even though their forms of government differed, and whether she would be willing to do so even though he had played a leading role in the rupture of Sino-Soviet relations. Stomoniakov had replied that "the Soviet government was never guided in its foreign policy by consideration of some social-economic differences or antipathies," but by "interests of state" and "interests of peace." "What's past is past," he had added; "we are not guided in our policy by remembrances and feelings."[29]

As the Japanese, in the summer of 1935, moved to gain control of North China, Soviet press comments remained remarkably mild.[30] "As long as Japan does not actually invade Russian territory, in a definite manner, Moscow will presumably continue to follow a policy of least resistance, as she has done since 1931, and be careful to avoid a 'show down'," Gascoigne commented. "Clearly China has nothing to hope for from Moscow," Randall added; "only if Japan appeared to be drawing near to Germany would Russia, I imagine, begin to concern herself with China's fate."[31] That is, of course, what was to happen in 1936, when Japan joined the Anti-Comintern Pact, and

[28] Bogomolov to Foreign Commissariat, June 22, 1934, DVP, XVII, 406–407.
[29] Record of Stomoniakov's conversation with Ch'en, October 16, 1934, DVP, XVII, 640–44.
[30] Lord Chilston to Sir Samuel Hoare, No. 252, Moscow, June 17, 1935, FO 371/19347–713.
[31] Comments in minutes, dated June 26 and July 2, 1935, respectively, pertaining to Chilston to Hoare, No. 252, Moscow, June 17, 1935.

the Japanese invasion of China the next year was to trigger Russian military aid to the Nationalist government, completing a full cycle in the shifting relations between Moscow and Nanking.

* * *

The statements and interpretations of Soviet diplomats and historians are often dismissed in the West as following the ideological line. The impression is left that the utterances are not believed by the authors, but made exclusively for purposes of propaganda. Yet Soviet diplomatic correspondence reveals that similar views were expressed in confidential dispatches and that the Russians truly felt as threatened by the Western powers as they contended. They were convinced that Finland and Poland would attack the Soviet Union if she became involved in war with Japan and that Great Britain was inciting Germany and Japan against the USSR.[32]

The British sought to allay Soviet suspicions, partly for fear that if Litvinov concluded that the French and British would leave the USSR without support in the face of a German "Drang nach Osten," he might "throw in his hand altogether in the Far East in order to be able to turn his undivided attention to the West." "This, of course, would not suit our book at all," Collier reflected, "any more than the reverse situation—which is also a possibility, though a more remote one—in which a Soviet-German détente in Europe might be brought about through Soviet fear of isolation in the face of Japan in the Far East."[33]

A Foreign Office memorandum over the name of Vansittart deemed it not impossible that the Soviet

[32] See, for example, Ambassador V. P. Potemkin's record of his conversation with the Italian statesman Fulvio Suvich, June 11, 1934, DVP, XVII, 383–85.

[33] Minutes, January 30 and 31, 1935, regarding Clive to Foreign Office, No. 32, January 29, 1935.

government, "if really hard-pressed in Europe, would completely throw in their hand in the Far East, and allow the Japanese a free field in those regions in return for a guarantee of the security of their own territory—which, of course, is not a situation that we would wish to see brought about." Likewise the possibility of a détente between Germany and the USSR could not be neglected as more and more people in both countries came to realize that "common sense and the lessons of past history argue that Germany cannot afford an enemy west *and* east, and that Russia cannot afford an enemy east *and* west."

In their quest for security, the memorandum noted, the Soviets had changed their policy from a revisionist one to an antirevisionist one. Great Britain had gained thereby much directly by the increase in her trade with the USSR, the cessation of Soviet pressure on Afghanistan, the comparative consideration by the USSR of British interests elsewhere in Asia,[34] and by the diminution of anti-British propaganda. She had gained perhaps even more indirectly "through the effect in Europe of the general realisation of the fact that the Soviet government are now seeking the friendship of those Powers which are opposed to any change in the *status quo*."[35]

While Soviet statesmen and diplomats sought to assure their British and French counterparts of their

---

[34] "For example," the report stated, "their desire to stand well with us has probably been a main factor in deterring them from detaching Chinese Turkestan from China as completely as Mongolia, which they could easily have done at any time in the past year."

[35] "International Position of the Soviet Union in relation to France, Germany, and Japan," Foreign Office Memorandum, N 880/135/38, dated February 21, 1935, FO 371/19460–881. The French chargé d'affaires in Moscow described the transformation of the USSR from "*dynamisme pertubateur*" to "*statisme stabilisateur*." (Jean Payart to Paul-Boncour, No. 150, Moscow, June 2, 1933, DDF, First Series, III, 634.)

sincerity in seeking to improve relations between their
countries, Soviet propagandists described the new policy to fellow-Communists as a temporary and limited
measure and justified it on the ground that the ultimate
aim of world revolution could best be served by such
a change in tactics. R. L. Speaight dismissed the propaganda as "little more than eyewash, designed to
satisfy the many non-Russian Communists who are
not unnaturally inclined to interpret the present Soviet
hobnobbing with Paris and London as a betrayal of
their cause." "I do not think the Soviet Government
are really as subtle as they would like their friends
to believe," Speaight wrote. "All our information goes
to show that their changing foreign policy is due to
hard necessity rather than to cunning, and that,
frightened of Germany and Japan and realizing that
peace is at present essential for their own internal purposes, they are now genuinely anxious for good relations with this country and France. Future developments (e.g. a victorious war with Japan) may well cause
them to return to their former policy of encouraging
revolution in all capitalist countries whenever and
wherever opportunity offers, but for the time being
it looks as if Mr. Litvinov (whose control of Soviet
policy, although challenged, seems still unbroken) is
bent on playing the European political game without
cheating."[36] "I agree," Collier added. "Every government which compromises with hard facts always says
the compromise doesn't affect its ultimate aims; but
it often *does* affect them, all the same."[37]

While the British did not use their influence in Tokyo
to set Japan against the USSR, as the Soviets sus-

[36] Minutes, January 9, 1935, regarding Captain Liddell to Norton, No.
420/Gen/1/DS8, January 7, 1935, FO 371/19460.
[37] January 11, 1935.

pected, neither did they use it to act as peacemakers. As James Dodds observed on August 12, 1935: "If the Japanese and Russians cease to suspect each other, another barrier to Japanese aggression in the Far East disappears as well as to Russian aggression in Afghanistan and Sinkiang. The argument [for acting as peacemaker] is presumably, that we want Russia to be free of entanglements in the Far East in order that she may be able to pull her weight against Germany. I venture to suggest that she should be allowed to work out this problem in her own way without too much pushing from us." "From a purely Far Eastern point of view I can only agree with Mr. Dodds," Orde commented. "We shall be better off there if relations between Japan and the Soviet Union are bad. Desire for good relations with Russia for their own sake and desire for her influence against Germany has caused us to take some pains to assure her that it is not our desire that Japan should attack her. Truthfully so, for we do not want a war between them. The ideal from our point of view would be a continued state of nervousness in Japan about Russia, but no commitment of Russia's strength that could not be liquidated at a moment's notice if the European situation made it desirable. We also want good relations with Japan and can place no reliance on American cooperation against her or on Russian help. . . . But it seems unnecessary from either point of view to go out of our way to sooth Japanese fears. . . ."[38]

Towards the end of 1934 the British War Office had made an analysis of the radical changes that had recently taken place in Soviet domestic and foreign policy. While feeling that the policy of securing peace

[38] Minutes regarding Clive to Hoare, No. 338, Tokyo, June 29, 1935, FO 371/19347–713.

at almost any price was due solely to expedience and did not signify renunciation of the ultimate aim of world revolution, it had observed that "there was a tendency, exemplified often enough in history for changes of policy dictated by pure expediency to become permanent through sheer force of circumstances." In a secret memorandum, dated July 8, 1935, the War Office observed that since its analysis of the preceding year Hitler had denounced the military clauses of the Treaty of Versailles and the USSR had concluded a Treaty of Mutual Assistance with France. Taking note of the fact that "conversion by straightforward conquest" played no part in Soviet ideology and that the Soviet government, in pursuit of an "ultra-pacifist policy," had been indulging in "an orgy of pact-making," the memorandum concluded that "although world revolution remains the final objective of the Russian Communist Party, they have now been compelled by events in the Far East and in Europe since Hitler's rise to power, to insert an intermediate objective into their plans of attack, viz. the security of the Soviet Union, the parent body of World Communism." The USSR now wanted a settled, not a troubled Europe, because she believed that the slightest spark would suffice to set alight a general European conflagration of which Japan would take advantage to seek to gain domination of East Asia. If that happened, "the Soviet Union might well find herself engaged in war in the west and in the Far East simultaneously, a possibility that has for some time past constituted a nightmare for her leaders."[39]

[39] "The Policy of the Soviet Union," memorandum dated July 8, 1935, and classified "secret," sent by Colonel Ismay of the War Office to Collier, July 9, 1935, FO 371/19460–881. The Germans too were fearful at first of being drawn into a multipower conflict. In October 1934 Bernhard von Bülow, state secretary of the German Foreign Ministry, instructed Ambassador Dirksen to avoid any

The fear of being drawn into a two-front war continued to dominate Soviet thinking up to and throughout most of the Second World War. As one of the inducements for her entry into the Pacific War Prime Minister Winston Churchill and President Franklin D. Roosevelt agreed at Yalta to the joint operation of the Chinese Eastern Railway and of the South-Manchurian Railway by a newly established Soviet-Chinese Company, "it being understood that the preeminent interests of the Soviet Union shall be safeguarded and that China shall retain full sovereignty in Manchuria.[40]

The provision was incorporated in an instrument appended to the Treaty of Friendship and Alliance signed by the Soviet Union and the Republic of China on August 14, 1945, providing for the combining of the main trunk line of the CER and SMR into one system known as the Chinese Changchun Railway, owned and operated by the USSR and China jointly. The subsidiary railway enterprises also reverted to joint ownership and administration. Once again the president of the board of directors of the railway was to be a Chinese, the manager Russian, with China possessing sovereignty over the railway and being responsible for its protection. The agreement was to run for thirty years—until 1975—when the railway and

---

"close relations" with Japan, lest Germany be suspected of "wishing to render assistance against Russia." Viewing the interest of the United States and certain League powers in the USSR as part of an "encirclement" of Japan, Bülow saw danger for Germany in the outbreak of another Russo-Japanese War, because, as he put it, "in the case of conflict in the Far East moves would probably be made against us in order to make certain that we did not attack Russia in the rear or even merely cause disquiet." (Bülow to Oskar P. Trautmann, German minister in China, Berlin, October 12, 1934, "Personal and Confidential," *Documents on German Foreign Policy,* Series C, III, 480.)

[40] G. A. Lensen, "Yalta and the Far East," 150.

its property were to be transferred to China without compensation.[41]

Before the expiration of this term, however, the Japanese forebodings of a Communist victory in China materialized and on February 14, 1950, the USSR agreed to transfer to the Chinese People's Republic without compensation all her rights in the joint administration of the railway and in the subsidiary enterprises immediately upon the signing of a peace treaty with Japan "but not later than the end of 1952."[42] She did so on December 31, 1952, after having repaired once again the damage wrought by war and after having trained more Chinese in railway construction and operation. In a telegram to Stalin, Chairman Mao Tsetung praised the return of the railway as a "tremendous contribution to railway construction in China."[43]

At last, it seemed, the USSR had succeeded in divesting herself of the "damned inheritance" with grace and good purpose.

[41] Clubb, *China and Russia,* 346–47; Henry Wei, *China and Soviet Russia,* 340–43.

[42] *Ibid.,* 384; O. B. Borisov and B. T. Koloskov, *Sovetsko-kitaiskie otnosheniia 1945–1970,* 47; Wei, 345–46.

[43] Borisov and Koloskov, 56.

Appendix

A

ECONOMIC RELATIONS

Soviet economic relations with Japan may be divided into three categories: trade, fisheries, and the oil and coal concessions on Sakhalin Island. While trade relations were not substantial in the 1930s, their tremendous potential had been demonstrated during the First World War when Russia, isolated from the West, had temporarily become Japan's number one customer.[1] The lure of the vast Russian market and of possible participation in the economic development of Siberia was a positive force in Soviet Japanese relations, for economic transactions of this sort presupposed peace, if not amity. The fisheries rights and oil and coal concessions, on the other hand, constituted a source of constant friction because the Japanese regarded them as "captured by blood" in the Russo-Japanese War and were prone to resort to force in their defense. The belligerent attitude with which the Japanese responded to any Soviet effort to modify the conditions under which the fisheries were conducted and the concessions exploited, prompted Karakhan to write to Troianovskii: " . . . we must determinately oppose any attempts of further expansion by Japan

[1] G. A. Lensen, "The Russian Impact on Japan," 344–46.

in our Far East and strive in every way to strengthen our own positions in those regions which the Japanese regard almost as their own monopoly."[2]

When a delegation from the Okura company in May 1933 wanted to lease the Soviet half of Sakhalin, Iuren'ev replied that the Soviet government was itself increasing the economic development of the island and that the proposal was tantamount to his asking that one of the important Japanese islands be leased to the USSR.[3]

Yet the Japanese kept toying with the idea. Baron Iwakura Michitaro, president of the Hokuyo Kyokai (the Northern Seas Society), worked on a plan for the purchase of the oil-producing rights in North Sakhalin and the land and sea fishing rights in the north with the support of Barons Kuroda Nagakazu, Shijo Takahide, Watanabe Tei, Yabuki Shozo, and Shiba Chuzaburo. His scheme was much favored also by Admiral Saito, Count Uchida, Minister for Overseas Affairs Nagai, Minister for Agriculture and Forestry Goto Fumio, General Araki, Admiral Osumi and Minister for Commerce and Industry Baron Nakajima. It was even discussed at a Cabinet meeting, and the Ministries for Foreign Affairs and Agriculture and Forestry were asked to study the matter thoroughly.[4]

Between 1930 and 1935 Soviet-Japanese relations had been marred by numerous incidents on land and at sea linked to the fisheries question. For example, in the wake of an intensive campaign by Japanese fisheries interests for a "firm policy" toward the USSR, an assassin had wounded the Soviet commercial counselor and trade representative Pavel Anikeev on March 16, 1931, and the Kenkokukai, an ultranationalist society, had organized a march on the Soviet embassy on April 24.[5]

[2] Karakhan to Troianovskii, June 13, 1930, DVP, 336–37. For the Japanese point of view, see *Hirota Koki,* 82–85.

[3] Telegrams from Iuren'ev to Foreign Commissariat on May 11 and 15, 1933, DVP, XVI, 834, note 123.

[4] Resumé of article in *Hochi Shimbun* of August 17, 1933, in Snow to Simon, No. 503, Tokyo, August 31, 1933, FO 371/17151–858.

[5] Ambassador Hirota denied that the attack on Anikeev had been an anti-Soviet

In his talks with Fujiwara Ginjiro at the beginning of 1933 Troianovskii vainly tried to link the sale of the CER with the settlement of the fisheries problem. "The fishery right is Japan's right, making inroads into Russia's interests, and the Chinese Eastern Railway is Russia's right, eating into Japan's interest," he argued. "If Russia will buy up the fishery rights and surrender the Chinese Eastern Railway to Japan, i.e. if Japan buys it, the problem will be simplified." He estimated that the Japanese fishery rights in Soviet waters were worth 50 million yen—that Japan could apply this amount toward the purchase of the CER if she gave them up.[6]

When Ota, on his own initiative, raised the subject of a commercial agreement with Karakhan on April 24, 1933, Karakhan reminded him that the Soviet Union had more than once proposed the conclusion of a commercial treaty with Japan, but she had not received a favorable reply. She considered the absence of such a treaty between their countries as abnormal and would be willing to begin discussions concerning one if an official proposal were made in the name of the Japanese government.[7]

---

act. It was common for murderers, he said, to cloak their personal grudges in public issues and that the situation in Japan was "difficult and abnormal," two premiers having been killed and a third seriously injured. (Two telegrams from Troianovskii to Foreign Commissariat on March 16, 1931, DVP XIV, 201–202; *Izvestiia* and *Pravda,* March 17, 1931; Karakhan's record of his conversation with Hirota, March 17, 1931, DVP, XIV, 203–204; Troianovskii to Foreign Commissariat, April 24, 1931, DVP, XIV, 277–78. For further details about the attempt on Anikeev's life and the trial of the assassin, Sato Nobukatsu, see Troianovskii to Shidehara, March 23, 1931, and Shidehara to Troianovskii, April 7, 1931, DVP, XIV, 218–21; also DVP, XIV, 786, note 71.)

[6] "Saionji-Harada Memoirs," 375. For details concerning fisheries incidents, including the firing on Japanese fishermen, the seizure of Japanese fishing vessels and the deployment of Japanese guard ships and destroyers, as well as for negotiations concerning fishery auctions, see *Nisso kosho-shi,* 346–60; J.W.C., June 30, 1933, p. 896; June 29, 1933, p. 903; *Izvestiia,* June 27, 1933; JWC, July 6, 1933, pp. 4, 11, 22; July 13, 1933, p. 46; documents in DVP, XVI, pp. 455–57, 470–72, 515–16, 566–68, XVII, 160–63, 190, 382–83, and notes in DVP, XVI, nos. 183, 194, 239, XVII, nos. 86, 87, 178, 179. For detailed discussions concerning the exchange rate of the AKO bonds, see documents in DVP, XVII, pp. 168–89, 175–77, 326–27, 344–45, 348–49, 558–59 and notes in DVP, XVII, nos. 148, 149, 165, 166, 179.

[7] DVP, XVI, note 832.

In a letter to Iuren'ev on May 16 Karakhan expressed the view that should the political situation improve with the sale of the CER, the Soviet Union would have "a serious basis for the development of commercial relations with Japan." "Japan can be one of the serious users of our lumber, our oil and wheat," he noted, expressing particular interest in the latter, because "Anglo-Canadian circles" were seeking to close European markets to Soviet wheat.. While Soviet imports from Japan had heretofore been of a local character—to serve the economic development of the Russian Far East—the products of such Japanese industries as the shipping, railway equipment, electrical machinery, and chemical industries could be included among the general imports of the USSR, particularly as they could be obtained cheaper in view of the fall in the exchange rate of the yen, but for this a commercial treaty would be necessary. Since the Soviet government had no idea whether the overtures of Ota and Counselor Sako reflected the thinking of the Japanese government or were merely good intentions of their own, or whether the feelers were but a strategem to sweeten the "bitter pills" that Japanese policy constituted for the USSR, Karakhan instructed Iuren'ev to try to determine with utmost caution the actual intentions of government and business circles, being careful not to give the impression that the Soviet Union was showing increased interest in the matter, for the initiative in considering a commercial treaty or agreement had been and must remain Japanese. In asking Iuren'ev to furnish the Foreign Commissariat with the necessary material to make a preliminary study of the question, he requested not only the latest data about the economic development of Japan and her foreign trade, but the text of Japanese commercial agreements with other countries and details about Soviet trade with Japan, specifically about Soviet trade practices. He revealed that the Foreign Commissariat had absolutely no knowledge of the general "commercial-political practice" of Japan and of the nature of credits used by the USSR in Japan, as well as of the extent to which the credit guarantee by the Japanese government was being used.[8]

Asked by Karakhan for his views concerning a commercial treaty with Japan,[9] Iuren'ev replied on July 5 that the question was "a very important and delicate problem." It had not yet been adequately studied either by the Soviet embassy or the trade mission and until this was done there could be no more-or-less serious discussions of this subject with the Japanese, nor had any responsible Japanese government leader posed the question in "any official or even semi-official form."[10]

In an interview granted to special correspondent Maruayama of the *Tokyo Asahi* and the *Osaka Asahi* in April, 1935, Commissar of Foreign Trade A. P. Rozengol'z held forth on the prospects of Soviet-Japanese economic relations in the wake of the sale of the CER. Noting that the wide range of products which the USSR planned to buy for the sum it was to receive as part payment for the railway would allow a large number of Japanese factories to participate in the transaction, Rozengol'z announced that the Commissariat of Foreign Trade would shortly dispatch to Japan a commission of commercial and technical experts led by F. G. Kiselev, chairman of the All-Union Society of "Tekhnopromimport" (Technical and Industrial Import), to assist the trade representative stationed in Tokyo. He expressed confidence that the familiarity with Japanese products and firms that would result from these purchases would lead to increased Japanese trade in the future as well.[11]

A nine man purchasing mission, headed by Kiselev, duly arrived in Japan that month to collect information about

[8] Karakhan to Iuren'ev, May 16, 1933, DVP, XVI, 294–97. A year earlier Troianovskii had complained to Moscow that no one from the Soviet trade mission, except for the commercial counselor, had attended an important meeting of the Japan-Soviet Society on June 11, 1932. "They plead that they do not have morning coats," he wrote. "That is no reason; one must sew morning coats." (Troianovskii to Foreign Commissariat, June 11, 1932, DVP, XV, 356–58.)

[9] Karakhan to Iuren'ev, May 16, 1933, DVP, 294–97.

[10] DVP, XVI, 833, note 121.

[11] *Izvestiia*, April 5, 1935.

Japanese goods and prices. Since Japan was already one of the leaders in the electrical industry, the Russians displayed particular interest in electrical machinery.[12] But difficulties arose because the Soviets refused to recognize the control of transactions by Japanese export guilds, such as the Tai-Ro Yushutsu Kumiai (Export Guild to Russia). They demanded free competition between Japanese suppliers[13] and preferred to come to terms with individual companies rather than a combined export sales committee. "On principle, the Soviet officials might be expected to prefer collective dealing to transactions with capitalists," the *Japan Weekly Chronicle* reflected, "but the Soviet trade commissioners have found it easier to make a contract with the Mitsubishi company for 25,000 tons of cement than with the export sales committee." "The Soviet people are to be envied" the paper remarked tongue-in-cheek. "They can deal with whom they please, but the ordinary buyer is not so free. Is it a dangerous thought that Communism, after all, has some advantages in business?"[14]

On May 8 Ambassador Iuren'ev visited Nagoya, accompanied by his wife, by Consul General Petr Krauze, Embassy Second Secretary Boris Gintse, Embassy Translator Boris Rodov, and Consulate Translator Fukami Kobe to select merchandise as part payment for the railway. A luncheon in their honor at the Municipal Hall, sponsored jointly by Aichi Prefecture, Nagoya Municipality, and the Nagoya Chamber of Commerce and Industry, was attended by the governor of Aichi Prefecture and the mayor of Nagoya City and by leading industrialists and financiers.[15]

The purchasing mission met with groups of businessmen in various cities. On May 31, for example, Commercial Counselor Vladimir Kochetov arranged for a round-table

[12] JWC, May 2, 1935, p. 581. Of the nine industrial experts, four were specialists in heavy machinery, one in textiles. (Takashima Seichi, "Several Methods Seen of Improving Trade Between Soviet Russia and Japan," JTM, May 31, 1935.)

[13] JWC, May 9, 1935, 608.

[14] JWC, May 30, 1935, 685–86.

[15] For the list of luncheon guests, see JTM, May 16, 1935.

discussion with members of the Kobe Chamber of Commerce and Industry, followed by a luncheon the next day, to which he invited some forty local officials and businessmen. The Japanese reciprocated with a reception, given jointly by the Japan-Russia Trade Association and the Kobe Chamber of Commerce and Industry on the thirty-first. Among those present on the Soviet side, in addition to Kochetov, Kiselev and suite, were Petr Krauze and an engineer by the name of Garlin, who was to test the quality of the products to be considered for purchase. Japanese participants included managing directors of export associations and of manufacturing companies.[16]

In the "Soviet-Japanese Friendship Number" of the *Japan Times and Mail,* Kadono Chokyuro of the Okura Company described the arrival of the Kiselev mission as a "splendid opportunity" to develop Soviet-Japanese trade on a firm basis.[17] Kawatani Kozaemon, commercial secretary of the Japanese embassy in Moscow, decried that trade with the Soviet Union had not developed according to expectations, firstly because there was no credit system to facilitate transactions, and secondly because the Russians knew very little of Japan's industrial progress and the Japanese equally little about economic conditions in the USSR. For the next three years Japanese companies would furnish the Soviet Union with a large number of goods as partial payment for the CER. Pessimists predicted that trade with the Soviet Union would wither away as the payments were completed. "I cannot share such pessimism," Kawatani wrote. "On the contrary, I believe that the transfer of the North Manchuria Railway will prove a turning point for the advancement of trade between the two countries and that trade will prosper even after the termination of the three years."[18]

Baba observed that the attitude of the purchasing commis-

[16] JWC, June 6, 1935, 738–39.
[17] "Trade Ties," ITM, May 31, 1935.
[18] "Commercial Relations," JTM, May 31, 1935.

sion had contributed to better relations by holding out hope for long-term economic collaboration.[19]

The industrial advance achieved by the Soviet Union in the eighteen years since the revolution and the priority given to internal development by Stalin encouraged some Japanese to be optimistic about the possibilities of large-scale commercial transactions. Kawatani wrote full of hope: "From the point of view of trade, the Soviet Union is full with possibilities and, therefore, it is advisable that Japan, instead of merely seeking immense profits, should sell merchandise superior in quality and cheaper in price. With this in mind, the Japanese merchants must lay the foundation for better commercial relations with this great Communist State."[20]

Takashima Seichi, the director of the Japan Economic Federation, proposed four steps for promoting trade between the two countries: (1) to show to the Soviet economic commission then in Japan every convenience so that the Russians would become acquainted with the superior industrial techniques of the Japanese and continue to buy their goods even after the completion of the railway payments and to try to prevail upon Soviet Russia to employ Japanese experts in her factories; (2) to counteract the bargaining advantage held by Soviet Russia in view of her state monopoly of foreign trade by establishing central control over Japanese transactions, expanding the authority and scope of the Guild of Exporters to Soviet Russia, established in 1926; (3) to devise a long-term credit system, such as Germany and Italy had instituted in 1931 for Soviet purchases, and to subsidize the trade by increasing the amounts of state compensation paid to Japanese companies for losses sustained in their export to the Soviet Union; and (4) to maintain the most cordial relations with the USSR.[21]

---

[19] "Effect of NMR Sale on Relations Between Japan and USSR,"JTM, May 31, 1935.

[20] JWC, July 4, 1935, 26.

[21] JTM, May 31, 1935, p. 6. For a discussion of the question of granting credits to the USSR, see Hirooka Mitsuharu, "Nichi-Ro Kankei no seicho."

B

ANTI-COMMUNISM IN JAPAN

The Communist Party of Japan agitated against Japanese imperialism among soldiers and sailors as well as workers in Manchuria. "Do not transport a single soldier," Japanese Communists exhorted their countrymen. "Oppose all military actions of Japanese imperialism and Chinese reaction-[aries]. Collaborate with the Red Army in the defense of the USSR. Down with imperialist Japan! For a Soviet Japan!"[1] Such subversive activity could not but fan the ire of Japanese patriots and compromise the USSR.

The Japanese Communist leaders seriously undermined Soviet policy when they turned the public trial, at which they were being prosecuted since June 1931 for subversion, into a propaganda platform, boasted of their affiliation with the Comintern, and took the side of the USSR and China against Japanese imperialism. "It becomes the task of the Japanese proletariat and the Communist Party," the 1932 theses of the Comintern proclaimed, "to combine the struggle against war [in China] with the struggle of the

[1] M. Mariev, *Imperialisty gotoviat voinu i interventsiiu protiv SSSR,* 131–32. For a striking photograph of a Communist meeting in Tokyo at that time, with almost everyone very bourgeois in appearance, in Western hats, see *ibid.,* 132.

477

workers, the peasants, and all the toilers against their economic and political enslavement in order to convert the imperialist war into civil war and overthrow the bourgeois-landlord monarchy."[2]

The political utterances of Soviet statesmen at home also hindered Soviet diplomacy. Lazar Kaganovich, a member of the Politburo, for example, used the same language as the Comintern in a speech to Soviet Communists on January 17, 1934, when he praised the work of fellow-Communists in other countries, notably the Communists of Japan who, in spite of their relatively small number, worked energetically "to turn the imperialist war into a civil war."[3]

Troianovskii reported that Araki's attitude toward the Soviet Union had visibly worsened as he had become familiar with the proceedings of the Communist trial.[4] He wrote that Araki and his group had revived their campaign for war with the USSR because of the findings of the trial and from fear of the Sovietization of China, stemming from the failure of Chiang Kai-shek's campaign against "the Soviet part of China."[5]

Convinced that Communist activities in Japan were the result of Soviet prompting, Japanese ultranationalists opposed the conclusion of a nonagression pact with the USSR on the ground that "the resulting closer intercourse between the two countries will bring Japanese and Russian Communists into closer contract, adding fresh cause of trouble to the Japanese world of thought." Noting that in the latest Communist case, a professor was found deeply involved as a Communist leader, four members of the House of Representatives asserted in a written interpellation: "Among the University professors there are some who hold ideas incompatible with the national polity, contemptuous of the army, and subversive of popular thought, and give public expression to them too. Such being the case, some

[2] George M. Beckmann and Okubu Genji, *The Japanese Communist Party*, 215–19.
[3] *Izvestiia,* January 22, 1934.
[4] Troianovskii to Foreign Commissariat, August 11, 1932, DVP, XV, 464.
[5] Troianovskii to Foreign Commissariat, August 19, 1932, DVP, XV, 479–81.

publicists regard the Departments of Economics, Law and Literature of the Imperial Universities as though they were the centre of the Bolshevisation of Japan, and even insist on their total abolition."[6]

The *Japan Weekly Chronicle* ridiculed the fear that closer relations with the USSR would lead to the infection of the Japanese people with Russian thought. It recalled the gist of the devastating reply made by the late Count Goto Shimpei when his own attempts to restore relations with Russia in the 1920s were criticized on similar grounds: "What is the use of constantly saying that the Japanese are the most loyal and patriotic people in the world if they have to be protected so carefully from the very breath of radicalism?" Turning to the attack on the intellectuals, the *Japan Weekly Chronicle* observed: "It is a curious paradox that the military men who have got their country into the most perfect state of defense always live in a panic fear of invasion, and that the men who are most boastful of their country's loyalty are always the first to think that there is a danger of revolution."[7]

As the year 1933 drew to a close, the *Japan Weekly Chronicle* reflected on the relentless war on "thought" that was being waged in Japan. Thousands of arrests had been made during the year, fifteen hundred in connection with one case alone. No longer was prosecution confined to professed Communists, but Communist sympathizers were also brought to trial.[8]

In an effort to root out subversion, officials struck out wildly at intellectuals and anyone appearing "red" in their eyes.[9] Proceeding from the premise that "the converse to patriotism is thought," the Japanese police and judiciary,

[6] JWC, March 16, 1933, p. 368.
[7] JWC, March 16, 1933, p. 360.
[8] JWC, January 4, 1934, pp. 3–4.
[9] Osamu Shimizu, the late director of the Orientalia collection of the Library of Congress and an old personal friend, told me that he was stopped by a Japanese policeman in the 1930s for carrying a book with a red binding.

in the words of a Western newspaper editor who knew Japan intimately, "pursued 'thought' with an implacable and almost insane severity." Even to "sympathize" with Communism became an offense. Communists found it difficult to obtain legal counsel, for it was regarded disloyal to defend persons accused of disloyalty. While "patriotic" murderers received light sentences, Communists were severely punished. The long sentence of one Communist was extended by two years' penal labor when he wrote "disrespectful" words on the wall of his cell. Another Communist was punished for writing disrespectful words in his private diary. When disrespectful words were found on the wall of a public urinal in another case, officials were so shocked that the news was banned from the press.[10]

In expounding to the British ambassador his peculiar political philosophy, which struck the latter as a "baffling mixture of mysticism and realism," Araki stressed on February 20, 1934, the "moral side of politics and the impossibility of cooperating with those who possessed no moral sense." He was referring to the Soviets, whom he branded as liars and whom he accused of seeking to undermine their neighbors by constant propaganda; he reiterated his concern at the spread of Communism in China.[11] When Araki expanded on his views toward the USSR to a number of British luncheon guests on March 23, Lindley commented in a cover letter accompanying the notes of the conversation that "General Araki has much the same idea regarding bolshevism as General Ludendorff had at the end of the Great War." "At the same time," he added, "I think Araki's nervousness is better founded than was Luden-

[10] A. Morgan Young, *Imperial Japan*, 242.

[11] Lindley to Simon, No. 123, Tokyo, March 1, 1934, "Very Confidential," FO 371/18181–810. Not everyone linked opposition to the growth of Communism in China necessarily with hostility toward the USSR. In a speech to the Diet on January 23, 1934, Foreign Minister Hirota expressed serious concern about the spread of Communism in North China, which bordered on Manchukuo, yet in the same breath called for good-neighborly relations with the USSR. (*Izvestiia*, January 24, 1934.)

dorff's; since the Soviets have obviously a far better chance of going ahead in China than they ever had in Europe."[12]

Proceeding from the conviction that so long as the USSR existed, all nations on earth would be threatened by bolshevization, Araki contended that the bolshevization of China would close the door to Japanese and Western business, thereby increasing the economic world crisis, and would lead to anti-Japanese uprisings in Korea and Formosa, cutting Japan off from vital raw materials. Japan was forced, therefore, to take "precautionary measures," the rather because her cities were within bombing range from Vladivostok. The formation of Manchukuo had been such a precautionary measure, the establishment of a steady, prosperous anti-Bolshevik state on the Soviet border serving as an inspiration to the Chinese people.

Likening the spread of Bolshevism in Asia to that of tuberculosis in the human organ, Araki declared that Japan felt it to be her mission to keep Bolshevism out of the Far East and to protect the rest of the moral world from the Red Terror. He advocated a strong line in dealing with Russia, for it was Japan's experience, he said, that the Soviets were audacious when treated mildly, but lost heart when confronted with strong resistance.

Since he viewed Japan's opposition to the Soviet Union as an act on behalf of "mankind and civilization," Araki argued that no international moral pressure should be put on Japan in her dealings with the USSR and that the latter should not be given any moral support by other powers. At the same time he sought the moral assistance of the British for Japan, confident that Bolshevism would be an equal threat to their "sacred tradition, Emperor, Religion, and Morale."[13]

[12] Lindley to Wellesley, Tokyo, April 12, 1934, "Very Confidential," FO 371/18176–776.
[13] Report by Captain Kennedy, Enclosure No. 2 in Lindley to Wellesley, April 12, 1934, "Very Confidential." The above views were contained in a memorandum given to Kennedy by Araki's "man of confidence." Although Araki had sent his son to study in Great Britain, the British were skeptical of Araki's professions

In response to a series of questions by Captain M.D. Kennedy, Araki declared, on one hand, that "Japan must be watching closely and [be] fully prepared for a good opportunity to crush the present Soviet system of Russia," and that on the other hand, "Japan does not plan to start an offensive war against the USSR, the attack must be expected from the USSR side." "It is very important to know that the foreign policy of Russia is not different from that of the time of the Tsar," Araki declared. "It is only the interior constitution that has changed in Russia. The USSR is an active volcano spouting its lava to any direction where there is the least resistance. The USSR, just like in old days Tsarist Russia, will maintain its offensive character."[14]

The British naval attaché commented that naval officers of high standing had expressed to him exactly the same opinions as Araki. "The burden of their song is that Russia must be pushed out of the Maritime Provinces in order that Japan Proper may be completely buffered from Bolshevism." "But," he added, "the Navy definitely does not want war yet for the curious reason that the Navy is intensely jealous of the Army which extracted the naval forces from a nasty hole at Shanghai and then obtained immense prestige with the nation over the Manchurian affair; the Navy got none because there was nothing for the Navy to do." He pointed out that "a Russo-Japanese war would in any event be a military affair and much as the Navy would like to hold Vladivostok, it dislikes the idea of that port being handed to it by the Army."[15]

---

of loyalty. When he argued in support of his contention that Japan had sided with Great Britain in the First World War out of her "deep sense of moral in meeting her pledged obligation" and that "had she been looking only for gain, she could have changed her mind and would have tried to make the best of the confusion in those days," one official scribbled in the margin, "particularly in the event of a German victory!"

[14] "Supplementary Deliberations," communicated by Kennedy, Enclosure No. 3 in Lindley to Kennedy, April 12, 1934, "Very Confidential."

[15] Notes by naval attaché, Enclosure No. 4 in Lindley to Wellesley, April 12, 1934, "Very Confidential."

Araki's views were not changed by Soviet sale of the CER. He continued to oppose the conclusion of a nonaggression pact with the USSR, lest the door be opened to the spread of Communism throughout the Japanese empire. He told Clive in June 1935 that there had been no Communism in Japan before she had renewed her relations with the USSR; then, within two or three years, the seeds of Communism had been found sown in the country. "This could only have been due to Soviet influence," he said. In vain Clive pointed out that the British had put a halt to Soviet subversion by making it clear that they would break off relations if they did not cease, and that the revolutionary zeal in the USSR would eventually fade, as it had in France after the fall of Napoleon.

Yet there was evidence that however genuine the aversion of many Japanese was toward Communism because of its denial of patriotism and its attack on the divine origin of the imperial family and of the Japanese people, the militarists and ultranationalists hoisted the banner of anti-Communism for purposes of their own. In his talk with Kennedy, Araki had admitted that he saw little difference between the USSR and Tsarist Russia. Clive realized (as did Iuren'ev) that "to the military mind a nonaggression pact—the proposal to live in perpetual peace—with her one perpetual enemy is almost inconceivable." "How could the Army continue to maintain its dominating position and where would be the justification for these ever increasing military estimates if Japan grasped the Soviet hand of peace and agreed to abjure warfare as a means of settling her differences?"[16]

In a personal letter to a fellow-diplomat, Shiratori Toshio made it plain that he regarded Russia, not Communism, as the enemy. Declaring that it was fated that "the Slavs and the Yamato race must eventually fight each other for supremacy on the Asiatic continent," he advocated a policy of "instantaneous removal of future calamity" while the Russians were "comparatively impotent." He did not

[16] Clive to Hoare, No. 338, Tokyo, June 29, 1935, FO 371/19347–713.

propose, he asserted, that Japan "unreasonably force a war" against the USSR. "I am only saying that we should start negotiations with her with determination, not refusing even war, if it is inevitable, to shut her out completely from advancing into East Asia." But what were the *minimum* demands that Shiratori wanted Japan to make without "unreasonably" forcing the USSR into war? That Russia give up entirely her subversive activities in East Asia; abolish the defenses of "Vladivostok, etc."; withdraw all her troops from Outer Mongolia, Sinkiang, and even the region east of Lake Baikal; and sell North Sakhalin and the Maritime Province to Japan. "These demands should be made with firm determination," Shiratori wrote. "There would be no possibility of success if we negotiated with such a generous attitude as was done during the negotiations concerning the purchase of the North Manchurian Railway." Realizing no doubt the futility of such demands, Shiratori urged (while admitting that "a diplomat should not talk rashly about such matters") that there be a thorough "liquidation of relations with Soviet Russia" to rid Japan "of the fears and worries from the northwest forever." Regarding the moment of the world depression, when the other powers were preoccupied with internal problems, as the most opportune, he warned that if Japan let this opportunity pass, she would never have another one "to oust the Slav peril forever."[17]

Shiratori urged war with the USSR while anti-Communist feeling was still strong in the United States and Europe. While he wanted to reduce Russia to "a powerless capitalistic republic," others did not wish to lose the Communist bogey. As Tani Masayuki, chief of the Asia Bureau of the Foreign Office had told Baron Harada on July 29, 1933: "It seems advantageous for Japan, from the standpoint of foreign policy, to leave Russia as Red Russia. If it changes to White Russia, the sympathies of the European powers

---

[17] Shiratori to Arita Hachiro, November 1935, Japanese Archives, reel WT 61, IMT document 474, pp. 19–29.

would all be transferred to Russia. It is advisable, in view of Japan's position, for Russia to be hated to a certain degree."[18]

[18] "Saionji-Harada Memoirs," 649–50.

C

THE SOVIET-JAPANESE-AMERICAN TRIANGLE

In February 1932 the publication of two documents aroused Japanese public opinion against the United States. One was a letter from Secretary of State Stimson to Senator William Edgar Borah, chairman of the Senate Foreign Relations Committee, branding Japan by implication as an aggressor and rejecting her proposal for a neutral zone at Shanghai; the other was a resolution by American educators and civic leaders calling for an economic blockade of Japan.[1] As W. Cameron Forbes, the American ambassador, reported from Tokyo, the Japanese regarded Stimson's letter as "distinctly provocative" and an economic boycott, if imposed, as "tantamount to war." "Many of the daily papers are talking now of war, some refer to it as another world war; but it is undeniable that the United States is looked upon as the probable enemy," Forbes cabled.[2] When the United States responded to Manchukuo's proposal for the establishment of diplomatic relations[3] with silence[4] and

---

[1] Forbes to Stimson, No. 79, February 26, 1932.
[2] Forbes to Stimson, No. 83, February 27, 1932.
[3] Hsieh Chieh Shih to Stimson, Changchun, March 12, 1932.
[4] Castle to American embassy in London, No. 113, April 7, 1932.

Acting Secretary of State William R. Castle, Jr., though he denounced the idea of a boycott against any nation, advanced the "Hoover Doctrine," that no territorial gain in violation of the Kellogg Pact should be recognized, as a new keystone of international law,[5] the embers of Japanese hostility were fanned. As Forbes's successor Joseph C. Grew reported, the Japanese army had since September portrayed the Manchurian enterprise to the Japanese public as an idealistic and humanitarian venture. "Failure to recognize would be misunderstood," he warned, "the people having been carefully guarded against any suspicion that the present regime in Changchun was in any sense a puppet government."[6]

When Lindley had sounded out Arita on August 31, 1932, about the possibility of war between Japan and the USSR, the vice minister of foreign affairs had asked with a smile whether there were rumors also of war between Japan and the United States and had expressed agreement with Lindley's assertion that "a Japanese-American war seemed . . . as improbable as a war with Russia."[7]

The American ambassador was not so sure. Reporting that military preparations were continuing steadily, he observed that "the Japanese regard the United States as their greatest stumbling block," while remarking that talk of friction with the Soviet Union was "comparatively quiescent."[8]

Amau Eiji, who was serving as counselor of the Japanese embassy in Moscow, attributed the false rumors about the true state of Soviet-Japanese relations to Duranty of the *New York Times* and to other American correspondents

---

[5] Perkins to Stimson, No. 503, Peiping, May 6, 1932. The Hoover Doctrine was known also as the Stimson Doctrine and as the Nonrecognition Doctrine. It had been enunciated originally by Stimson in identic notes sent to Japan and China on January 7, 1932. (DVP, XVI, 806–807, note 22.)

[6] Grew to Stimson, No. 161, Tokyo, June 20, 1932.

[7] Lindley to Simon, No. 452, Chuzenji, August 31, 1932, FO 371/16246–680.

[8] Grew to Stimson, Tokyo, September 3, 1932. The French chargé d'affaires reported that it would be easier for Japan to affect a reconciliation with the USSR than with the United States. (De Lens to Herriot, No. 415, Tokyo, October 23, 1932, DDT, vol. 1, p. 557.)

in Moscow who were "using the theme of Soviet-Japanese relations as a pawn in the present campaign for recognition of the USSR by the United States of America." They argued, when portraying the Soviet Union and Japan as on the brink of war, that United States recognition of the USSR would strengthen both countries vis-à-vis Japan, or, when portraying the Soviet Union and Japan as in agreement over Manchuria and China, that United States recognition of the USSR would place a restraining hand on the latter.[9]

In an analysis of the difficulties the United States had in conducting foreign policy during the "interregnum" between the election of a new administration and its inauguration, Boris Skvirskii, the unofficial representative of the USSR in Washington, reported on January 28, 1933, that "a whole number of Roosevelt's close advisers in matters of foreign policy, with the exception of Norman Davis, who is close to both administrations, regard the Hoover Doctrine as not only too general, academic and impractical, but also as dangerous, should one uphold it seriously and persistently till the end." It was their belief, Skvirskii wrote to Litvinov, that all that the Hoover administration had accomplished with its policy was to focus the hostility of Japan on the United States and increase the danger of conflict, which everyone in Washington sought to avoid, particularly in view of the inadequacy of the American navy. "To defend 'American interest' that is one thing; to lecture Japan and marshal world opinion against her is another thing. It is easier to reach an agreement in the first instance than in the second." There was awareness, Skvirskii observed, that an all-embracing doctrine could someday be turned against the United States, whose interests in the Far East would be greater in the future. Besides, there were such restraining considerations as the relatively large American trade with Japan, the danger of the Sovietization of China, and the inability, in the face of Roosevelt's pledge to reduce expenditures sharply, to launch at once a large

[9] Strang to Simon, No. 491, Moscow, September 5, 1932, "Confidential," FO 371/16178–665.

naval program. He speculated, therefore, that "Roosevelt will speak more . . . of American interests, the Open Door, [and] the Nine Power Agreement and will strive for a united front against Japan not on the basis of the academic doctrine, which the English, French, and Italians like no more than the Japanese, but on the basis of the Nine Power Agreement and all the other treaties of the Washington Conference." Expecting Roosevelt to be more practical than Hoover, Skvirskii observed that some influential Democrats believed that "the recognition of the USSR would strengthen the position of the United States vis-à-vis Japan as well as vis-à-vis England and France."

Skvirskii related in detail the view of Nathaniel Peffer, published in *Harper Magazine,* that Japanese expansion had been prompted in part by the fear that the Western powers would renew their inroads into China and that the only way to prevent war in the Far East was to halt annexation of Chinese territory by all countries, something the League had refused to consider. Peffer warned against continued application of the Non-Recognition Doctrine, by which the United States had unwittingly shouldered an obligation as binding as the Monroe Doctrine but far more burdensome, for it had made her the defender of the *status quo* in a region where the *status quo* was unavoidably unstable.[10]

Skvirskii added in cables on the twenty-ninth and thirtieth that senior officials of the State Department, feeling deceived by Japan, which had led them to believe that she would not expand beyond Manchuria, and feeling let down by England, France and Italy, which would not join the United States in halting Japan by an economic boycott or war, were watching the reaction of the USSR to the expansion of Japan with great interest. He telegraphed that he had told Senator Borah that American recognition of the Soviet Union at this moment would make the necessary impression on Japan. Borah had agreed, but had expressed

[10] Skvirskii to Litvinov, Washington, January 28, 1933, DVP, XVI, 57–65.

doubt about the statesmanship of President Herbert Hoover.[11]

On February 21, Skvirskii reported that the question of United States recognition of the USSR had not yet been decided definitively. "Senator Borah informed me yesterday," he cabled, "that he had been asked for his advice and that he had replied that America now was in greater need of the USSR than the USSR of America, and that one should recognize the USSR at once by the appointment of an ambassador and negotiate later."[12]

When Ota told Karakhan on February 27 that the meddling of the United States had aroused strong anti-American feeling in Japan, because the Japanese felt that the Far Eastern question was not truly vital for the United States, Karakhan asked whether it was for this reason that Matsuoka in recent press interviews had tried to depict Japan as a bulwark against Communist expansion. Why would the Japanese government and its delegate at the League wish to create an anti-Soviet atmosphere if, as he said, Japan was gripped by anti-American sentiments?

Ota denied that an attack on Communism was an attack on the USSR. Some Japanese were opposed merely to the Sovietization of Manchukuo and felt that such Sovietization could be prevented so long as Manchukuo was in Japanese hands.

Karakhan objected that this was a most dangerous theory, for according to it all strong capitalist countries would have to seize the weaker states bordering on the Soviet Union to prevent their Sovietization—the Germans or the English would have to take the Baltic states; England would have

[11] Slavutskii to Foreign Commissariat, January 29 and 30, 1932, DVP, XV, 69–70 and 71–72. Assistant Secretary of State James Grafton Rogers also expressed doubt that United States recognition of the USSR could occur until Hoover left office. So extreme had the Japanese military become, Rogers added, that he did not think American recognition of the USSR would restrain them from attacking the latter, if they had put their mind to doing so. In Rogers' words, "anything can be expected from them." (Skvirskii to Foreign Commissariat, June 4, 1932, DVP, XV, 351–52.)

[12] Skvirskii to Foreign Commissariat, February 21, 1933, DVP, XVI, 108.

to grab Afghanistan and Persia, etc. Yet no neighbors of the USSR were threatened with Sovietization. "It is sufficient to recall 1929, when the Chinese seized the CER and we had to cross into Manchuria as the result of their attacks on our territory," Karakhan pointed out. "We had the full possibility, and a better possibility than the Japanese have now, to take Northern Manchuria into our hands. We did not do this because this is not our policy. Japan knows this better than any other country; hence, I regard any such explanations as artificial explanations made up for the present situation in the Far East." Waxing sarcastic, Karakhan asked whether Japan had also intended to save Manchuria from Sovietization when she had tried to obtain it by the Twenty-one Demands, presented by her to China in 1915, before the USSR had come into existence?" "We are not at the League of Nations, but in my office, and there is no reason for us to deceive each other," Karakhan continued. "Japan took Manchuria for herself, for her military, political and economic benefits, just as she had wanted to do in 1915." He warned that such arguments as that Manchukuo constituted a barrier to the spread of Communism in China would not gain Japan the support of the United States or anyone else, but would only create a bad impression in the USSR, "which," he remarked, "would in no way contribute to the strengthening of our good-neighborly relations."

Ota admitted that it was fruitless to seek to justify Japanese actions with the argument that Japan was saving the civilized world from the spread of Bolshevism. He thought awhile and then said laughing, half-in-jest: "I sometimes wonder why the Third International needs to spread Communism in all countries. Is such a large country as the USSR not enough for the Third International?" He admitted that Karakhan had repeatedly declared that the Third International and the Soviet government were "different things," but he observed that many foreigners, the Japanese included, did not understand this. Karakhan replied that many foreigners linked the Third International with the USSR in order to arouse anti-Soviet feeling; others made an honest mistake, unable to understand much that was happening in the USSR because it was so different from what was taking place elsewhere.[13]

The prospect of United States recognition of the USSR alarmed a number of Japanese, even though their country had done the same. "In some quarters the view prevails that following better economic relations between America and Russia, the identity of interests in many respects will cause these countries to offer a united front on Far Eastern problems against Japan," the *Japan Weekly Chronicle* reported on February 9 on the basis of an *Asahi* dispatch from Moscow. But the *Asahi* correspondent believed, the *Chronicle* continued, that the Russian authorities, "hold peaceful relations with Japan to be absolutely necessary, despite Russia's future relations with America." "They know full well," he asserted, "that Russo-American cooperation in the political field will incur Japan's ire and the brunt of a collision with Japan will have to be borne by Russia, not by America which lies across the Pacific."[14]

When Ota told Karakhan on February 27 of reports in the Japanese press that the USSR was drawing nearer to the United States in order to attain American recognition, Karakhan retorted: "We are not drawing nearer to anybody, including America. Nor did we draw nearer to China when China wished to reestablish relations with us. The question is put incorrectly. China drew nearer to us, when she under-

[13] Karakhan's record of his conversation with Ota, February 27, 1933, DVP, XVI, 121–33.

[14] JWC, February 9, 1933, p. 199. The French chargé d'affaires in Moscow also believed that Soviet-American collaboration might incite Japan rather than intimidate her. (Jean Payart to Paul-Boncour, telegrams nos. 151–157, Moscow, May 30, 1933, DDF, vol. I, pp. 598–600.) "Relations with the United States are affected reciprocally by relations with Russia," Baron Harada recorded after a conversation with Lt. Col. Suzuki on July 29, 1933. "If there is a single misstep when we attack Russia, relations with the United States will become extremely delicate. . . .The Army said to the Navy, 'Our intention is to attack Russia to the end. We ask the Navy to take thorough care of America.' The Navy had agreed." ("Saionji-Harada Memoirs," 651–52.)

stood that she had acted foolishly and had made a mistake in breaking relations with us. And when China, drawing nearer to us, asked for the resumption of relations, we agreed." Noting that the USSR regarded the absence of diplomatic relations between two countries as abnormal and favored having normal relation with all countries, Karakhan stated that the Soviet Union had unofficial, private word from various sources that there was an increasing number of Americans, including people in the present administration, who admitted that America was mistaken in not having relations with the USSR. "Thus, if America wishes to correct her mistakes, we shall not hinder her doing so; if she wishes to reestablish relations with us, we shall, of course, gladly reestablish normal relations with America."

Ota agreed that it was the United States which wanted to draw near to the USSR. "It would be in America's interest, if relations between the USSR and Japan deteriorated," Ota contended. "You know that the press in America is in the hands of capitalists and they wage special propaganda against Japan," he stated. "They wish to acerbate relations between Japan and the USSR."

When Karakhan asked whether it was true that there was alarm in Japan concerning the possible resumption of diplomatic relations between the Soviet Union and the United States, Ota uttered, "Nothing of the sort." But Karakhan was not convinced and sought to reassure him. He was right, he said, that there were elements in America which wished to impair relations between the USSR and Japan. "But you understand, of course," he declared, "that relations between the USSR and Japan do not depend on what they want in America or any other country. Relations between Japan and the USSR depend on what is desired in the USSR and what is desired in Japan, and only on that."[15]

[15] Karakhan's record of his conversation with Ota, February 27, 1933, DVP, XVI, 121–33. The French ambassador in Moscow reported that it was the ambitions of the Japanese which had given rise in the USSR and the United States

Litvinov's visit to Washington prompted the *Manchuria Daily News* to warn the United States of the danger of recognizing such a state as the USSR. While this was "a remarkable thing for a Japanese paper to do, seeing that Japan is on friendly terms with the Soviet republic and exchanges ambassadors and consuls," the *Japan Weekly Chronicle* commented, the reason was plain enough. "There has been much talk of 'inevitable conflicts' of late in Japan, and these would not be undertaken half so lightheartedly if America and the Soviet [Union] were on friendly terms."[16]

Vice Minister Shigemitsu told Harada on October 19 that he thought the Soviet dispatch of troops to the Far East was due to American instigation. "There are signs of America and Russia getting together. That is, they may act against us in unison both peaceably and militarily."[17]

"I wonder if the time isn't coming when America will recognize Russia and, accompanied by China, will subject Japan to an ordeal just as they did at the Washington Conference," Hirota confided to Harada. "In order that such a situation will never develop, in other words, so that Japan will not be confronted with such a situation, we must act now on Japan's relations with America, China and also Russia. In order to bring the Manchurian problem to a solution, Russia must be handled harmoniously and the existing issues settled. These issues are the Chinese Eastern Railway and armaments."[18]

During his lengthy talk with Slavutskii on November 9, Komatsubara touched on Soviet-American relations. Slavutskii replied that the USSR was conducting an independent policy and was completely independent from anyone and ready, if the adventurous acts against her ceased, to be on friendly terms with Japan; if, on the other hand,

---

to "a certain feeling of solidarity in the face of a common danger." "The Japanese question dominates all others." (Charles Alphand to Paul-Boncour, No. 312, Moscow, November 6, 1933, DDF, First Series, vol. 4, pp. 713–16.)

[16] JWC, October 26, 1933, p. 513.

[17] "Saionji-Harada Memoirs," 719.

[18] *Ibid.*, 722–23.

Japan adopted the plans of the adventurous circles, which were openly discussed in the press, the Soviet Union would be completely free "both in the selection of the means of defense and in the selection of allies." "We do not seek them. On the contrary, we consider friendship with Japan as the best means of preserving peace in the Far East and as the best means of guaranteeing the interests of the workers in the [Soviet] Union and Japan, but when it will be necessary and when we shall be driven to it by the adventurous elements of Japan, we shall find allies everywhere, even in Japan herself."[19]

Transmitting excepts from Molotov's speech to London, Lord Chilston reported that it showed a less conciliatory and more defiant attitude towards Japan, due possibly to hope of recognition by the United States.[20]

In a conversation with Litvinov following the exchange of notes concerning the establishment of diplomatic relations between the United States and the USSR, Roosevelt suggested that the Soviet Union and America exchange information about Japan. "He supposes," Litvinov cabled, "that we need some 10 years to get Siberia ready, particularly to build roads, and America is ready to do everything to avert the Japanese danger from us. America will not fight, as not a single American will go for that, but Roosevelt is prepared to give us moral and diplomatic support 100%."[21]

Japanese fears of Soviet-American cooperation were reflected in a news dispatch from Hsinking that Soviet railway officials were considering the possibility of a temporary transfer of the control and management of the CER to the

---

[19] Slavutskii's record of his conversation with Komatsubara, November 9, 1933, DVP, XVI, 618–20.

[20] Chilston to Foreign Office, No. 622, November 15, 1933, FO 371/17152–858.

[21] Litvinov to Foreign Commissariat, Washington, November 17, 1933, DVP, XVI, 658–60. Roosevelt told Litvinov that while the United States and Great Britain had not built up to the limits set by the Washington Naval Conference, Japan had filled her quota and by building the newest vessels had reached a stage where her fleet could compete with the British navy and had overtaken the American navy.

United States in order to restrain Japanese and Manchukuoan pressure and give the Americans security for investments in the Soviet Far East.[22]

Ambassador Bullitt informed Karakhan on December 13 that according to what the United States had been able to learn, one faction of the Japanese leadership was planning an attack on the Maritime region in February; another faction, also rather influential, similarly favored an attack on the Maritime region but had not decided when. Bullitt thought that it might be possible to avert war, though there was a 40 percent chance that the Japanese would attack the Soviet Union in spring. Bullitt and Karakhan agreed that the restoration of diplomatic relations between their countries was bound to have a moderating effect on the Japanese.

Bullitt related that Japan had proposed to the United States the conclusion of a nonaggression pact, but that Washington had rejected the proposal, for had there been negotiations concerning such a pact, the Americans would have had to point out that Japan had already violated the Kellogg Pact and must withdraw her forces from Manchuria before the United States could sign a nonaggression pact. The Japanese, on the other hand, would want to extend the pact to Manchukuo, to which the United States could not agree. (In his record of the conversation Karakhan noted parenthetically that Litvinov had reported that Roosevelt had instructed Bullitt to investigate the idea of a pact between Japan, the USSR, and the United States, but that Bullitt's remarks now showed that he had found the idea impractical.)

Bullitt stressed that the United States did not want war with Japan, nor did she fear it, as neither side had anything to gain from it. "What would we gain," he asked, "if our navy could freely sail around the Japanese islands?"

Karakhan recorded that Bullitt had communicated to him "a curious detail," whose veracity must be left "completely

[22] JWC, December 7, 1933.

on his conscience." Roosevelt, Bullitt asserted, had not sent a message to President Mikhail Kalinin as soon as he had decided to do so, for fear that the Japanese might attempt to thwart the restoration of relations with the USSR; Roosevelt and he himself had feared in particular that the Japanese might send their fleet to Vladivostok. The message to Kalinin had been delayed until the Soviet port had been protected from the Japanese navy by a shield of ice.[23]

In a conversation with Molotov, Bullitt repeated that the United States was prepared to offer to the Soviet Union "every moral support" for the prevention of war in the Far East. When Molotov stated that it was very important for the American and Soviet governments to keep each other informed of circumstances that might impede the preservation of peace, Bullitt agreed wholeheartedly. "I must tell you of one disappointment that we recently experienced," he added. "We have become absolutely convinced that every time that our ambassador in London shares any information with Sir John Simon, this information appears totally and fully at the disposal of the Japanese. The English make use of this to give the Japanese evidence of their friendship toward them. I am telling you this so that you would see how one should not trust English diplomacy. Here, for a start, is the first information from me."

Molotov thanked Bullitt playfully.

The American ambassador realized that peace was all-important for the USSR. "Fifteen years of peace," he said, "and you will hold the whole world in your hands."

Molotov and Bullitt agreed that had the United States recognized the USSR a couple of years earlier, "events would have developed differently and the Japanese would not have become so impudent."[24]

[23] Karakhan's record of his conversation with Bullitt, December 13, 1933, DVP, XVI, 744–45.

[24] E. V. Rubinin's record of Molotov's conversation with Bullitt, December 15, 1933, DVP, XVI, 748–51.

In another conversation with Litvinov on December 21, Bullitt said that it would be difficult for the United States to conclude a nonaggression pact with the USSR after having rejected such a pact with Japan. The United States could not agree to a four power pact between the United States, the Soviet Union, Japan, and China without insisting on the immediate withdrawal of Japanese forces from Manchuria, whose occupation she regarded as aggression. The offer of a new pact might suggest that the United States was changing her position. Litvinov expressed doubt that even a three power pact (between the Soviet Union, the United States, and Japan) would be acceptable to Japan, but that such a proposal would have great propaganda value, as its refusal by Japan would underline her aggressive intentions.[25]

On February 23, 1934, Roosevelt asked Troianovskii whether he did not find that the Japanese had changed their tone lately and sought his view of their foreign policy.

> I told him [Troianovskii cabled to Stalin and Molotov], that I personally am relatively optimistic concerning the current year and very pessimistic about the future. I argued that at present the Japanese would try to improve their relations both with the United States and with us, because their policy for the immediate future consists in securing their position in Manchuria and in subjugating China as much as possible. . . . Roosevelt said that I was probably right, that the Japanese were conducting propaganda against the whites in Asia and were continuing their activity in China. In his opinion it will be very difficult next year. The United States cannot agree that Japan have a fleet equal to the American fleet, whose units are divided into the Atlantic [fleet] and the Pacific [fleet]. I told him that it would not be easy to restrain Japan and diminish her appetite. Japan will not listen either to America alone or to the USSR alone, but she will listen to the two together even at the last moment; therefore, we must maintain contact.[26]

[25] Litvinov's record of his conversation with Bullitt, December 21, 1933, DVP, XVI, 758–61.

[26] Troianovskii to Central Committee of Communist Party, addressed to Stalin and Molotov, February 23, 1934, DVP, XVII, 163–64.

The Soviet-American rapprochement enormously increased Japanese apprehension of the Soviet "menace." Rumors abounded that an air service would be instituted between Kamchatka and Alaska and that the Soviet authorities were considering American overtures for oil and other concessions on Sakhalin and in the Maritime Province. "The Soviet authorities have repeatedly denied the authenticity of such rumors, and it is probable that there has not been any such talk between Moscow and Washington," Fuse Katsuji wrote. "Nevertheless . . . what is impossible today may become quite possible tomorrow, if other circumstances breed more ill-blood between Tokyo and Moscow."[27]

On March 14 Bullitt told Litvinov that according to information obtained by the United States, Japan would not attack the Soviet Union that spring, partly because Japan feared the military preparations made by the USSR, partly because she feared American intervention in the war. But as one Japanese (Chargé d'Affaires Taketomi Toshihiko) had told him in Washington, some Japanese commander in Manchuria could suddenly send his forces across the Amur River and present his government with the *fait accompli* of war with the USSR. Bullitt told Litvinov that the Japanese were still trying to conclude a nonaggression pact with the United States, but that Roosevelt intended to propose to them the inclusion of the USSR and China in the pact without recognizing Manchukuo. He also spoke of the possibility of a Pacific pact of nonaggression, embracing the United States, Great Britain, France, Holland, the USSR, China and Japan, but when Litvinov asked whether the United States planned to make such a proposal to the Pacific powers, Bullitt did not give an "intelligible answer." "Bullitt did not impart anything interesting," Litvinov wrote to Troianovskii, "nonetheless it became clear that America does not intend to come forth with any new proposals on her own initiative."[28]

[27] JWC, March 15, 1934, pp. 354–55, reprinted from *Contemporary Japan*.
[28] Litvinov to Troianovskii, March 14, 1934, DVP, XVII, 179–82.

On March 18 and on March 21 Litvinov continued his conversation with Bullitt.[29] Bullitt repeated that Roosevelt was against bilateral nonaggression pacts, but was willing to consider a multilateral Pacific nonaggression pact. He made it clear, however, that Roosevelt was not prepared to propose such a pact, merely "to throw out the idea" for someone else to pick up. "In Bullitt's opinion," Litvinov recorded, "Japan is most impressed by what is said simultaneously from both sides of the Pacific Ocean and a declaration that will be made by us in Moscow and at the same time by Roosevelt in Washington cannot but have a great effect in Japan."[30]

The British were skeptical of American assistance in the restraint of Japan. "America has never done anything in the Far East but talk, and nothing follows, and I doubt if anything ever will," Clive opined. "If the Soviet is counting on American support in the event of serious trouble with Japan she is, I believe, leaning on a broken reed, as we should be if we were to stand in against Japan too solidly with America."[31] Sir Robert Craigie had a similar view of current American policy. "As things are at present it is of course impossible to count on the United States; the normal degree of unreliability is today enhanced by a foreign policy impregnated with indecision and nurtured in ignorance." "But I believe," he prophesied, "that the present phase of defeatism in respect of Japanese aggression in the region of the Eastern Pacific is likely to be a passing one and that there is more than an even chance that the United States would resist by force of arms an overt Japanese attack upon the Dutch East Indies—if only because of the future implications for the United States in the success of such a stroke by Japan."[32]

[29] On March 14 Litvinov, who was ill, had received Bullitt in his apartment, in bed; on the eighteenth and twenty-first he received him in the hospital.

[30] Litvinov's record of his conversation with Bullitt, March 18 and 21, 1934, DVP, XVII, 193–95.

[31] Clive to Wellesley, Tokyo, January 16, 1935, "Private and Confidential," FO 371/19347–713.

[32] Minutes, July 6, 1933, regarding Admiral Dickens to Orde, No. M. 00540/34, May 22, 1924, FO 371/18186–916.

Bibliography

A. V., "Ob opasnosti voiny na Dal'nem Vostoke" [Regarding the danger of war in the Far East], *Tikhookeanskii kommunist,* Khabarovsk, 1934, no. 2–3, pp. 35–46.

Ajia Kyokai [Asia Society]. *Japanese Fisheries, Their Development and Present Status.* Second edition. Tokyo, 1960.

Akagi, Roy Hidemichi. *Japan's Foreign Relations.* Tokyo: Hokuseido, 1936.

Alekseev, I. *Chto proiskhodit na K.-V. zh. d.* [What is happening on the Chinese Eastern Railway]. Khabarovsk, 1929.

Aoki, Senri. "Nichi-Ro fushinryaku kyotei teiketsu ron" [Controversy over the conclusion of a Russo-Japanese nonaggression pact], *Gaiko jiho,* 1932, no. 4, pp. 34–45.

Aprelev, V. "America and Japan in the Pacific," *Oriental Affairs,* vol. 1, no. 2 (Shanghai, January 1934). (Typescript in Aprelev Archive of the American Society for Russian Naval History.)

Asik, M. *Vooruzhennye sily Iaponii. Spravochnik* [The armed forces of Japan. Reference book]. Moscow, 1934.

Bakhmetieff, Boris A. "The Issue in Manchuria," *The Slavonic and East European Review,* vol. 8, no. 23 (December 1929), pp. 305–14.

Balakshin, Petr. *Final v Kitae. Vozniknovenie, razvitie i ischeznovenie Beloi Emigratsii na Dal'nem Vostoke*

[Finale in China. The appearance, development and disappearance of the White (Russian) Emigration in the Far East]. San Francisco: Knigoizdatel'stov Sirius, 1958. 2 vols.

Barnes, Kathleen. "Japanese-Soviet friction," *Far Eastern Survey*, vol. 4, no. 19 (September 25, 1935), pp. 148–52.

Beckmann, George M. and Okubo Genji. *The Japanese Communist Party 1922–1945*. Stanford: Stanford University Press, 1969.

Beloff, Max. *The Foreign Policy of Soviet Russia, 1929–1941*. Vol. I (1929–1936). London: Oxford University Press, 1947.

Bennett, Edwin Moore. "Franklin D. Roosevelt and Russian-American Relations, 1933–1939." MS, doctoral dissertation, University of Illinois, 1961.

Berton, Peter, Paul Langer and Rodger Swearingen. *Japanese Training and Research in the Russian Field*. Los Angeles: University of Southern California Press, 1956.

Bessedovsky, Grigory. *Revelations of a Soviet Diplomat*. London: Williams and Norgate, 1931.

Bilibin, J. "Soviet Russia and Japan," *The Nineteenth Century and After*, July 1932, pp. 50–59.

Bisson, Thomas Arthur, "Soviet-Japanese Relations, 1931–1938," *Foreign Policy Reports*, vol. 14, no. 22 (February 1, 1939), pp. 258–72.

Boldyrev, Prof. G. I. "Dal'nevostochnyi krai. (Ekonomicheskii ocherk)" [Far Eastern region. (Economic survey)], *Tikhii Okean* 1935, no. 2, pp. 155–58.

Boorman, Howard L. and Richard C. Howard (eds.). *Biographical Dictionary of Republican China*. New York: Columbia University Press, 1967–71. 4 vols.

Borg, Dorothy. *The United States and the Far Eastern Crisis of 1933–1938*. Cambridge, Mass.: Harvard University Press, 1964.

Borisov, O. B. and B. T. Koloskov. *Sovetsko-kitaiskie otnosheniia 1945–1970* [Soviet-Chinese relations 1945–1970]. Moscow: Mysl', 1972.

Borodin, B. A. *Pomoshch SSSR kitaiskomu narodu v antiiaponskoi voine 1937–1941* [Assistance of the USSR to the Chinese people in the anti-Japanese war 1937–1941]. Moscow: Mysl', 1965.

Borton, Hugh. *Japan's Modern Century*. Second edition. New York: Ronald Press, 1970.

Brandt, Conrad. *Stalin's Failure in China, 1924–1927*. Cambridge, Mass.: Harvard University Press, 1958.

Budkevich, Sergei Leonidovich. "Razvitie iaponoameri-kanskikh protivorechii na Dal'nem Vostoke v 1931–1941 gg." [Development of Japanese-American contradictions in the Far East in 1931–1941]. MS, doctoral dissertation, Institut Vostokovedeniia Akademii Nauk SSSR (Moscow), 1953.

Butlitskii, E. and D. Teplov. *Voennaia ugroza na Dal'nem Vostoke. Chto proiskhodit na Sovetsko-kitaiskoi granitse* [War threat in the Far East. What is happening on the Soviet-Chinese frontier]. Moscow: GIZ, 1929.

Carr, Harry. *Riding the Tiger*. Boston: Houghton Mifflin, 1934.

Castle, William R., Jr. "Castle Papers. Sino-Japanese Incident." MS, Herbert Hoover Presidential Library.

Chamberlain, William Henry. *Japan over Asia*. Boston: Little, Brown, 1938.

Chang, Tao Shing. "International Controversies over the Chinese Eastern Railway," MS, doctoral dissertation, University of Iowa, August 1934.

Chang, Yüan-fu. *Chung-Su wen-t'i* [Sino-Soviet problems]. Shanghai: Commercial Press, 1937.

Ch'en, Po-wen. *Chung-O wai-chiao shih* [A history of Sino-Russian diplomatic relations]. Shanghai: Commercial Press, 1929–1931.

Cheng, Tien-fong. *A History of Sino-Russian Relations*. Washington: Public Affairs Press, 1957.

China. Ministry of Foreign Affairs. *Documents with Reference to the Sino-Russian Dispute, 1929*. Nanking, 1929.

"China's Case Against Soviet Russia: Evidences of Communist Conspiracies," *Chinese Social and Political Sci-*

ence Review, vol. 13, no. 4 (October 1929), Public Documents Supplement, pp. 131–58.

Christopher, James William. *Conflict in the Far-East. American Diplomacy in China 1928–1933.* Leiden: Brill, 1950.

Chu, Pao-chin. "V. K. Wellington Koo: A Study of the Diplomat and Diplomacy of Warlord China, During His Early Career, 1919–1924," MS, doctoral dissertation, University of Pennsylvania, 1970.

Clark, Grover. "The Sale of the Chinese Eastern," *Current History,* vol. 42, May 1935, pp. 221–23.

Clayberg, Anna Marie Anderson. "Soviet Policy Toward Japan, 1923–1941." MS, doctoral dissertation, University of California, 1962.

Clubb, O. Edmund. *China and Russia: The "Great Game."* New York: Columbia University Press, 1971.
———. *Twentieth Century China.* New York: Columbia University Press, 1964.

Clyde, Paul Hibbert. "Manchuria and Siberia: 1918. Diplomatic Backgrounds," *Contemporary Japan,* vol. 3, no. 1 (June 1934), pp. 51–65.

Condliffe, J. B. (ed.). *Problems of the Pacific 1929.* Chicago: University of Chicago Press, 1930.

Current, Richard. "The Hoover Doctrine and the Stimson Doctrine," *The American Historical Review,* vol. 59, no. 3 (April 1954), pp. 512–42.

Dallin, David J. *Soviet Russia and the Far East.* New Haven: Yale University Press, 1948.

Dean, Vera Micheles. "The Soviet Union and Japan in the Far East," *Foreign Policy Reports,* vol. 8, no. 12 (August 17, 1932), pp. 136–46.

Demidov, A. P. *Sovremennyi Kitai i Rossiia* [Contemporary China and Russia]. Paris: Librairie "La Source," 1931.

Diplomaticheskii slovar' [Diplomatic dictionary]. Moscow: Politizdat, 1971. 3 vols.

Dirksen, Herbert von. *Die Wechselwirkung zwischen Aussenpolitik und Strategie in Japan von 1931–1941, von Botschafter z.v. dr. von Dirksen* [The correlative effect of foreign policy and strategy in Japan from 1931–1941, by Ambassador von Dirksen]. Heidelberg: Heidelberger Institut für politische Auslandskunde, 1941(?).

"Dogovor SSSR s Kitaem. Soglashenie ob obshchem printsipe dlia uregulirovaniia voprosov mezhdu SSSR i Kitaiskoi respublikoi, zakliuchenoe v Pekine 31/V 1925g." [Treaty of the USSR with China. Agreement of a common principle for the regulating of questions between the USSR and the Chinese republic, concluded in Peking on May 31, 1925], *Mezhdunarodnaia letopis* 1925, no. 3, pp. 21–30.

Doi, Akira. "Shina no genjo to Sovietto kuiki no mondai" [The present condition of China, and the problem of the frontier with the Soviet Union], *Gaiko jiho,* vol. 62, no. 5 (June 1932), pp. 122–130.

Dorfman, Ben. "White Russians in the Far East. Would they join in a war against the Soviet Union?" *Asia,* March 1935, 166–72.

Doronin, M. *Zakhvat Kitaisko-Vostochnoi zheleznoi dorogi* [The seizure of the Chinese Eastern Railway]. Novosibirsk, 1929.

Eidus, Khaim Tevel. *Iaponiia ot Pervoi do Vtoroi Mirovoi Voiny* (Japan from the First to the Second World War). Moscow: Izdatel'stvo Politicheskoi Literatury, 1946.

Erickson, John. *The Soviet High Command: A Military-Political History.* New York: St. Martin's Press, 1962.

Escarra, Jean. *Le Conflit Sino-Japonais et la Société des Nations.* Paris: Conciliation Internationale, 1933.

Etherton, Colonel P. T. and H. Hessell Tiltman. *Manchuria: The Cockpit of Asia.* London: Jarrolds Publishers, 1932.

Eudin, Xenia Joukoff and Robert C. North. *Soviet Russia*

and the East 1920–1927. A Documentary Survey. Stanford: Stanford University Press, 1957.

Ferrell, Robert H. *American Diplomacy in the Great Depression: Hoover-Stimson Foreign Policy, 1929–1933.* New Haven: Yale University Press, 1957.

Filippovich, K. "Sovetskie i kitaiskie shkoly na KVzhd" [Soviet and Chinese schools on the Chinese Eastern Railway]. *Vestnik Man'chzhurii* 1926, no. 5, pp. 27–39.

Fischer, Ruth. *Stalin and German Communism.* Cambridge: Harvard University Press, 1948.

Foreign Policy Association. "The Chinese Eastern Railway," *Foreign Policy Association Information Service,* vol. 2, no. 1 (February 27, 1926).

France, Ministry of Foreign Affairs, Commission de Publication des Documents Relatifs aux Origines de la Guerre. *Documents Diplomatiques Français 1932–1939.* First Series (1932–1935). Paris: Imprimerie Nationale, 1966–1970. 5 vols.

Fuji, Tatsuma. "Nisso fushinryaku joyaku no igi" [The meaning of a Soviet-Japanese nonaggression pact], *Gaiko jiho,* vol. 64, No. 3 (December 1932), pp. 133–146.

———. "So-Man kankei no ittembo" [A prospect of Soviet-Manchurian relations], *Gaiko jiho,* vol. 63, No. 6 (September 15, 1932), pp. 154–64.

Funaoka, Seigo. *Japan im Sternbild Ostasiens* [Japan in the constellation of East Asia]. Tokyo, 1941–42. 2 vols.

Furaev, Viktor Konstantinovich. *Sovetsko-amerikanskie otnosheniia, 1917–1939* [Soviet-American Relations, 1917–1939], Moscow: Mysl', 1964.

Gaimusho Hyakunen-shi Hensan I-inkai (comp.). *Gaimusho no hyakunen* [A century of the Foreign Office]. Tokyo: Harashobo, 1969. 2 vols.

Gamazkov, K. A. *Iz istorii rasprostraneniia marksizma-leninizma v Iaponii (1932–1938 gg.)* [From the history of the dissemination of Marxism-Leninism in Japan (1932–1938)]. Moscow: Nauka, 1971.

Georgiev, Iu V. "Bor'ba kommunisticheskoi partii Iaponii

za revoliutsionnyi put' razvitiia Iaponskogo profes-
sional'nogo dvizheniia (1922–1928 g.g.)'' [The struggle
of the Communist Party of Japan for the revolutionary
way of development of the Japanese trade union movement (1922–1928)],'' MS, doctoral dissertation, Moscow
State University, 1954.

Gilbert, Lucien. *Dictionnaire Historique et Géographic de
la Mandchourie*. Hongkong: Imprimerie de la Société
des Missions-Étrangères, 1934.

Gilbert, Carl L., Jr. "The Hirota Ministries: An Appraisal.
Japan's Relations with China and the USSR, 1933–1938."
MS, doctoral dissertation, Georgetown University, 1967.

Gladstern, Alexander. "Der Kampf um die Chinesische
Osteisenbahn" [The fight for the Chinese Eastern Rail-
way], *Ost-Europa,* vol. 4, no. 1 (October 1928), pp. 1–20.

Glushakov, P. I. *Man'chzhuriia. Ekonomiko-geografi-
cheskoe opisanie* [Manchuria. Economic geographical
description]. Moscow: OGIZ, 1948.

Graham, Malborne Watson. "A Decade of Sino-Russian
Diplomacy," *The American Political Science Review,*
vol. 22, no. 1 (February 1928), pp. 45–69.

Gorshenin, I. *Man'chzhuriia i ugroza Iapono-Ameri-
kanskoi voiny* [Manchuria and the threat of a Japanese-
American war]. Moscow: Partiinoe izdatel'stvo,
1933.

Great Britain, Foreign Office Archives.

Grew, Joseph C. *Ten Years in Japan*. New York: Simon
and Schuster, 1944.

Hanaoka Shiro. "Sovieto Yunion to Manshu mondai" [The
Soviet Union and the Manchurian problem], *Gaiko jiho,*
vol. 63, no. 6 (September 15, 1932), pp. 38–53.

Hata, Ikuhiko. "Reality and Illusion. The Hidden Crisis
between Japan and the USSR 1932–1934," *Occasional
Papers of the East Asian Institute*. New York: Columbia
University, 1957.

Hauser, Ernst Otto. *Gefährlicher Osten* [Dangerous East].
Zürich, 1935.

Hayashi Nobuo. "Rono Rokoku sekka senden no shinso

to waga taisaku" [The truth about the Red propaganda of the Workers and Peasants of Russia and our counter-policy], *Gaiko jiho,* vol. 51, no. 2 (July 15, 1929), pp. 85–116; no. 4 (August 15, 1929), pp. 83–105.

————. "To-Shi Tetsudo wo chushin to suru Ro-Shi funso" [Russo-Chinese conflict centering about the Chinese Eastern Railway], *Gaiko jiho,* vol. 53, no. 6 (March 15, 1930), pp. 74–92.

Heller, Otto. *Die rote Fahne am Pacific. Zehn Jahre Sowjetmacht im Fernen Osten* [The red flag on the Pacific. Ten years of Soviet power in the Far East]. Moscow, 1933.

Hirai Tomoyoshi. "Manshu jihen to Nisso kankei" [The Manchurian Incident and Japanese-Soviet relations], in Nihon Kokusai Seiji Gakkai (comp.). *Nichi-Ro Nisso kankei no tenkai* [The development of Japanese-Russian and Japanese-Soviet relations](Tokyo, 1966), 99–113.

Hiratake Denzo. "Man-So kokkyo mondai to gaiko kosho" [Manchukuo-Soviet border problems and their diplomatic negotiation], *Gaiko jiho,* No. 5 (March 1937), pp. 49–59.

Hirooka, Mitsuharu. "Nichi-Ro kankei no seicho" [Furthering Russo-Japanese relations], *Gaiko jiho,* vol. 59, no. 2 (July 15, 1931), pp. 118–128.

Hirota Koki Denki Kanko-kai (comp.). *Hirota Koki.* Tokyo, 1966.

Ho, Han-wen. *Chung O wai chiao chih* (History of Chinese-Russian foreign relations). Shanghai: Chung Hua Bookstores, 1936.

Hoetzch, Otto. "Der Konflikt zwischen Russland und China [The conflict between Russia and China]. *Ost Europa,* vol. 4 (Berlin, 1928–29), pp. 727–41.

Holcombe, Arthur N. "Japanese and Russian Interests," *Current History,* vol. 35, December 1931, pp. 345–50.

Hornbeck, Stanley K. "American Policy and the Chinese-Russian Dispute," *Chinese Social and Political Science Review,* vol. 14, January, 1930.

Hoshida Nobutaka. *Ro-Shi kokkyo fusa to to-shi oyobi man-tetsu ni oyobosu eikyo* [The blockade of the Russian and Chinese frontiers and its effect upon the Chinese Eastern and South Manchurian Railways]. Dairen: South Manchurian Railway, 1929.

Hosokawa Kameichi. *Kindai Nihon gaikoshi kenkyu* [Studies in modern Japanese diplomatic history]. Tokyo, 1942.

Houang, Tchang-sin. *Le Problème du Chemin de Fer Chinois de l'Est* [The problem of the Chinese Eastern Railway]. Paris: Les Écrivains Réunis, 1927.

Hsü, Immanuel C. Y. *The Rise of Modern China.* New York: Oxford University Press, 1970.

Hudson, G. F. *The Far East in World Politics.* Oxford, 1937.

Hudson, Manley O. *The Verdict of the League. China and Japan in Manchuria.* The official documents with notes and an introduction. Boston: World Peace Foundation, 1933.

Iavdynskii, J. *The Chinese-Eastern Railway Problem in Contemplation of Law.* Shanghai, 1934.

Ichikawa Tagui. *To-Shi tetsudo kaisha gaiyo* [Sketch of the Chinese Eastern Railway Company]. Dairen: South Manchurian Railway, 1929.

Inozemtsev, N. *Vneshniaia politika SShA v epokhu imperializma* [The foreign policy of the United States in the age of imperialism]. Moscow: Gospolitizdat, 1960.

Ioffe, A. E. *Internatsional'nye, nauchnye i kul'turnye sviazi Sovetskogo Soiuza 1928–1932* [International, scholarly and cultural contacts of the Soviet Union 1928–1932]. Moscow: Nauka, 1969.

Istoriia diplomatii [History of diplomacy]. Second edition. Vol. 3. Moscow: Gospolitizdat, 1965.

Istoriia voiny na Tikhom okeane [History of the Pacific War; translation of *Taihei-yo senso-shi*]. vols. 1 and 2. Moscow: Izdatel'stvo inostrannoi literatury, 1957.

Ivanov, S. *V bor'be za mir. O Krasnoznamennoi Dal'nevos-*

tochnoi [In the struggle for peace. About the Red-banner Far Eastern (Army)]. Khabarovsk, 1930.

Ivanov, V. and V. Leonian. *V interesakh narodov. K voprosu ob ustanovlenii diplomaticheskikh otnoshenii mezhdu SSSR i SShA v 1933 g.* [In the interest of the peoples. Regarding the question of the establishment of diplomatic relations between the USSR and the United States in 1933]. Moscow, 1957.

Ivin, Aleksei. *Kitai i Sovetskii Soiuz* [China and the Soviet Union]. Moscow, 1925.

Izvestiia. 1919–35.

Japan, Foreign Office, O-A Kyoku. *Nisso kosho-shi* [History of negotiations between Japan and the Soviet Union]. Compiled by Tanaka Bunichiro. Tokyo, 1942, classified "Secret"; declassified and reprinted 1969.

Japan, Foreign Office (comp.). *Nihon gaiko nempyo narabi ni shuyo bunsho* [Chronology and main documents of Japanese foreign relations]. Tokyo, 1965. 2 vols.

Japan, Foreign Office Archives, 1868–1945. Microfilmed for the Library of Congress, Washington, D.C., 1949–1951.

Japan, National Diet Library, Chosa Oyobi Rippo Kosa Kyoku. *Nisso kokko chosei mondai kiso shiryo-shu* [Collected basic materials for the study of Japanese-Soviet diplomatic relations]. Tokyo, 1955.

Japan, Toa Keizai Chosakyoku [East-Asiatic Economic Investigation Bureau]. *The Manchuria Year Book 1931.* Second Edition. Tokyo, 1931.

Japan Advertiser.

Japan Weekly Chronicle. 1929–1935.

Jones, F. C. *Manchuria Since 1931.* New York: Oxford University Press, 1949.

Kaji, Ryuichi. "Nisso fushinryaku joyaku seiritsu e no michi" [A way to the establishment of Soviet-Japanese nonaggression pact], *Kaizo,* vol. 14, no. 12 (December 1932).

Kaji, Takaichi. "Manshukoku no shutsugen to rono rempo

no taido" [The appearance of the Manchurian state and the attitude of the Soviet Union], *Chuo koron,* vol. 47, no. 5 (Tokyo, May 1932), pp. 147–58.

Kajima Morinosuke. *Teikoku gaiko no kihon seisaku* [Fundamental Foreign Policy of the Japanese Empire]. Tokyo, 1938.

Kantorovich, Anatolii. *Amerika v borbe za Kitai* [America in the struggle for China]. Moscow: Sotsekgiz, 1935.

Kapitsa, Mikhail Stepanovich. *Sovetsko-kitaiskie otnosheniia v 1931–1945 gg.* [Soviet-Chinese relations in 1931–1945]. Moscow: Gospolitizdat, 1956.

———. *Sovetsko-kitaiskie otnosheniia* [Soviet-Chinese relations]. Moscow: Gospolitizdat, 1958.

Kasai, Jiuji G. *The United States and Japan in the Pacific. American Naval Maneuvers End Japan's Pacific Policy.* Tokyo: Kokusai Press, 1935.

Kawakami, K. K. "A Japanese Journalist Looks at Soviet Russia," *Contemporary Japan,* vol. 3, no. 4 (March 1935), pp. 624–35.

———. "The Russo-Chinese Conflict in Manchuria," *Foreign Affairs,* vol. 8, no. 1 (October 1929), pp. 52–69.

Kellock, H. "The USSR and the Chinese Eastern Railway," *Nation,* August 7, 1929, pp. 140–41.

Kennan, George F. *The Decision to Intervene.* Princeton: Princeton University Press, 1958.

Kennedy, Malcolm Duncan. *A History of Communism in East Asia.* New York: Praeger, 1957.

Khardzhiev, N. *Osobaia Dal'nevostochnaia* [The Special Far Eastern (Army)]. Moscow, 1930.

Kingman, Harry L. *Effects of Chinese Nationalism upon Manchurian Railway Development, 1925–1931.* (Vol. 3, no. 1 of *University of California Publications in International Relations.*) Berkeley, September 8, 1932.

Kitaiskaia vostochnaia zheleznaia doroga. K sobytiiam 1929 goda [The Chinese Eastern Railway. Regarding the events of 1929]. Khabarovsk, 1929.

Kokushi dai-nempyo [Large chronology of Japanese his-

512   THE DAMNED INHERITANCE

tory]. Tokyo: Heibonsha, 1940–41. 9 vols.
Kommunisticheskaia akademiia, Institut mirovogo khoziaistva i mirovoi politiki, Kolonial'nyi sektor. *Okupatsiia Manchzhurii i bor'ba imperialistov* [The occupation of Manchuria and the struggle of the imperialists]. Moscow: Partizdat, 1932.
Komuro Makoto. "Nichi-Ro-Man no fushinryaku joyaku ron" (Discussion of a Japanese-Russian-Manchukuoan nonaggression pact), *Gaiko jiho,* vol. 64, no. 3 (November 1932), pp. 68–82.
Konev, N. *Na sovetsko-kitaiskoi granitse* [On the Soviet-Chinese border]. Moscow, 1930.
Kostarev, Nikolai A. *Granitsa na zamke. (Ob ODVA)* [The border under lock and key. (Concerning the Special Far Eastern Army)]. Moscow: Molodaia gvardiia, 1930.
Kreitner, Gustav, Ritter von. *Hinter China steht Moskau* (Behind China stands Moscow). Berlin, 1932.
Kulagin, Vladimir Mikhailovich and Nikolai Nikolaevich Iakovlev. *Podvig Osoboi Dal'nevostochnoi* [Campaign of the Special Far Eastern (Army)]. Moscow: Molodaia gvardiia, 1970.
Kutakov, Leonid N. *Istoriia sovetsko-iaponskikh diplomaticheskikh otnoshenii* [History of Soviet-Japanese diplomatic relations]. Moscow: Izdatel'stvo Instituta mezhdunarodnykh otnoshenii, 1962.
———. *Portsmutskii mirnyi dogovor 1905–1945* [The Portsmouth Peace Treaty 1905–1945]. Moscow: Izdatel'stvo sotsial'no-ekonomicheskoi literatury, 1961.
Kyozawa Kiyoshi. *Gaiko-shi* [History of foreign relations]. Tokyo, 1941.
L., J. "Die Sowjetgefangenen in Harbin" [The Soviet prisoners in Harbin], *Ostasiatische Rundschau,* no. 23 (December 1, 1929), pp. 663–64.
Langer, Paul F. *Communism in Japan. A Case of Political Naturalization.* Stanford: Hoover Institution Press, 1972.
Lattimore, Owen. *Manchuria Cradle of Conflict.* Revised edition. New York: Macmillan, 1935.

―――. "Russo-Japanese relations," *International Affairs,* vol. 15 (July 1936), pp. 525–537.

Latyshev, I. *Vnutrennaia politika iaponskogo imperializma nakanune voiny na Tikhom okeane 1931–1941* [The foreign policy of Japanese imperialism on the eve of the Pacific War 1931–1941]. Moscow, 1955.

League of Nations. *Official Journal.* Geneva, 1929–1935.

Lebedev, Dm. "Nankinskie napoleonchiki" [The little Napoleons of Nanking], *Iunyi Kommunist,* 1929, no. 19, pp. 10–15.

Lensen, George Alexander. "Japan and Manchuria: Ambassador Forbes' Appraisal of American Policy Toward Japan in the Years 1931–32," *Monumenta Nipponica* 1968, vol. 23, no. 1–2, pp. 66–89.

―――. *Japanese Recognition of the USSR: Soviet-Japanese Relations, 1921–1930.* Tallahassee: Diplomatic Press, 1970.

―――. "The Russian Impact on Japan," in Wayne S. Vucinich (ed.), *Russia and Asia. Essays on the Influence of Russia on the Asian Peoples* (Stanford: Hoover Institution Press, 1972), pp. 338–68 and 457–65.

―――. (ed). *Russia's Eastward Expansion.* Englewood Cliffs, N.J.: Prentice-Hall, 1964.

―――. *The Russo-Chinese War.* Tallahassee: Diplomatic Press, 1967.

―――. *The Strange Neutrality: Soviet-Japanese Relations during the Second World War, 1941–1945.* Tallahassee: Diplomatic Press, 1972.

―――. "Yalta and the Far East," in John L. Snell (ed.), *The Meaning of Yalta: Big Three Diplomacy and the New Balance of Power* (Baton Rouge: Louisiana State University Press, 1956), pp. 127–66.

Leshko, O. *Russkie v Man'chzhugo* [Russians in Manchukuo]. Shanghai, 1937.

Levi, Werner. *Modern China's Foreign Policy.* Minneapolis: University of Minnesota Press, 1953.

Li, Dun J. *The Ageless Chinese, A History.* New York:

514 THE DAMNED INHERITANCE

Charles Scribner's Sons, 1965.

Li, Ping-jui (Edward Bing-Shuey Lee). *Two Years of the Japan-China Undeclared War and the Attitude of the Powers.* Second edition. Shanghai: Mercury Press, 1933.

Liang, Chia-pin. "History of the Chinese Eastern Railway. A Chinese Version." *Pacific Affairs,* vol. 3, no. 2 (February 1930), pp. 188–211.

Lif, Sh. *Voina i ekonomika Iaponii* [War and the economy of Japan]. Moscow: Politizdat pri TsK VKP (b), 1940.

Ling, Chong-yun. *La position et les droits du Japon en Mandchourie* [The position and the rights of Japan in Manchuria]. Paris: A Pedone, 1933.

Lipman, N. *Zapiski krasnoarmeitsa-dal'nevostochnika* [Memoirs of a Red Army soldier of the Far Eastern Army]. Moscow: Molodaia gvardiia, 1930.

Lobanov-Rostovsky, A. *Russia and Asia.* New York: Macmillan, 1933.

Lory, Hillis. "Recognition of Manchukuo," *Contemporary Japan,* vol. 3, no. 4 (March 1935), pp. 611–23.

Louis, Wm. Roger. *British Strategy in the Far East 1919–1939.* Oxford: Clarendon Press, 1971.

Loviagin, A. "Plany iaponskikh imperialistov. (K sobytiiam na KVZhD)" [Plans of the Japanese imperialists. (Concerning the events on the Chinese Eastern Railway)], *Morskoi Sbornik,* October 1934, no. 10, pp. 13–21.

Mad'iar, L. "General'naia repetitsiia budushchei voiny. (K sobytiiam na K.-V. zh. d.) [Dress rehearsal of the next war. (Regarding the events on the Chinese Eastern Railway)], *Bol'shevik* 1929, no. 15, pp. 36–59.

―――. "Proletarskaia pobeda na Dal'nem Vostoke" [The proletarian victory in the Far East], *Bol'shevik* 1930, no. 2.

Makita, Yutaro. *Ro-Shi kokkyo danzetsu ni itaru made no keika gaiyo* [The events leading to the rupture of the Russian and Chinese frontiers]. Dairen: South Manchurian Railway, 1929.

Mallory, Walter H. "The Permanent Conflict in Manchuria," *Foreign Affairs,* vol. 10, no. 2 (New York, January 1932), pp. 220–230.

Manshu Jijo Annai-jo. *Rokoku no Toa seisaku to Manshu* [Russia's Far Eastern Policy and Manchuria]. Hsinking, 1942.

Mariev, M. *Imperialisty gotoviat voinu i interventsiiu protiv SSSR* [The imperialists prepare war and intervention against the USSR]. Leningrad: Lenpartizdat, 1934.

Matsubara, Kazuo. "Ro-Shi funso ni taisuru Nihon no kyoso" [Sino-Russian difficulties and the attitude of Japan], *Gaiko jiho,* vol. 51, no. 4 (August 15, 1929), pp. 1–4.

Maxon, Yale Candee. *Control of Japanese Foreign Policy: A Study of Civil-Military Rivalry, 1930–1945.* Berkeley: University of California Press, 1957.

McLane, Charles B. *Soviet Policy and the Chinese Communists 1931–1946.* New York: Columbia University Press, 1958.

Meng, Chü-ju. *La position juridique du Japon en Mandchourie* [The legal position of Japan in Manchuria]. Paris: A. Pedone, 1933.

Michael, Franz. *Der Streit um die Mandschurei* [The Struggle for Manchuria]. Leipzig: Robert Noske, 1933.

Mikhailov, M. *Chto proiskhodit na Kitaisko-vostochnoi zheleznoi doroge. K poslednim sobytiiam na KVZhD* [What is happening on the Chinese Eastern Railway. Concerning the latest events on the Chinese Eastern Railway]. With a foreword by D. F. Sverchkov. Moscow, 1926.

Mitarevskii, N. *World-wide Soviet Plots. As Disclosed By Hitherto Unpublished Documents Seized at the USSR Embassy in Peking.* Tientsin, 1927.

Mohr, F. W. "Tatsachen und Entwicklungen im Konflikt um die ostchinesische Eisenbahn" [Facts and developments in the conflict over the Eastern Chinese Railway], *Ostasiatische Rundschau,* August 1, 1929, pp. 407–409.

Moore, Harriet Lucy. *Soviet Far Eastern Policy, 1931–*

1945. Princeton: Princeton University Press, 1954.

Moscow Daily News.

Mossdorf, Otto. "Der mandschurische Konflikt des Jahres 1929" [The Manchurian conflict of 1929], *Zeitschrift für Politik,* vol. 20 (Berlin, 1931), pp. 50–63.

Mughal, Nazir A. "The Manchurian Crisis, 1931–33: The League of Nations, the World Powers, and the United States." MS, doctoral dissertation, Southern Illinois University, 1972.

Murakawa, Kengo. *Nihon gaiko shi* [History of Japanese diplomacy]. Tokyo, 1940.

Murata, Shiro. "Ro-Shi kokko kaifuku no kiun" [The opportunity for the restoration of Sino-Russian relations], *Gaiko jiho,* vol 57, no. 6 (March 15, 1931), pp. 137–144.

Nakayama, Sadao. "Sorenpo wa Manshu wo shonin suru ka?" [Will the Soviet Union recognize Manchukuo?], *Gaiko jiho,* vol. 63, no. 4 (August 15, 1932), pp. 66–72.

Nakayama, Shiro. *Semari yuku Nichi-Ro saisen* [The imminent second Russo-Japanese War]. Tokyo: Shinkosha, 1932.

Nampo Doho Goka (comp.). *Hoppo ryodo no chii. Chishima, Karafuto wo meguru shomondai* [Status of the Northern Territories. Various problems concerning the Kuril Islands and Sakhalin]. Tokyo, 1962.

Nevins, Allan. "League Gains from Russia," *Current History,* vol. 41, November 1934, pp. 143–48.

Nezadorov, G. V. "Amerikanskii istorik o sovetsko-iaponskikh otnosheniiakh 20-kh godov" [An American historian concerning Soviet-Japanese relations in the 1920s], *Istoriia SSSR,* no. 3 (May-June 1972), pp. 169–72.

Nichi-Ro Tsushin-sha (comp.) *Nichi-Ro nenkan* [Japan-Russia yearbook]. Tokyo, 1933.

Nihon Kusai Seiji Gakkai (comp.). *Nichi-Ro Nisso kankei no tenkai* [The development of Japanese-Russian and Japanese-Soviet relations]. Tokyo, 1966.

Nishi, Masaaki. "Rokoku wa Shina wo enjo suru ka?" [Does Russia aid China?], *Gaiko jiho,* vol. 60, no. 6 (December 15, 1931), pp. 117–23.

Nishinoiri, Aiichi. "Tai-Ro kosho wo do suru?" [What are we to do about our negotiations with Russia?], *Gaiko jiho,* vol. 57, No. 2 (January 15, 1931), pp. 106–12.

Nixon, Edgar B. (ed.). *Franklin D. Roosevelt and Foreign Affairs.* Vol. 1 (January 1933–February 1934). Cambridge, Mass: Harvard University Press, 1969.

North, Robert C. *Moscow and the Chinese Communists.* Second edition. Stanford: Stanford University Press, 1963.

North China Daily News.

North China Standard.

Ogata, Sadako N. *Defiance in Manchuria: The Making of Japanese Foreign Policy, 1931–1932.* Berkeley: University of California Press, 1964.

Ogata, Taketora. "War or Peace with Soviet Russia?," *Contemporary Japan,* vol. 3, no. 3 (December 1934), pp. 357–64.

Okonishnikov, Aleksei Petrovich. "Iaponskii imperializm v gody podgotovki vtorzheniia v Severo-Vostochnyi Kitai (Man'chzhuriia) 1929–1931 gg." [Japanese imperialism during the years of preparation for the thrust into Northeastern China (Manchuria) of 1929–1931], MS, doctoral dissertation, Moskovskii Institut Vostokovedeniia, 1952.

An Old Emigrant. "The Truth About the Russian Emigrants in Manchoukuo," *Contemporary Manchuria* 1939, vol. 3, no. 3.

Otake Hirokichi. "Nichi-Ro fushinryaku joyaku wo chishin to shite" (Focusing on the Soviet-Japanese nonaggression pact), *Keizai orai,* vol. 7, No. 12, December 1932.

———. "Nisso tatakau beki ka?" [Must Japan and the Soviet Union fight?], *Gaiko jiho,* vol. 63, no. 1 (July 1, 1932), pp. 197–201.

Parlett, Sir Harold. *A Brief Account of Diplomatic Events in Manchuria.* London: Oxford University Press, 1929.

Peffer, Nathaniel. "The Reckoning of Conquest," *Asia,* April 1935, pp. 197–201.

Peking and Tientsin Times.

Peking Leader.

Perleberg, Max (comp.). *Who's Who in Modern China.* Hong Kong: Ye Olde Printerie, 1954.

Pevtsov, A. "Iaponiia i sovetsko-kitaiskii konflikt" [Japan and the Soviet-Chinese conflict], *Mirovoe khoziaistvo i mirovaia politika* (World economy and world politics). 1930, no. 2, pp. 77–83.

Pollard, Robert T. *China's Foreign Relations 1917–1931.* New York: Macmillan, 1933.

Powell, John Benjamin. *My Twenty-five Years in China.* New York: Macmillan, 1945.

―――. "Russo-Japanese relations," *China Quarterly,* vol. 1, no. 1 (September 1936), pp. 29–49.

―――. "The truth about the Sino-Soviet dispute in Manchuria," *China Weekly Review,* September 14, 1929.

Pozharskii, Nikolai. *Liudi OKDVA* [People of the Special Red Banner Far Eastern Army]. Leningrad: Izd. "Krasnoi gazety," 1930.

―――. *Osobaia Dal'nevostochnaia* [The special Far Eastern (Army)]. Leningrad, 1930.

Predin, O. *Imperializm SShA na Dal'nem Vostoke* [Imperialism of the United States in the Far East]. Moscow: Mezhdunarodnyi Agrarnyi Institut, 1933.

Price, Willard De Mille. *Japan Rides the Tiger.* New York: Day, 1942. 228 pp.

Primakov, V. *Iaponiia i SSSR.* [Japan and the USSR.] Sverdlovsk: Uralgiz, 1932.

Quigley, H. Scott. "Kellogg Pact invoked in the Soviet-Chinese dispute," *Current History,* January 1930.

―――. "The Struggle to Control the Chinese Eastern Railway," *Current History,* vol. 30, no. 6 (September, 1929), pp. 1100–10.

Rea, George Bronson. *The Case for Manchukuo.* New York: D. Appleton-Century, 1935.

Royal Institute of International Affairs. *Survey of International Affairs.* Edited by Arnold J. Toynbee. Vols. for 1926–1936. London: Oxford University Press, 1928–1937.

Rozenfel'd, Mikhail. *Za arkoi granitsy. ODVA v Man'-chzhurii* (Beyond the arch of the frontier. The Special Far Eastern Army in Manchuria.) Moscow, 1931.

"The Saionji-Harada Memoirs." Exhibit 3751 of the International Military Tribunal of the Far East, Japanese Archives, reel SP 161.

Saito, Yoshie. *Sovieto Rokoku no Kyokuto shinshutsu* [Soviet Russia's Far Eastern advance]. Tokyo, 1931.

Sakamoto, Giko. "Ro-Shi funso to rekkoku no taido" (Russian-Chinese complications and the attitude of the powers), *Gaiko jiho*, vol. 51, no. 4 (August 15, 1929), pp. 111-117.

Sansom, Katharine. *Sir George Sansom and Japan: A Memoir*. Tallahassee: Diplomatic Press, 1972.

Sato Keijiro. *Tai-Ro gaiko no koshin* [Renovation of policy toward Russia]. Tokyo, 1933.

Semenov, B. "Kitai i SSSR" [China and the USSR], in A. Lozovskii (ed.) *O Kitae* [About China] (Moscow, 1928), pp. 141–60.

Shen, Mo. *Japan in Manchuria. An Analytical Study of Treaties and Documents*. Manila: Grace Trading Company, 1960.

Shidehara, Kijuro. *Gaiko gojunen* [Fifty years of foreign relations]. Tokyo, 1951.

Shigemitsu, Mamoru. *Japan and Her Destiny. My Struggles For Peace*. Edited by Major-General F. S. Piggott. Translated by Oswald White. New York: E. P. Dutton & Co., 1958.

―――. *Revolutionary Foreign Policy of China. A Report Submitted to the Japanese Government*. Tokyo, 1931.

―――. *Showa no doran* [The Showa upheaval]. Tokyo, 1952. 2 vols.

Shigemori, Tadashi. "Nichi-Ro-Shi kankei no shin tenkai" [New developments in Sino-Russian-Japanese relations], *Kaizo*, vol. 14, no. 3 (March 1932), pp. 147–58.

―――. *Nihon to Sorempo* [Japan and the Soviet Union]. Tokyo, 1934.

520   THE DAMNED INHERITANCE

"The Sino-Soviet Crisis," *The Chinese Social and Political Science Review,* vol. 13, no. 4 (October 1929), Public Documents Supplement, pp. 116–30.
Skalov, G. *KVZhD. Imperialisty i kitaiskaia reaktsiia v sobytiiakh na KVZhD* [The Chinese Eastern Railway. Imperialists and Chinese reactionaries in the events on the Chinese Eastern Railway]. Moscow: Gosizdat, 1930.
————. *Sobytiia na Kitaiskoi Vostochnoi zheleznoi doroge* [Events on the Chinese Eastern Railway]. Moscow, 1929.
Skliarov, D. *Ekonomicheskaia politika iaponskogo imperializma v Man'chzhurii* (The economic policy of Japanese imperialism in Manchuria). Second edition, Moscow: Partizdat, 1934.
Smith, Sara. *The Manchurian Crisis, 1931–1932; A Tragedy in International Relations.* New York: Columbia University Press, 1948.
Sobranie dokumentov, kasaiushchikhsia deiatel'nosti Rossiiskoi Missii v Kitae za period 1 Noiabria 1917 g.-po 31 Dekabria 1920 g. [Collection of documents, concerning the activity of the Russian Mission in China for the period of 1 November 1917 to 31 December 1920]. Peking: Tipolitografiia Russkoi Dukhovnoi Missii, 1920.
Sokolov, B. "Sovetskii Soiuz i imperialisticheskaia Iaponiia (20 let sovetsko-iaponskikh otnoshenii)" [The Soviet Union and imperialist Japan (20 years of Soviet-Japanese relations)], *Tikhii Okean,* vol. 3–4, no. 13–14 (July-December, 1937), pp. 88–105.
Serizawa, Shinichi. "Ro-Shi funso to Nichi-Bei-Shi no kankei" [The Sino-Russian conflict and the relations of Japan, the United States and China], *Gaiko jiho,* vol. 51, No. 6 (September 15, 1929), pp. 91–106.
Shanghai, Bureau of Industrial and Commercial Information. International Relations Committee, *The Sino-Russian Crisis; The Actual Facts Brought To Light.* Nanking, 1929.
Sorge, Wolfgang. *Erlebtes Mandschukuo* [Witnessed

Manchukuo]. Berlin: Kommodore Verlag, 1938.

Soviet Plot in China, Documents 1–32 inclusive. Peking: Metropolitan Police Headquarters, 1927. 2 vols.

Stimson, Henry L. *The Far Eastern Crisis. Recollections and Observations.* New York: Harper and Brothers, 1936.

Storry, Richard. *The Double Patriots. A Study of Japanese Nationalism.* London: Chatto and Windus, 1957.

Suehiro, Shigeo. "Ro-Shi shototsu yori Nissi kenan no shorai wo omou" [The Russo-Chinese conflict and its possible effect upon pending Sino-Japanese plans], *Gaiko jiho,* vol. 52, No. 1 (October 1929), pp. 104–12.

Suntsov, N. P., A. I. Teleshenko, and M. P. Khvostikov. *Krasnoznamennyi Dal'nevostochnyi* [The Red Banner Far Eastern (Military District)]. Moscow: Voennoe izdatel'stvo, 1971.

Swearingen, Rodger and Paul Langer. *Red Flag in Japan; International Communism in Action, 1919–1951.* Cambridge: Harvard University Press, 1952.

Takeuchi, Ayayoshi. "The CER Negotiations," *Contemporary Japan,* vol. 3, no. 3 (December 1934), pp. 374–80.

Tamura, Kosaku. *Taiheiyo senso gaiko-shi* [Diplomatic history of the Pacific War]. Tokyo, 1966.

Tanaka, Tokichi, "Soviet-Japanese Relations," *Contemporary Japan,* vol. I, no. 1 (June 1932), pp. 16–22.

Tanakamaru, Sukeatsu. *Tairo gyogyo kosho o supaisuru* [Spying on Russian fishery negotiations]. Tokyo, 1932.

Tang, Peter S. H. *Russian and Soviet Policy in Manchuria and Outer Mongolia 1911–1931.* Durham: Duke University Press, 1959.

Terent'ev, N. *Ochag voiny na Dal'nem Vostoke* [Hotbed of war in the Far East]. Moscow, 1934.

T'ien, Hsiao-sheng. *Chung O chan shih* (History of the Sino-Soviet War). Shanghai, 1930.

Tompkins, Pauline. *American-Russian Relations in the Far East.* New York: Macmillan, 1949.

Tong, Hollington K. *Facts About The Chinese Eastern*

Railway Situation (*With Documents*). Published under the auspices of the Committee for Public Enlightenment of the Northeastern Provinces. Harbin, 1929.

Toynbee, Arnold J. *A Journey to China or Things which are seen.* London: Constable and Co., 1931.

Treadgold, Donald W. *Twentieth Century Russia.* Chicago: Rand McNally, 1959.

Tsai, Wei-ping. "The Russo-Japanese conflict in the Far East." MS, doctoral dissertation, University of Illinois, Urbana, 1938.

Tsao, Lien-en. *The Chinese Eastern Railway. An Analytical Study.* Shanghai: Bureau of Industrial and Commercial Information, Ministry of Industry, Commerce and Labor, 1930.

————. "The Settlement of the Sino-Soviet dispute," *Chinese Economic Journal,* vol. 6, no. 3 (March 1930), pp. 290–330.

Tullie, A. R. *La Mandchourie et le conflit devant la Société des nations* (Manchuria and the conflict before the League of Nations). Paris: Librairie du Recueil Sirey, 1935.

Ueda, Sentaro. *Tai-Ro seisaku* [Policy toward Russia]. Tokyo: Gaimusho, 1932.

Ulam, Adam B. *Expansion and Coexistence. The History of Soviet Foreign Policy 1917–67.* New York: Frederick A. Praeger, 1968.

Union of Soviet Socialist Republics, Academy of Sciences. *Sovetskaia istoricheskaia entsiklopediia* [Soviet historical encyclopedia]. Moscow: Sovetskaia entsiklopediia, 1961– .

————. Institut Istorii. *Istoriia vneshnei politiki SSSR* [History of the foreign policy of the USSR]. Moscow: Nauka, 1966–1971. 2 vols.

————. Glavnoe upravlenie pogranichnykh voisk, Politicheskoe upravlenie pogranichnykh voisk. *Pogranichnye voiska SSSR 1929–1938. Sbornik dokumentov i materialov* [The frontier forces of the USSR 1929–1938. Collection of documents and material]. Moscow: Nauka, 1972.

————. Institut Kitaevedeniia. *Russko-kitaiskie otnosheniia 1689–1916. Ofitsial'nye dokumenty* [Russo-Chinese Relations 1689–1916. Official documents]. Moscow: Izdatel'-stvo vostochnoi literatury, 1958.

————. *Sovetsko-kitaiskie otnosheniia 1917–1957. Sbornik dokumentov* [Soviet-Chinese relations 1917–1957. Collection of documents]. Moscow: Izdatel'stvo vostochnoi literatury, 1959.

Union of Soviet Socialist Republics, Ministry of Foreign Affairs. *Dokumenty vneshnei politiki* [Foreign relations documents]. Moscow: Gosudarstvennoe izdatel'stvo politicheskoi literatury, 1957– .

————. Monopoly of Foreign Commerce. *Torgovye otnosheniia SSSR so stranami vostoka* [Commercial relations of the USSR with the countries of the East]. Moscow: Mezhdunarodnaia kniga, 1938.

————. People's Commissariat of Foreign Affairs. *Sovetsko-kitaiskii konflikt 1929 g. Sbornik dokumentov.* [The Soviet-Chinese conflict of 1929. Collection of documents]. Moscow, 1930.

United States, Department of State. *Documents on German Foreign Policy 1918–1945.* Series C (1933–1937). Washington, D.C.: Government Printing Office, 1959–66. 5 vols.

————. *Foreign Relations of the United States: Diplomatic Papers.* Volumes for 1929 through 1935. Washington: United States Government Printing Office, 1943–53.

————. *Manchuria. Report of the Commission of Enquiry Appointed by the League of Nations.* Washington: United States Government Printing Office, 1932.

————. National Archives.

Ventsel', A. N. "Znachenie Kitaiskoi Vostochnoi zheleznoi dorogi v dal'nevostochnom voprose" [The significance of the Chinese Eastern Railway in the Far Eastern question], *Ekonomist* 1922, no. 4, pp. 177–99.

Vinogradov, A. (comp.). *Konflikt na KVZhD 1929 g.* [The conflict on the Chinese Eastern railway of 1929]. Moscow, 1932.

Voitinskii, G. *K.V.Zh.D. i politika imperialistov v Kitae* [The Chinese Eastern Railroad and the policy of the imperialists in China]. Moscow, 1930.

————. "Zakhvat KVzhd i politika SSSR" [The seizure of the Chinese Eastern Railway and the policy of the USSR], *Krasnaia nov'*, 1929, no. 9, pp. 142–150.

Voronchanin, I. *Iaponiia i SSSR v konventsionnykh vodakh. Ekonomicheskii ocherk* [Japan and the USSR in convention waters. An economic sketch]. Khabarovsk: Dal'kraiotdelenie Ogiza, 1931.

Voroshilov, K. E. *Eshche sil'nee budem krepit' oboronu Sovetskoi strany. Rech' na XVII sezde VKP(b). 31/I– 1934g.* [We will further strengthen the defense of the Soviet land. Speech at the XVII's meeting of the All-Union Communist Party (Bolsheviks), January 31, 1934]. Moscow: Partizdat, 1934.

Vygodskii, S. Iu. *Vneshniaia politika SSSR 1924–1929 gg.* [The foreign policy of the USSR 1924–1929]. Moscow: Gospolitizdat, 1963.

Wada, Kihachi. "Soren no tai-Nichi-Man keizai kankei" [Economic relationship of Soviet Russia to Japan and Manchukuo], *Gaiko jiho,* vol. 77, no. 5 (March 1935), pp. 45–66.

Wang, Chi. "Young Marshal Chang Hsueh-liang and Manchuria: 1928–1931." MS, doctoral dissertation, Georgetown University, 1969.

Wang, Ching-chun. "The Dispute between Russia and China," *Nineteenth Century and After,* February 1930, pp. 167–78.

————. *Japan's Continental Adventure.* New York: Macmillan, 1941.

————. "The Sale of the Chinese Eastern Railway," *Foreign Affairs,* vol. 12, no. 1 (New York, October 1933), pp. 57–70.

————. "A Solution of the Chinese Eastern Railway Conflict," *Foreign Affairs,* vol. 8, no. 2 (New York, January 1930), pp. 294–96.

Wei, Henry. *China and Soviet Russia*. Princeton: D. Van Nostrand Co., 1956.

Weigh, Ken Shen. *Russo-Chinese Diplomacy*. Shanghai, 1928.

Wende-Textor. "Die chinesische Ostbahn im Jahr des russischen Konflikts 1929" [The Chinese Eastern Railway in the year of the Russian conflict 1929], *Archiv für Eisenbahnwesen,* Berlin, September-October 1931.

"The White Russians in Manchukuo," *Contemporary Manchuria,* vol. 1, no. 3 (September 1937), pp. 16–33.

Whiting, Allen S. *Soviet Policies in China 1917–1924*. New York: Columbia University Press, 1954.

Wilbur, C. Martin and Julie Lien-ying How. *Documents on Communism, Nationalism and Soviet Advisers in China 1918–1927*. New York: Columbia University Press, 1956.

Williams, William Applemen. *American-Russian Relations, 1781–1947*. New York: Rinehart, 1952.

———. "China and Japan: a Challenge and a Choice of the Nineteen Twenties," *Pacific Historical Review,* vol. 26 (August 1957), pp. 259–79.

Willoughby, Westel W. *The Sino-Japanese Controversy and the League of Nations*. Baltimore: Johns Hopkins Press, 1935.

Wu, Aitchen K. *China and the Soviet Union. A Study of Sino-Soviet Relations*. New York, 1950.

Yakhontoff, Victor A. *Eyes on Japan*. New York: Coward-McCann, 1936.

———. *Russia and the Soviet Union in the Far East*. London: George Allen and Unwin, 1932.

Yoshihashi, Takehiko. *Conspiracy at Mukden. The Rise of the Japanese Military*. New Haven: Yale University Press, 1963.

Yoshimura, Chuzo (Ryuri). *Nichi-Ro no genzai oyobi shorai* [The present and future of Japanese-Russian (relations)]. Tokyo, 1934.

———. "Saikin no Nisso kankei" [Recent Japanese-Soviet

relations], *Gaiko jiho,* vol. 76, no. 6 (December 1935), pp. 90–97.

Young, A. Morgan. *Imperial Japan 1926–1938.* New York: William Morrow, 1938.

Young, C. Walter. *The International Relations of Manchuria. A Digest and Analysis of Treaties, Agreements, and Negotiations Concerning the Three Eastern Provinces of China.* Chicago: University of Chicago Press, 1929.

———. *Japan's Special Position in Manchuria; Its Assertion, Legal Interpretation and Present Meaning.* Baltimore: Johns Hopkins Press, 1931.

Zhukov, E. M. *Mezhdunarodnye otnosheniia na dal'nem vostoke (1870–1945 gg.)* [International relations in the Far East (1870–1945)]. Moscow: Gospolitizdat, 1951.

———. (ed.). *Iaponskii militarizm* [Japanese militarism]. Moscow: Nauka, 1972.

Zotov, K. "Dal'nevostochnyi teatr voennykh deistvii" [The Far Eastern theater of military action], *Morskoi sbornik* 1929, no. 10, pp. 93–113.

Index

527

BOOKS FROM THE DIPLOMATIC PRESS, INC.

1102 BETTON ROAD, TALLAHASSEE, FLORIDA 32303, U.S.A.

Satow, Sir Ernest. *Korea and Manchuria between Russia and Japan 1895–1904. The Observations of Sir Ernest Satow, British Minister and Plenipotentiary to Japan and China.* Selected and edited with a historical introduction by George Alexander Lensen. First published 1966; second printing 1968. 300 pp., collotype frontispiece. cloth. ISBN 0–910512–01–9. $12.50.
". . . a welcome addition to primary source material for the study of Far Eastern diplomatic history."—*The Journal of Asian Studies*
". . . full of interesting and illuminating views from a diplomat of experience and wisdom. . ."—*The American Historical Review*

D'Anethan, Baron Albert. *The d'Anethan Dispatches from Japan 1894–1910. The Observations of Baron Albert d'Anethan, Belgian Minister Plenipotentiary and Dean of the Diplomatic Corps.* Translated and edited with a historical introduction by George Alexander Lensen. 1967. 272 pp., collotype frontispiece. cloth. ISBN 0–910512–02–7. $15.00.
"A companion volume to . . . Sir Ernest Satow . . . Masterfully selected excerpts of heretofore unpublished official dispatches . . ."— *Historische Zeitschrift*
"Valuable to students in East Asian international relations."— *Choice*

Lensen, George Alexander. *The Russo-Chinese War.* 1967. 315 pp., collotype frontispiece, maps, extensive bibliography. cloth. ISBN 0–910512–03–05. $15.00.
"The first full-length treatment of Sino-Russian hostilities in Manchuria during the Boxer Rebellion of 1900 . . . Lensen writes clearly, vividly, and with full mastery of his subject."—*Choice*

Will, John Baxter. *Trading Under Sail off Japan 1860–1899.* The Recollections of Captain John Baxter Will, Sailing-Master and Pilot. Edited with a historical introduction by George Alexander Lensen. 1968. 190 pp., lavishly printed and illustrated, cloth. ISBN 0–910512–04–3. $12.50.
". . . this extremely interesting story . . . ranks with the few which, while not perhaps of the type to keep young children from play, should keep most men 'in the chimney corner.'"—*The Japan Times*

Lensen, George Alexander (comp.). *Japanese Diplomatic and Consular Officials in Russia. A Handbook of Japanese Representatives in Russia from 1874 to 1968.* 230 pp., hardcover. ISBN 0–910512–05–1. $15.00.
"A useful handbook for every serious student of the relations between Japan and the U.S.S.R."— *Narody Azii i Afriki*

Lensen, George Alexander (comp.). *Russian Diplomatic and Consular Officials in East Asia. A Handbook of the Representatives of Tsarist Russia and the Provisional Government in China, Japan and Korea from 1858 to 1924 and of Soviet Representatives in Japan from 1925 to 1968.* 1968. 294 pp., hard-cover. ISBN 0–910512–06-X. $15.00.
"The two handbooks are essential reference works for every library of East Asian or Russian history: for specialists in the field of Russian-East Asian relations where the author is known as a distinguished pioneering scholar, they will be indispensable companions."— *Pacific Affairs*

Westwood, J.N. *Witnesses of Tsushima* 1970. xiv, 321 pp. plus 38 illustrations, cloth. ISBN 0–910512–08–06. $15.00.
"Dr. Westwood by interweaving his own narrative with eyewitness accounts and the official reports both Russian and Japanese gives us a far more accurate version of the famous Russian voyage out of Kronstadt to the Straits of Tsushima and the subsequent battle than has been available heretofore."— *Journal of Asian Studies*

Lensen, George Alexander. *Japanese Recognition of the U.S.S.R.: Soviet-Japanese Relations 1921–1930.* viii, 425 pp. illustrated. cloth. ISBN 0–910512—09–4. $15.00.
"The book is a careful detailed treatment of an important period in Russo-Japanese relations. It will be of special interest to diplomatic and economic historians and of more general interest to those concerned with Japan's position in East Asia or the Soviet Union's relations there."— *Choice*

McNally, Raymond T. *Chaadayev and his Friends. An Intellectual History of Peter Chaadayev and his Russian Contemporaries.* 1971. vi, 315 pp., frontispiece, imitation leather. ISBN 0–910512–11–6. $15.00.
A new and highly readable interpretation of the place of Peter Chaadayev (1794–1856), the first Russian Westernizer and a unique thinker, in intellectual history, based on research in Soviet archives.

Poutiatine, Countess Olga. *War and Revolution. Excerpts from the Letters and Diaries of the Countess Olga Pontiatine.* Translated and edited by George Alexander Lensen. 1971. vi, 111 pp., illustrated, cloth. ISBN 0–910512–12–4. $12.50.
A moving eyewitness account of the Russian Revolution and of conditions in Russian and Anglo-Russian military hospitals during the First World War by the granddaughter of the Russian admiral who competed with Commodore Perry in the opening of Japan.

Sansom, Lady Katherine. *Sir George Sansom and Japan.* A memoir of Sir George Sansom, G. B. E., K. C. M. G., Diplomat Historian, by his wife. 1972. 183 pp., illustrated, cloth. ISBN 0–910512–13–2. $15.00.
The diplomatic and scholarly life of Sir George Sansom, the foremost Western authority on Japan, mirrored in the letters and diary entries of his wife and himself, with unforgettable thumbnail sketches of leading diplomatic, political, military and literary figures in Japan from 1928–1950.

Kutakov, Leonid N. *Japanese Foreign Policy on the Eve of the Pacific War. A Soviet View.* 1972. pp., frontispiece, cloth. ISBN 9105012–15–0. $15.00.
". . . a tightly knit interpretation of an epochal aspect of modern history (par-

ticularly the long essay on Japanese-Russian relations) which will intrigue students of the background of World War II."— *Library Journal.*
"Of special interest to students of East Asian international relations and to diplomatic historians generally."— *Choice.*

Lensen, George Alexander. *The Strange Neutrality: Soviet-Japanese Relations During the Second World War, 1941–1945.* 1972. xii, 335 pp., illustrated, cloth. ISBN 910512–14–0. $15.00.
"A dispassionate and authoritative account which has a place in every collection on the history of World War II in Asia and the Pacific."— *Library Journal*
". . . written with cogency, balance, and depth."— *History*
"A first rate historical work."— *Choice.*

Vishwanathan, Savitri. *Normalization of Japanese-Soviet Relations 1945–1970.* 1973. About 200 pp. illustrated, cloth. ISBN 910512–14–0. $15.00.
An examination of the political, economic and diplomatic relations between Japan and the U.S.S.R. since the Pacific War, with chapters on trade, fisheries, and the territorial dispute. Written by an Indian scholar on the basis primarily of Japanese sources.

Lensen, George Alexander. *The Damned Inheritance: The Soviet Union and the Manchurian Crises, 1924–1935.* 1974. About 500 pp., illustrated, cloth. ISBN 910512–17–5. $19.80.
An account of the triangular Russo-Chinese-Japanese struggle over Manchuria and the Chinese Eastern Railway and of American and British reaction thereto, written on the basis of Soviet, Japanese, and British documents.

*   *   *

Lensen, George Alexander. *Faces of Japan: A Photographic Study.* 154 large collotype reproductions, beautifully printed in a limited edition. 1968. 312 pp., cloth. ISBN 0–910512–07–8. $25.00 (originally $30.00).
Japanese of all walks of life at work and at play, as seen through the eyes of a historian.
"A terrifically beautiful book."—*Wilson Hicks*

Lensen, George Alexander. *April in Russia: A Photographic Study.* 100 large collotype reproductions, beautifully printed in a limited edition. 1970. 208 pp., cloth. ISBN 0–910512–10–8. $30.00 (originally $40.00).
A historian's view of daily life in the U.S.S.R.
"An enlightening educational tool as well as an artistic, almost poetic, addition to personal libraries."—*Tallahassee Democrat*
". . . this historian has the soul of a poet and the eye of an artist."—*Novoye Russkoye Slovo*